Hotel Operations Management

David K. Hayes, Ph.D.

Jack D. Ninemeier, Ph.D.

PEARSON

Prentice Hall

Upper Saddle River New Jersey, 07458

Library of Congress Cataloging-in-Publication Data

Hayes, David K.
    Hotel operations management / By David K. Hayes and Jack Ninemeier.
    p. cm.
    ISBN 0-13-099598-3
    1. Hotel management.   I. Ninemeier, Jack D.   II. Title.
TX911.3.M27 H39 2003
647.64'068—dc21
                                      2003011010

This book is dedicated to E. Ray Swan, former executive director of the Educational Institute of the American Hotel and Lodging Association, and his recognition of the importance of the individual manager entrepreneur ("the Little Guy") to the hotel industry.

Editor-in-Chief: Stephen Helba
Executive Assistant: Nancy Kesterson
Executive Acquisitions Editor: Vernon R. Anthony
Director of Manufacturing and Production: Bruce Johnson
Editorial Assistant: Ann Brunner
Managing Editor: Mary Carnis
Production Liaison: Adele M. Kupchik
Senior Marketing Manager: Ryan DeGrote
Production Management: Pine Tree Composition, Inc.

Production Editor: Marianne Hutchinson, Pine Tree Composition, Inc.
Manufacturing Manager: Ilene Sanford
Manufacturing Buyer: Cathleen Petersen
Creative Director: Cheryl Asherman
Senior Design Coordinator: Christopher Weigand
Printer/Binder: Phoenix Color Book Technology Park
Cover Illustration: Photo courtesy of Belinda Lazaro
Cover Printer: Phoenix Color Book Technology Park

Cover photo: The "oasis" from the hustle and bustle of Bourbon Street, the lobby of the Royal Sonesta Hotel. Courtesy of the Royal Sonesta.
Text photo credits appear on page 487, which constitutes a continuation of this copyright page.

Pearson Education LTD.
Pearson Education Australia PTY, Limited
Pearson Education Singapore, Pte. Ltd
Pearson Education North Asia Ltd
Pearson Education Canada, Ltd.
Pearson Educación de Mexico, S.A. de C.V.
Pearson Education—Japan
Pearson Education Malaysia, Pte. Ltd
Pearson Education, Upper Saddle River, New Jersey

10 9 8 7 6 5 4 3
ISBN 0-13-099598-3

Contents

Companion website available at http://www.prenhall.com/hayes

Foreword

I have been fortunate during the more than twenty-five years of my career to have managed activities at some of the finest luxury hotels in the world. I know that a hotel general manager (GM) has one of the most challenging, exciting and rewarding positions in the entire hospitality industry. General managers become outstanding as a result of a combination of real-world experience and careful study; and I know that never ends.

The world of hotel administration is interdisciplinary. It draws upon economics, management theory, mathematics, food science, chemistry, microbiology, physics, engineering, accounting, marketing, law, psychology, sociology and, increasingly, technology. As Sinclair Lewis wrote in his 1934 book *(World of Art)* about hotel managers, "*If you can do all of this, . . . you'll have a good time.*"

The truth is that, while hotel G.M.s truly can (and do!) "have a good time," they cannot ever truly know or "do" it all. Fortunately, they do not need to know everything to be successful. Rather, successful G.M.s rely on a talented group of other managers and team members to provide superlative service to guests, superior financial returns for owners, and fulfilling careers for their staff members.

If you want to become a hotel G.M. or want to better understand what G.M.s must do to be successful, you'll get a great start on your journey by studying the book you now hold in your hands. It is, in fact, a primer, which describes the role and responsibilities of G.M.s in today's lodging properties.

Most G.M.s are unlikely to know more about heating and cooling systems than their Chief Engineer. It is also the rare G.M. who can produce a Crème Brulee with a better flavor and texture than that of their property's best Chef. Likewise, the skills and "tricks of the trade" that are required of today's professional Executive Housekeeper may not be fully known (or even understood!) by the G.M. Interestingly, however, it the G.M.'s job to supervise all of these highly skilled managers as well as their peers. The GM must know how to evaluate and even assist in the professional development of these specialized and highly skilled professionals. This book will show you how to do just that.

Hotel Operations Management takes its readers on a by-department tour of a full-service hotel. Along the way, it consistently answers two questions: *what* do GMs need to know about each department, and *why* do they need to know it? These questions are addressed by information that emphasizes philosophy rather than details. In each chapter, a "Managers at Work" section outlines a "challenge" (some would call it a problem!), and allows readers to think and act like a GM to address the issue by applying what they learned from the chapter. Extensive and up-to-date glossaries provide insight on the language of hotel management, and the web sites referenced by the authors point readers to valuable resources literally at the effective G.M.'s fingertips. As well, another section ("Issues at Work") provides additional opportunities for readers to practice the art and science of a GM's work by applying real-world information to real-world problems.

Hotel Operations Management is a unique and long overdue text. The value of any book, whether it consists of poetry, a biography, or management principles, can be, in part, assessed by the number of people who could benefit from reading it. In the case of *Hotel Operations Management,* there are many types of potential readers. Hotel owners and investors who read it will better understand the many tasks and responsibilities of the G.M.s they employ. Practicing G.M.s will be able to compare their own activities with those of their colleagues. Hotel department managers including those in the Front Office, Food and Beverage, Sales and Marketing and others will learn what their own G.M.s should expect from them and, in turn, what they should expect from their G.M.

Most importantly, tomorrow's G.M.s, whether they are currently "working their way up" in the industry and/or participating in a formal education program before they begin their careers, will learn much and benefit from reading *Hotel Operations Management.* They will discover information, which will help them to, someday, be a successful member of one of the most exclusive groups within the vast hospitality management industry.

I am proud to be a member of a cadre of G.M.s worldwide who cares deeply about their own properties, their guests, their on-site team of professionals and the entire hospitality industry. As a G.M., I thank the authors for their hard work, and I welcome you, the reader, into the fascinating study of what I believe to be the world's greatest profession. "Have a good time!"

Luis Argote
General Manager
Four Seasons Hotel, Mexico City, Mexico

(The only AAA Five Diamond Hotel and Restaurant in México City. Voted # 21 on the 2001 Institutional Investor world's best hotel list. Top Latin Hotel and Hotel Restaurant, and # 2 in the Americas, Conde Nast Reader's Choice Awards (2001). World's Best Service in Mexico, Central and South America, Travel and Leisure Magazine (2000).)

Preface

Hotel managers in today's rapidly changing technological world hold some of the most complex, yet rewarding, jobs in the hospitality industry. The hotel general manager, as the on-site leader of all the hotel's other managers, has the most challenging job. Ultimately, it is the responsibility of the general manager to ensure that each area within the hotel is running smoothly, profitably, and in a manner consistent with the guest service goals of the hotel. This book has been written to help present and future general managers do just that.

Historically, hotel general managers have risen in the ranks from a variety of hotel departments. Thus, for example, an excellent director of hotel sales and marketing might become a hotel general manager. Such an individual will likely have an excellent grasp of hotel sales yet lack experience or expertise in food and beverage, housekeeping, accounting, and other areas. Similarly, a general manager who has been promoted from a prior job as director of food and beverage may find his or her knowledge of hotel sales, as well as other hotel departments, lacking. *Hotel Operations Management* has been written to fill a void for individuals such as these.

Just as the conductor in an orchestra need not be an expert player of each musical instrument to ensure the orchestra's outstanding sound, the hotel general manager need not have the most technical expertise in, for example, the food and beverage department, to guarantee the production of quality food. In this book, the reader will learn what general managers need to know and do to properly supervise and monitor the activities of the food and beverage, housekeeping, sales and marketing, and engineering departments, to name but a few of the areas of general manager responsibility. To further clarify the purpose of the book, consider the case of carpet stains in a guestroom corridor. It is not the intent of this book to detail the best procedures for removing the stains. That is the responsibility of the housekeeping department and the specialists within that area who are charged with the task of keeping the hotel clean. It *is* the general manager's job, however, to monitor the effectiveness of the housekeeping department and to ensure that the department has the funding, supervisory personnel, and equipment required to keep the carpets clean. Thus, readers seeking a book that explains "how to" operate individual hotel departments will be better served selecting books on those specific departments. For the general manager, however, this book is a first compilation of the skills and knowledge required to effectively supervise *all* of the activities in a midsize full-service hotel. As a result, the book is comprehensive and detailed.

Hotel general managers are often perceived as the "best of the best" within the hospitality industry. The authors believe that this perception is most often accurate. Outstanding hotel managers ensure that their hotels prosper by their attention to detail, support of the managerial and hourly staff within the hotel, and the vision they exhibit for the hotel's goals and achievements. In this book, current and future hotel general managers will learn about the procedures effective managers use to ensure their hotel's, and thus their own, ultimate success.

INTENDED AUDIENCES

Instructors

Instructors will find, for the first time, a comprehensive text that addresses all of the operating departments of a full-service hotel. The key word is comprehensive because *Hotel Operations Management* is detailed in its coverage of the general manager's responsibilities. It is intended to be so. It is not, however, redundantly laden with information on "how-to" perform tasks that are addressed in other hospitality courses or in hotel departmental-specific textbooks. It is unique in that it addresses hotel management from the viewpoint of the general manager, a position to which many hospitality students aspire.

Students

Serious hospitality students quickly learn that few individuals can be experts in every area of hotel management. It is simply unrealistic, for example, to assume that a hotel front office manager will have the same technical knowledge as the hotel's chief maintenance engineer. Front office managers are experts in their own functional areas, which include managing Internet reservation sites and sophisticated computerized property management systems, whereas the chief maintenance engineer stays current on topics such as the availability of improved building materials and energy conservation techniques. Either of these two individuals, however, may be promoted to the job of hotel general manager. At that time, they each need to understand what they must do to properly manage the new areas they will administer.

It is also unrealistic to assume that one's first hotel job will be that of general manager. In most cases, students will start in a functional area of the hotel, and as their careers progress, they will gain added expertise. This book will be of critical assistance when the student actually reaches the position of general manager. Thus, it should be an important addition to any hotel management student's professional library.

Industry Professionals

There are many parties interested in how effective managers do their work. Hotel investors need to understand what general managers *should* be doing to help ensure the quality and growth of the hotel investment. Those lenders to the hotel industry can also make better lending decisions if they analyze the activities of a general manager. This book presents, in copious detail, the systems a general manager should have in place to monitor departmental effectiveness. Lenders who are aware of such systems and can verify their presence are in a better position to make quality lending loan decisions.

Those individuals in the franchise community, such as franchise sales representatives, inspectors, franchise services directors, and others in corporate franchisor positions may not always have a strong background in hotel operations. This book will help those individuals better understand the challenges facing the modern hotel general manager.

Within a hotel, department heads and assistant managers benefit if they understand how the segment of the hotel they manage meshes with all other areas within the hotel. The general manager has that perspective, and it is presented in this book. In addition, department heads and those that aspire to become department heads need to know what a general manager will expect from them. In this way, they can better develop their own skills and thus improve the quality of their work and their career advancement potential.

CHAPTER ORDER AND CONTENT

An important decision to be made in the production of a book such as *Hotel Operations Management* relates to the proper sequencing of information. There is no uniform agreement on this sequence. Thus, for example, some would state that a thorough knowledge of front office management should precede learning about the sales and marketing department, whereas others would maintain that the reverse order best ensures understanding. The authors realize that there is honest disagreement on how best to "learn" the hotel business and celebrate the differences of opinion as healthy and quite beneficial to the field of study. In the final analysis, however, sequencing decisions do have to be made, and in this book the authors elected to begin with a history of the industry (Chapter 1), followed by specific information about the role of the general manager (Chapters 2–3), information related to the actual management of the functional areas of the hotel (Chapters 4–11), a chapter related to the unique situations of hotel franchising and operating under a management contract (Chapter 12), and, finally, a review of the processes encountered when buying a hotel (Chapter 13), a long-term personal goal of many individual hotel general managers.

CHAPTER FUNDAMENTALS

There is not, the authors believe, another book that takes the unique approach to hotel management presented in *Hotel Operations Management*. Because this is true, the authors were free to create a new, and first of its kind, user-friendly book, and they were also challenged to produce the book in a way that could serve as a model for the efforts of future authors. As a result, the book includes the following fundamental components.

"This Chapter at Work"

Each chapter begins with a narrative summary that describes what will be presented in the chapter, as well as why the information is important to the success of a general manager.

"Tiered Content Outline"

Each chapter's outline has been carefully developed to provide the maximum ease in finding important information. The outline also provides a detailed preview of the chapter's content.

"Hotel Terminology at Work"

As is true in many professional fields, hotel managers often speak their own unique language. Thus, for example, guests may be "walked," "par levels" will be established for laundry items, "STAR" reports will be analyzed, and the "GDS" will ensure reservation connectivity. When hotel specific terms are used in the book (and they are used extensively), they are defined at the time of usage, often with direct usage examples that help to further clarify their meaning. The special language of hoteliers is both creative and extensive. In this book, the reader is thoroughly exposed to that language without being burdened by definitions of common words that are not unique to the hotel industry.

"Managers at Work"

Hotel General Managers routinely face unique problems and situations that require outstanding decision-making skills. The "Managers at Work" component of this text places the reader in the position of general manager through vignettes that require decisions to be made to solve realistic problems of the type that must be faced now or in the future. The situations presented are often complex, reflecting the fact that in many cases, the problems presented to the general manager are not easily addressed, or require an analytical solution that can best be provided only by a manager with thorough knowledge of the goals of the entire hotel.

Instructors will find that the assignment of these problems as homework, in-class essays, or use as in-class discussion items will allow student knowledge and understanding of concepts to be readily assessed. Multiple numbers of this important text element are contained in every chapter.

"The Internet at Work"

In many cases, the amount of additional information a specific Web site could provide to a General Manager was so significant that the site was presented at the point in the chapter where the information would be most useful. Thus, for example, in a description of the tasks and qualifications of a competent concierge, a reference to the organizational Web site of Les Clefs d'Or (the International Order of Concierges) at www.lesclefsdor.com provides additional information to the interested reader, as well as content that can be regularly reviewed as long as the Web site remains active. In many cases, the addition of Web resources enhanced the book's own content. The Web references in this book are purposefully extensive and exist in every chapter.

Managerial Tools

Where it was deemed helpful, checklists, forms, and step-by-step procedures that help general managers better do their jobs were included. For example, inspection sheets that general managers would use to evaluate the effectiveness of a housekeeping department were included, as well as sample Pace reports used for monitoring the quality of the hotel sales effort. These examples are only a few of the dozens included in the book. As a result, readers will be saved the trouble of "reinventing the wheel" in the many situations where a common form or procedure is the industry standard, or where such information can be easily modified to meet the needs of a specific hotel.

"Hotel Terminology at Work Glossary"

At each chapter's end, a complete listing of the industry-specific terms defined in the chapter is presented. As a result, readers can quickly review these terms to ensure they are understood and can be used in their proper context.

"Issues at Work"

This chapter-concluding feature encourages students to think about the material they have mastered in that chapter. The questions and issues presented allow the student/ reader the opportunity to reflect on and develop their own views of hospitality management, as well as challenge them to express themselves clearly to others.

The production of a book such as this is truly the culmination of the efforts of many. The authors' thanks go to Vernon Anthony, our editor, for his belief in the project; Ann Brunner for her outstanding assistance in text development; and the entire production staff at Prentice Hall for its tireless efforts. In addition, our text reviewers, Peter Ricci, University of Central Florida; Kimberly A. Boyle, University of Alabama; John Knight, Indiana University-Purdue University of Fort Wayne; and Candice Clement, Virginia Polytechnic Institute, added much to improve both the structure and content of the text. For their efforts we are truly grateful.

The authors believe that *Hotel Operations Management* describes, in great detail, exactly what the general manager of a midsize full-service hotel must know and do to be successful. Its up-to-date and comprehensive coverage of all areas of hotel operations make it an essential addition to the professional library of the serious hospitality student. It is our hope that students, instructors, and industry professionals will find it to be a significant contribution to the field of hospitality management. If they do, its success is assured.

David K. Hayes, Ph.D.
Jack D. Ninemeier, Ph.D.

1
The Hotel Industry: Overview and Professional Career Opportunities

This Chapter at Work

The hotel industry has evolved from the very modest beginnings of families and landowners who opened their homes to travelers to the high-rise properties of today which contain thousands of guest rooms. This chapter will help you understand the environment within which hotel managers operate modern hotels. Managers of lodging facilities work in the tourism industry. It is exciting to be part of tourism, one of the largest industries in the world, and to gain the knowledge and skills that can be transferred to hotels of many types and sizes.

Lodging facilities can be classified by location, by room rate (the amount charged for a guest room), and by the number of rooms they contain. They can also be classified by the type of guests they serve (e.g., business or leisure travelers) or by who owns and manages them. Fortunately, there are many common management principles that can be utilized regardless of the type of hotel being managed.

The purpose of this book is to help you understand what a general manager (G.M.) in today's hotel environment must know, and do, to be successful. As your career in the lodging industry progresses, you will be able to build on the base of information found here. As your personal experiences add to this foundation, you will find yourself able to manage more effectively in a wider range of positions with ever-increasing responsibility.

The hotel industry is, first, a service industry. There is an attitude or philosophy about serving guests that is critical to success in the hotel industry. As a hotel G.M., you cannot "fake" your concern about your guests. There must be a genuine enthusiasm to please people who are visiting your property. This concern must be held by you and by the hotel staff working with you because your employees will interact with guests far more than you will.

This chapter will help you begin your journey of emphasizing quality guest service as you learn how effective general managers manage their properties, using advanced technology and excellent human resource management skills. It concludes with a brief discussion about career opportunities in the lodging industry because there are numerous kinds of management positions available. An advantage of working within the lodging industry already noted—useful knowledge and skills can be transferred from one type of hotel organization to another—will make it easier for you to have a diverse and exciting career in this vibrant industry.

Chapter 1 Outline

LODGING IS PART OF THE TOURISM INDUSTRY

We are beginning a journey to explore the world of tourism and hospitality with a focus on lodging operations. Our journey will be long (there is a lot of information to cover because hotel management is complex). It will also be fun and exciting because those are typical ways that professional hoteliers describe their work.

HOTEL TERMINOLOGY AT WORK

Hoteliers: Those who work in the hotel business.

■

We will discuss hotel management by telling you, the reader, what a general manager of a 350-room property must know, do, and be concerned about. By focusing on a property of this size, we can present *practical* information that is applicable to the majority of lodging businesses in the United States. Each of the policies and practices discussed are, in many ways, relevant to a property of any size. Therefore, as you study this information, you will be learning how to be an effective manager regardless of the size hotel you will manage.

The Tourism Industry

Lodging properties are a segment within the **tourism industry.** Figure 1.1 (Segments in the Tourism Industry) provides an overview of the different types of organizations that make up the tourism industry.

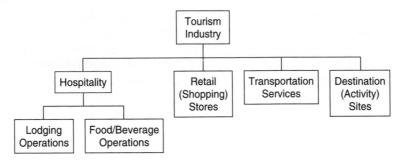

FIGURE 1.1   Segments in the Tourism Industry

HOTEL TERMINOLOGY AT WORK

Tourism Industry: All businesses that cater to the needs of the traveling public.

■

   When reviewing Figure 1.1, note that there are four major segments. One (hospitality) is comprised of lodging and food and beverage operations. This book is about the "lodging operations" sector. Retail (shopping) stores include a wide variety of gifts/souvenir shops, retail shopping malls, markets, and other businesses offering products for sale to the public (both to those who reside within a geographic area and those who travel to it). Transportation services include airplanes, rental cars, trains, ships, and alternative ways that people travel between their homes and their destinations. Finally, destination (activity) sites include the many places that the traveling public visits. These include locations offering sporting, ethnic, entertainment, cultural, and other events. In addition to travel for personal reasons, people also travel to professional meetings and conventions. Facilities that host these meetings include convention centers and private retreats, as well as hotels.

   In the United States, the tourism industry is the third largest retail industry following automotive and food stores. It is the nation's largest service industry and one of the country's largest employers. It is also the second or third largest employer in twenty-nine of the fifty-two states.[1]

Lodging (Hotel) Sector

When most people think about "hotels," they think about a building containing guest rooms for sleeping. In its narrowest sense, this definition may be correct. However, today's traveling public has a wide variety of lodging alternatives, and the definition just cited is of limited use. For example, on

---

[1]American Hotel and Lodging Association. *Lodging Industry Profile.* 2001 (www.ahla.com; statistics are for 2000).

one extreme, a person may choose a lavish destination resort in an exotic location that, in addition to sleeping rooms, offers many recreational alternatives, food and beverage outlets, and numerous other amenities. Other travelers prefer a **full-service hotel** that offers, in addition to sleeping rooms, a variety of food and beverage services. These may include operating a dining room, coffee shop, or lounge, and providing **room service** and banquet facilities. Still other travelers may prefer a **limited-service hotel** that simply provides sleeping rooms with no food and beverage outlets except a limited breakfast offered in the morning. On the farthest end of our lodging alternative continuum are sleeping spaces, some without even rest room facilities, rented on a short-term (ranging up to six or more hours) basis at airports and other locations (see Figure 1.2).

HOTEL TERMINOLOGY AT WORK

Full-Service Hotel: A lodging property that offers complete food and beverage services.
■

HOTEL TERMINOLOGY AT WORK

Room Service: Food and beverage services delivered to a guest's room.
■

HOTEL TERMINOLOGY AT WORK

Limited-Service Hotel: A lodging property that offers no or very limited food services; sometimes a complimentary breakfast is served, but there is no table service restaurant.
■

The range of lodging options noted earlier is still not inclusive. For example, facilities other than those commonly referred to as hotels may offer sleeping accommodations. These include private clubs, casinos, cruise ships, time-share condominiums, and campground lodges, among many others. In addition, there are unique hotels such as those that consist only of **suites** (known as all-suites hotels), those designed to attract guests who tend to stay for a long time (extended-stay hotels), and very small hotels usually operated out of converted homes (bed and breakfast hotels).

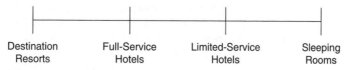

| Destination Resorts | Full-Service Hotels | Limited-Service Hotels | Sleeping Rooms |

FIGURE 1.2   Range of Lodging Property Alternatives

HOTEL TERMINOLOGY AT WORK

Suite: While there is no universally agreed-upon definition, in most cases this term refers to a guest room consisting of at least two physically separated rooms or, at the very least, a hotel room that is extra large when compared with the hotel's standard guest room.

■

To this point we have been discussing lodging operations open to all of the traveling public. Some other types of facilities offer sleeping accommodations for people away from their homes. These include schools, colleges, and universities offering residential services, health care (hospital and nursing homes) facilities, correctional institutions (prisons), and military bases.

A Brief History of Hotels

Travelers have always required places where they could rest at the end of the day. For the earliest travelers, this place was a campsite with, good fortune permitting, a campfire. Over time, places of rest became available at the crossroad centers of travel and, in between these centers, persons living along travel routes frequently made a room (lodging) and board (meals) available in their own homes. Hotels in the United States have a tradition of innovation and orientation to guest service that is worth noting. Highlights of the growth of the hotel industry in the United States since 1900 are shown in Figure 1.3

CLOSE LOOK AT LODGING ORGANIZATIONS

Figure 1.4 (2001 Property/Room Breakdown) classifies lodging properties in the United States by location, by the price they charge for rooms and by size. Note that, when analyzed by location, the vast majority of all lodging properties (approximately 75% of properties with 61% of rooms) are in suburban and highway locations. The center city (urban), airport, and destination (resort) properties comprise a relatively small percentage of lodging properties and room inventory in the United States.

When reviewing lodging industry rate structures, note that the majority of guest rooms (approximately 78% of the properties representing about 65% of rooms) are sold at a per night rate ranging from $30 to $85 per room. Some hotel operators classify hotels by the rates they charge for rooms. This is difficult because the terms "upscale," "midprice," "economy," and "budget" will vary by geographic regions. For example, a very nice room in a smaller agricultural community may be less than $60 per night. In New York City, it may be difficult to find a nice room for even five times this rate!

The hotel industry can be segmented by size. Figure 1.4 indicates that 85 percent of all properties (which contain approximately 58% of all rooms) are relatively small (less than 150 rooms).

FIGURE 1.3   Highlights in the Modern History of the United States Hotel Industry[1]

1900 Fewer than 10,000 hotels 750,000–850,000 rooms	**1900**—A typical first-class hotel offers steam heat, gas burners, electric call bells, baths and closets on all floors, billiard and sample rooms, barbershops and liveries. **1904**—New York City's St. Regis Hotel provides individually controlled heating and cooling units in each guest room. **1908**—The Hotel Statler chain begins in Buffalo. All guest rooms have private baths, full-length mirrors, telephones and built-in radios, serving as the model for hotel construction for the next forty years.
1910 10,000 U.S. hotels 1 million rooms 300,000 employees Average size: 60–75 rooms	**1910**—Electricity is beginning to be installed in new hotels for cooking purposes, as well as for lighting. However, most hotels place candle sticks, new candles, and matches in every room—electric lightbulb or no.
1920 Occupancy: 85% Hotel construction reaches an all-time peak as thousands of rooms are added along the new state and federal highways	**1920**—Prohibition begins. **1922**—The Treadway Company has some of the first management contracts on small college inns. **1925**—The first roadside "motel" opens in San Luis Obispo, California, for $2.50 a night. **1927**—The Hotel Statler in Boston becomes the first hotel with radio reception; rooms are equipped with individual headsets to receive broadcasts from a central control room. **1929**—The Oakland Airport Hotel becomes the first of its kind in the country.
1930 Occupancy: 65% AHA's Hotel Red Book lists 20,000 hotels Typical hotel: 46 rooms Average room rate: $5.60	**1930**—Four out of five hotels in the United States go into receivership. **1933**—Due to the Great Depression, hotels post the lowest average occupancy rate on record (51%). Construction grinds to a halt. **1934**—The Hotel Statler in Detroit is the first to have a central system to "air condition" every public room.
1940 Occupancy: 64%	**1940**—Air conditioning and "air cooling" become prevalent. **1945**—Sheraton is the first hotel corporation to be listed on the New York Stock Exchange. *(continued)*

FIGURE 1.3   *(Continued)*

Average room rate: $3.21	**1946**—Westin debuts first guest credit card. The first casino hotel, the Flamingo, debuts in Las Vegas.
	1947—Westin establishes Hoteltype, the first hotel reservation system. New York City's Roosevelt Hotel installs television sets in all guest rooms.
	1949—Hilton becomes the first international hotel chain with the opening of the Caribe Hilton in San Juan, Puerto Rico.
1950 Occupancy: 80% Typical hotel: 17 rooms Average room rate: $5.91	**1951**—Hilton is the first chain to install television sets in all guest rooms.
	1952—Kemmons Wilson opens his first Holiday Inn in Memphis, Tennessee.
	1954—Howard Dearing Johnson initiates the first lodging franchise, a motor lodge in Savannah, Georgia. Conrad Hilton's purchase of the Statler Hotel Company for $111 million is the largest real-estate transaction in history.
	Mid-1950s—Atlas Hotels develops the first in-room coffee concept.
	1957—J.W. Marriott opens his first hotel, the Twin Bridge Marriott Motor Hotel in Arlington, Virginia, and Jay Pritzker buys his first hotel, The Hyatt House, located outside the Los Angeles Airport. Hilton offers direct-dial telephone service.
	1958—Sheraton introduces Reservation, the industry's first automated electronic reservation system, and the first toll-free reservation number.
1960 Occupancy: 67% $3 billion in sales Total hotel rooms: 2,400,450 Typical hotel: 39 rooms, independent and locally owned Average room rate: $9.99	**Early 1960s**—Siegas introduces the first true minibar (a small refrigerator displaying products).
	1964—Travelodge debuts wheelchair-accessible rooms.
	1966—Inter-Continental introduces retractable drying lines in guest showers, business lounges, ice and vending machines in guest corridors, and street entrances to hotel restaurants.
	1967—The Atlanta Hyatt Regency opens, featuring a twenty-one-story atrium and changing the course of upscale hotel design.
	1969—Westin is the first hotel chain to implement twenty-four-hour room service.

FIGURE 1.3   *(Continued)*

1970 Occupancy: 65% $8 billion in sales Total hotel rooms: 1,627,473 Average room rate: $19.83	**1970**—Hilton becomes the first billion-dollar lodging and food-service company and the first to enter the Las Vegas market. **1973**—The Sheraton-Anaheim is the first to offer free in-room movies. **1974**—The energy crisis hits the industry. Hotels dim exterior signs, cut heat to unoccupied rooms, and ask guests to conserve electricity. **1975**—Four Seasons is the first hotel company to offer in-room amenities such as name-brand shampoo. Hyatt introduces an industry first when it opens a concierge club level that provides the ultimate in very important person (VIP) service. Cecil B. Day establishes the first seniors program.
1980 Occupancy: 70% $25.9 billion in sales Total hotel rooms: 2,068,377 Average room rate: $45.44	**1983**—Westin is the first major hotel company to offer reservations and checkout using major credit cards. VingCard invents the optical electronic key card. **1984**—Holiday Inn is the first to offer a centralized travel and commission plan. Choice Hotels introduces the concept of market segmentation. Choice Hotels offers no-smoking rooms. Hampton Inns is the first to offer a set of amenities. **1986**—Teledex Corporation introduces the first telephone designed specifically for hotel guest rooms. Days Inn provides an interactive reservations capability connecting all hotels. **1988**—Extended stay segment introduced with Marriott's Residence Inns and Holiday Corporations Homewood Suites. **1989**—Hyatt introduces a chainwide kids program for ages three to twelve and a business center at the Hyatt Regency Chicago. Hampton Inns is the first hotel chain to introduce the 100% satisfaction guarantee.
1990 Occupancy: 64% $60.7 billion in sales Total hotel rooms: 3,065,685	**1990**—Loews Hotels' Good Neighbor Policy becomes the industry's first and most comprehensive community outreach program. **1991**—Westin is the first hotel chain to provide in-room voice mail. Industry sees record losses (61.8%). **1992**—Industry breaks even financially after six consecutive years of losses. *(continued)*

FIGURE 1.3 *(Continued)*

45,020 properties	**1993**—Radisson Hotels Worldwide is the first to introduce business-class rooms.
Average room rate: $58.70	**1994**—First on-line hotel catalog debuts—TravelWeb.com. Promus and Hyatt Hotels are the first chains to establish a site on the Internet.
	1995—Choice Hotels International and Promus become the first companies to offer guests "real-time" access to its central reservations system. Choice and Holiday Inn are the first to introduce on-line booking capability.
	1999—Choice Hotels International is the first chain to test making in-room PCs a standard amenity for guests.
2000	**2000**—Hilton unveils plans for the first luxury hotel in space.
Occupancy: 63%	**2001**—September 11 destruction of the World Trade Center in New York causes occupancy rates to plummet
$97 billion in sales	**2002**—Travel industry recovers from terrorist attacks amid heightened airport security.

[1] http://www.ahma.com/infocenter/lodging_history.asp.

FIGURE 1.4   2001 Property/Room Breakdown

By Location	Property[*]	Rooms[+]
Suburban	13,660 (33.0%)	1,231,682 (29.4%)
Highway	17,454 (42.2%)	1,327,518 (31.7%)
Urban	4,453 (10.8%)	666,820 (15.9%)
Airport	3,401 (8.2%)	469,247 (11.2%)
Resort	2,425 (5.0%)	490,496 (11.7%)
By Rate		
Under $30	1,695 (4.1%)	95,378 (2.3%)
$30–$44.99	7,101 (17.2%)	503,167 (12.0%)
$45–$59.99	13,722 (33.2%)	1,017,463 (24.3%)
$60–$85	11,563 (27.9%)	1,200,559 (28.7%)
Over $85	7,312 (17.7%)	1,369,058 (32.7%)
By Size		
Under 75 rooms	21,580 (52.1%)	954,057 (22.8%)
75–149 rooms	13,820 (33.4%)	1,479,206 (35.3%)
150–299 rooms	4,397 (10.6%)	878,724 (21%)
300–500 rooms	1,091 (2.6%)	404,967 (9.7%)
Over 500 rooms	505 (1.2%)	468,671 (11.2%)

[*]Based on a total of 41,393 properties.
[+]Based on a total of 4.2 million rooms.
Please note: Total percentages may not add up to 100 because of rounding.

Figure 1.4 also indicates that, in 2001, there were 41,393 properties containing 4.2 million rooms; the average lodging property size was, then, 101.5 rooms (4.2 million rooms ÷ 41,393 properties). This information should be of interest to those aspiring to careers as hotel general managers. Many young persons see themselves as the G.M. of a very large, luxurious property in a large city. There are, of course, many properties of this type and managing one of them is an excellent goal. However, the "average" property is smaller, is in a nonurban location, and sells its rooms for a modest price. Realistic expectations of employment opportunities, especially early in one's career, are important. The good news is that excellent opportunities exist in all types of properties of all sizes in all locations and the principles required to operate a smaller hotel are the same ones used to operate large properties.

Typical Lodging Guests

Who stays in hotels? A profile of the "average" **guest** who stays in a hotel is shown in Figure 1.5 (Typical Lodging Guests).

HOTEL TERMINOLOGY AT WORK

Guest: A hotel visitor. Most guests rent rooms and/or purchase food or beverages in a hotel outlet or a banquet function.

■

Throughout this book we refer to the person renting the hotel room as a "guest"—not a "customer." In everyday usage, these terms are often used interchangeably. However, in the language of the hospitality industry—including lodging—the terms have different meanings. For example, to the extent practical, hoteliers treat persons visiting the property the same as they would treat friends visiting in their own homes. (The service attitude is discussed later in this chapter.) In contrast, the term "customer" implies someone whose relationship with the property is based only upon the exchange of money for products and services that are provided. Yes, "guests" must pay for the products and services they receive; however, the tactic of treating visitors as "guests" rather than "customers" helps establish the service philosophy, which is very important to a hotel's success.

FIGURE 1.5   Typical Lodging Guests

28.8%	are transient business travelers
25.3%	are attending a conference/group meeting
24.6%	are on vacation
21.8%	are traveling for other reasons (for example, personal, family, or special event)

When reviewing Figure 1.5, note that those traveling for the four purposes (business, conference/group meeting, vacation, and other reasons) are approximately equal. Some hotels may cater to one category of guests all the time. However, it is just as likely that a hotel may generate much business from two or more types of guests. This occurs, for example, when business travelers visit the property during the workweek and other persons visit the hotel on the weekend when they are in the area for personal reasons. Increasingly, travelers combine conference/group meeting attendance with vacations. They may, for example, bring their families, attend meetings during part of their stay, and enjoy a family vacation for the remainder of the visit.

Who travels for business and pleasure? The "typical" business guest is just about equally likely to be a male (60%) or female (40%), is thirty-five to fifty-four years (52%), is employed in a professional/managerial position (48%), and earns an average yearly household income of $72,240. Typically, these guests travel alone (81%), make reservations (91%), and pay $91 per room night. Approximately 61 percent of business travelers spend one or two nights at a property. Business guests value hotel features such as oversize work areas, high-speed Internet access, and two line telephones.

By contrast, the typical leisure room night is generated by two adults (50%), ages thirty-five to fifty-four years (42%), earning an average yearly household income of $74,386. The typical leisure traveler travels by auto (75%), makes reservations (83%), and pays $84 per room night. Most (71%) leisure travelers spend one or two nights at the property. Leisure travelers, more so than business travelers, look for facilities such as swimming pools, saunas, tennis courts and game rooms.[2]

THE INTERNET AT WORK

Current statistics about the United States hotel industry are from the American Hotel & Lodging Association (AH&LA). Check out their Web site at:

www.ahla.com.

Lodging Industry Characteristics

As seen earlier, we can classify hotels by location, rate, size, or the type of guest served. However, there are common characteristics all good properties share. These include:

• Emphasis on safety, cleanliness, and service. Few, if any, guests consider only the room and other physical attributes of the property when making a will-stay/will not–stay decision. For example, safety and

[2]See reference 1.

cleanliness are very important considerations. Friendliness (hospitality) of property staff is also an important issue which, along with the physical aspects (size, quality of maintenance, furnishings, and other factors), is part of the guests' evaluation mix. By contrast to their retail store counterparts, then, there are intangible (difficult to quantify) aspects of the purchase decision, which potential hotel guests consider.

- Inseparability of manufacture and sales. It is not possible to separate the "manufacture" (production) of a guest room with its "sale." A room exists and is sold at the same site. Contrast this with, for example, the manufacture/sale of an automobile, shirt, or a television set. Cars, shirts, and TVs are typically manufactured at one site and sold at another. The hotel G.M. and his/her staff, then, must be an "expert" at both manufacture and sales. Their counterparts in the auto/clothing/electronic industries must normally be an "expert" in only one aspect of either manufacturing products or selling them to the consumer in the marketplace.

- Perishability. If a guest room is not rented on a specific date, the **revenue** is lost forever. By contrast, an automobile/shirt/television can be sold "tomorrow" if it is not sold "today." In this regard, empty sleeping rooms are similar in nature to empty airline seats on a flight that has just taken off.

HOTEL TERMINOLOGY AT WORK

Revenue: Money the hotel collects from guests for the use of rooms or from the purchase of hotel goods and services.

Examples include guest room revenue, meeting room revenue, and food and beverage revenue.

■

- Repetitiveness. The steps involved in making a guest room ready for sale or for preparing a specific meal or drink are basically the same every time these items are sold. These routines (operating procedures) allow for some standardization. At the same time, however, they create challenges because it is always important to focus on the individual needs of guests and because standardization provides less opportunity for creativity in the decision-making processes used to perform required work.

- Labor intensive. In many industries, for example, automotive and electronics, technology and sophisticated equipment have replaced people in many work activities. By contrast, in the lodging industry, less of this has occurred. That is because much of a hotel's daily work involves employees providing services. Beds are made, rooms are cleaned, and food is prepared. The traveling public increasingly wants and is willingly to pay for services that must be "delivered" by employees. As is discussed in chapter 4 (Human Resources), a hotel's ability to attract and retain qualified staff who can consistently deliver excellent service is a key to the success or failure of a hotel.

Lodging Industry Overview

Two ways to consider the vast lodging industry are to learn about how hotels are:

1. Affiliated
2. Owned and managed

Largest Hotel Affiliations

Who are the largest lodging companies? Figure 1.6 (Top Five Lodging Companies) answers this question. When reviewing Figure 1.6, note that many of the most popular **brands** are part of the same organization. For example, many more persons probably know familiar hotel names such as Days Inn, Ramada, Super 8 Motels, and Howard Johnson International more than they know the parent company of all these hotel chains (Cendant Corporation). Likewise, many travelers will be less familiar with "Choice Hotels International"—the parent company for Comfort Inns, Suites & Hotels, Quality Inns, Suites and Hotels, EconoLodge, Clarion Hotels, Inns and Suites, Sleep Inns and Rodeway Inns, among others.

HOTEL TERMINOLOGY AT WORK

Brand: The name of a hotel chain. Sometimes referred to as a "flag."

■

When reviewing Figure 1.6, note that the ranking is based upon the total number of domestic and nondomestic (international) hotel rooms in each organization. The largest lodging organizations are, in fact, very large. For example, the five largest companies that are reported in Figure 1.6 (Cendant Corporation, InterContinental Hotels, Marriott International, Choice Hotels International, and Hilton Hotels Corporation) had 14,884 domestic hotels with 1,708,617 rooms. First, note that the average room size (115 rooms: 1,708,617 rooms ÷ 14,884 properties) is appreciably larger than the "average" domestic hotel (101 rooms as noted earlier in this chapter). Note also that these top five lodging organizations represent a significant percentage of all domestic properties/rooms. As Figure 1.4 noted, there are 41,393 properties with 4.2 million rooms in the United States. These five largest companies, then, represent almost 36 percent of all domestic properties (14,884 properties ÷ 41,393 properties) and 41 percent of rooms (1,708,617

FIGURE 1.6   Top Five Lodging Companies[1]

1. CENDANT CORPORATION	Rooms	Properties
Domestic	515,537	6,105
Nondomestic	39,297	435
Total	554,834	6,540
Days Inn Worldwide	**Rooms**	**Properties**
Domestic	152,319	1,785
Nondomestic	9,457	116
Total	161,776	1,901
Ramada Franchise Systems	**Rooms**	**Properties**
Domestic	120,414	975
Nondomestic	7,339	60
Total	127,753	1,035
Super 8 Motels	**Rooms**	**Properties**
Domestic	119,993	1,919
Nondomestic	4,672	82
Total	124,665	2,001
Howard Johnson International	**Rooms**	**Properties**
Domestic	41,830	420
Nondomestic	8,209	80
Total	50,039	500
Travelodge Hotels	**Rooms**	**Properties**
Domestic	36,340	469
Nondomestic	9,210	91
Total	45,550	560
Knights Franchise Systems	**Rooms**	**Properties**
Domestic	17,858	224
Nondomestic	143	3
Total	18,001	227
Wingate Inns	**Rooms**	**Properties**
Domestic	10,801	115
Nondomestic	0	0
Total	10,801	115
Villager Franchise Systems	**Rooms**	**Properties**
Domestic	9,329	106
Nondomestic	267	3
Total	9,596	109
AmeriHost Franchise Systems, Inc.	**Rooms**	**Properties**
Domestic	6,653	92
Nondomestic	0	0
Total	6,653	92
2. InterCONTINENTAL HOTELS AND RESORTS	Rooms	Properties
Domestic	316,572	2,202
Nondomestic	164,910	828
Total	481,482	3,030

(continued)

FIGURE 1.6   *(Continued)*

Holiday Inn	Rooms	Properties
Domestic	185,526	990
Nondomestic	69,940	385
Total	255,466	1,375
Holiday Inn Express	**Rooms**	**Properties**
Domestic	79,365	1,019
Nondomestic	12,686	132
Total	92,051	1,151
Crowne Plaza	**Rooms**	**Properties**
Domestic	21,927	71
Nondomestic	23,537	84
Total	45,464	155
Inter-Continental Hotels & Resorts	**Rooms**	**Properties**
Domestic	4,461	10
Nondomestic	39,034	121
Total	43,495	131
Holiday Inn Select	**Rooms**	**Properties**
Domestic	18,281	70
Nondomestic	2,005	9
Total	20,286	79
Holiday Inn Garden Court	**Rooms**	**Properties**
Domestic	0	0
Nondomestic	10,099	77
Total	10,099	77
Holiday Inn Sunspree Resort	**Rooms**	**Properties**
Domestic	4,308	20
Nondomestic	1,756	6
Total	6,064	26
Forum Hotels & Resorts	**Rooms**	**Properties**
Domestic	0	0
Nondomestic	5,853	14
Total	5,853	14
Staybridge Suites by Holiday Inn	**Rooms**	**Properties**
Domestic	2,704	22
Nondomestic	0	0
Total	2,704	22
3. MARRIOTT INTERNATIONAL	**Rooms**	**Properties**
Domestic	297,250	1,598
Nondomestic	76,760	248
Total	374,010	1,846
Marriott Hotels, Resorts, & Suites and Ritz Carlton	**Rooms**	**Properties**
Domestic	121,541	297
Nondomestic	39,724	120
Total	161,265	417

FIGURE 1.6   *(Continued)*

Courtyard by Marriott	Rooms	Properties
Domestic	63,997	433
Nondomestic	6,818	36
Total	70,815	469
Renaissance Hotels and Resorts/		
Ramada International	Rooms	Properties
Domestic	16,561	35
Nondomestic	29,151	85
Total	45,712	120
Fairfield Inns by Marriott	Rooms	Properties
Domestic	41,346	412
Nondomestic	0	0
Total	41,346	412
Residence Inn by Marriott	Rooms	Properties
Domestic	39,841	316
Nondomestic	1,067	7
Total	40,908	323
TownePlace Suites by Marriott	Rooms	Properties
Domestic	7,481	59
Nondomestic	0	0
Total	7,481	59
Spring Hill Suites by Marriott	Rooms	Properties
Domestic	4,019	34
Nondomestic	0	0
Total	4,019	34
Marriott Conference Centers	Rooms	Properties
Domestic	2,464	12
Nondomestic	0	0
Total	2,464	12
4. CHOICE HOTELS INTERNATIONAL	Rooms	Properties
Domestic	257,705	3,115
Nondomestic	79,521	1,104
Total	337,226	4,219
Comfort Inns, Suites, & Hotels	Rooms	Properties
Domestic	115,265	1,457
Nondomestic	23,675	337
Total	138,940	1,794
Quality Inns, Suites, & Hotels	Rooms	Properties
Domestic	49,397	433
Nondomestic	29,426	295
Total	78,823	728
EconoLodge	Rooms	Properties
Domestic	43,847	685
Nondomestic	1,277	27
Total	45,124	712

(continued)

FIGURE 1.6   *(Continued)*

Clarion Hotels, Inns, & Suites	Rooms	Properties
Domestic	19,028	115
Nondomestic	3,629	29
Total	22,657	144
Flag Hotels, Suites & Inns	**Rooms**	**Properties**
Domestic	0	0
Nondomestic	20,692	406
Total	20,692	406
Sleep Inns	**Rooms**	**Properties**
Domestic	16,917	221
Nondomestic	444	5
Total	17,361	226
Rodeway Inns	**Rooms**	**Properties**
Domestic	10,387	163
Nondomestic	360	4
Total	10,747	167
MainStay Suites	**Rooms**	**Properties**
Domestic	2,584	28
Nondomestic	0	0
Total	2,584	28
Friendship Inns	**Rooms**	**Properties**
Domestic	280	6
Nondomestic	18	1
Total	298	7
Royal Inns	**Rooms**	**Properties**
Domestic	0	7
Nondomestic	0	0
Total	0	7
5. HILTON HOTELS CORPORATION	**Rooms**	**Properties**
Domestic	321,553	1,864
Nondomestic	11,557	46
Total	333,110	1,910
Hampton Inns	**Rooms**	**Properties**
Domestic	110,421	1,063
Nondomestic	1,949	15
Total	112,370	1,078
Hilton Hotels	**Rooms**	**Properties**
Domestic	94,206	225
Nondomestic	3,208	10
Total	97,414	235
Doubletree Guest Suites & Hotels	**Rooms**	**Properties**
Domestic	41,889	156
Nondomestic	505	2
Total	42,394	158

FIGURE 1.6   *(Continued)*

	Rooms	Properties
Embassy Suites	**Rooms**	**Properties**
Domestic	38,915	159
Nondomestic	950	4
Total	39,865	163
Hilton Garden Inns	**Rooms**	**Properties**
Domestic	12,174	86
Nondomestic	405	3
Total	12,579	89
Homewood Suites by Hilton	**Rooms**	**Properties**
Domestic	10,024	89
Nondomestic	0	0
Total	10,024	89
Harrison Conference Centers & Independents	**Rooms**	**Properties**
Domestic	8,527	53
Nondomestic	0	0
Total	8,527	53
Red Lion Hotels & Inns	**Rooms**	**Properties**
Domestic	5,377	33
Nondomestic	0	0
Total	5,377	33
Conrad International Hotels	**Rooms**	**Properties**
Domestic	0	0
Nondomestic	4,540	12
Total	4,540	12

[1]http://www.ahma.com/infocenter/top50.asp

rooms ÷ 4,200,000 rooms). The dominance of large hotel organizations and lodging chains is obvious. What is less obvious, however, is that in the great majority of cases, these brands do not "own" their hotels. Instead, owners of hotels elect to affiliate, for a fee, with the brand. This arrangement is discussed in great detail later in this text (Chapter 12) because the relationship between those who manage the brands (**franchisors**) and those who actually own and operate the hotels within the brand (**franchisees**) is quite unique.

HOTEL TERMINOLOGY AT WORK

Franchisor: Those who manage the brand and sell the right to use the brand name.

■

HOTEL TERMINOLOGY AT WORK

Franchisee: Those who own the hotel and buy the right to use the brand name for a fixed period of time and at an agreed-upon price.

■

Hotel Ownership/Management

A motorist is driving along the highway and sees the name of a popular hotel chain. The name is easily recognizable due, in part, to an extensive nation-wide advertising campaign. A typical comment of this driver is likely to be: *"I guess that hotel company purchased some land and built another hotel to operate in this location."* In fact, that is not likely to be the case. It is more likely that an independent investor or company has built the property on owned (or leased) land, and signed an agreement with those who own the brand to operate the hotel in a manner consistent with that brand's standards. In some cases, the investor may hire a third party to manage the hotel.

There are numerous ways that hotels are owned and managed (see Figure 1.7) including:

- *Single-unit property not affiliated with any brand.* Some single-unit properties have been in business for many years, are extremely success-ful and may be the pre-eminent hotel in a community or area. This, however, is the exception. These properties capture an ever-smaller **market share** in the lodging industry nationwide.

HOTEL TERMINOLOGY AT WORK

Market Share: The percentage of the total market (typically in dollars spent) captured by a property.

For example, a hotel generating $200,000 in business traveler guest room rental annually in a community where business travelers spend $1,000,000 per year will have a 20 percent market share.

■

- *Single unit properties affiliated with a brand.* Properties that are part of a **hotel chain** are most prevalent. This brand affiliation, whether inter-national, nationwide, regional, or located within an even smaller area, is successful because of name recognition, and because it is often easier to receive financing for businesses affiliated with a brand.

HOTEL TERMINOLOGY AT WORK

Hotel Chain: A group of hotels with the same brand name.

■

Of course, some owners have multiple hotels and when they do, they have a variety of options available to them. These include:

- *Multiunit properties affiliated with the same brand.* Some owners own several hotels and affiliate them all with the same brand. This often makes managing them easier because the expectations of the brand's owners are well known.

- *Multiunit properties affiliated with different brands.* Some owners elect to choose several brands. Sometimes this is done because they own more than one hotel in a market area and feel that two hotels with the same brand would not be best. In other cases, the owners may have some limited-service and some full-service hotels, and the same brand name would not represent both these types of properties well.
- *Multiunit properties operated by the brand or others.* Some brands will, for a fee, offer management services to hotel owners. Also, some companies neither own the brands nor the hotels, but simply provide, for a fee, management services to the hotel's owners. These companies are known as **management companies.** There are many management companies that operate hotels of numerous brands owned by many separate owners. This special arrangement will also be examined more fully later in this text (chapter 12).

HOTEL TERMINOLOGY AT WORK

Management Company: An organization that operates a hotel(s) for a fee.

Also sometimes called a "Contract Company."

■

- *Multiunit properties owned by the brand.* Some brands do own some of their own hotels. Independent (not controlled by the brand) ownership, however, is most common in the United States.

THE INTERNET AT WORK

Want to learn more about many of the franchise lodging organizations and management companies in the United States? If so, check out, *Lodging News of American Hotel & Lodging Association:*

www.lodgingnews.com/subs/fd/md09.asp

Hotel Organizational Structures

From the guest's perspective, the primary functions of hotel personnel remain the same regardless of property size. Guests, many of whom make advanced reservations, want to be checked into a safe and clean room and expect to make payment upon departure. They may expect the food and beverage services offered in a full-service property as well. As the number of rooms in a hotel increase, the number of staff it employs grows, and the staff work in increasingly more specialized positions.

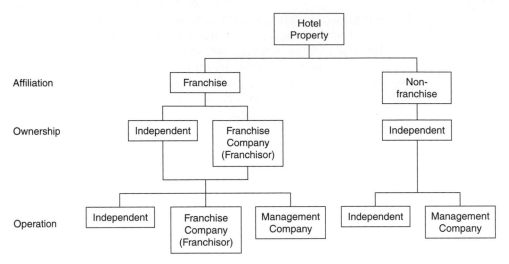

FIGURE 1.7 (Hotel Ownership/Management Alternatives) is a summary of the possible ownership/management arrangements possible today. It confirms that the ownership/management of a hotel can be complex because of the many possible ownership/management alternatives.

MANAGERS AT WORK

J. D. Ojisama is the assistant general manager of an independent (privately owned) full-service hotel with 250 rooms. The present general manager, the son of the hotel's founder, has expressed an interest in early retirement; he has two children, one of whom is a department head in the property.

J. D. has been approached by a management company to assume the position of general manager of a 350-room property in another city. The recruiter has noted the company's track record in quickly promoting its managers to larger properties with increasingly higher salaries. J.D. believes this to be true because of the increasing number of hotel management contracts the company is acquiring.

J.D. discusses the situation with the general manager who, in addition to being the boss, is also a friend. "You should do what is best for you," said the G.M. "However, you have a secure position here. Your salary increases are fair; and I promise they will keep coming. Besides, you grew up around here, and all your friends and relatives are here. If you move on with the management company, you will have to move from the area. Then, what will happen later if they lose some properties or are acquired by another company? You have a good job with almost guaranteed employment here. Why jeopardize it?"

If you were J.D., what issues would affect your decision. Why might J.D. want to move on to employment with the contract management company? Why might J.D. want to stay with his present employer? What would you do?

To understand the differences in hotels of varying sizes, consider the organizational charts that are typical in a small hotel (less than 75 rooms), large hotel (350 rooms), and mega property (3,000 rooms).

Small Hotel

Figure 1.8, an organization chart for a smaller, limited-service hotel, shows the possible organizational structure for a ±75-room property. The property owner may even be the general manager. Such a hotel is likely to have an individual in charge of maintenance, as well as maintenance support staff, an executive housekeeper who supervises those hourly employees who work to clean the hotel's rooms and public space, and a front office manager who supervises the staff working at the hotel's front desk. There may or may not be a designated individual responsible for hotel sales. A bookkeeper/accountant (typically part time) is retained for completion of financial reports and tax returns.

Large Hotel

Figure 1.9, an organization chart for a larger, full-service hotel, illustrates the departments and functions that are discussed in detail in the chapters that follow. With increased size, specialists (department heads) are hired by the general manager to perform front office, housekeeping, food/beverage, safety/security, engineering/maintenance, marketing, accounting, and, perhaps, other functions. These top-level officials require assistance from managers and supervisors who, in turn, manage the day-to-day work of entry-level staff members.

Mega Hotel

Figure 1.10, an organization chart for a mega, full-service hotel, shows the possible organization for a very large hotel. Note, for example, the food/beverage department and its many specialized positions. Specialized positions for the other departments are also necessary to handle the increased work

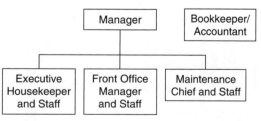

FIGURE 1.8   Organization Chart for Small (75-Room), Limited-Service Hotel

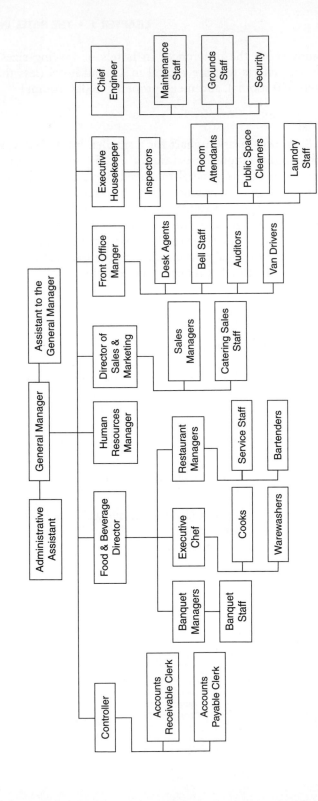

FIGURE 1.9 Organization Chart for Large (350 Room), Full-Service Hotel

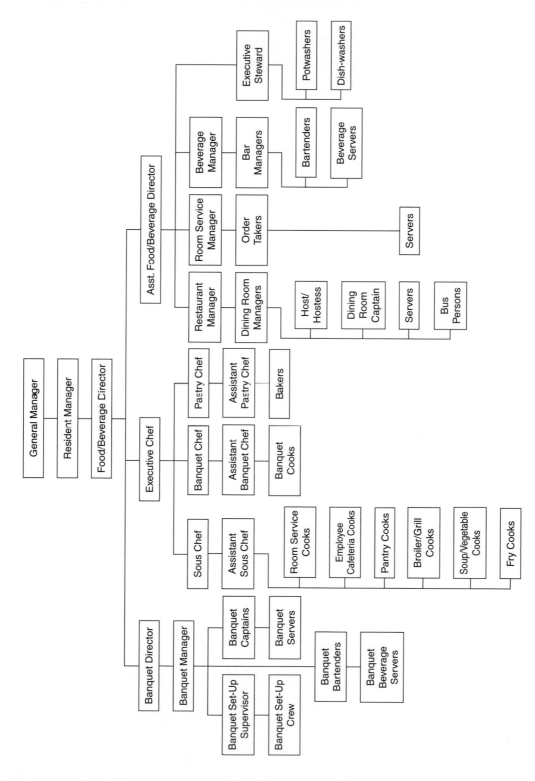

FIGURE 1.10 Organization Chart for Mega (3,000-Room) Hotel

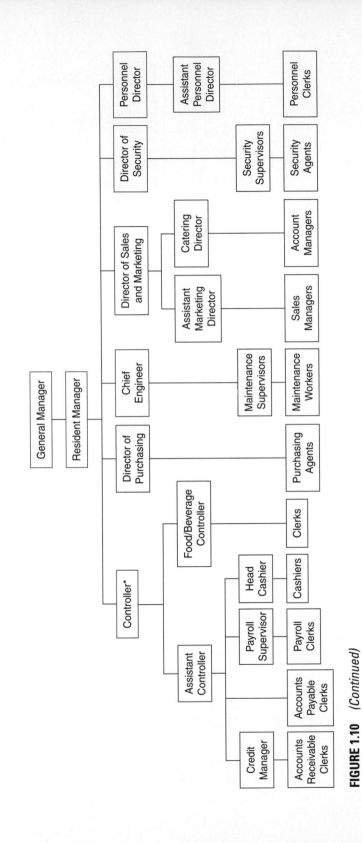

FIGURE 1.10 *(Continued)*

26

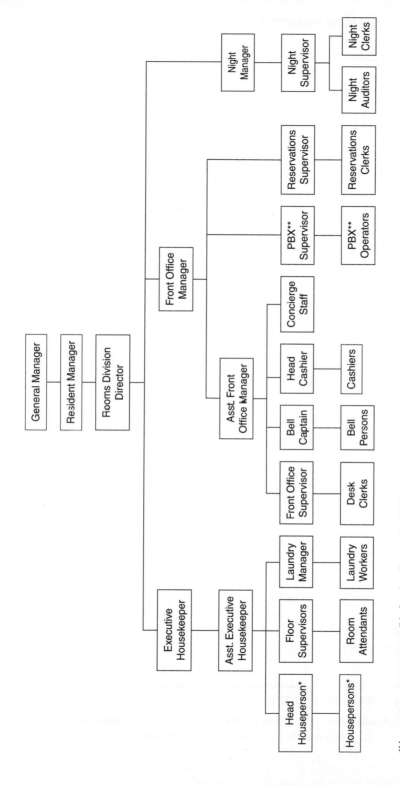

*Housepersons are responsible for cleanliness of public/group function spaces.
**Public Broadcast Exchange—a technology relating to the within-hotel communications (telephone) system.

FIGURE 1.10 *(Continued)*

required to effectively operate a hotel property with this many (or more) rooms.

Hotel Departments

Future chapters in this book discuss hotel departments in detail, as well as how G.M.s can best manage them. However, the concepts of line and staff departments and revenue and cost centers can be examined now.

Line and Staff Departments

Hotel departments can be classified according to line and staff functions. **Line departments** are those directly involved in the "chain of command." Managers in these departments are responsible for making the direct operating decisions that impact the success of the property. Examples of line departments are the front office and the food and beverage departments.

HOTEL TERMINOLOGY AT WORK

Line Departments: Hotel divisions that are in the "chain of command" and are directly responsible for revenues (such as front office and food/beverage) or for property operations (such as housekeeping and maintenance and engineering).

■

Managers in line departments need the specialized and technical assistance of persons in **staff departments.** These specialists provide information to support the line decision makers. Typical staff departments in a hotel relate to purchasing, human relations, and accounting. For example, the purchasing staff buys those items needed by line menu planners. Human relations personnel do not "hire and fire employees"; their role is to provide personnel needed by line departments and to provide technical advice about labor laws, training, and related specialized activities. Finally, accounting personnel are responsible for developing accounting systems, collecting financial information, recording data in financial statements, and making recommendations to (but not decisions for) line decision makers in line departments.

HOTEL TERMINOLOGY AT WORK

Staff Departments: Hotel divisions that provide technical, supportive assistance to line departments, for example, the human resources department.

■

Revenue and Cost Centers

Another way to think about hotel departments is to consider whether they generate revenue or, alternatively, whether they incur costs to support the departments that do generate revenue. The two most obvious examples of **revenue centers** are the front office department, which generates revenue from the sale of guest rooms, and the food and beverage department that sells products in dining rooms, lounges, room service, and banquets.

HOTEL TERMINOLOGY AT WORK

Revenue Center: A hotel department that generates revenue. Two examples are the front office and food and beverage departments.

■

A hotel also may receive revenues from telephone services, space rental (such as leasing a gift shop or other space), and could include revenue sources such as fees from parking garages, vending machines, golf courses, and other areas that will vary by the hotel's product offerings.

A **cost center** exists to help revenue centers generate sales. Examples include the marketing, maintenance, accounting, human resources, and security departments. Today and in the future, cost centers will be increasingly required to quantify exactly how they provide value to the organization. Managers will challenge the cost effectiveness of all money spent for salaries and wages and to purchase other resources required by all departments within the hotel.

HOTEL TERMINOLOGY AT WORK

Cost Center: A hotel department that incurs costs in support of a revenue center. Two examples are the housekeeping and maintenance departments.

■

LODGING IS A SERVICE BUSINESS

Earlier in this chapter we suggested that a hotel is more than just a building with guest rooms. Successful hotels are increasingly differentiated from their unsuccessful counterparts by an emphasis on serving their guests. Although the brand name a hotel uses is important, it is not the most important factor in a hotel's success. Guests return to good hotels for the same reasons they return to good restaurants. These reasons include personalized service, quality products and fair prices. Today's hotel guests desire good service, and they are willing to pay for it. Effective managers continually ask the question: *"What's best for our guests?"*

When hoteliers make decisions based on putting guest's needs first, their hotels do well. When decisions made put the hotel first by attempting to maximize revenue, minimize costs, and do "what's easiest" or what has always been done, invariably guest service will suffer, as will the long-term financial health of the hotel.

Successful hotels implement effective strategies to consistently deliver quality guest service. In today's marketplace, technological advancements can help this process, and we discuss many of these in this book. In addition, staff development will become increasingly important as hotel managers seek to effectively train their staff to deliver the quality guest service that will make their hotels excel.

As they seek to deliver quality service, the questions that must be addressed by hotel managers include:

- How will we demonstrate to our own staff members the need for high-quality guest service?
- How exactly will we evaluate the level of service quality being provided to our guests?
- What exactly are our service strategies and our service procedures?
- How will we train our staff about service concerns and the tactics to deliver service?
- How will we reinforce our service strategies?
- What can we do to emphasize service as a philosophy rather than as a program with a definite start and end time?
- What can we do to excel in the guests' **moments of truth**?

HOTEL TERMINOLOGY AT WORK

Moments of Truth: Any (and every) time that a guest has an opportunity to form an impression about the hotel. Moments of truth can be positive or negative.

■

The most important ingredient for a successful service emphasis within a hotel is (and will continue to be) top-level commitment. As this occurs, general managers will:

- Have a strong vision and a strategy for service that is clearly developed and clearly communicated
- Practice visible management
- "Talk" service routinely
- Have guest-friendly systems
- Balance "high-tech" with "high-touch" (in other words, to balance sophisticated systems and methods with personal factors)
- Recruit, hire, train, and promote for service quality

- Market service to guests
- Measure service and make the results available to service staff

Unfortunately, some general managers think only about tactics to generate revenues and to reduce costs. These are, of course, important. However, issues relating to the consistent delivery of the proper quality of products and services to guests must first be addressed. As this is done, the foundation for a successful hotel organization will then be in place.

CURRENT ISSUES CONFRONTING HOTELIERS

There are many issues and challenges confronting hoteliers in today's competitive hotel environment. This section contains a special focus on operating, marketing, technology, industry consolidation, and economic issues.

MANAGERS AT WORK

J.D. Ojisama accepted a general manager's position at a very nice hotel. The property was a good one: It had a great staff, a high occupancy rate, and consistently met budgeted revenue and profit goals. The previous general manager had retired and had left J.D. with an excellent property with which to hone the skills he learned as the assistant general manager at the previous property.

Within a week on the job, J.D. had an opportunity to make some decisions that would help set the pace for the staff's attitude toward guest service.

"Here's the situation," said the front office manager. "The couple in our Bridal Suite was due to check out at noon today. Their wedding generated about twenty sold guest rooms for their relatives and the bride's father spent several thousand dollars on their wedding reception in our ballroom yesterday."

"Well," said J.D., "Sounds like the event was a big success. I hope they feel the same way."

"Yes, they do," replied the front office manager. "The problem isn't them; It's the weather. All outbound flights are delayed—they'll probably be canceled—because of the snowstorm we are having. I don't think they really care; they're enjoying our hotel and the groom just called to inform me that they were planning to stay the second night—tonight—and he was looking for a good deal on the room rate."

"No problem; let's give him a good rate," said J.D.

"That's where the problem arises," said the front office manager. "Another couple living here in town is scheduled to hold their reception here tonight and have booked the Bridal Suite for *this* evening. It's the only Bridal Suite with all the appropriate amenities that we have. It looks like we're going to have tonight's couple very mad at us. I hope they don't have lots of friends in the community . . . so they can't tell them we didn't give them the room they reserved on their Wedding night!"

"Well," said J.D., "let's think about this. I wonder if there is a way to please both couples rather than to disappoint one of them. Let's put our heads together and see if we can come up with a solution."

What are some alternatives that J.D., working with the front office manager, might consider? What might the hotel offer to the couple currently occupying the Bridal Suite to encourage them to move to another room? What might the hotel offer the incoming couple as an incentive to select another room? What other issues might be addressed by J.D. and the front office manager?

Operating Issues

Concerns confronting hoteliers as they consider the day-to-day operation of their properties are many. Among these are:

- Labor shortages. Hoteliers almost everywhere are faced with the on-going problem of finding enough good employees. This is especially true for some hourly paid positions. Managers can address this concern by implementing procedures to (a) reduce turnover levels to minimize the number of new staff members that must be recruited, (b) increase productivity levels so that fewer employees are needed to effectively operate the hotel, and (c) recruit from nontraditional employee labor markets, including younger, inexperienced workers, the elderly, and also physically challenged individuals.

- Cost containment. Good hoteliers are continually examining all possible ways to reduce costs without impacting quality. Interestingly, **downsizing**, which involves reducing the number of staff members employed, has been met with only limited, if any, success.

HOTEL TERMINOLOGY AT WORK

Downsizing: Reducing the number of employees and/or labor hours for cost-containment purposes.

■

This may speak to the effectiveness of past hotel management practices. Despite the fact that "all hotel rooms look alike when the guest is sleeping," the fact is that the traveling public pays for both a product (the room) and services provided with the room. An excessive emphasis on cutting the quality of either the product or service will ultimately result in reduced hotel revenue.

- Increased competition. Hoteliers in almost every geographic area in the United States indicate that their community is **overbuilt.** That is, that there are too many hotel rooms for the number of guests wanting to rent them. This has led to intense competition between properties in an effort to provide greater value to their guests and also greater profits to the hotel's owners.

HOTEL TERMINOLOGY AT WORK

Overbuilt: The condition that exists when there are too many hotel guest rooms available for the number of travelers wanting to rent them.

■

Marketing Issues

Properly managed hotels capture their fair share of the market. This becomes increasingly difficult to do, however, as competition increases. Effective managers need to be aware of the marketing issues that will affect them and respond properly. Current issues include:

- **Market segmentation** is increasing. Some lodging chains are attempting to focus on a specific niche of travelers (business, long term, vacation travelers, etc.). In addition, limited service properties are increasing in popularity in many markets. These are frequently of interest to senior citizens, travelers on "minivacations," and others who are very budget conscious.

HOTEL TERMINOLOGY AT WORK

Market Segmentation: Efforts to focus on a highly defined (smaller) group of travelers, for example, "executives desiring long-term stays" rather than "business travelers" (some of whom might only desire short-stay accommodations).

■

- Brands are overlapping. There is great concern, especially among those in the limited service markets, that some franchisors are expanding their number of brands to a point that franchisees purchasing franchises from the same franchisor are in direct competition with each other. In addition, as the number of brands increase, it becomes harder for consumers to differentiate between them.
- Increased sophistication of consumers. Internet use for the reserving of hotel rooms has increased dramatically, resulting in a better informed consumer but a more competitive selling environment for hoteliers.
- Increased number of **amenities**. Hotels are offering numerous new types of amenities, including business centers, exercise/recreational facilities, and creative innovations within guest rooms. These amenities increase costs for hotel owners, yet sometimes appeal to only a small segment of the hotel's market.

HOTEL TERMINOLOGY AT WORK

Amenities: Hotel products and services designed to attract guests.

Popular amenities include items such as free continental breakfasts, in-room coffee makers, exercise rooms business centers.

■

Technological Issues

Recent technological innovations include:

- Interactive reservation systems that allow potential guests to quickly make reservations at preferred room rates in reduced time (fewer "clicks" on their computer keyboards).
- Guest room innovations that include two (or more) telephone lines enabling Internet access, interactive menu ordering for room service, electronic games, and guest room checkout.
- **Data mining** technology that allows hotel marketing/sales personnel to utilize guest-related data in new and creative ways. This allows properties to learn more about guest needs and to then use this information for marketing and advertising purposes and to better serve current guests.

HOTEL TERMINOLOGY AT WORK

Data Mining: Using technology to analyze guest (and other) related data to make better marketing decisions.

■

- **Yield management.** Hotels, like airlines, are increasingly matching guest demand with room rates. When demand for rooms is high, discounts for room purchases are eliminated. When demand is low, discounts are implemented. This concept is discussed further in chapter 6, The Front Office. Advances in technology make yield management practices more common than ever before.

HOTEL TERMINOLOGY AT WORK

Yield Management: Demand forecasting systems designed to maximize revenue by holding rates high during times of high guest room demand and by decreasing room rates during times of lower guest room demand.

■

Economic Issues

"As goes the economy, so goes the lodging industry" is an observation that is generally true. During "good" times business travel is up, and business travelers tend to utilize higher-priced guest rooms. The reverse is also true: weakened economies equate to lessened business travel with a negative impact on hotel revenues. Also, like many areas of business, fewer and fewer companies franchise or own more and more hotels. As noted earlier in this chapter, today's hotel organizations frequently grow larger by buying other hotels. There are fewer independent properties, fewer franchisors, and fewer management companies as this consolidation trend continues. The result is not always good for consumers or the industry.

Today, with the impact of **globalization**, economies of the United States (and all other nations) and the communities within them are increasingly interrelated to the economic status of other countries throughout the world. As stated at the beginning of this chapter, the lodging industry is an integral part of the tourism industry. As such, it is affected by the extent to which travelers both within the country and around the world travel. Although this is obvious, it is also important to recognize the significant influence that the economies of the world, the country, the state, and the community play on the financial success of a lodging organization and the individual properties that comprise it.

HOTEL TERMINOLOGY AT WORK

Globalization: The condition in which countries and communities within them throughout the world are becoming increasingly interrelated.

■

PROFESSIONAL CAREER OPPORTUNITIES IN THE LODGING INDUSTRY

If you are serious about the hospitality industry, this book will confirm your interest because it demonstrates how hotel management is both exciting and rewarding. What's next? How can you plan for and implement a professional development program leading to a professional career in the lodging industry?

Alternative Management Positions

The lodging industry is vast and, therefore, so are the alternative management positions available within it. Figure 1.11 (Alternative Management Positions in the Lodging Industry) illustrates many of these positions. Those listed under multiunit exist when a hotel company owns or manages multiple (multi) properties. Regardless of your vocational/professional preferences, there is likely to be a rewarding position available in the fast-paced and exciting lodging industry. As you read this book, you will become familiar with many of these management positions. It is important to realize, however, that this book examines hotel management from the unique perspective of the individual seeking to be a hotel general manager.

FIGURE 1.11   Alternative Management Positions in the Lodging Industry

- General Manager
- Rooms division manager
- Front office manager
- Controller
- Executive housekeeper
- Catering manager
- Executive steward
- Food and beverage manager
- Banquet manager
- Chef
- Executive chef
- Food production manager
- Pastry chef
- Sous chef
- Room service manager
- Food and beverage controller
- Restaurant manager
- Beverage manager
- Purchasing director
- Human resources manager
- Credit manager
- Executive assistant manager
- Convention manager
- Marketing/sales manager
- Auditor
- Director of security
- Convention services director
- Resident manager
- Chief engineer

Typical Multiunit Positions
- Area general manager
- Regional general manager
- Director of training
- Vice president, finance
- Vice president, real estate
- Director of franchising

Get Started with Career Planning

How does one start to plan for a career in the lodging industry? Here are some suggestions:

- Many secondary and postsecondary schools offer hospitality-related programs of study. Although enrollment in and graduation from these programs is not absolutely critical to a successful career in the lodging industry, they can help greatly by providing job-related knowledge and by allowing you to express your early interest in the lodging/hospitality industry.

- Working in a variety of lodging positions (including educational internships) provides additional job-related knowledge. This will help you to develop important skills and get to know people in the lodging industry that can help you advance your career.

- Developing a **career ladder** for professional development within the lodging industry can also be helpful. This is a graphic "road map" that indicates possible career progression through a lodging organization. Career ladders can help you to rationally plan career advancement strategies. Working with a **mentor**, you can develop a long-range career plan that will enable you to advance between desired positions within planned time frames.

HOTEL TERMINOLOGY AT WORK

Career Ladder: A plan that projects successively more responsible professional positions within an organization/industry. Career ladders also allow one to plan/schedule developmental activities judged necessary to assume more responsible positions.

■

HOTEL TERMINOLOGY AT WORK

Mentor: A senior employee of a hotel who provides advice and counsel to less experienced staff members about matters relating to the job, organization, and profession.

■

- If you seek a management career within the lodging industry, it will be helpful to talk with general managers at hotels near you, industry leaders, and educators and to get suggestions from those currently employed within the lodging properties within your own community.

THE INTERNET AT WORK

Want to learn more about careers in the lodging industry? Check out the Council of Hotel, Restaurant and Institutional Educators Internet homepage at:

http://www.chrie.org

HOTEL TERMINOLOGY AT WORK GLOSSARY

The following terms were defined within this chapter. If you are not familiar with each of them, please review the segment of the chapter that contains the term.

Hoteliers	Franchisee	Overbuilt
Tourism industry	Market share	Market segmentation
Full-service hotel	Hotel chain	Amenities
Room service	Management company	Data mining
Limited-service hotel	Line departments	Yield management
Suite	Staff departments	Globalization
Guest	Revenue center	Network
Revenue	Cost center	Career ladder
Brand	Moments of truth	Mentor
Franchisor	Downsizing	

ISSUES AT WORK

1. You've learned about a wide variety of lodging properties, all of which must be managed. What type of hotel would you like to work in as you begin your career and as you gain more experience within it? Think about unique characteristics applicable to the management of a large urban property versus an isolated resort facility. Consider preferences of guests renting rooms for $40 per night versus $400 per night. Think about management concerns in a property with fifty rooms and one with 5,000 rooms. Each of these and related examples illustrates unique opportunities and challenges that must be managed by those in charge. What are some of these unique management concerns? What are some guest-related concerns and management principles that apply regardless of the hotel's location, guest room charge, or size?

2. This chapter has emphasized the need to consistently deliver guest service. If you were a general manager, what kind of guest relations training would you provide to your employees? What are principles that you would incorporate into the training? In addition to training, what other tactics could you use to consistently emphasize quality guest service at your hotel? (Think about contests, role modeling in which you as General Manager "walk the talk," and coaching sessions in which you reinforce desired service tactics as you see employees perform them.)

3. Hotels exist in every city. Where would you like to work in your management career? Why? What types of hotels are operated there? Name three advantages to becoming a general manager in the area you have selected. Are there disadvantages?

4. What would you do to address a labor shortage problem in your hotel? First, think about tactics you might use to retain current employees. (If they did not leave, there would be lesser need to recruit new staff members.) Then, think about tactics you could use to recruit new employees. How would you advertise employment opportunities in your hotel? What could you offer potential applicants that they might not receive from other employers that would help to make your hotel an "employer of choice" within the community?

5. The chapter briefly discusses career opportunities in the lodging industry. Think about what you would like to do in your career. What progressively responsible positions would you like to attain? What would you need to do, beginning now, to prepare yourself for these positions?

2
The Hotel General Manager

This Chapter at Work

Every hotel and lodging facility, regardless of its size, has a leader on the property that makes the final day-to-day decisions about how that property will operate. From the largest mega-hotel to the smallest Bed and Breakfast (B and B), this individual is critical to the hotel's image in the community, its reputation for guest service, and, most important, its ultimate profitability.

While the title of this person may vary depending on the hotel's size, the traditional term used is general manager (G.M.). In this chapter you will learn about the responsibilities of the G.M. and why the execution of these responsibilities is so important to the ultimate success of the property.

The G.M.'s role as a hotel property manager is significant. Equally important, however, are other abilities, including serving as a liaison with the property's owners (and, in many cases, the property's franchise organization and/or operating company) and representing the property to the local community. Another important responsibility involves training and facilitating the work of other managers.

In addition to understanding what a G.M. does, in this chapter you will discover alternative ways to develop the skills needed to become a G.M. These include formal education offered by both two-year (Associate degree) and four-year (Bachelor degree) programs and advanced degrees. Another option—On-the Job Training offered by hotel companies—is also discussed.

Your development as a G.M. will continue long after you assume responsibility for your first property. Therefore, the chapter concludes with a discussion of the opportunities and career paths for continued professional development offered by those organizations and trade associations dedicated to the advancement of the lodging profession.

If your goal is to become a G.M., this chapter will help you better understand the types of daily activities you will oversee on a continuous basis and what you can do now to prepare yourself for the job.

Chapter 2 Outline

RESPONSIBILITIES
  Investor Relations
  Brand Affiliation Management
  Community Relations
  Executive Committee Facilitation
  Property Management
SKILLS DEVELOPMENT
  Formal Education
    Two-year degree
    Four-year degree

  Advanced degrees
  On-the-Job Training
  Professional Development
    Business associations
    Trade associations
    Trade publications
HOTEL TERMINOLOGY AT WORK
  GLOSSARY
ISSUES AT WORK

RESPONSIBILITIES

A **general manager** is, arguably, the single most important human variable affecting a hotel's short-term profitability. If you aspire to be a G.M., you should know that the way you will do your job will directly affect the owners of the hotel, your community, your employees, and, of course, your guests.

HOTEL TERMINOLOGY AT WORK

General Manager (G.M.): The traditional title used to identify the individual at a hotel property who is responsible for final decision making regarding property-specific operating policies and procedures. Also the leader of the hotel's management team.

■

Property G.M.s "wear many hats" in the fulfillment of their duties. While it may not really be possible to identify any one role that is most important, the responsibilities involved in any G.M. position will vary based upon many factors, including ownership structure, location, and type of property. In some hotels, the G.M may be very guest oriented and spend a great deal of time with the guests; in others, the G.M. may view their role to be one of a staff development specialist who guides the growth of other managers in the hotel. Despite the demands of a particular hotel and the preferences of individual G.M.s, nearly all G.M. positions consist of some combination of the following significant tasks:

- Investor relations
- Brand affiliation management
- Community relations
- Executive Committee development
- Property management

Investor Relations

The G.M.'s role in investor relations is tremendously important. Investor relations include all communications between the G.M. and those who own the property. Property ownership can take many forms. A hotel may be owned and operated by the G.M. More often, however, the G.M. is employed either directly by the hotel's owners or by a management company that has been selected to operate the hotel for the owner (in some cases, the management company may own all or part of the hotel).

Individuals or corporations who own or invest in the hotel property will look to the G.M. to positively influence the hotel's standing in the market, its physical condition, and, of course, its profitability. Note: A hotel consists of both an ongoing service business and a real estate asset. Some owners may view the hotel primarily in terms of its business success; others will focus on the real estate/physical asset worth of the hotel property. The G.M. must continually inform ownership about the condition of both.

When the hotel requires additional investment in either the business (such as additional staff or more advertising) or the real estate asset (such as new **FF&E,** roof repair, parking lot resurfacing and the like), it is most often the G.M. who communicates that information to ownership.

HOTEL TERMINOLOGY AT WORK

FF&E: The term used to refer to the furniture, fixtures, and equipment used by a hotel to service its guests.

■

Owners/investors are usually willing to make additional investments in a property when doing so makes good economic sense. However, they generally must be presented with a persuasive case that additional investment is, in fact, a worthwhile course of action. It is an important part of the G.M.'s job to help make that case. If this is not done, the hotel's infrastructure may deteriorate, resulting in a declining quality of service for guests and, ultimately, reduced business volume.

The talents required to successfully manage the owner/investor relations' portion of the G.M.'s job include financial analysis, proficiency in written communication, and, often, effective public speaking/presentation skills. Owners want to know about the performance of their properties. No one will have a better idea of how the hotel is performing than its G.M. The ability to effectively inform investors and owners about the current performance and future needs of their hotel will be critical to that property's long-term success.

Brand Affiliation Management

Clarion, Comfort, Best Western, Hawthorn, Microtel, Holiday Inn, Ramada, Marriott, and Hilton are just a few examples of the many franchise brands in the market today. (Chapter 1 presents a more detailed overview of lodging brands.) Most hotels operated today are, in fact, affiliated with a franchise brand. The reason becomes very clear when you learn about front office operations and guest room sales in chapter 6, The Front Office. Sometime during your career you will likely manage a franchised property. Therefore, you should be aware that an important part of the G.M.'s job is to manage the brand at the property level. This includes continually monitoring operational standards set by the brand to ensure property conformance, communicating effectively with franchise brand officials about marketing and sales programs, and by using activities and programs offered by the brand that can improve the profitable operation of the hotel.

G.M.s who have worked with various franchise companies will verify that different brands have differing "personalities." Some brands attempt to exert extreme influence on day-to-day property operations; others take a more hands-off approach. In either case, it is up to you as a G.M. to manage the franchise relationship for the good of your investors, community, employees, and, most important, your guests.

To illustrate just one aspect of brand affiliation management, consider the quality inspection scores (sometimes called quality assurance [QA] scores) regularly given to properties by the franchise brand.

HOTEL TERMINOLOGY AT WORK

Quality Inspection Scores: Sometimes called quality assurance (QA) scores, these scores are the result of annual (or more frequent) inspections conducted by a franchise company to ensure that franchisor-mandated standards are being met by the franchisee. In some cases, management companies or the property itself may establish internal inspection systems as well. In general, however, it is the franchise company's quality inspection score that is used as a measure of the effectiveness of the G.M., the hotel's management team, and the owner's financial commitment to the property.

■

Quality inspection scores are the result of annual (or more frequent) inspections conducted by a franchise company to ensure that their mandated standards are being met by the franchisee. In the typical case, a franchise brand inspector arrives at the hotel property (either with or without prior notification) and in the presence of the G.M. undertakes a complete property inspection. The property then receives a "score" based on its compliance with established brand standards that have previously been communicated to the hotel. If a property consistently scores too low on these inspections, it runs the risk of being dropped as a franchisee by the brand's managers.

In some cases, management companies or the property itself may establish standards and inspection/rating systems in addition to, or in preparation for, the brand inspection. Often the resulting scores of brand inspections are used in property ratings, marketing efforts, and even by owners to partially determine the G.M.'s and other hotel managers' compensation/bonuses. Therefore, quality inspection scores become an important example of how the G.M. interacts with franchisors and/or management companies.

The talents required to successfully handle the brand affiliation management portion of the G.M.'s job include well-developed interpersonal skills, persuasive ability, listening skills, and the ability to write effectively.

Community Relations

In many communities, a hotel is more than merely another service business. In fact, the hotels in an area, collectively, dictate in large measure how those outside the community view the area. There is no doubt, for example, that

---

THE INTERNET AT WORK

For an example of one company (United States Franchise System's Best Inn and Suites) that mandates the public reporting of the summary results of individual property Quality Inspection (Assurance) scores go to:

www.bestinn.com.

---

the hotels located in the French Quarter of New Orleans lend ambiance to the entire area. This is just as true of hotels in nontourist areas. Therefore, local government and community leaders often look to local hotel G.M.s to become leaders in efforts to attract new businesses, expand tourism opportunities, and provide input as to the needs of the local business community. All these tasks are important because the health of any local hotel industry is partially dependent on the health of the overall local economy.

As a G.M., the opportunities to assist your local community will be varied and significant. Consider, for example, the hotel G.M who gets a call from the local mayor asking if the hotel can assist in hosting a gathering for the representatives of a manufacturing business that is considering building a new manufacturing facility in the community. The manufacturer's decision to do so would mean many jobs for the local community (as well as the opportunity for increased guest room sales by the hotel). Obviously, the G.M. would want to assist and, in fact, be a very visible host and community representative.

Additional community efforts that often involve a G.M. include charity events, fund-raisers held at the hotel, and interactions with community organizations seeking activity sponsorships from area businesses.

The talents required to successfully perform the community relations segment of the G.M.'s job include an outgoing personality, well-developed social skills, and, very often, effective public speaking and presentation skills.

Executive Committee Facilitation

While G.M.s are leaders in the community, it is on the hotel property itself where their leadership skills should be most readily apparent. In today's rapidly advancing technological world, it is unlikely that a G.M. will be the most knowledgeable expert in each functional (departmental) area of the hotel. (For example, in a large property, the G.M.'s knowledge of the intricacies of the specific electronic lock system will probably be less than that of the chief maintenance engineer or the director of security.) However, the G.M. is still the recognized leader of the managers who supervise the engineering and security departments. The G.M. is partially responsible for their professional development. The G.M. may not, in this example, be able to provide technical assistance even for a task as simple as the replacement of batteries in the actual locking device. The G.M. could, however, instruct the managers who are responsible for this activity about the best way to train their staff members to replace the batteries with a minimum amount of guest disruption.

Although larger properties may have more departments than smaller properties, the hotel G.M. in both is generally responsible to provide direction to the departmental managers within the hotel. Each of the departments are examined in detail in the following chapters. The goal is to identify the key aspects of each area that should be monitored by an effective G.M.

Functional Area	Responsible For
Human Resource Manager	Hotel staffing needs
Controller	Accounting for hotel assets and liabilities
Front Office Manager	Guest services and sales
Executive Housekeeper	Property cleanliness
Food and Beverage Director	Food and beverage production and service
Director of Security	Guest, employee and property safety/ security
Director of Sales and Marketing	Revenue production and hotel promotions
Chief Engineer	Upkeep of the hotel's physical facility

Each of the department heads in these functional areas report directly to the G.M. as seen in Figure 2.1 below.

Note: To more effectively demonstrate the purpose of this book and the manner in which a G.M. interacts with departmental managers, let's look at housekeeping—a typical department within every hotel. There is a chapter relating to housekeeping in this text. However, it is *not* the purpose of this book to explain how to be an executive housekeeper or how to properly clean

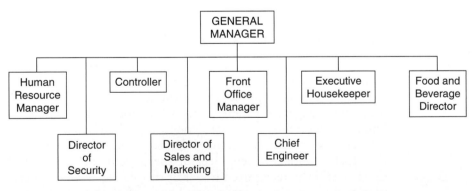

FIGURE 2.1 Typical Midsize, Full-Service Hotel Department Organizational Chart

a room. In fact, to attempt to do so in a relatively few pages would trivialize and play down the importance of the housekeeping department. Housekeeping is a tremendously complex area, and to do an excellent job as an executive housekeeper requires a unique individual with can-do attitude, detailed technical information, years of experience, and, most important, a commitment to the profession of executive housekeeper. What then, is the role of the G.M. in housekeeping? A G.M. without a strong housekeeping background should first learn the basics of the area, determine how best to monitor the effectiveness of the team performing housekeeping duties, and then develop his or her own role as a leader of, and mentor to, the executive housekeeper. This book, then, is written from the viewpoint of the general manager. It is *not* intended to be a quick overview of each hotel department but, rather, an in-depth look at how a G.M. manages each area.

A football coach may lack the ability to play all the positions on the field as proficiently as the individual players who make up the coach's team. Similarly, the G.M. is not expected to be an expert in the specific day-to-day operation of each hotel department. The G.M. is, however, expected to work with hotel managers that make up the executive operating committee (EOC) to improve their skills and the efficiency of the departments these individuals manage.

HOTEL TERMINOLOGY AT WORK

Executive Operating Committee (EOC): Those members of the hotel's management team (generally department heads) responsible for departmental leadership and overall property administration.

■

When you become a G.M., you will need to take the time to become familiar with the tasks being performed within each department. Hopefully, you will have gained some experience in many of the departments during earlier career training and experience. Also, effective G.M.s have a genuine interest in the professional development of the managers reporting to them. (Most successful managers can point to one or more individuals in their lives who took the time to "show them the ropes." As a G.M., you have a responsibility to be that person for the managers who work with you.)

The talents required to successfully handle this part of the G.M.'s job include good listening skills, the ability to evaluate and implement managerial training and development programs, and a desire to assist in the professional improvement and growth of your EOC team. The EOC members will count on you to help them advance in their own careers. Your demonstrated interest in them will be immediately reflected in how they treat their own staff and, in turn, how their staff members treat your hotel guests.

Property Management

If you ask the average person on the street what hotel G.M.s do in their jobs, the property management function is most likely to be mentioned. Indeed, while this chapter points out that a G.M. performs multiple tasks, certainly one of the most important is that of "managing" the hotel.

As noted earlier, a G.M. is not likely to possess all of the highly technical skills required to directly manage each hotel department. However, as the title implies, the G.M. should be able to direct the overall **management** of the property. In this book, you will learn what a G.M. needs to know to effectively manage each of the functional areas of a hotel.

HOTEL TERMINOLOGY AT WORK

Management: The process of planning, organizing, staffing, directing, controlling, and evaluating human, financial, and physical resources for the purpose of achieving organizational goals.

■

The property management goals of a hotel (as well as the goals of each department) will vary. However, it is the G.M.'s job to help achieve those goals. Goals may be related to profitability, service levels, efficiency, or any other objective set by the G.M. and/or the property owners. Traditionally, those who study the management of hotels or any other enterprise have described the management process as consisting of the following distinct functions:

Functional Area	Purpose
Planning	To establish goals and objectives
Organizing	To maximize the deployment of resources
Staffing/Directing	To provide leadership
Controlling/Evaulating	To measure and evaluate results

These are presented in Figure 2.2. Let's look at each management function more specifically.

Planning. Planning is the process of creating goals and objectives and then designing action plans/strategies and tactics to achieve those goals and objectives. G.M.s engage in the planning function when they establish the philosophical and operational direction of the hotel. They also help departmental leaders plan for their respective departments. In most cases, the planning activities undertaken by the G.M. cut across hotel departmental areas and require an overall, integrated approach to planning.

Consider, for example, the process by which you as G.M. might evaluate the goal of improving your property's competitiveness in the marketplace by

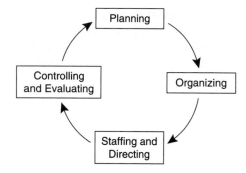

FIGURE 2.2   The Management Process

implementing a new guest service (improving your guests' ability to access the Internet from guest rooms). Also, assume the proposed service is the provision of unlimited, high-speed Internet access.

Sample questions you might consider in the planning (goal setting) portion of your role include:

- Why does it appear that this service enhancement is desirable?
- What *exactly* is the service to be provided to the guests?
- What are the technological/physical facility requirements to add the service?
- Which operational department(s) will be responsible for implementing the new service?
- Which operational department(s) will be responsible for ensuring the continued quality of the new service?
- How will the hotel fund the cost of providing the service? (Will the service be **"free-to-guests"** or will there be a specific charge for use of the service?)
- What are the marketing implications of providing the service? What are the marketing implications of *not* providing the service?
- How will the hotel measure the sales volume or reputation value gained versus the cost of providing the service?

HOTEL TERMINOLOGY AT WORK

Free-to-Guests: A service provided at no additional charge (beyond normal room rental charges) to the hotel guest. Examples could include making local telephone calls, access to premium cable television channels such as HBO or Showtime, and use of the hotel's pool or workout facilities. (Ultimately, the hotel must absorb the cost(s) of providing these services to guests, but guests are not charged on a per usage basis. Therefore, the term does not mean that the services that are provided are free to the hotel.)

If, as you plan, you determine that the provision of in-room, high-speed Internet access is a goal you desire, you will have completed this phase of the planning process. It is then your responsibility to move to the next step of the management process: organizing resources that allow you to achieve your objective.

Organizing.   The organizing function of management relates to arranging and deploying resources in a manner that most efficiently helps to achieve goals. When some managers think of the term "organizing," they think of a business's organizational chart. Even though an organizational chart is an effective way of showing how "human" resources are organized, nonhuman resources such as financial capital and the hotel's property and equipment also must be organized.

Back to our example of providing high-speed Internet access to guest rooms. If the decision has been made to implement this goal, all the hotel's resources must be organized and deployed to best achieve the goal. Staff members may be given assignments to begin implementing the service; dollars will be required to fund the process; and the property itself may need physical reconfiguration to accommodate the service. (For example, recabling of guest rooms to provide for the data transmission requirements or satellite installation for high-speed access will be required.)

Organizational skills are one of a G.M.'s most important talents. For most hotel G.M.s, the reality is that they have approximately the same amount of resources available to them as did the property's prior G.M. and the G.M. who will follow. It is the skillful deployment of human, financial, and equipment resources that can markedly affect the profitability of the hotel. Some G.M.s can create great visions and plans for their property, but lack the organizational skills required to effectively implement those plans. Other G.M.s seem to have a great talent for organizing resources in a way that results in achieving (and often exceeding!) the goals set for the property.

Organizing always follows planning. That is, the hotel G.M. plans and develops the objective, then organizes resources to realize the objective. The next step in the managerial process involves directing those who will attain the objective.

Staffing/Directing.   This concept relates, in its most comprehensive sense, to the G.M.'s recruiting, motivational, and leadership characteristics. In fact, some management experts use the terms "coaching" or "leading" rather than "directing" when referring to this area of management. (They do so because coaching and leading implies the teaching and encouraging of skills, which will successfully impact the actions and attitudes of staff members.)

In most hotels, the G.M. is the "coach" or "leader" of the entire staff. From the clothes the G.M. wears, to picking up debris in the corridor, to the way the G.M. greets the hotel's guests, the entire staff looks to the G.M. to set the personal and service standards for the entire property.

THE INTERNET AT WORK

To read an account of how the "directing" actions of the G.M. profoundly affect the entire staff, read "Think Strawberries." This account, by James Levenson, past president and chief executive officer of the New York Plaza Hotel, describes his own hotel management experience. It was originally published in the October 1974 issue of the *Saturday Evening Post*. This timeless, insightful, and often humorous classic can be accessed at:

www.easytraining.com/strawberry.htm.

The attitudes of employees reflect the attitudes of management in the hotel business. Department heads and **line-level** staff look to their G.M. for leadership.

HOTEL TERMINOLOGY AT WORK

Line-Level: Those employees whose jobs are considered entry level or nonsupervisory. These are typically positions where the employee is paid an hourly (rather than salary) compensation. Examples include positions such as guest service agents, room attendants, and food and beverage servers.

■

In our high-speed Internet example, leadership occurs as the G.M. keeps individual staff members "on task" with project completion timelines, undertakes efforts to build team spirit, engages in coaching for maximum staff performance, and sets an example by indicating how important successful completion of the project is to the hotel's overall success.

Successful hotel managers know what needs to get done in their properties. They can identify needed improvements in operations. A few typical examples illustrate that G.M.s can identify when:

- Cleaning procedures used in the banquet kitchen must be improved
- The maintenance tool storage area should be reorganized
- Room attendants must be better trained in the proper disposal of hypodermic needles found in guest rooms
- Room-type preferences of top-client, frequent-stay guests should be tracked and reported weekly (not quarterly)
- **"Comp"** room reports need to be submitted, with a justification for each comp, to the G.M.'s office on a daily basis when this is not currently done

Knowing what needs to be done is actually an easy part of the management process. Knowing how to get managers in each functional area to address the tasks in their respective departments is the hard part. It is here

---

HOTEL TERMINOLOGY AT WORK

Comp: Short for "complimentary" or "no-charge" for products or services.

Rooms, food, beverages, or other services are often given to guests by management if, in their opinion, the "comp" is in the best interests of the hotel.

The term can be used as either an adjective (e.g., "I gave them a comp room") or a verb (as in "I told the assistant manager to comp the room").

■

---

that the G.M. demonstrates real leadership, and often, through willpower, motivates a hotel staff to achieve things that were never before considered possible.

In review, managerial planning addresses what to do while organizing and directing how to do it. The next step in the management process involves control.

Controlling and Evaluating.   When most managers think of controlling and evaluation, they think of finances and accounting. Earlier in this discussion, however, you learned that the purpose of the controlling and evaluating function is to measure and assess results. The complete controlling task for the G.M., then, involves much more than journal entries, ledger balances, and changes in cash flow.

Again, consider our high-speed Internet service example. Perhaps none of the high-speed Internet service-related questions listed earlier are more important than this one: *How will the hotel measure the sales volume or reputation value gained versus the cost of providing the service?* This question is important because, generally, even the least effective G.M. can achieve increases in sales volume or service levels if unlimited resources are available. The reality, however, is that over the long term resources are not unlimited. In fact, the excessive expenditure of resources is wasteful, inefficient, and reduces the assets of the hotel.

During the controlling process the G.M. assesses the effectiveness of his or her own actions as well as that of the management team. Were room revenue budgets met? Did sales productivity in the Food and Beverage department meet expectations? Did quality inspection scores increase or decrease from the previous inspection? Were maintenance costs related to the swimming pool incurred as planned? Or, as in our high-speed Internet example, *Was the high speed Internet service installed in the guest rooms at the proper cost to the hotel, marketed to guests within budget guidelines, and was the final outcome a measurable improvement in room sales and/or guest satisfaction?* A G.M. controls the effectiveness of personal staff efforts. It is an important role that must be attended to on a continuous basis.

The actual management of the hotel property is one of the most visible and challenging aspects of a G.M.'s job. It is also one of the most exciting.

The talents required to successfully handle this part of the job include organizational and coaching skills, analytical and financial analysis skills, an ability to anticipate guest needs, competitive spirit, and tremendous attention to detail. In addition, a truly effective G.M. has the near-magical ability to inspire the staff to make guests feel truly welcome when they stay at the property.

It may seem somewhat odd to warn an aspiring G.M. about spending too much time "managing" the property, but this can happen. Remember, it is a well-trained staff, directed by highly motivated departmental leaders, that will best ensure guests receive reliably excellent service. After all, no G.M. can consistently be on the property twenty-four hours per day, seven days a week.

Similarly, a G.M. who spends too much time in investor relations or any other job task may find that some other important job area(s) will suffer from neglect. G.M.s are challenged to define their own role while considering the best use of their time in the critical areas of investor relations, brand management, community activities, EOC development, and property operations to maximize the long-term value of the hotel, as well as their own career.

SKILLS DEVELOPMENT

The training and experience required to become a G.M. vary based on the size and complexity of the property to be managed: it takes more experience, preparation, and skill to effectively manage a 2,000-room resort than to operate an eighty-room limited service hotel. While the manager of the latter property certainly has a complex job, the manager of the resort property

---

MANAGERS AT WORK

J.D. Ojisama is the G.M. of a full-service hotel owned by Partner's Equity Group (a collection of investors who have pooled their money to purchase the hotel).

Because of the excellent way the property has been managed, J.D.'s hotel has achieved quality scores among the top 5 percent in the franchise chain each year J.D. has been the property's G.M.

At their annual convention, the franchise company announces a change in franchise standards that mandates all properties offer twenty-seven-inch televisions in their guest rooms within twelve months. This mandate represents a change from the current standard of simply providing each guest room with a traditional twenty-five-inch TV. Any property that does not comply with the new policy within the twelve-month time frame will face the certainty of reduced quality inspection scores. J.D.'s annual salary bonus is dependent, in part, on the quality scores achieved by the property.

Whose role is it to "sell" the owners on the expenditure required to implement the new standard? What would you advise J.D. do to help make the case for the improvement?

What specific skills will J.D. likely need to achieve the goal of communicating the property's need for this mandated guest service enhancement? Where might J.D. have obtained these skills?

will be compensated to a higher degree and will find that the career path required to secure the position is longer. In both cases, however, the managers of these two types of properties, as well as all other properties, will find that the preparation required in their positions consists of some combination of formal education, on-the-job training, and continued professional development.

Formal Education

If you are interested in pursuing a formal educational degree that has traditionally helped prepare individuals for the role of G.M., you are in good company. There are literally hundreds of such schools, and thousands of such students, in the United States. Formal hospitality education most often occurs at either a two-year, four-year, or advanced degree program.

Two-Year Degree

Programs offering a two-year Associate's degree in hotel (hospitality) management can be found in many local community colleges. Typically, these programs are designed for both traditional college students and more nontraditional working students. Required classes are often offered on the weekends or evenings. Program titles are not standard in hospitality education; it may be possible to find relevant programs under any of the following names (or variations of them):

- Hotel Administration
- Hotel and Restaurant Management
- Hospitality Administration
- Restaurant, Hotel, and Institutional Management
- Food Service Management
- Hospitality Business
- Tourism Administration
- Culinary Arts

A two-year Associate's degree in hotel administration is a good choice for those individuals who wish to terminate their formal education after several years of study. In addition, the two-year degree may be a good choice for those individuals who already have a Bachelor's degree in another subject and simply wish to gain knowledge of the hotel industry in an academic setting.

Classes required to complete the two-year degree generally consist of some general education courses (English, writing, math, history, etc.) and some courses specific to the hospitality industry. These are likely to include classes such as Introduction to the Hospitality Industry, Hospitality Operations Management, Cost Control, Hospitality Law, Marketing,

Human Resource Management, Food and Beverage Production/Management, and others designed to teach students how to manage a hospitality operation. The largest two-year programs may allow students to select a concentration of courses specifically designed for hotel managers. Often courses will be applicable for both restaurant and hotel managers, so it is important to carefully select a program that has sufficient hotel emphasis.

Typically, hospitality-related courses at the two-year level are taught by a combination of full-time faculty and practicing professionals from the local hospitality community. This educational approach is usually very practical and current. An additional advantage of practicing professional instructors is that they may be well connected in the community and so will be able to assist you in seeking temporary or even permanent job placement in the local area.

Four-Year Degree

Four-year degree programs are less available than two-year programs; however, about every state has at least one or more quality institutions offering the Bachelor (four-year) degree in hotel, restaurant, or hospitality administration. Some programs are better known than others, and the price students will pay to attend depends, in part, on the institution's status as a public or private school. The best of the four-year schools have a diverse faculty, quality facilities, and offer an excellent learning environment.

Although most students today take longer than four years to complete a Bachelor's degree, the course of study is roughly twice as extensive as the typical two-year degree. As with the two-year degree, students pursuing a four-year degree will find about one-half of the coursework involves general education. The balance of the courses will be either hospitality related, general business, or electives.

Although the time commitment is significant, the four year degree is a good choice for students who wish to complete a Bachelor's degree, who seek to learn from a larger number of qualified faculty, and who wish to obtain a degree that is generally considered "more advanced" than the two-year degree.

Advanced Degrees

For some people, an advanced (graduate) degree in hospitality management makes sense. The typical advanced degree completed by students is the Master's in hospitality administration, and at least one college or university in each state generally offers it.

Entrance to a Master's degree in hospitality administration at most educational institutions is highly competitive. Admission typically requires that a student previously completed an undergraduate degree and achieved excellent grades while doing so.

Generally, the requirements for completing the Master's degree vary both by the educational institution offering the degree and the background of the student pursuing it. A typical Master's degree program consists of one to two years of study beyond the Bachelor's degree. In nearly all cases, faculty in charge of the degree program will require that students demonstrate that they have achieved mastery of the required subject matter and the ability to communicate effectively before the degree is granted.

Regardless of the degree you may wish to pursue, it is important to realize that formal education will not "make" you a qualified hotel G.M. Formal education can, however, provide excellent tools with which to perform the job of G.M. when you attain this position.

THE INTERNET AT WORK

For current information on educational institutions in the United States offering two- and four-year degrees in your geographic area (as well as advanced degree programs) go to:

www.hospitalitylawyer.com

and click on "Schools."

On-the-Job Training

Most hotel management companies realize that, to be the very best, they must continually update and sharpen the skills of their G.M.s. Consider for a moment the challenge facing the president of a hotel company operating one hundred properties when an advancement in data file server technology allows information on an individual guest's room preferences to be shared across the hundred properties. The opportunities to better serve the guest become significant but can only be achieved if each G.M. understands what must happen on their own property to fully utilize the benefit of a shared file environment. A situation such as this calls for **on-the-job training (OJT)**. That is, the company itself must provide the learning experiences needed for G.M.s to learn how to implement the property-level changes required to effectively share the guest information.

HOTEL TERMINOLOGY AT WORK

On-the-Job Training (OJT): Learning activities designed to enhance the skills of current employees. OJT programs are typically offered by management with the intent of improving guest service and employee performance at the hotel. There is generally no charge to the employee for the training.

■

For hotel G.M.s, on-the-job training in recent years has focused on two major industry trends:

- The impact of advancing technology
- The impacts of a changing workforce

This book addresses many of the results of these trends in each chapter because advancements in technology and the changing workforce affect every area of the hotel. As a future G.M., you need to be aware of these changes and the role that OJT programs offered by your company can play in improving your skills. Just as important, when you lead a hotel, you'll need to create and implement OJT programs for your own management staff to keep their skills up-to-date and your property running smoothly.

Professional Development

The hotel industry is dynamic; G.M.s must constantly stay abreast of the business, societal, workforce, and increasingly, technological changes that affect how they do their jobs. In some companies, sufficient OJT programs to fully develop needed skills simply may not exist. If so, you must manage your own professional development. Fortunately, there are many resources available, including business and trade associations and industry publications.

Business Associations

In nearly every community large enough to support a hotel, you will be able to join local business associations. Local Chambers of Commerce and related business associations can be a critical part of your overall efforts to keep your skills "up-to-speed" without leaving your community. Chamber members benefit from business/skills enhancement programs, networking opportunities, timely publications, and seminars that include local economic data and best management practices.

Additional membership features include professional development opportunities to make you a better manager and, in some cases, provide low- or no-cost training for your entry-level workers. Other Chamber activities include lobbying for business interests and facilitating public-private employment initiatives. Chambers of Commerce and other professional service organizations often hold meetings and schedule speakers to update you on the newest business thoughts and methods. While it is unlikely that these sessions will be hotel-specific, many topics, especially those related to human resources and technology, will be generally applicable. Given all that they do and can help you accomplish, membership in local business associations is generally well worth the modest cost.

Trade Associations

As a G.M., you will likely belong to one or more professional trade associations in addition to the American Hotel and Lodging Association (AH&LA). Trade associations typically serve the certification, educational, social, and legislative needs of their members. Associations usually hold monthly and annual gatherings and, in conjunction with these meetings, often offer educational seminars/workshops to improve the knowledge and skills of their members.

In addition, most trade associations, in conjunction with their annual meetings, invite companies who sell products and services of interest to the membership to participate in a trade show. These shows bring together a variety of vendors, all of whom are interested in exhibiting their latest product offerings. Trade shows are an extremely efficient way to see new products and service offerings of a large number of vendors in a very short time. Many trade associations also have both state- and local-level chapters, some of which host their own trade shows. Vendors can be an excellent source of information about new developments in the industry, and you should make an effort to attend association-sponsored meetings and trade shows when possible.

THE INTERNET AT WORK

For information on some of the professional associations you may wish to join, go to:

American Hotel and Lodging Association: www.ahla.com
International Hotel & Restaurant Association: www.ih-ra.com
National Restaurant Association: www.restaurant.org
American Culinary Federation: www.acfchefs.org
Hospitality Financial and Technology Professionals: www.iaha.org
Professional Convention Management Association: www.pcma.org

The hotel industry is fortunate to have an additional resource for professional development that exists in only a few other industries. It is called the Educational Institute of the American Hotel and Lodging Association, or **E.I.** for short.

HOTEL TERMINOLOGY AT WORK

E.I.: The shortened version of the name given to the Educational Institute of the American Hotel and Lodging Association (AH&LA). Located in Orlando, Florida, and Lansing, Michigan, E.I. is the professional development and certification subsidiary of the AH&LA.

■

The mission of E.I. is to help hotel owners and managers become better trained and to provide resources that allow these individuals to better train their own staffs. In addition, E.I. provides certification services for a variety of management, supervisory, and line-level industry positions including the CHA (certified hospitality administrator), the CFBE (certified food and beverage executive), the CLSS (certified lodging security supervisor), and the registered Guest Room Attendant.

THE INTERNET AT WORK

For information on the professional development programs for G.M.s offered by the Educational Institute of the American Hotel and Lodging Association, go to:

www.ei-ahla.org.

Trade Publications

Trade publications take many forms. The book you are currently reading is a type of trade publication because it has been published specifically for those interested in the hotel industry. There are a variety of books and publishers in the hospitality field. Many of them, including this one, can be excellent additions to your own professional library.

THE INTERNET AT WORK

For a look at other hospitality books published by Prentice Hall, visit their Web site at:

www.prenhall.com.

Select the discipline, "Hospitality & Travel/Tourism."

Many industry publications are produced monthly or more frequently. Some are offered free of charge to industry professionals. Typically, these publications are produced in either newspaper or magazine formats, and the best of them can be an excellent source of information on the latest hotel industry news, trends, and practices. Sometimes technology applications have become a large part of the editorial interest of these publications, and a technology editor is employed to monitor technological changes for the publication's readers. Human resources developments are also an important part of most trade publications.

While hotel G.M.s often find that there are not enough hours in the day to complete all the tasks they wish complete, those professionals who take the time to stay up-to-date by reading industry books and publications find the time is exceptionally well spent. These individuals are well informed, ahead of their competitors relative to current information, and ultimately are more successful with both their employees and guests.

THE INTERNET AT WORK

For a look at some of the important issues facing today's hotel G.M., as well as publications that you may find helpful in your career development, go to:

www.bpubs.com/industry_publications/hospitality/.

HOTEL TERMINOLOGY AT WORK GLOSSARY

The following terms were defined within this chapter. If you are not familiar with each of them, please review the segment of the chapter that contains the term.

G.M. (general manager)
FF&E (furniture, fixtures, and equipment)
Quality inspection scores

EOC (Executive Operating Committee)
Management
Free-to-guests
Line-level

Comp (complimentary)
OJT (on-the-job training)
E.I. (Educational Institute of the AH&LA)

ISSUES AT WORK

1. A G.M. has responsibilities to guests, employees, owners, and, of course, to themselves. What are some reasons these interests might come into conflict? If that were to happen, whose interests do you think you would consider to be the most important? Why?

2. The late 1990s saw tremendous technological advancements in the hotel industry which continue today. Which two departmental areas in a hotel do you believe have been most affected by technological advancements during the past ten years? Why? Did you find that your lack of knowledge about a specific area resulted in your believing that few technological advances occurred in that area? How can effective G.M.s prevent these types of blind spots?

3. It has been said that 10 percent of a manager's time should be spent on preparing themselves for the next higher level job, 80 percent of their time doing their current job, and 10 percent of their time helping those individuals who are at the level below them to prepare for advancement to the

next level (their current) job. Do you think this is true for a G.M.? How would you modify the equation in your own situation?

4. Some practicing G.M.s elect to pursue four-year or higher degrees that they believe will assist in their career advancement. What are some of the advantages and potential disadvantages of such a career advancement strategy? What alternatives would you suggest to a G.M. whose geographic location prevents such an approach?

5. The Educational Institute of the American Hotel and Lodging Association offers the certified hotel administrator (CHA) designation for professionals who meet established standards and pass a competency exam appropriate for a hotel G.M. Do you think that the CHA is a designation that would be valuable for you to seek? Why or why not?

3

Management and Supervision Skills for the G.M.

This Chapter at Work

In this chapter you will learn more about the management principles and procedures you will use as a G.M. to interact with the department heads and other staff you supervise. This is important because the way you manage those reporting to you will heavily influence how those managers will, in turn, supervise their own staffs. The chapter begins by emphasizing that the G.M. is a significant influence on the organizational culture of the property. Good or bad, the G.M. serves as a key role model to a hotel organization.

Effective hoteliers manage staff members and other resources such as money, equipment, energy and time according to basic, proven management principles. This chapter provides a short overview of these management basics.

There has been a significant evolution of traditional hotel human resources practices. In the "old days," the G.M. was the ultimate authority and let everyone know it! Today, increasingly, there is a focus on employees input, both as individuals and as members of the hotel team. While it is true that successful G.M.s can practice a variety of management styles, good G.M.s know that creating a thriving hotel is very much a team effort and that every member of the team is important to the property's ultimate success.

Some G.M.s spend very little time "planning for things" and much time "doing things." This chapter emphasizes the need for up-front planning to precede the management of any asset, including human resources. Principles of decision making, organizing, and delegation are presented. A brief overview of the flow of communication up, down, and across the hotel organization is also presented, as is essential information about the principles of motivation, leadership, and discipline.

G.M.s must have some information about how to build and make the most effective use of employee teams. As well, they must utilize proven tactics for selecting, orientating and training staff members. These, too, are presented in this chapter.

Finally, while there is probably no such thing as an "average" day for a G.M., this chapter concludes by providing examples of what G.M.s do every day in the course of their normal duties.

Chapter 3 Outline

THE G.M. SETS THE PACE
G.M.s MUST MANAGE
    G.M. Functions
    G.M. Skills
    G.M. Relationships

G.M.s Manage in Times of Change
EVOLUTION OF TRADITIONAL HOTEL HUMAN RESOURCES PRACTICES MANAGEMENT BASICS

THE G.M. SETS THE PACE

The old saying in the hospitality industry that "it all starts at the top" is true. For example, how the G.M. feels about and acts regarding issues such as sanitation, safety, or providing excellence in guest service will very likely impact the attitude of the hotel's staff when they address these same issues. So it is with a focus on **human relations** within the hotel.

HOTEL TERMINOLOGY AT WORK

Human Relations: Skills needed to understand and effectively interact with other people.

■

Throughout this book we have emphasized that the hospitality industry is very labor intense: It takes a large number of staff members to produce the services and products guests seek. The G.M. must be able to effectively manage this staff. Typically, the G.M. will only direct personally the work of department heads and, perhaps, a relatively few other staff. The importance of the G.M.'s supervision style, however, cannot be overstated. By contrast, the department head in the housekeeping or food and beverage department directly supervises many more staff members. However, the manner in which the G.M. interacts with department heads will most often set the pace for the relationship between the department heads and their own staff members.

Consider, for example, a G.M. who genuinely respects the department heads, who values and solicits and, when possible, utilizes their input and effectively communicates with them. Contrast this G.M. with one who doesn't respect or seek advice from the department heads and who "communicates" only one way: *"Do it my way, or I'll replace you!"* Department heads that, like the first G.M., are effective "people persons" would not be able to work well with a G.M. of the second type. They would leave and would eventually be replaced by others who, not surprisingly, treat their subordinates exactly as their own boss treats them.

The G.M., then, has a direct impact upon how managers in the property interact with their employees. This, in turn, influences the level of morale, the employee turnover rate, and the extent to which products and services of desired quality are consistently delivered to the guests. This is true because inexperienced staff members, in any department, are often slower, and make more mistakes than their equally talented, but more experienced coworkers.

The remainder of this chapter focuses on basic principles, strategies and tactics that effective G.M.s utilize as they interact with those they supervise. As a result, the chapter also provides ideas about how department heads, managers, and supervisors should interact with those for whom they are responsible.

G.M.s MUST MANAGE

The process of management involves using resources to attain organizational goals. Of the resources available to hospitality managers, people (human resources) are clearly the most complex and important for success. From the perspective of a specific hotel property, the G.M. is considered the top-level manager.[1] Figure 3.1 reviews four organizational levels within a hotel.

As seen in Figure 3.1, G.M.s represent the highest management level on the property. They direct the work of department heads. Department heads are considered middle-level managers who, in turn, direct the work of supervisors and managers who then oversee the work of entry level employees.

FIGURE 3.1 Organizational Levels in a Hotel

G.M. Functions

G.M.s (and all other managers in any type of organization) must perform several management functions which were reviewed in the previous chapter. Figure 3.2, the Basic Functions of a G.M.'s Role, reviews each of the basic management functions and provides an example of work activities applicable to each. The figure illustrates that all of a G.M.'s broad and complex management activities can be categorized into one or more of these basic management functions.

G.M. Skills

Hotel G.M.s, like managers in other organizations, must be able to utilize four basic types of skills to be effective:

- Conceptual skills. The ability to collect, interpret and use information in a logical way. An example occurs as a G.M. learns about a new, competing hotel opening nearby and makes future marketing decisions accordingly.
- Interpersonal skills. The ability to understand and interact well with people, including guests, employees, and suppliers.
- Administrative skills. The ability to organize and direct work efforts required by the hotel; an example is the ability to develop policies and operating procedures needed for ensuring guest safety within the property.
- Technical skills. The ability to perform hotel management-specific aspects of the job. Examples include forecasting guest demand for rooms, establishing room rates, and perhaps checking in a guest in the absence of a front desk clerk.

FIGURE 3.2 Basic Functions of a G.M.'s Role

Management Function	Example of Activity; Working with Department Head (If Applicable) to:
Planning	Develop an operating budget or a marketing plan
Organizing	Assign responsibilities for an upcoming banquet or conference event
Staffing	Recruit, select, orientate, and train a new department head
Directing	Supervise the work of department heads in each department
Controlling	Take corrective action(s) when budgeted financial plans are not attained
Evaluating	Assess the extent to which long- and short-range plans were attained.

G.M. Relationships

G.M.s, like other hotel employees, must be able to effectively interact with many groups of persons including:

- Staff members whom they supervise. In the "old days," many managers in hotels and other organizations used a dictatorial style of leadership. By the power of their position, they were the "boss" and made that fact clear. Today managers in all types of organizations, including hotels, tend to be facilitators. They assist those whom they supervise by providing them with necessary resources and by giving advice and help as necessary. "Tomorrow," many observers believe, managers will increasingly practice the art of **empowerment**. This is done by working with employees to plan broad goals and then to give these employees discretion on how to achieve the goals while remaining in the background ready to provide assistance if needed.

HOTEL TERMINOLOGY AT WORK

Empowerment: The act of granting authority to employees to make key decisions within the employees' areas of responsibility.

■

- Other hotel employees. Every day, G.M.s come in contact with hotel employees. Good G.M.s make sure that they do. As they "manage by walking around," there are many opportunities to interact with staff members in numerous ways.

- Guests. Outstanding hoteliers take every possible opportunity to interact with guests and on a basis that extends far beyond the *"How was everything?"* comments often heard in hotel lobbies, dining rooms, and at the front desk. G.M.s must make a serious effort to learn about what their own guests want and how the hotel can best meet and exceed guest's expectations.

- External organizations. G.M.s represent their hotels when, for example, they join professional business organizations, community service organizations, interact with suppliers, and meet with representatives of community government.

- Others in the community. Effective G.M.s are often well recognized in their own communities. They are known as the manager of the "XYZ Hotel" as they participate in their community's social events, attend school and athletic events with their children, interact with their neighbors, and otherwise live their personal lives. Almost everything they do, in subtle or overt ways, impacts the reputation and, therefore, the success of the hotel they manage.

G.M.s Manage in Times of Change

The world of hotel management is changing, and G.M.s must keep up with these changes. Many examples of change are addressed throughout this book as technical aspects of the job are discussed. Many others relate to changes in the world in general and to the business world more specifically. All these changes can impact the way managers interact with people. For example, relative to their counterparts in years past, G.M.s must:

- Interact with a more diverse workforce.
- Emphasize teams rather than the performance of individual employees.
- Cope with the fast-paced change of technology.
- Adjust to workplace changes, including, sometimes, **reengineering** and/or downsizing.
- React to global challenges. The impact of one country's economy in another part of the world can often have a direct impact on the economy of a local community and other areas from which the hotel attracts its business and pleasure travelers.
- Improve quality while increasing productivity. "Doing more and better with less" is no longer a set of buzz-words, but rather, it is a philosophy and a work objective in many organizations, including hotels.
- Improve ethical/social behavior. Hoteliers must be fair to all and must ensure that the hotel organization is a good "citizen" within the community.

HOTEL TERMINOLOGY AT WORK

Reengineering: Reorganizing hotel departments or work sections within departments.

■

EVOLUTION OF TRADITIONAL HOTEL HUMAN RESOURCES PRACTICES

Like managers in other organizations, hotel G.M.s have had to revise "how things are done" with regard to employees. Figure 3.3, the Evolution of Hotel Human Resources Practices, reviews some of the changes that are applicable to the management of people in a hotel.

When reviewing Figure 3.3, consider that not all changes have fully taken place in all hotels by all G.M.s. Rather, the figure indicates an evolution from a traditional approach or viewpoint to a more modern one. This evolution is likely to continue so that, over time, there will be a significant difference in the way G.M.s utilize their interpersonal skills as they interact with their staff members.

FIGURE 3.3 Evolution of Hotel Human Resources Practices

Approach/Viewpoint	
Traditional	**Contemporary**
Manager-focused work unit	Team-focused work unit
Manager is dominant	Manager is supportive
Emphasis on technical skills	Emphasis on employee facilitation skills
Manager seeks stability	Manager encourages change
Manager tells and sells their own views	Manager listens
Manager personally responsible for results	Manager shares responsibility for results
Manager personally solves problems	Team problem solving is employed
Fear and pressure are used to motivate staff	Pride, recognition, and growth are used to motivate staff
Autocratic (dictatorial) decision style	Participative decision style
Individual behavior	Team behavior
G.M. forces compliance	G.M. earns the team's support
What one *says* is inconsistent with what one *does*	What one *says* is consistent with what one *does*
Inconsistent "moments of truth"	Consistent "moments of truth"
Reactive management/supervision style	Proactive management/supervision style
Bureaucratic "rituals"	Flexible routine
Top down—one-way communication	Multidirectional communication
Hierarchy of control	Empowerment
Power	Consensus
Short-term human resources strategies	Long-term human resources strategies

MANAGEMENT BASICS

Hotel G.M.s, like their counterparts in other organizations, must possess and consistently use a wide range of management skills. There is, at its most basic level, a universal process of management. These basics represent a range of **strategies** and **tactics** that managers use to attain organizational goals. This section reviews some of these management basics.

HOTEL TERMINOLOGY AT WORK

Strategy: A method or a plan developed to achieve a long-range goal.

For example, one hotel strategy to attain financial success may be to significantly increase revenue from room-service sales.

■

HOTEL TERMINOLOGY AT WORK

Tactic: An action or method used to attain a short-term objective.

For example, a tactic to improve room service revenue might be to design an appealing menu.

■

Planning

Figure 3.2 indicated that planning was the first management function. Unfortunately, it is an activity that is frequently overlooked or ignored by many G.M.s. In practice, there are many types of planning tools that G.M.s, with help from their staff, must develop and utilize. Some of the most important planning tools are illustrated in Figure 3.4, a Flowchart of Management Planning Tools.

Let's look at Figure 3.4 to review how planning activities are interrelated. First, the hotel's owners will have specific goals set for the financial performance of the property. That is, hotel owners invest in hotels with the expectation that their **ROI** will be attractive and as good or better than alternative investments they can make.

HOTEL TERMINOLOGY AT WORK

ROI: Short for "return on investment." The percentage rate of return achieved on the money invested in a hotel property, as in *"We expect our hotel to have an ROI of 12 percent this year."*

■

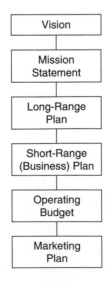

FIGURE 3.4 Flowchart of Management Planning Tools

To achieve ROI goals, owners, G.M.s, and Executive Operating Committee members, among others, will develop broad, but generally less quantifiable, visions about what the hotel will strive to be. For example, the vision of management may be that the property be perceived as the "preferred" destination in the community for corporate business travelers. In all cases, the vision of management must support the goals of the hotel's owners.

Second, a mission statement is developed which is driven by the vision. It becomes more specific and indicates what the hotel must do to be successful and how this will be accomplished. For example, planners may want the hotel to be the destination of choice for business travelers by providing exemplary products and services at competitive prices.

Third, the mission statement drives a long-range plan. For example, within five years, the hotel may wish to have a 55 percent market share of all business traveler stays in the community.

Fourth, the short-range (business) plan indicates the hotel's goal within a one-year time span. For example, by the end of the year, the hotel will be successful if it has attained a specified percentage of the desired market share of business travelers.

Fifth, an operating budget is developed to indicate the amount of revenues and associated expenses that are anticipated to arise as the short-range (business) plan is implemented.

Finally, a marketing plan is developed to indicate what must be done to generate the revenue anticipated by the operating budget.

Clearly, there is a wide-range of interrelated planning tools, which are required for successful hotel operation. The G.M. works with the Executive Operating Committee to develop, implement, and monitor progress toward goals by using these planning tools. This is best accomplished by a team-oriented, "democratic" approach in which input is solicited from all affected personnel. Then, those ideas that are judged to be best are selected and utilized.

Decision Making

As noted earlier in this chapter, G.M.s utilize resources (money, people, time, etc.) to attain objectives. However, all resources are in limited supply. Therefore, G.M.s must constantly make decisions about how to best use these limited resources as attempts are made to maximize the chances of attaining the G.M.'s planned objectives.

There are two basic types of decisions that G.M.s make. These are **programmed decisions** and **nonprogrammed decisions**.

HOTEL TERMINOLOGY AT WORK

Programmed Decisions: Routine or repetitive decisions that can be made after considering policies, procedures, or rules.

■

HOTEL TERMINOLOGY AT WORK

Nonprogrammed Decisions: Decisions that occur infrequently and require creative and unique decision-making abilities.

■

Programmed decisions are routine and repetitive and can typically be made by considering guidelines such as policies, rules, and other requirements. An example would be enforcing a policy found in the employee handbook. By contrast, nonprogrammed decisions occur infrequently; there are few, if any, systems in place to deal with them. Examples include addressing issues such as "Should we extend the hours of operation for the dining room?" or "What can we do to reduce guest complaints generated at time of check-in?" The most effective G.M.s are successful at making nonprogrammed decisions and, in fact, look forward to the challenges and opportunities for the creativity these decision-making occasions present.

As a G.M., there are numerous factors that you would consider before making a decision that affects your hotel. These include:

- Who is the correct person to make the decision? Typically, the person with authority or power closest to the point of action is the best person to make the decision. Thus, good decisions related to food and beverage are likely to best be made by those working daily in the food and beverage department.

- Will a decision about a specific issue bring the hotel closer to attaining its objectives and goals?

- How will the decision affect guests? Often decisions made to "improve" the hotel do so at the expense of guests. For example, if guests are currently allowed to make free local telephone calls, but the hotel's managers are contemplating whether to begin charging for these calls, the hotel might consider the additional telephone revenue it would gain from the change, but it could come at the expense of increased guest dissatisfaction and thus potentially reduced hotel room sales revenue. The net result could well be a decline in overall hotel revenue because the decision negatively affected the guest. Management decisions that negatively affect guests will, in nearly every case, have a negative long-term impact on the hotel.

- Is there only one acceptable alternative? Typically, as alternatives for decision making are generated, several might be applicable. Frequently, the "best" decision is arrived at as a result of utilizing "parts" of several different alternatives.

- Should the decision be based upon objective facts and analysis alone or, alternatively, can some subjective ("common sense") issues also be addressed?

- How much time and effort can be spent on the decision? In the fast-paced hotel business, the issue creating the greatest problem at the moment typically gets priority in the decision-making process. Some decisions, such as what to do with a burst water pipe, must be made quickly. Others, such as which local radio station to use to advertise a Valentine's Day room special, can be made more slowly.

- How does my experience help with decision making? Through practice and experience, G.M.s become better decision makers. As a G.M., what has or has not worked for you in the past can be very helpful as you make decisions about what to do today.

- Must the decision please everyone? Often "good" decisions do not uniformly please all persons who are affected by them.

- What, if any, are the ethical aspects to the decisions being made? **Ethics** relates to the "rightness" or "wrongness" of one's behavior and frequently involves judgments about "fairness." Decisions should not be arbitrary or revengeful.

HOTEL TERMINOLOGY AT WORK

Ethics: Standards used to judge the "right" and "wrong" (or fairness) of one's actions when dealing with others.

■

Many decisions can be made by the G.M. alone or by using a team approach. This is illustrated in Figure 3.5 (Continuum of Decision Making).

As noted in Figure 3.5, managers have traditionally made unilateral decisions. That approach evolved into a modified team method in which the manager solicited input from others and then utilized it to the extent desired. The manager utilizing the contemporary approach realizes the worth of the team decision-making process and allows the team to make decisions.

There are advantages and disadvantages, however, to the use of a group decision-making process. First, consider the advantages. They include:

- The group will likely have a broader range of information that can be considered, because each group member brings unique information to

FIGURE 3.5 Continuum of Decision Making

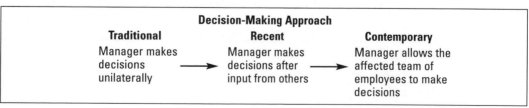

the group decision-making process. This is similar to the old problem-solving saying that "two (or more) heads is better than one."

- More creative alternatives can be generated.
- The entire team becomes aware of issues and problems that need to be addressed and this may, in the long run, make the team more supportive of the final decision made.
- There can be higher morale levels since team members who are involved in the decision-making process appreciate the fact that their ideas are considered to have merit.
- The decision will be easier to implement because the team helped to develop it.

There are, however, several potential disadvantages to a team decision-making approach:

- The manager will ultimately be accountable for the group's decisions and, perhaps even held responsible for it, yet it may conflict with that manager's own ideas of what should have been decided.
- Team members will spend time on decision making, which otherwise could be used for other purposes.
- The manager may be forced to "choose sides" if alternative opinions are expressed.
- Staff members with the strongest personalities may dominate the decision-making process.
- The manager will need excellent leadership skills simply to facilitate the group's decision-making process.
- Group decision making is often time-consuming and may not be applicable when fast decisions must be made.

In fact, an effective G.M. often utilizes all three of the approaches to decision making presented here. The situation and the issue being addressed frequently determine the specific process used.

Organizing

G.M.s must know and practice several organizing principles. For example, they must recognize the concept of **unity of command:** every employee in the hotel should report to/be accountable to only one boss when performing a specific activity.

HOTEL TERMINOLOGY AT WORK

Unity of Command: Each employee should report to/be accountable to only one boss for a specific activity.

■

MANAGERS AT WORK

"He is really mad!" said the sales manager.

"Who is mad?" asked J. D. Ojisama, the hotel's G.M. as he watched the man the sales manager had been talking to enter the hotel elevator.

"The couple in room 531," replied the sales manager. "They checked in at 3:30 this afternoon. They're here for tonight's New Year's Eve package. But the champagne and Strawberries that were *supposed* to be in their room are not there."

"Why not?" asked J.D.

"Well, I guess, from what I can gather, the Front Desk reserved their room for them this morning, and then notified food and beverage that they would be in that room . . . so the wine and berries could be put in it . . . but when the couple checked-in, he wanted to be on a higher floor, not the ground floor. . . . So, the desk agent moved them to an upper floor room."

"OK," said J.D. "That's the right thing to do."

"Well, I guess the food and beverage department was never notified about the change. And then, when the guests complained and the front desk manager called the food and beverage department, the food and beverage director said he was too busy preparing for tonight's dinner event to fix some other department's screw up!"

"What is the current status on the guest?" asked J.D.

"Well," replied the sales manager, "it's been two hours and the items are still not in his room. He just said if they are not there in 15 minutes he's leaving. . . . The bad news is that he is head of the corporate travel department for Tech-Mar Industries, one of our largest corporate clients."

What are decisions that J.D. must make unilaterally and immediately in this situation? What decisions would best be made after consulting with others in the hotel? Last, what decisions could best be made by the managers and employee team members involved? As a G.M., how would you go about creating and managing such a decision-making group?

They should also know about the principle of **span of control;** that is, there is a limit to the number of staff members that one supervisor can effectively manage. Generally, top-level managers can supervise the work of fewer persons (who perform widely diverse duties) than can subordinates at lower levels (who generally supervise staff members who perform more similar duties).

HOTEL TERMINOLOGY AT WORK

Span of Control: The number of people one supervisor can effectively manage.

■

G.M.s also must know how to avoid conflict between line and staff personnel. They define levels of **authority,** and they assure that there is ongoing and effective communication between personnel in all departments.

HOTEL TERMINOLOGY AT WORK

Authority: The power to tell others to do or not to do something in efforts to attain the hotel's objectives.

■

FIGURE 3.6 Types of Authority in a Hotel

Type of Authority	Used By	Example
Advisory	Staff (rather than line) managers	Development of an orientation program for use by all hotel employees
Line	Line managers (in their own departments)	Hiring and firing the employees needed to operate the department
Functional	Line managers (assisting other departments)	Executive housekeeper establishes the schedule for cleaning table linens used by the food and beverage department

Figure 3.6, the Types of Authority in a Hotel, provides benchmarks that G.M.s can use as they organize the distribution of authority within their property. It reviews the types of authority, by whom each type is used, and it provides an example of each.

Delegation

G.M.s are too busy to do all the work for which they are responsible. Effective managers, then, delegate some work assignments to others. **Delegation** is the process of assigning authority (power) to others to do required work.

HOTEL TERMINOLOGY AT WORK

Delegation: The process of assigning authority (power) to others to enable subordinates to do work that a manager at a higher organizational level would otherwise do.

■

G.M.s benefit in several ways as they delegate:

- It allows them to do the most important things first.
- It is an effective process to train employees so they can grow in their jobs.
- It allows more work to be accomplished.
- It improves control because, when effective, delegation focuses on results confirmed through feedback. It does not focus on activities.

When managers delegate, responsibilities are assigned and, in turn, those to whom work is delegated are held **accountable** for the work. Accountability, then, flows upward throughout the hotel organization. A person who delegates an assignment is still accountable to his or her own manager for performance of the work.

What work might be delegated by the G.M.? Examples include:

HOTEL TERMINOLOGY AT WORK

Accountability: An obligation created when a person is delegated duties/responsibilities from higher levels of management.

■

- Work that others can do as well as the G.M.
- Work that is less important than other work, that is, other higher priority tasks
- Work that should be learned by more than one person

Figure 3.7 (Steps in Effective Delegation) reviews how delegation should be undertaken.

Flow of Communication

G.M.s must effectively communicate with staff members, guests and others outside of the hotel organization. A G.M.'s ability to effectively communicate is critical to professional success. Figure 3.8, Multidirectional Communication, illustrates the multidirectional flow of communication that is required.

When reviewing Figure 3.8, notice that there is vertical communication to and between personnel at each organizational level. Policies, rules, and procedures applicable to all staff members flow through the hotel organization from the G.M. and department heads to all employees at all organizational levels. Also, staff members receive instructions, such as assignments and work schedules, from their immediate supervisors. Communication,

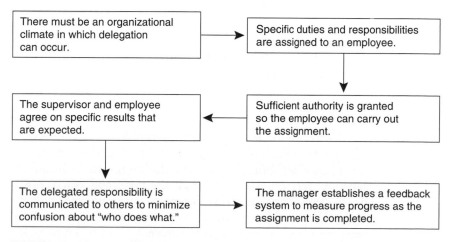

FIGURE 3.7   Steps in Effective Delegation

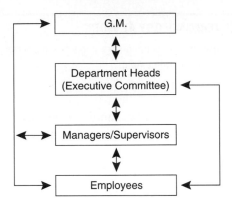

FIGURE 3.8   Multidirectional Communication

however, also goes up through the organization by use of formal communication channels, for example, through on-the-job feedback between staff members and their immediate supervisor and, as well, through other opportunities such as performance evaluation sessions and "suggestion box" and "open door policy" alternatives.

In addition to **vertical communication** (up and down the organization) channels, there is also **horizontal communication** which occurs, for example, when department heads, managers, or supervisors communicate with others at their same organizational level.

HOTEL TERMINOLOGY AT WORK

Vertical Communication: Communication between individuals that flows up and down throughout the organization.

■

HOTEL TERMINOLOGY AT WORK

Horizontal Communication: Communication between individuals at the same organizational level.

■

To this point, we have been examining formal communication channels. There is another informal communication channel commonly referred to as the "grapevine." Sometimes called the "rumor mill," informal communication can flow very quickly throughout the hotel and, often, can be very accurate. Employees often use the grapevine to communicate "politics and personnel" topics. Wise G.M.s "listen" to the grapevine and use it both to assess employee perceptions of the hotel's "current events" and to know when accurate information required to counter grapevine rumors must be communicated.

Effective G.M.s recognize barriers that can prevent or inhibit effective communication. Examples include the impact of distortion as communication flows between organizational levels, the impact of employees who may be anxious about "telling the truth" to supervisors, and the recognition that hotel jargon (specialized terms or specialized work-related tasks) can leave communication muddled. An example of jargon occurs when a food server says "86" to imply that a menu item is no longer available, and/or a front desk clerk says they are "short" to communicate that his or her cash drawer does not match its expected dollar value.

Cultural differences, language barriers, and the hotel environment itself can impact the effectiveness of communication. G.M.s should be aware of these and related factors and must continually emphasize the need for feedback from employees. This is because employees are often very aware of guest perceptions and "challenges" in their work areas and can, if encouraged, share valuable information with their supervisors and managers.

It is important that information about the hotel's mission statement be effectively communicated to all staff members because it provides the foundation upon which other planning tools will be developed and implemented. How can the mission statement be "communicated" throughout the hotel? Some G.M.s simply hang a copy on their office wall, place a statement in the preface to the employee handbook, or explain it during new employee orientation sessions. This, however, is far different from "walking the talk" which occurs as managers make frequent reference to the mission and continually discuss ways to better attain it with employees at all organizational levels. Unfortunately, in some hotels, G.M.s may know and actually believe in the mission. However, department heads may have only a vague idea about its content, and, increasingly, its spirit and intent become even more abstract for employees at lower organizational levels. Even more unfortunate is the all-too-frequent situation in which entry-level employees are unaware that the hotel even has a mission statement, much less know what it is! Communication in words and actions is the way that the mission statement is effectively conveyed down and throughout the hotel's organization.

Motivation

The term "**motivation**" refers to an inner drive that a person has to attain a goal.

HOTEL TERMINOLOGY AT WORK

Motivation: An inner drive that a person has to attain a goal.

■

Poorly motivated staffs do not consistently perform work that meets required quality or quantity standards. Therefore, guest dissatisfaction is likely to result, operating costs are likely to increase, and, at some point, other, more motivated, employees leave the organization. As these good employees leave, the hotel suffers.

We have suggested that the G.M. is probably in the best position to influence, by words and actions, how other managers and supervisors within the hotel will treat staff members because it is the G.M. that most strongly influences the hotel's organizational culture. A "proemployee" philosophy, along with supportive rules, policies, and procedures, helps recognize the worth and dignity of employees and encourages their active participation as a productive member of the hotel's staff.

Figure3.9, "Common Sense" Tactics to Motivate Employees, lists numerous no- and low-cost techniques, which can be used by hotel managers as they interact with their employees.

Leadership

The G.M. must be a leader. While entire books, and even bookshelves, have been devoted to leadership, most successful leaders would agree that an effective leader will:

- Have a good understanding of the hotel's values and be able to translate these values into practice. In other words, the G.M. must be able to implement the property's mission statement.
- Have an objective and measurable "picture" of the desired future for the hotel.
- Help others develop the knowledge and skills needed to attain the hotel's vision. This is done, in part, through orientation, training, and follow-up **coaching** activities.
- Utilize the empowerment process to help others move toward the vision by enabling them to use discretion.
- Develop a team of staff members who are committed to the hotel's success.
- Achieve a reputation for quality service consistently delivered to guests.
- Cultivate a reputation for fairness and honesty.

HOTEL TERMINOLOGY AT WORK

Coaching: A process whose goal is helping staff members, and the hotel team, reach their highest possible levels of performance.

■

FIGURE 3.9   "Common Sense" Tactics to Motivate Employees

Strategy 1: Follow Sound Management Advice
Serve first and lead second
Learn your turnover costs
Eliminate workers who won't
Eliminate managers who can't
Manage your guests

Strategy 2: Effective Orientation
Understand the role of starting wages
Inform employees about their total compensation
Explain the long-term benefits of staying
Share your vision
Motivate entry-level employees
Conduct an entrance interview
Create career ladders

Strategy 3: Train Correctly
Invest in training
Encourage employees to try your hotel
Train trainers to train
Reward your trainers
Relieve trainers of other job duties
Conduct preshift training

Strategy 4: Manage a Professional Hotel
Strictly enforce a zero-tolerance harassment policy
Create a culturally diverse workforce
Make employee safety a top priority
Ensure reasonable accommodations for disabled employees
Share financial numbers with employees

Strategy 5: Supervise Like You Want to Be Supervised
Enforce "on-time" policies fairly and consistently
Be careful not to overschedule
Give employees a personal copy of their work schedule
Seek out employee assistance programs
Invite "fast track" employees to attend management meetings
Implement a "catch the employee doing something right" program
Conduct an exit interview with employees who leave

Strategy 6: Encourage Effective Communication
Hold employee-focused meetings for nonmanagement staff
Communicate the benefits of your hotel
Create an employee retention committee
Recognize employee birthdays
Make daily "howdy" rounds

Strategy 7: Manage a Friendly Hotel
Use employee recognition programs
Build a great team and praise it often
Write a personal letter to parents of teenage employees
Share scheduling responsibilities with employees
Reward employees who work on nonscheduled days   *(continued)*

FIGURE 3.9   *(Continued)*

Invite family members of new employees to visit your hotel
Make the hotel a fun place to work

Strategy 8: Help Your Employees Succeed
Identify state-approved (licensed) child care options
Help employees learn about public transportation systems
Reward success in each employee
Recognize your employees' elder care responsibilities
Don't punish your best for being good
Stay in touch by going to lunch with hourly and supervisory employees

---

THE INTERNET AT WORK

One of the most popular books about leadership ever written is Steven Covey's *The Seven Habits of Highly Effective People* published by Simon & Schuster. Amazon.com displays 40+ pages of this popular book at their Web site. To view these pages, go to www.amazon.com. Then, under the "Books" search field, enter the name "Stephen R. Covey."

Discipline

Discipline is one of a manager's most important, but sometimes most uncomfortable, tasks. It refers to specific management actions designed to reinforce desired performance (positive discipline) and to correct or eliminate undesired performance (negative discipline).

HOTEL TERMINOLOGY AT WORK

Discipline: Activities designed to reinforce desired performance (positive discipline) or to correct undesired performance (negative discipline).

■

Some managers think of discipline only in its negative context, that is, that discipline exists only to punish a staff member for doing something wrong. A much better approach is to view discipline as one part of the coaching process with the goal of helping staff members to reach for their highest levels of performance. It is generally true that highly motivated employees are much less likely to need negative discipline than are their lesser-motivated counterparts. As a G.M., motivating staff properly is a much more rewarding task than enlisting negative discipline to solve problems.

When negative discipline is required, enlightened G.M.s use a **progressive discipline** process in which a graduated scale of penalties is applied.

Figure 3.10, Steps in a Progressive Discipline Process, details typical steps in a progressive discipline program.

FIGURE 3.10   Steps in a Progressive Discipline Process

Step 1:	Oral warning (no entry in employee's record).
Step 2:	Oral warning (with entry in employee's record).
Step 3:	Written reprimand (often from a manager at an organizational level above that of the employee's immediate supervisor).
Step 4:	Suspension for a specified number of days.
Step 5:	Discharge from the organization.

HOTEL TERMINOLOGY AT WORK

Progressive Discipline: A process of negative discipline in which repeated infractions result in an increasingly severe penalty.

■

For discipline to be effective, the G.M. must:

- Assure that there is a clear communication of expectations. Staff members must truly know what is and is not expected of them.
- Begin the disciplinary process as soon as possible after the problem has occurred.
- Assure that the discipline is similar when the same offense is committed by two or more persons in the same situation.
- Assure the discipline addresses only an employee's behavior and not the employee as a person.

Effective G.M.s ensure that a fair, even-handed, progressive discipline program is in place in their hotels.

TEAM BUILDING TACTICS

Figure 3.3 indicated that contemporary management focuses on team behavior rather than upon individual behavior. A **team** is a group of individuals who accomplish mutually agreed-upon goals through cooperation.

HOTEL TERMINOLOGY AT WORK

Team: A group of individuals who place the goals of the group above their own.

■

As with many other concepts applicable to the hotel's staff members, teamwork will only be effective to the extent that it is part of the hotel's culture that is established in large measure by the G.M.

In its broadest sense, the G.M. is the leader of the hotel's entire team of staff members. Excellent staffs want to work for excellent G.M.s. In addition, excellent G.M.s care about their team members and do what is possible to help those team members advance in their own careers.

To be a good team leader, the G.M. of a hotel, as well as any organization, must:

- Have high standards and expectations
- Support individual members of the teams and maintain relationships of trust and respect
- Practice participative management and solicit input from team members as goals and objectives are established and as plans to achieve them are implemented
- Demonstrate that their own personal goals, like those of the individual team members, should not be placed before the goals of the team
- Share credit for the success the team achieves

Perhaps "tomorrow's" G.M. will facilitate the work of self-directed teams which have significantly more control over their work responsibilities than do present-day teams in many hotels. For example, team members in the future may, within the team, make work assignments, schedule themselves, evaluate each other's work, assign compensation increases, and identify priorities for studying ways to improve the work processes done by the team. Traditional G.M.s and, perhaps, many others probably believe that the hotel industry is far from attaining this level of team-led responsibilities. It is true, however, that there has been, and may well continue to be, an evolution in hotel management toward interaction with teams of staff members and away from individual employees.

THE INTERNET AT WORK

Some organizations organize exotic trips and extensive activities and games to help build teamwork among their members. One company that specializes in developing such activities is "Team Builders." To view their Web site and examine their product offerings, go to:

http://www.teambuilding.org/teambuilding.htm.

EMPLOYEE SELECTION, ORIENTATION, AND TRAINING

In today's increasingly cost-conscious lodging environment, it is necessary to maximize use of people because they are the hotel's most valuable resource. Staff at all organizational levels must be effectively recruited and selected, appropriately oriented to their department, and properly trained to consistently produce results that meet established standards and guest expectations. As will be emphasized in the next chapter, some of these duties may be within the responsibility of the human resources department. However, the G.M. will still be very influential in assuring that the methods used in this process are effective. As well, G.M.s should personally employ these tactics as they interact with department heads and others who report directly to them.

Figure 3.11, Personnel Tactics Checklist, reviews procedures that can be helpful as the G.M. ensures that new employees receive a favorable first impression of the hotel and get off to a good start in their jobs.

G.M. INTERACTIONS

G.M.s never have a daily routine; every day is different. This is one attraction of the job because it helps ensure that the work is never boring. On the other hand, it can bring surprises daily (or more frequently!).

The responsibilities of a G.M. are widely diverse. There is no textbook or course (or even postsecondary school curriculum!) that can totally prepare you for your career as a G.M. In this section, however, we will explore examples of a "What G.M.s do" by looking at a monthly professional "diary" and by reviewing typical examples of the G.M.'s interactions with employees and guests. These examples will illustrate some of less frequently identified activities of a G.M.

G.M.'s Monthly Diary

The actual daily activities undertaken by a G.M. vary from day-to-day and month-to-month as well as from property-to-property. The tasks involved in managing a hotel are numerous. Some, such as daily involvement in guest relations, are quite visible. Others, such as emotionally supporting a key department head who is implementing an important, but potentially unpopular, hotel policy are much less noticeable.

Much of the general manager's job involves the day-to-day management of the hotel property itself. The following entries in the daily schedule for the G.M. of a full-service hotel suggest the range of activities that may be encountered in a typical month:

Day 1:   Conduct an all-employee meeting; explain changes in health insurance benefits. Submit a ninety-day room revenue reforecast to the hotel's owner.

Day 2:   Review previous month's income statement with the controller. Contact bank branch president to review hotel bank statement mailings schedule changes.

Day 3:   Lunch with director of sales and marketing and potential high-volume client (in hotel's dining room) after the director's sales presentation to the prospective client.

FIGURE 3.11 Personnel Tactics Checklist[1]

Recruitment/Selection Tactics
- Human resources officials, if applicable interview applicants, before being referred to line department personnel for a second selection interview.
- The department head interviews all applicants for positions within the department.
- The applicant's potential supervisor conducts a preselection interview with the applicant.
- Background checks, including validation of references, are made.
- Tests for job knowledge/skills are administered to applicants for positions in which experience is required.
- Interview discussions about job-related topics including use of "open-ended" questions are used to reveal information relating to job applicants' attitudes.
- Human resources personnel conduct the initial interview of all applicants for supervisory/management positions.
- The department head and other interviewers attend special training sessions to learn procedures helpful in questioning applicants during employment prescreening.
- Paperwork that must be signed by new employees is completed with the department head present to show his or her interest in and concern about the new staff member.

General Orientation Tactics
- All new employees participate in a general orientation program conducted, at least in part, by human resources officials.
- Content of the orientation program includes:
  - Overview of the department
  - Detailed explanation of employees' benefits
  - Applicable policies and procedures (including handbook)
  - General guest relations training
  - Safety and security issues
  - Emphasis on teamwork and cooperation
  - Property tour
- Teamwork is addressed through small-group training activities.
- The hotel's mission statement is discussed in detail and is referred to frequently as the orientation program is presented; a copy is provided to employees.
- The concept of a "career—not a job" begins during orientation; new employees can schedule vocational counseling sessions with department personnel at any time.

Departmental (Workstation) Orientation (Induction) Tactics
- New employees receive an introduction to department members (especially peers) and a tour of their workstation.
- New staff members receive a review of department-specific policies/procedures; written information is also provided.
- Employees are assigned to a mentor (who will not be their trainer).
- Employees work in, or observe at least briefly, other related positions that are affected by their work, in efforts to develop teamwork/corporation.
- A detailed departmental induction checklist helps assure that all employees receive the same basic information about the department.

FIGURE 3.11   *(Continued)*

Trainer-the-Trainer Tactics

- The department has selected one or more departmental trainer(s).
- Personnel who train have received *extensive* train-the-trainer information.
- Human resources officials, if applicable, randomly/routinely monitor departmental on-the-job trainers/training.
- Trainers receive ongoing recognition (certificate, promotional priority, etc.) for their training efforts.
- Trainers are relieved of some job duties while training to reduce the pressure to get their own work done first.
- Trainers from each department meet together regularly to learn more about training techniques.
- Training projects (e.g., developing a job breakdown for or conducting a group training session within their department) must be completed before trainers are eligible to conduct on-the-job training.
- Experienced trainers belong to a trainers' club, which meets regularly; trainers receive a certificate of completion when they are certified eligible for training.
- An award (Trainer of the Year) is given for the best trainer.
- A competency test comprised of a videotaped training session evaluated by human resources staff and the G.M., among others, is used for all trainers before they are certified to train.
- Employees formally evaluate their on-the-job training/trainer.
- Trainees attending group-training sessions formally evaluate their trainer/training; this information is used by human resources and/or other personnel to counsel trainers about possible improvements.

On-the-Job Training (OJT) Tactics

- A task list noting each task for which training is required is available for each position.
- A job breakdown explaining (a) how each task is to be done and (b) observable standards that must be consistently attained has been developed and is used by the trainer to help teach/evaluate each job task.
- Both the trainer and the trainee sign off after each/all tasks identified in the training task list is/are addressed.
- Employees are encouraged to participate in cross-training (job rotation) activities within and between departments.
- Initial on-the-job training involves observing—not physically performing—required tasks.
- Written materials are available for all identified tasks for which on-the-job training is necessary.
- When applicable, initial tasks for which on-the-job training is required do not involve contact with the guests being served.
- Training manuals based upon departmental operating manuals are used as part of the OJT process.
- A department official visits with each new staff member at least by the end of the first month of employment.
- Entry-level employees receive a certificate of completion when their initial training is successfully completed.
- A detailed training schedule is developed that indicates both the sequence of and completion dates for successful performance of job tasks.
- Employees being trained do not replace employees required for a specific shift; their presence is in addition to the required number of staff members so that standards are not reduced during training.

(continued)

FIGURE 3.11   *(Continued)*

Supervisory/Other Training Tactics
- Employees nominated by the department head can begin supervisory training *before* they are promoted to supervisory positions.
- Employees are encouraged to obtain education/training external to the department; a full/partial reimbursement program is in effect.
- Group training about selected, modularized topics is *continually* available for employees nominated by department officials.
- Nominated employees are allowed to attend selected managers' meetings.
- Qualified employees participate in ad hoc (task force) activities that are an integral part of their planned professional development program.
- A monthly training schedule lists topics and times for generic training and is used by schedule planners to release trainees for required training.
- A promotion test is given after required supervisory training and must be successfully passed before promotion is granted.
- Before being appointed to a supervisory position, those being considered for promotion serve as acting supervisors and receive special guidance/evaluation from an experienced supervisor.

Training Budget
- A list of recommended training activities on a by-employee (position) basis is used to help build the department's annual training schedule and budget.
- A significant amount of the training budget is spent for management training.
- Funds for the annual training budget are driven by a specified percentage of payroll or another objective formula.
- *All* employees receive some training for which funds are budgeted each year.

Other Training Issues
- Employees formally evaluate their supervisors.
- Career development planning is available for staff at midlevel management positions and above.
- A promotion track has been developed that suggests advancement opportunities for personnel in specific positions.
- Some career planning is done during formal performance appraisal sessions.
- Extensive training about the department's goals and limits of employee discretion precede empowerment and/or delegation activities.
- Managers understand the importance of role-modeling: they act the way they desire their employees to act!
- Performance appraisal addresses the extent to which career development goals made at the previous performance appraisal sessions have been attained.
- General staff meetings are held for all employees.
- Employee reward programs are in place to motivate employees.
- Exit interviews given to department staff address, in part, training activities.
- Group training (especially involving employees from more than one department) is scheduled during times of slow business volume and at slow shift times, when possible.
- The facility offers afterwork activities (special interest groups) to help facilitate socialization (teamwork).
- The department maintains a library of professional books, magazines, videotapes, etc., which are loaned to employees for professional development and personal enjoyment purposes.

FIGURE 3.11 *(Continued)*

- Before new employees are granted permanent employee status, they must be interviewed by the department head and department trainer and are given paper/pencil tests addressing training topics.
- Recognizing that training never ends, training opportunities are constantly available for all position-competent employees in the department.
- A formal empowerment training program is conducted for all employees.
- An internship program is available for selected entry-level employees to be trained for fast progression into supervisory (and higher) positions.
- Each department head is responsible for conducting some group training programs on a regular basis.
- An official from each department randomly/routinely attends training sessions conducted throughout the department.
- Information from employee performance appraisals relative to training needs is accumulated by each department and is used in planning generic training programs for the next year.
- The department's mission statement is translated into training objectives and is broken down into small parts, and each part is addressed each year in planned training programs.

[1]From Jack Ninemeier, *Training Strategies in World-Class Asian Hotel: Relevance to the United States Lodging Industry. Hospitality and Tourism Educator* 7, no. 7 (fall 1995).

Day 4:   Prepare owner's month-end revenue and expense re-cap report for prior month.

Day 5:   Attend franchisor's co-op advertising meeting to discuss recommendations about the next fiscal quarter's advertisement placements.

Day 6:   Attend the mayor's gala fund-raising dinner at the convention center.

Day 7:   OFF (but makes one call to and takes two calls from hotel staff).

Day 8:   Review prior meeting's minutes and attend the property's Safety Committee meeting. Review all department heads quarterly staff wage increase recommendations.

Day 9:   Conduct weekly room inspections with executive housekeeper and supervisors. Meet with food and beverage director to review bids from new linen supplier.

Day 10: Accept award from City Council for chairing Community Beautification Committee (breakfast).

Day 11: Meeting with front office manager; telephone call to long-distance calls vendor to discuss new contract as well as interstate, intrastate, and international long-distance phone rates.

Day 12: Work half day (review month's trade journals); OFF half-day.

Day 13: Serve as weekend property manager on duty (MOD).

Day 14: OFF (only one call from a department head!).

Day 15:   Begin work on developing long-range plans resulting in a capital improvement budget to be used in the next fiscal year.

Day 16:   Meet with the hotel's insurance company representative to review hotel swimming pool policies and safety procedures. Review disputed invoice from furniture vendor related to poor product quality.

Day 17:   Proof proposed new menu copy; taste test new menu items with director of food and beverage.

Day 18:   Attend Chamber of Commerce Member Mixer (evening reception).

Day 19:   Review monthly employee turnover statistics with human resources director; evaluate annual community salary survey results.

Day 20:   OFF (golf vacation out-of-state; no telephone contact).

Day 21:   OFF (see day 20).

Day 22:   Meet with the city fire marshal and hotel's chief engineer to review the first draft of the safety/evacuation portion of the hotel's emergency plan.

Day 23:   Inspect boiler area, heating, cooling units with city building inspector.

Day 24:   Weekly Executive Committee staff meeting to choose employee of the month and review upcoming convention meetings schedule.

Day 25:   OFF (but come to office because of some forgotten "paperwork").

Day 26:   Review previous results and prepare documentation for next week's quality review (inspection) by franchisor.

Day 27:   Present employee of the month award to staff member.

Day 28:   Attend Hotel and Lodging Association luncheon.

Day 29:   Attend sales and marketing client appreciation reception and dinner.

Day 30:   OFF.

Day 31:   Meet with the director of sales and marketing and sales team to review Smith Travel Research (Star) reports.

When reviewing these activities note that the daily entries only record one or two unique activities for each date. In fact, the G.M. is on duty eight or more hours daily and is often on-call even when not on the property.

You will also note that the schedule above indicates that the G.M. is off work for six-and-a-half days during the thirty-one-day period. Many persons hold a stereotype of a hotel G.M. who works very long hours and with very few days off. Unfortunately, in the past, this has been true in many properties and hotel organizations. Increasingly, however, employers recognize that the position of G.M. must be competitive with other employment options. While there are "peaks and valleys" of busy and slow times and while there may be some work duties (such as telephone calls on days off), today's G.M.s enjoy a shorter work week than did their counterparts in the past. To be successful a G.M. must enjoy the work. The G.M. must also, like other management and nonmanagement staff, have an appropriate amount of time away from the job for rest and relaxation. Effective G.M.s, simply do not work themselves into exhaustion! Those who do so demonstrate a lack of managerial ability or unrealistic expectations on the part of the hotel's ownership.

Employee and Guest Relationships

We have noted elsewhere that an effective G.M. is a good "people person." Successful G.M.s enjoy interacting with employees, guests, and others, and this enjoyment is a significant factor in the level of job satisfaction for many managers. The range of potential interactions is broad and results in very rewarding, but sometimes discouraging or even unpleasant experiences. Even the most seasoned G.M.s will, on occasion, be confronted with an interpersonal experience unlike any they have ever encountered. Figure 3.12 (Possible Interactions with Employees) and Figure 3.13 (Possible Interactions with Guests) illustrate examples of these positive and negative experiences that, as a G.M., you may encounter.

FIGURE 3.12   Possible Interactions with Employees

Positive Examples	Negative Examples
Daily conversations with long-term staff members	Disciplining or terminating staff members
Learning suggestions about possible operating improvements from employees	Confronting staff members known to be stealing
Welcoming new staff members to the team	Learning about illegal acts committed off-property by staff members
Congratulating personnel about significant events in their/their families' lives	Assigning work responsibilities to cover "no-show" employees
Mentoring younger workers	Discovering employee "sabotage"
Following the careers of employees as they are promoted within the hotel organization and industry	Supervising employees who consistently violate the hotel's policies/rules and personnel requirements
Providing non-job-related advice when requested	Comforting an employee whose only child has passed away
Observing staff members who participate in community organizations/activities	Explaining to a staff member why they did not get a promotion they sought
Observing employees at a company picnic enjoy themselves	Observing an intoxicated employee attempting to come to work

FIGURE 3.13   Possible Interactions with Guests

Positive Examples	Negative Examples
Interacting with frequent guests	Interacting with police called to the hotel for disturbances and/or illegal guest activities
Receiving spontaneous "thank you notes" from happy guests	Guest deaths in sleeping rooms or in the hotel's public spaces
Observing guests celebrate significant family or professional occasions in the hotel	Dealing with obviously and visibly intoxicated guests
Providing assistance (service) to guests who require it	Preventing on-site prostitution activities
Receiving guest input about hospitable staff members	Discovering overt guest room damage
Receiving input from guests who genuinely want the hotel to be successful	Preventing guest theft of money, products, and/or services from the hotel
Interacting with guests as peers at community/professional meetings	Preventing property vandalism
Providing accommodations to grateful guests stranded by adverse travel conditions	Calming irate guests stranded by adverse travel conditions

Fortunately, there are many more positive than negative interactions with the hotel's employees and guests. The job of the G.M. is often not easy, but it is always challenging and rewarding. The remainder of this book will teach you many (but never all!) of the things you must learn if you are to achieve the honor of becoming a hotel general manager.

MANAGERS AT WORK

"It's in his car," said the room attendant. "I saw him take the television set out of his room and put it in his car trunk. He didn't see me. I'm in a nearby guest room and immediately called you."

The call was placed to the front desk clerk who transferred it to J.D. Ojisama, the hotel's G.M.

By the time J.D. arrived in the wing of the hotel where the room with the stolen television set was located, the guest had already left. "What happened? What did you see?" asked J.D.

"Well, I saw Mr. Dolcifino just as he was going through the exit door carrying a television set. That's when I went back into the room I was cleaning and called the front desk."

"How do you know it was Mr. Dolcifino?" asked J.D.

"I've seen Mr. Dolcifino many times; he stays here at least a couple of times per month. Besides, he reminds me of a guy I know. . . . It was him for sure."

A review of front desk records indicated that, in fact, Mr. Dolcifino had stayed at the hotel the previous evening. However, he did *not* stay in the room from which the television was missing. In fact, his room was in another wing and on another floor.

What should J.D. do now? What, if any, difference does it make if Mr. Dolcifino is a frequent guest? Should the police be called in response to this (alleged) guest theft? How would J.D. ensure that the staff member reporting the theft was not involved? How would knowing the most possible about the hotel's security policies and procedures help J.D. respond in the best manner possible?

HOTEL TERMINOLOGY AT WORK GLOSSARY

The following terms were defined within this chapter. If you are not familiar with each of them, please review the segment of the chapter that contains the term.

Human relations	Ethics	Motivation
Empowerment	Unity of command	Coaching
Reengineering	Span of control	Discipline
Strategy	Authority	Progressive discipline
Tactic	Delegation	Team
ROI	Accountability	
Programmed decisions	Vertical communication	
Nonprogrammed decisions	Horizontal communication	

ISSUES AT WORK

1. This chapter has established that the G.M. needs conceptual, interpersonal administrative, and technical skills to be effective. It also provides an example of each type of skill. What are three additional examples of each type of skill? How can a G.M. increase his or her skills in each of these areas? Which type of skill do you believe is the most important? Why? Which type of skill, if any, is the least important? Why?

2. There has been an evolution of hotel human resources practices from the G.M. as "boss" to the G.M. as a facilitator and/or team leader. Why has this occurred? Will this trend continue? Explain why you believe it will or will not.

3. There are several types of authority in a hotel: advisory, line, and functional. What are some examples of advisory authority? What can you as a G.M. do to assure that line and staff personnel recognize their responsibilities and the limitations involved when this type of power is used? Functional authority was also defined. What are examples of functional authority between departments? How, if at all, does a G.M. help to assure that there are clear distinctions about duties and responsibilities as functional authority within the hotel is established?

4. G.M.s do not have enough time to do all the work that is required of them. Some tasks simply must be delegated. What are three specific things you could do when delegating work to a subordinate to help ensure that that staff member does not think you are "dumping" additional work onto them? If an employee is already busy with assigned tasks (and every staff member should be!), how can you explain to the staff member that you expect them to do all of their current work and, in addition, take on the newly delegated work?

5. Motivation has been defined as "an inner drive that a person has to attain a goal." If this is the case, how can a G.M. "motivate" an employee? What motivates you? To what extent do you think a motivated employee will be more likely to remain with the property than an unmotivated counterpart? How could you discover what motivates an employee? Do you think the goals that motivate people change over time?

4
Human Resources

This Chapter at Work

Hotel organizations are very labor intensive. People, in addition to machines, are needed to perform many of the tasks leading to the delivery of quality products and services for the hotel's guests. Employees at all organizational levels must be recruited and trained to consistently perform their jobs well if guests are to come back and the hotel is to gain a reputation for providing quality service. An effective human resources department helps a G.M. ensure that the staff employed by the hotel is truly the best it can be.

In this chapter you will learn about many of the tasks assigned to this important department. In addition to direct employee development issues, there are many other activities, including performance evaluations, safety and benefit concerns, and governmental regulations compliance that must be managed as hotel employees go about their work. Hotels typically employ one or more persons to administer these human resources–related responsibilities and to assist line-operating managers with employee-related issues.

Employee-related legal issues can drastically impact the workplace. In this chapter you will learn about the most important of these. In addition, you will discover the process by which a human resources department fulfills its most significant role. That role is the recruitment, selection, orientation, training, and evaluation of staff.

Dynamic human resources departments also plan for future staff needs. This may involve either staff size increases or decreases. In addition, employees' safety and health concerns fall within the responsibilities of the human resources department. An aggressive human resources department serves as an employee advocate, dedicated to helping ensure safe and healthy working conditions for all employees.

Other important functions of an effective human resources department include long-range planning for staffing needs and the development of programs that help improve the quality of workers, as well as the work they do. The human resources department, while one of the smallest in the hotel, is vitally important to the success of the staff and thus your work as the hotel's G.M.

Chapter 4 Outline

THE ROLE OF HUMAN RESOURCES DEPARTMENT

STAFFING THE HUMAN RESOURCES DEPARTMENT

LEGAL ASPECTS OF HUMAN RESOURCES
    Employee Selection
    Employment Relationships

THE ROLE OF THE HUMAN RESOURCES DEPARTMENT

Good managers in every department in the hotel care about their own employees. The human resources department and its department head are responsible for caring about every hotel employee. In fact, in a well-run hotel, this department is a vocal advocate for the fair treatment of staff, and good G.M.s ensure that this is so. Personnel in this department also assist other departmental managers with human resources concerns, including recruitment, selection, orientation, training, performance evaluation, compensation, labor relations, safety and health, legal, and a wide range of other specialized tasks.

In years past, the term "personnel" or "personnel management" was the name given to describe the human resources function. Regardless of the term used, however, there are many important activities performed by human resources staff in support of all of the hotel's operating departments. Some, such as involvement in getting paychecks to workers, make the department very visible; others, such as filing required paperwork with governmental agencies, go on "behind the scenes" of the hotel's day-to-day operations.

Hotels of all sizes cannot be successful unless human resources activities are attended to. In most limited service and smaller full-service hotels, the G.M. and perhaps one additional full- or part-time staff person will be responsible for the administration of the **H.R.** department.

HOTEL TERMINOLOGY AT WORK

H.R.: Short for human resources, for example, "When is H.R. going to distribute the results of the turnover study?"

■

In larger properties, H.R. may consist of a director or department head and several additional staff members. Regardless of the hotel's size, however, other hotel department heads and supervisors often misunderstand the H.R. function. This can be seen by the type of manager's comments about H.R. that can commonly be heard, including:

"Our work would be much easier if only those H.R. people would send us better applicants."

"How in the world did this guy (or girl) pass the H.R. screening?"

"We're busy serving guests and putting out fires; it is the job of the H.R. department to train our employees!"

"Who do those H.R. people think they are wanting to train my employees? What do they know about our area?"

"I wish the H.R. department would do something to motivate my employees!"

"We just don't have enough staff members. Why doesn't the H.R. department send us more people?"

"We're doing all the work around here. What does the H.R. department do? All they can do is think up more paperwork for us."

The above and related statements and questions suggest the unfortunate relationship that sometimes exists between H.R. and other operating departments in the hotel. The G.M. must work hard to prevent this type of relationship. Throughout this book we have noted that a hotel is a very labor-intensive operation. Most of a hotel's work must be done by and through people. A successful hotel, like any other service organization, must treat every staff member like the important resource they can become, even if not all members of the staff are not yet achieving all that they can.

H.R. activities in hotels are actually performed by two groups of staff members. The first group consists of the operating managers in line departments and the second consists of the specialist(s) in the H.R. department.

Activities of line managers include making the final employee selection decision, providing some departmental-specific orientation, and initiating ongoing training. They must also undertake numerous supervision activities, including performance appraisal, scheduling, and discipline. H.R. specialists help these managers and supervisors with these and many other H.R.-related activities that otherwise would not get done, or possibly might not be done properly or legally.

Because H.R. is both a line and staff function, sometimes conflict occurs between line managers and their H.R. counterparts. This can be due to confusion about the boundaries of authority. For example, the question of who determines the content of new employee orientation programs is one such possible conflict. Conflicts of this type, however, can be rather easily resolved if the G.M. clearly defines the role of the H.R. department. When that happens, the H.R. department becomes a true asset to line managers.

Examples of ways that H.R. personnel assist in the overall operation of the hotel include:

- Implementing policies and tactics to effectively recruit, select, motivate, and retain the most qualified management and nonmanagement staff members
- Developing and delivering orientation, safety, security, supervisory, and some departmental specific training programs
- Developing and communicating H.R. policies that are equitable and fair to all employees while protecting the rights of the hotel
- Interpreting, implementing, and enforcing the ever-increasing body of laws and regulations that affect people at work
- Helping to maintain appropriate standards of work-life quality and ethical business policies and practices

The H.R. department does not unilaterally develop policies and mandate "how things should be done" relative to the management of employees. Rather, it has an important role to play in working closely with all employees of the hotel. This includes those who are managers and those who are not. When an H.R. department is successful, the chances the hotel will be successful increase greatly.

STAFFING THE HUMAN RESOURCES DEPARTMENT

In most cases, the H.R. director reports directly to the hotel's G.M. In larger hotels the director may have a professional assistant to do interviewing, personnel records management, and other tasks and may also have an associate to perform word processing, filing, and other clerical-related duties. Regardless of the specific staffing levels, however, the tasks related to H.R. must be done. Typical tasks are identified in Figure 4.1, Job Description of a Human Resources Director.

When reviewing Figure 4.1, note that the terms **"job description"** and **"job specification"** are used.

HOTEL TERMINOLOGY AT WORK

Job Description: A list of tasks that an employee working in a specific position must be able to effectively perform.

■

FIGURE 4.1   Job Description of a Human Resource Director

JOB TITLE: H.R. DIRECTOR

General Job Description:

Performs responsible administrative work managing the H.R. of the hotel. Responsibilities involve the planning and administration of a H.R. program that includes recruitment, selection, evaluation, promotion, and other change of status of all employees. Must also develop and implement a system of communication to provide necessary information to staff. Works under general supervision. Exercises initiative and independent judgment when performing assigned tasks.

Job Activities:

- Participates in overall planning and policy making to yield effective and consistent H.R. services.
- Communicates applicable policies through all organizational levels by use of bulletins, meetings, and personal contact.
- Interviews applicants, evaluates qualifications, and classifies applications.
- Recruits and screens applicants to fill vacancies.
- Reviews applications of qualified persons.
- Meets with departmental managers and supervisors on personnel-related matters, including hiring, retention, or release of probationary employees, transfers, demotions, and dismissals of permanent employees.
- Develops and delivers orientation and training activities and coordinates these activities with managers in all departments.
- Establishes and maintains an effective performance appraisal system and assists departmental supervisors in making employee evaluations.
- Maintains employee personnel files.
- Supervises staff employees in the H.R. department directly and through subordinates.
- Performs related work and undertakes special H.R. projects as assigned.

General Qualifications (Job Specifications):

Should have considerable experience in area of H.R. management and administration.

<u>Preferred Education</u>:

Graduation from a four-year college or university with major work in human resources, business administration, hospitality management, or related field.

<u>Knowledge and Skills</u>:

Considerable knowledge of principles and practices of H.R. management.
Basic word processing and spreadsheet development skills highly desirable.

<u>Responsibility</u>:

Supervises H.R. professional and supportive staff.

HOTEL TERMINOLOGY AT WORK

Job Specification: A list of the personal qualities judged necessary for successful performance of the tasks required by the job description.

■

The job description in Figure 4.1 suggests the very broad range of tasks that must be performed by the H.R. director. Like all department heads, this individual is typically a member of the hotel's Executive Operating Committee.

The job specification noted in Figure 4.1 provides some general suggestions about knowledge and skills necessary for a successful H.R. director. Some industry observers believe that a law degree is increasingly important. Others believe that a working background in H.R. leading to increasingly more responsible positions in larger hotels provides a good background. Still other observers believe that the "best" H.R. directors have "come up through the ranks" by working in several operating departments. The manager with this experience is thought to have a better perspective about the work done in the departments and the type of employees most likely to succeed in the department. In fact, there is probably no one best type of H.R. director. Regardless of the person selected for the job, the G.M. must have trust in the director, value his or her opinions, and see that person as a true partner in the hotel's success.

LEGAL ASPECTS OF HUMAN RESOURCES

There are numerous legal matters that impact hotel employees. These change rapidly. Hotels and hotel management teams that do not pay attention to the law spend too much of their time involved in employee related disputes, grievances, and lawsuits. This distracts the hotel from its goal of serving guests. There are several areas of H.R. that involve legal aspects of management that must be understood by H.R. directors as well as G.M.s.

Employee Selection

The importance of job descriptions was noted earlier. These tools are also important because they help to confirm that job requirements were established prior to making employee selection decisions. The job specification, which is driven by tasks identified in the job description logically, not arbitrarily, identifies a candidate's job qualifications, as well.

Job specifications must address **bonified occupational qualifications (BOQs)**.

HOTEL TERMINOLOGY AT WORK

Bonified Occupational Qualifications (BOQs): Qualifications to perform a job that are judged reasonably necessary to safely or adequately perform all tasks within the job.

■

As a competent G.M., you should carefully review all hotel job descriptions with H.R. personnel to assure that your job specifications list only BOQs that are truly legitimate and that do not unfairly or illegally screen out qualified candidates. Legitimate BOQs include:

- Education or certification requirements
- Language skills
- Previous experience
- Minimum age requirements (for jobs such as waitress or bartender)
- Physical attributes needed for a job (amounts to be lifted, carried, etc.)
- Licensing

However, it is important to realize that a legitimate BOQ cannot be used inappropriately to illegally deny employment opportunities to a candidate. For example, a food and beverage manager who prefers to hire male wait staff rather than females cannot list as a BOQ "must be able to lift fifty pounds" in an attempt to unfairly discriminate against females, because wait staff typically do not have to lift items of that weight. On the other hand, a manager in the maintenance department may well specify that lifting furniture weighing fifty pounds is a BOQ for a specific job in that department.

In addition to proper job specifications, there are laws that impact the following tools used to screen employee applicants as part of the selection process.

For example:

- Applications. Applicants should only be required to provide data about their name, address, work experience, and other information directly related to the job for which they are applying. (*Note:* Proposed application forms should be reviewed by a qualified attorney to assure that they are in compliance with applicable federal and/or state laws.) Figure 4.2 lists the type of data that are permitted on a hotel's employment application form.

FIGURE 4.2   Informational Areas Included in Employment Applications

- Demographic information (such as name, address, dates available for work, and social security number)
- Employment history
- Educational background and skills
- Criminal history and pending criminal charges
- Employment status/authorization
- References
- Drug/background testing and authorizations

THE INTERNET AT WORK

For a free, downloadable copy of a "legal" application form related to the hospitality industry, go to:

www.hospitalitylawyer.com.

This helpful site, operated by Stephen Barth, an attorney for hospitality companies, is an excellent source of legal information related to H.R. and employment issues.

- **Interviews.** It is important that questions asked of job applicants be written down to help assure that all applicants are asked the same questions. Questions should not screen out any class of applicants and should be directly related to judging the applicant's competence for the job. Questions about race, religion, and physical traits (height and weight) should not be asked. Questions of age can be asked only to the extent that they relate to the hotel's legal requirements. For example, it is certainly legal to ask, in a state where bar wait staff must be eighteen or older to serve alcohol, if an applicant for a cocktail servers job is "over eighteen."

- **Testing.** Some hotels use skill, psychological, and/or drug screening tests. While preemployment drug testing is allowed in most states, there are typically strict guidelines that must be followed when it is implemented. A good H.R. director will know and follow these guidelines. As a G.M., if your hotel utilizes drug screening or testing, you, too, should be familiar with your state's requirements.

- **Background checks.** The only information that should be sought should be that directly applicable to the position for which an applicant is applying. A consent form authorizing a background check should be signed by the applicant before background checks are made.

- **References.** As with background checks, the applicant's permission to check references should be obtained in writing. In addition, your own hotel should never provide information about a previous employee of your hotel without having received a copy of that person's signed release. Even then, many hotels prefer not to divulge information about past employees other than their name and dates of employment.

There are numerous laws and regulations that affect a hotel's employee selection process. The Federal Civil Rights Act of 1964 did many things, one of which was to form the Equal Employment Opportunity Commission (EEOC) which administers and enforces laws relating to employment. Under federal law, hoteliers and other employers with fifteen or more staff members, who are engaged in **interstate commerce,** cannot discriminate against employees or others on the basis of race, color, religion, sex, or national origin.

HOTEL TERMINOLOGY AT WORK

Interstate Commerce: The commercial trading or transportation of people or property that occurs between and/or among states.

■

In addition, many states have specific civil rights laws that address or prohibit discrimination. As a result you may encounter state antidiscrimination laws that include categories such as marital status, arrest records, or sexual orientation.

Another example of a law affecting hotel staffing practices is the Americans with Disabilities Act (ADA). Enacted in 1990, it prohibits discrimination against persons with disabilities who are seeking employment. The ADA does not require the employment of an applicant who is not qualified to perform necessary work. It does, however, prohibit the elimination of applicants simply because they have disabilities covered by the act. In some situations, the hotel may be required to make a reasonable accommodation to enable a disabled staff member to perform the job. For example, perhaps modifications could be easily made to a front desk area, which would enable a front desk clerk in a wheelchair to perform necessary guest check-in and check-out duties.

The Age Discrimination in Employment Act (ADEA) applies to employers with twenty or more staff members and protects individuals forty years of age or older from employment discrimination based on age. Of course, this law affects staffing decisions also.

A competent H.R. director knows that before a qualified applicant can be selected, it is necessary to determine that the potential staff member is legally allowed to accept the position. This involves verification of work eligibility and compliance with applicable child labor laws. The Immigration Reform and Control Act (IRCA) of 1986 prohibits employers from knowingly hiring illegal persons to work in the United States, and all employers, including hoteliers, must verify that those staff members hired are legally authorized to work in the United States. A Form 1-I developed by the Department of Immigration and Naturalization Services (INS) must be completed. Applicants must have one or more of several approved documents to establish eligibility for employment:

- Social Security card
- Original/certified copy of birth certificate
- Unexpired INS employment authorization
- Unexpired reentry permit

- Unexpired refugee travel document
- Birth certificate issued by Department of State
- Certificate of Birth abroad issued by the Department of State
- United States citizen identification
- Native American tribal document
- Identification used by resident citizen in United States

The Fair Labor Standards Act passed in 1938 protects young workers from employment that interferes with their education and/or that is potentially hazardous to their health or well-being. Persons age 16 and 17 can work for unlimited hours at any time in jobs if the U.S. secretary of labor has declared that they are not hazardous. Youths age 14 to 15 may work in selected jobs during nonschool hours under specified conditions.

THE INTERNET AT WORK

There are numerous regulations involved in the employment of minors that are provided in the Fair Labor Standards Act (FLSA). To review basic information and to learn answers to frequently asked questions go to:

http://www.dol.gov/elaws/flsa.htm.

As seen in the above discussion, there are many laws that impact how hoteliers can make employee staffing decisions. There can also be other, perhaps more strict, state and/or local laws and regulations. Unfortunately, legal restraints do change, can be open to interpretation, and may have serious consequences for noncompliance. The G.M. must work with the H.R. director and other knowledgeable professionals to ensure those employee selection procedures, as well as all other procedures used in the H.R. department, are indeed legal and defensible.

Employment Relationships

As a G.M., you and your managers likely have the right to hire/terminate staff members as you see fit because, in most states, the relationship with the employee is **"at-will" employment.**

HOTEL TERMINOLOGY AT WORK

At-Will Employment: The employment relationship that exists when employers can hire any employee as they choose and dismiss that employee with or without cause at any time. The employee can also elect to work for the employer or terminate the work relationship anytime he or she chooses.

■

Assuming that no antidiscrimination laws are violated, this allows an employer to hire and dismiss an employee at any time if it is in the best interests of the business. In situations where an employee's union or other contractual agreement is in place, this relationship may, of course, be modified.

After an employee has been legally selected, an **employment agreement** can be drafted to specifically indicate the terms of the employment relationship.

HOTEL TERMINOLOGY AT WORK

Employment Agreement: A document specifying the terms of the work relationship between the employer and employee that indicates the rights and obligations of both parties. The employment agreement often takes the form of an official written offer letter.

■

The Law in the Workplace

There are numerous other laws that can have a significant impact upon the management of employees after they are hired. These laws and regulations change constantly. H.R. directors must stay abreast of these changes and keep the G.M. and others in the hotel informed of them. As a G.M., one way to help ensure that your H.R. director, and thus your hotel, stays up-to-date in the H.R. area is to encourage his or her membership in the Society for Human Resource Management.

THE INTERNET AT WORK

The Society for Human Resource Management (SHRM) is the professional association for H.R. directors and staff. To view their Web site, go to:

http://www.shrm.org.

Note that this group produces *HR Magazine,* a monthly information publication distributed to its membership.

While there are far too many specific H.R. issues to include in a chapter such as this one, there are some legal issues that are so significant they simply must be addressed. For example, discrimination was noted in an earlier section. Additional important legal issues include those related to sexual harassment, family and medical leave, compensation, employee performance, unemployment, and required employment records.

Sexual Harassment

One cannot ask a subordinate for sexual favors in exchange for employment benefits; neither can one punish an employee if an offer is rejected. As well, environmental harassment including the use of improper language or conduct are additional examples of prohibited harassment. To protect against liability that can result from allegations of discrimination or harassment, it is important that **zero tolerance** policies and procedures be in place.

HOTEL TERMINOLOGY AT WORK

Zero Tolerance: The total absence of behavior that is objectionable from the perspectives of discrimination or harassment. This is done through the issuing of appropriate policies, the conduct of applicable workshops, the development of procedures for employees alleging discrimination or harassment to obtain relief and written protocols for reporting, investigating and resolving incidences and grievances.

■

Today's professional G.M. strongly supports and aggressively follows a strict zero tolerance policy related to sexual and other forms of harassment.

Family and Medical Leave Act (FMLA)

Signed by President Clinton in 1993, this law states that hotels employing fifty or more staff members are required to provide up to twelve weeks of leave (unpaid) to an employee if the time is needed for the birth, adoption, or, in some cases, the foster care of a child. The act also applies when the employee or one of his/her family members has a serious illness.

Compensation

The Fair Labor Standards Act (FLSA) was discussed earlier relative to child labor standards. It also established a **minimum wage** to be paid to employees covered by the act and rates that must be paid for **overtime** work.

HOTEL TERMINOLOGY AT WORK

Minimum Wage: The lowest amount of compensation that an employer may pay to an employee covered by the FLSA or applicable state law. Minimum wage provisions cover most hotel employees; however, exceptions can include youthful employees being paid a training wage for the first ninety days of employment and some tipped employees.

■

HOTEL TERMINOLOGY AT WORK

Overtime: The number of hours of work after which an employee must receive a premium pay rate. This premium rate is generally one and one-half times the basic hourly rate.

■

Another provision of the FLSA relates to equal pay. Regardless of their gender, employees who hold essentially the same job must be equitably compensated with both financial and nonfinancial rewards.

In the United States, there are laws related to compensation and laws related to taxes. This is so because there are numerous taxes and credits that employers must pay based upon the compensation paid to employees. Employees must pay taxes as well, and the employer must withhold many of these taxes from the employee's paycheck. Tax credits are also sometimes granted to employers and employees. Examples of these taxes and tax credits include:

- Income tax. State, federal, and, sometimes, local income taxes must be withheld from employee paychecks.
- Federal Insurance Contribution Act (FICA). Taxes must be contributed by both employers and employees to fund the federal Social Security and Medicare programs.
- Federal Unemployment Tax Act (FUTA). This mandates that employers contribute a tax that is based on the employer's total payroll to help care for persons who are out of work through no fault of their own.
- Earned Income Credit (EIC). This is a refundable credit for employees whose incomes fall below preestablished levels.
- Work Opportunity Tax Credit (WOTC). This provides employers with tax credits for hiring disadvantaged workers.

Specific requirements related to the above tax and credit programs are complicated and change often. It is important for G.M.s to confirm that their H.R. directors interact closely with the hotel's accounting (payroll) employees to help ensure full compliance with all provisions of these tax-related laws.

Employee Performance

Hoteliers must comply with laws relating to the management of employee performance. These include;

Employee Evaluation. Hotels violate the law if it can be demonstrated that a performance assessment system is biased against a class of employees who are protected by the law. It is always important to assure that work performance, and nothing else, forms the basis for employee evaluations.

Discipline. Workplace rules and policies must be established that do not violate the law. They must be effectively communicated and consistently enforced. Some hotels use a progressive discipline system such as that described in chapter 3 to encourage employees to improve and to help ensure that managers and others who discipline employees do so fairly. ***Termination.*** The at-will employment relationship discussed earlier does *not* allow a hotelier to terminate employees for any reason. *Unacceptable* reasons to terminate an employee include the following:

- Actions that are approved in the hotel's employee manual
- In an effort to deny benefits
- For allowed work absences
- Because of attempts to unionize staff members
- For reporting violations of the law
- For being a member of a protected class of worker(s) (e.g., race, sex, or religion)
- When an oral promise of continued employment has been made
- In violation of a written employment agreement or contract

Unemployment Issues

Unemployment insurance is a large cost to hotels and can be difficult to administer. Federal and state governments operate this program. Each state requires employers to pay different costs to maintain the state's share of funds used to assist workers who have temporarily lost jobs.

HOTEL TERMINOLOGY AT WORK

Unemployment Insurance: Funds provided by employers to make available temporary financial benefits to employees who have lost their jobs.

■

Employees can file an **unemployment claim,** and as this is done, a series of steps mandated by states will be used to determine whether an applicant is eligible and, if so, (a) for how much, (b) the length of time payments will last, and (c) the length of time an employee must work for an employer to qualify for assistance.

HOTEL TERMINOLOGY AT WORK

Unemployment Claim: A claim made by an unemployed worker to the appropriate state agency asserting that the worker is eligible for unemployment benefits.

■

Employment Records

Federal and state agencies require that selected employee records be maintained. It is the H.R. director's job to ensure that this is done. Penalties for noncompliance can be severe. There are many requirements related to record keeping. Examples include:

- Department of Labor records. The Fair Labor Standards Act requires that numerous records be maintained for each employee, including information about the employee's name, address, gender, job title, work schedule, hourly rate, regular and overtime earnings, wage deductions, and dates of pay days.

- Records must be kept of any deductions from wages for meals, uniforms, and/or lodging.

- Records for tipped employees must include the amount of tips reported.

- Records applicable to the Family and Medical Leave Act require information about dates that FMLA-eligible employees take a covered leave, the amount of leave (in hours or days), as well as other documentation.

- The Immigration Reform and Control Act requires that an Employment Eligibility Verification (I-9) Form be completed and retained for each employee.

- The Age Discrimination and Employment Act requires that employers retain certain records, including those related to personnel matters and benefit plans.

As can be seen in this section, there are a wide variety of laws and regulations that impact how hoteliers can interact with applicants before employment and with employees after selection decisions are made. G.M.s count on an effective H.R. department and staff to ensure the hotel stays in complinace with these.

It is easy to see why extensive knowledge about employment laws and the need to spend significant amounts of time to keep up with legal aspects as they (seemingly) constantly change are integral requirements for an effective H.R. director. G.M.s, too, must know the basics of these laws, know when to ask H.R. personnel questions about the hotel's policies and practices, and, perhaps most important, know when external legal assistance is warranted.

THE HUMAN RESOURCES DEPARTMENT AT WORK

The legal aspects of managing H.R. discussed earlier provide some of the context for and, sometimes, many of the limitations within which personnel in the hotel's H.R. department must work. In this section we review some of the day-to-day activities performed by personnel in the H.R. department as they help line operating managers do their job.

Recruitment

In many hotels, the employee **turnover rate** is extremely high. The high turnover rate suffered by some hotels makes recruiting employees a seemingly never-ending and absolutely critical part of the work done by the H.R. department.

HOTEL TERMINOLOGY AT WORK

Turnover Rate: A measure of the proportion of a workforce that is replaced during a designated time period (i.e., month, quarter, year).

This measure can be computed as:

$$\frac{\text{Number of employees separated}}{\text{Number of employees in the workforce}} = \text{Employee turnover rate}$$

■

Recruitment can be especially tough in areas when the **unemployment rate** is low and because of common stereotypes suggesting that entry-level positions in hotels are undesirable.

HOTEL TERMINOLOGY AT WORK

Unemployment Rate: The number, usually expressed as a percentage, of employable persons who are out of work and looking for jobs.

As the unemployment rate decreases, it becomes more difficult to attract job applicants because employers must increasingly compete with other potential employers for those relatively few persons looking for work.

■

An astute G.M. recognizes that the need to recruit for vacant positions is directly related to the hotel's turnover rate. If fewer employees leave, the need to recruit for vacant positions will be lessened. There are many things that the hotel's EOC, along with all other managers at the property, can do to influence turnover rates. The H.R. department, however, does not control most of these. The point to be made here is that while H.R. is indeed responsible for recruitment, it is the operation of the individual hotel departments that will most influence turnover rates.

Close interaction between the G.M. and the H.R. director can lead to hotel policies, procedures, and standards that will help the hotel recruit effectively in its own community or market. As this occurs, the need for recruitment activities is lowered.

Often, a good mix of **internal recruiting** and **external recruiting** techniques is best. As the names imply, internal recruiting focuses on currently employed employees (internal applicants) for vacant positions; by contrast, external recruiting focuses on searching for applicants who are *not* currently employed by the hotel.

HOTEL TERMINOLOGY AT WORK

Internal Recruiting: Tactics to identify and attract currently employed staff members for job vacancies that represent promotions or lateral transfers to similar positions.

■

HOTEL TERMINOLOGY AT WORK

External Recruiting: Tactics designed to attract persons who are not current hotel employees for vacant positions.

■

The concept of "promotion from within" is an example of an internal recruiting technique. Many hotels look first to high-performing current staff members when management positions become vacant. This is an excellent idea. Promotional opportunities are incentives for many employees to remain with the hotel and to make efforts to excel while they are employed. Other staff members may want to make transfers to other positions and to other departments and should be allowed to do so whenever they are qualified and it is in the best interest of the hotel.

Alerting friends and relatives of current employees about position vacancies is another example of internal recruiting. Often, bonuses are paid to staff members who nominate applicants who then are employed at the hotel for a specified time period.

There are a wide range of external tactics that may, or may not, be effective. Some of these are well known. They include newspaper and other media advertisements, job fairs, the use of employment or executive search firms for management positions, recruiting at community schools and colleges, and the all-too-frequently used "Help Wanted" signs placed outside or inside the hotel.

Only shortsighted G.M.s think that "recruitment is the job of the H.R. department." In fact, all employees, by what they do and what they fail to do, make an impression on current staff members that, in turn, impacts the hotel's turnover rate. As well, they influence the perceptions of potential applicants because employees will certainly talk to candidates about how "great" or "terrible" it is to work for the hotel.

Selection

Selection involves evaluating applicants for positions to determine those most likely to be successful in the position. Hotels are sometimes criticized for hiring any "warm body" that applies for work. Unfortunately, however, if the recruitment process is not effective, those selecting employees may not have many candidates to choose from. It is from this situation that the "warm body" criticism typically surfaces.

HOTEL TERMINOLOGY AT WORK

Selection: The process of evaluating job applicants to determine those more qualified (or potentially qualified) for vacant positions.

■

Simply put, an effective selection process helps to ensure that the best candidate for the job is chosen. Typically, the selection decision is made by the appropriate manager in the line operating department and not by H.R. staff.

To make an appropriate selection decision, information about each candidate's eligibility for a position must be gathered. This may be done by use of several selection devices:

- Preliminary screening, including reviewing the candidate's application.
- Employment interviews.
- Employment tests. Sometimes tests are given to applicants, especially when experience is required. For example, an applicant may be given a paper and pencil test that addresses the arithmetic involved in cashiering skills or the spelling and grammar skills required of a typist. Alternatively, a skills test could be given. An "experienced" cook could be asked to prepare a sauce that an experienced cook should know how to prepare.
- Reference checks. These can be done to confirm employment dates and positions held.
- Drug screening. If used by the hotel.

As a result of the screening process done by H.R. staff, those applicants judged most qualified and potentially successful in vacant positions are referred to the department head or supervisor in the department where the vacancy is located. There, additional interviewing can be done, and the selection decision is made.

Orientation

After applicants are recruited and new staff members are selected, **orientation** becomes important. Orientation is the process of providing basic information about the hotel that should be known by all of its employees. Effective orientation is critical because it helps to establish the long-term relationship between the hotel and its employees.

HOTEL TERMINOLOGY AT WORK

Orientation: The process of providing basic information about the hotel which must be known by all of its employees.

■

Orientation programs must be well thought out. They cannot be done in an inconsistent, haphazard fashion, depending, in part, on how the busy the hotel staff is when a new staff member begins. The G.M., as part of a concern for the hotel's staff, must assure that the orientation program conducted by the H.R. department is organized, consistently comprehensive, and professionally well done.

Important goals of an effective orientation program are:

- To reduce anxiety. New staff members are looking for reinforcement that their decision to work for the hotel was a good one. The new employees' evolving impressions of the hotel will be enhanced as they learn about the organization and as they observe the genuine respect and attention given to them by H.R. staff and other managers.

- To improve morale and to reduce turnover. Studies have shown that the quality of an orientation program directly affects turnover.

- To provide consistency. An effective orientation process will yield a team of employees who are aware of and believe in the property's goals; who know what to do, for example, in the case of a fire or other emergency; and who understand the hotel's personnel policies about issues such as vacation, sick leave, and benefits.

- To develop realistic expectations. New employees want to know what the hotel and its management staff expect of them. Orientation programs can help to provide this information.

The H.R. department should conduct the general orientation program. This does not, of course, prevent individual departments from initiating their own departmental specific orientation programs. In most departments there should, in fact, be such a program. For example, while all employees in the hotel must know about guest security and safety, generally only food and beverage personnel must know about safety concerns in food preparation areas.

For an effective G.M., there are two critical orientation issues. The first is that of content, the second is attendance. Topics that a G.M. should ensure are covered in an orientation program include:

- A hotel overview, including a presentation of the mission statement, the importance of effective guest service, and the emphasis on teamwork
- A review of important policies and procedures (many hotels specifically address their harassment polices at this time)
- A detailed discussion about compensation, including fringe benefits and pay periods
- Guest safety and security concerns
- A review of employee and union relations (if applicable)
- A facility tour of all hotel areas (sometimes a meal in the hotel's restaurant is included as part of the tour)
- Any special topics related to the specific hotel

Attendance relates to who should be present. Obviously, the new employees should be there. Just as obviously, it is unquestionable that the G.M. should make at least some appearance at every orientation program. The G.M. is the hotel's leader and new employees want to meet the leader.

Many hotels have an **employee handbook**, or manual, that is provided to staff members during orientation.

HOTEL TERMINOLOGY AT WORK

Employee Handbook: Written policies and procedures related to employment at a hotel. Also sometimes called an employee "manual."

■

The purpose of the employee handbook is to provide details of the basic subject matter covered during orientation. For example, handbooks often contain information about the hotel's mission statement and goals, as well as details about its policies and procedures relating to compensation, benefits, and work-related behavior.

In some hotels, a follow-up orientation is held several weeks or months after the initial orientation session. This allows employees to provide input about their initial job experiences and can be used to revise and improve the initial orientation program.

Training

Training is designed to help improve the knowledge or skills of the hotel's staff. Some, but not all, observers also believe that training can be used to modify attitudes, such as those related to providing guest service or working closely with a team of fellow employees. Regardless of what you believe are the limitations of training, all of your hotel employees will require training of some type throughout their careers. In fact, even G.M.s require training as new operational techniques and management approaches change in response to advances in technology or modifications of hotel goals.

It is obvious that new employees must be trained to perform their required job tasks. When these employees are trained well, quality and quantity standards can be consistently attained. However, even experienced staff members need training as, for example, new equipment is purchased or as revised operational procedures are implemented. As well, ongoing professional development opportunities can motivate individuals and help the hotel by preparing employees for advancement opportunities.

Employee training can be done in groups or on an individual basis.

The role of the H.R. staff in training depends on the type of training undertaken.

Group training is an effective method when several or more staff members must learn the same thing. For example, consider a front office department interested in providing **upselling** training for front desk agents. In this example, the manager of the area may request assistance from H.R. personnel to assist with training efforts.

HOTEL TERMINOLOGY AT WORK

Upselling: Tactics used to increase the hotel's average daily rate (ADR) by encouraging guests to rent higher-priced rooms with better or more amenities (view, complimentary breakfast and newspaper, increased square footage, etc.) than those provided with lower-priced rooms.

■

H.R. personnel could request and preview potentially applicable training programs developed by professional associations or commercial training organizations. They could also provide some property-specific elements of the program, such as developing suggested upselling dialog, which might be used in a **role-play** or other group training activity.

HOTEL TERMINOLOGY AT WORK

Role-play: A training activity that allows trainees to practice a skill by interacting with each other in simulated roles (such as pretending that one trainee is a guest and the other is an employee interacting with the guest).

■

Individualized on-the-job training is a one-on-one training method that involves, for example, teaching a new staff member how to make a bed or providing instruction to an experienced maintenance staff member about how to maintain a new piece of equipment. Individualized training is most frequently the responsibility of line department managers and their staff. In fact, in most individualized training situations, the individual departments prefer to be responsible for the development of the training.

The H.R. department can play an additional training role by implementing "Train the Trainer" programs designed to teach individual department managers how to better implement training for their own staffs.

THE INTERNET AT WORK

One of the most important training roles that H.R. can play is that of teaching other managers how to train employees well. Crisp Publications produces an excellent tool for just this purpose. To view it go to:

http://www.crisplearning.com.

Type "Training Managers to Train" in the search field when you arrive there.

THE INTERNET AT WORK

More than ever, the Internet is being utilized to train hotel employees. To view a Web site developed just for that purpose go to:

http://www.hoteltraining.com.

G.M.s should assign the training responsibilities of H.R. staff and line managers. Training is absolutely critical to your hotel's success, and as the G.M., you must assure that it is being done as effectively as possible.

Performance Evaluation

Most employees want to know how their boss views their performance. Staff members in the H.R. department may be responsible for ensuring the consistency of the hotel's employee performance evaluation process. Essentially, there are two types of evaluation approaches that can be used. As a G.M., it is important that you know and support the approach in use at your hotel.

The first type of system requires managers to compare employees to a standard. In this case, managers evaluate employees individually without regard to other staff members. In the second approach, managers rank employees in comparison to other employees in their department. That is, the employee's performance is "good" or "bad" in comparison with that of other workers with similar responsibilities.

─────────────────────── **MANAGERS AT WORK** ───────────────────────

J.D. Ojisama was having lunch with the H.R. director in the hotel's dining room.

"I've got some possible budget problems," the director said. "Remember our 'pep talk' at last month's Executive Operating Committee meeting? The one where we all agreed that we needed to do more staff training?"

"Yes," agreed J.D., "I recall the meeting."

"I've had the department heads from food and beverage, housekeeping, and the Front Office visit me since then to request help in finding training materials for their entry-level staff—and they are asking my department to pay for it. You know there's not much in the budget for the purchase of materials from external suppliers."

"I do know that," J.D. responded, "but I also know that not training our staff will cost those departments more money than training them."

J.D. and the director flinched a bit as they heard, from the dining room busser's area, a drinking glass and several plates break with a loud, shattering sound.

"I hope no one got hurt," said J.D., getting up from the table and moving quickly toward the sound of the broken dishes.

What can J.D. do to ensure that department specific training occurs in the hotel?

How might inexpensive training materials be secured or developed?

What can be done with department heads that maintain they have neither the time nor the funds needed to undertake training efforts? Where do the costs of "not training" in a business show up?

───

Regardless of the evaluation approach used in a hotel, a regular system of employee evaluation can:

- Help determine where, if at all, staff members can improve their performance
- Help assess who will be eligible for raises in pay and promotions
- Improve morale because effective performance evaluation systems show employees that they are respected and that their supervisor wants to help them get better at their jobs
- Help assure legal compliance because a written record of information supporting promotions, rewards, disciplinary actions, and the like is available if employees make legal challenges

A systematic performance appraisal system involves at least six steps:

1. Performance standards are established for each position.
2. Policies relating to the frequency of rating and the persons responsible for them are established.
3. Data are gathered about an employee's performance.
4. The raters, and sometimes the employee, must evaluate performance.
5. A performance evaluation discussion is held with the employee.
6. Evaluation information is filed.

While the task of evaluating a staff member's performance is clearly the responsibility of his or her boss, the H.R. department has an important role to play in:

- Developing policies and procedures for a propertywide system
- Communicating these policies and procedures to all managers and staff
- Addressing and resolving employee concerns as they arise
- Filing performance evaluation results in the employee's records

For some employees, performance evaluations are a difficult procedure. Few people like to be told that they are doing anything other than an excellent job, even when they are not! Also, many managers find it uncomfortable to periodically "rate," then communicate that rating "face-to-face" with the employees they must work with every day. A good H.R. department recognizes the importance of an effective evaluation system, as well as the challenges faced by both employees and managers as they participate in the process. The value to the hotel of an effective performance appraisal system is certainly worth facing the challenges that operating such a system presents.

Compensation

Administration of a hotel's **compensation** program is a primary function of the H.R. department.

HOTEL TERMINOLOGY AT WORK

Compensation: All financial and nonfinancial rewards given to management and nonmanagement employees in return for the work they do for the hotel.

■

When many staff members think of "compensation," they often think of the **salaries** and **wages** that they are paid.

HOTEL TERMINOLOGY AT WORK

Salary: Pay calculated at a weekly, monthly, or annual rate rather than at an hourly rate.

■

HOTEL TERMINOLOGY AT WORK

Wage: Pay calculated on an hourly basis.

■

While these are the most significant forms of compensation paid to most staff, **benefits** can also be significant.

HOTEL TERMINOLOGY AT WORK

Benefits: Indirect financial compensation consisting of employer-provided rewards and services other than wages or salaries.

Examples include life and health insurance, paid vacations, and employer-provided meals.

■

Salaries and wages are examples of direct financial compensation, which also includes bonuses and commissions that are often paid to hotel sales personnel. By contrast, benefits are an indirect financial compensation.

Compensation is a necessity of life and the primary reason the majority of people work. Pay is important because, of course, employees require money to purchase food, shelter, clothing, and other necessities. However, it is also important because it indicates an individual's worth to the organization. For this reason, it is important that employees consider the hotel's compensation program fair. The G.M. and the H.R. director must work together to ensure that they do.

Well-conceived compensation programs are important to the hotel because, typically, the "average" property pays approximately 30 to 35 percent of its total revenue to employees in the form of payroll and related costs.[1] As well, the level of pay attracts or repels qualified applicants and either motivates or alienates employees as managers attempt to attain work quality and quantity goals.

Compensation must be equitable from the perspectives of both the hotel and its employees. Effectively administered, the compensation program will be:

- Legal—it will meet any requirements imposed by governmental agencies.
- Fair—each employee will be paid relative to input.
- Balanced—financial and nonfinancial rewards will represent a balanced part of the total reward package.
- Cost-effective—the hotel will receive reasonable productivity for the labor costs that are incurred.
- Viewed as reasonable by staff—employees will perceive that their compensation is equitable in relation to the work they do and relative to what they would be paid by competitive employers.

It is difficult to administer a compensation program that adequately addresses all the above factors. Doing so provides an ongoing challenge for

---

[1]1999 data from Hospitality Asset Advisors International, Inc., San Francisco, California, 2000 (p. 8).

the H.R. director and other hotel managers who must make compensation decisions. H.R. personnel work with the G.M. and other managers in the hotel to establish pay for specific positions based upon:

- What other employers attempting to attract the same applicants pay in their hotels.
    It is a good idea to use local salary and wage surveys for this purpose.
- What employees working on different jobs within the hotel are paid.
    For example, those doing cleaning work in the food and beverage department should be paid a reasonable amount relative to those doing cleaning in another department. Differences between pay must be reasonable and defensible and must be based upon the worth of the position to the hotel.
- What other employees working on the same job within the hotel are paid.
    This decision is often based upon the length of time the employee has worked for the hotel and evaluations made during an individual's employee performance appraisal.

H.R. officials can provide a significant service to line department managers as they provide information about the financial compensation practices of competitive hotels and other potential employers. In addition, information about benefits programs offered by other employers in the community will be of interest to the G.M. and others as compensation decisions are made.

Other Compensation (Benefits)

Different employees will receive different salaries and wages based upon factors such as the position they hold and their length of time with the hotel. Thus, the executive housekeeper's annual salary will be much greater than a laundry worker's annual income. The benefits package these two employees enjoy, however, may be very similar. While full- and part-time employees may qualify for different types of benefits, most of these benefits are available to all employees as long as the hotel has employed them for a specified period of time.

The G.M., the H.R. staff, and others in the EOC will typically work together to make benefits decisions. Top-level management, however, approves the benefits budget. As noted earlier in this chapter, the federal or state governments mandate some benefits programs. These include those benefits relating to unemployment insurance, Social Security and Medicare programs, and workers' compensation programs. There are, in addition, a wide range of voluntary benefits that hotels can offer employees in an effort to attract and retain qualified employees. Figure 4.3 lists examples of these.

An effective H.R. staff, along with the G.M., has a variety of responsibilities as they manage a benefits program. They should:

FIGURE 4.3   Examples of Employee Benefits Programs

Paid Leave Benefits
- Holidays
- Vacations
- Sick Leave
- Jury Duty
- Funerals
- Military Service
- Personal
- Breaks
- Maternity
- Paternity

Unpaid Leave Benefits
- Maternity
- Paternity

Life Insurance Benefits
- Wholly employer-financed
- Partly employer-financed

Medical Care Benefits
- Employee Coverage:
  Wholly employer-financed
  Partly employer-financed
- Family Coverage:
  Wholly employer-financed
  Partly employer-financed

Dental Care
- Employee Coverage:
  Wholly employer-financed
  Partly employer-financed
- Family Coverage:
  Wholly employer-financed
  Partly employer-financed

Other Insurance Benefits
- Sickness/Accident:
  Wholly employer-financed
  Partly employer-financed
- Long and/or Short-Term Disability:
  Wholly employer-financed
  Partly employer-financed

Retirement Benefits
- Defined Benefit Pensions:
  Wholly employer-financed
  Partly employer-financed
- Defined Contributions:
  Savings and thrift
  Deferred profit sharing
  Employee stock ownership
  Money purchase pension

Other
- Reimbursement Accounts
- Flexible Benefit Plans

Services
- Tuition Reimbursement
- Child Care
- Elder Care
- Financial Services
- Relocation Services
- Social/Recreational Programs

- Determine the objectives for the benefits programs. Most hotels desire to match the benefits they offer with those of competing hotels. However, hotels compete with other industries for potential employers and what these competitive industries offer employees should also be considered.
- Facilitate discussions with employees about desired benefits desired. This can be done through employee surveys and advisory committees.

- Communicate the "benefit" of benefits. Many staff members think of their compensation as their hourly pay or salaries only, yet benefits comprise a large and growing proportion of the total compensation provided by employers. Therefore, the types and especially the value of benefits provided by the hotel should be effectively and consistently communicated to staff members. These efforts should begin at the time of orientation, be included in the employee handbook, and should, for example, continue with presentations at employee meetings.

- Monitor costs. An aggressive assessment of labor costs and how they might be reduced or more effectively managed is an important ongoing activity of H.R. staff. Benefit costs related to medical insurance coverage are rising at an especially rapid rate. Programs designed to control costs such as these have a direct and positive affect on the hotel's bottom line.

Historically, hotels and other hospitality organizations have been very conservative in offering benefits programs. Other than granting some vacation and holiday time and limited medical coverage, few additional benefits were made available. Increasingly, however, hospitality businesses including hotels are offering a wider range of benefits opportunities to their staff members. This trend will continue as hotels are forced to compete with other employers to fill staff positions.

MANAGERS AT WORK

J.D. Ojisama was holding the weekly Executive Operating Committee meeting. Almost before J.D. could finish saying, "Good morning," the questions began:

"What are we going to do about that new hotel opening across town? They're stealing all our employees!" said the food and beverage director.

"One of my housekeepers said she was offered 25¢ more per hour to work there!" said the executive housekeeper.

"And . . . they're offering transportation reimbursement for local employees and free bus tokens for employees they recruit from the inner city," said the front office manager. "We've got to raise our employee's pay or we won't be able to keep anyone. I say forget any increases in our benefit package this year. We've got to raise our hourly rates."

Everyone in the room looked toward the H.R. director and J.D.

J.D.'s community, like many others, has a labor shortage problem. What are specific steps J.D. can take to ensure that the hotel retains its best staff and effectively recruits for those employees it will need in the future. How important is employee compensation in this process? What do you believe makes employees elect to stay at current jobs or more to new ones? Are benefits more important than hourly wages? To whom?

OTHER HUMAN RESOURCE ACTIVITIES

Our study of the H.R. department continues as we review its role in planning for future H.R. needs and in protecting the health and safety of the hotel's employees.

Planning for Human Resources

The high rates of turnover experienced by many hotels and other hospitality organizations require H.R. staff members to spend significant amounts of time in recruitment activities to fill vacant positions needed for day-to-day operations. Some jobs are filled from outside the hotel while, of course, some are filled by promoting from within. Most smaller and even medium-size hotels do not spend significant amounts of time in formalized H.R. planning. All, however, probably do informal planning as they anticipate how the future may impact upon the hotel's need for staff.

Traditionally, hotels have not needed to undertake long-term H.R. planning because most positions required only physical or entry-level technical skills, which could be learned on the job. Historically, as well, there has been an abundant supply of these applicants. Today, however, with increasingly intense competition for staff members with entry-level skills, this approach does not work well. Also, with the advent of technology, many staff and nearly all supervisors in hotels need to have some, if not extensive, computer-related abilities. Given this situation, it is easy to see that the H.R. training function is very much related to its long-range planning function and will continue to be.

Employee Safety and Health

All hoteliers, including the general manager, H.R. staff, and managers/supervisors in line operating departments, must be concerned about employees' safety and health. Many persons do not think of a hotel environment as being unsafe or unhealthy, but some jobs, improperly performed, can be. Many work-related accidents and illnesses in hotels relate to:

- The work to be done. For example, cooks may need to work with knives and meat slicers, housekeepers may need to use potentially hazardous chemicals when cleaning guest rooms and maintenance staff operate power equipment in their daily jobs.
- Working conditions. Greasy floors and wet, slippery surfaces can cause accidents for those in kitchens or cleaning floors anywhere in the hotel.

Managers in line operating departments are responsible for maintaining their workplaces and conditions to minimize accidents. As well, they should be responsible for safety and other training for staff members. However, H.R. personnel should also help by facilitating hotelwide safety efforts. In addition, employees need a place to go to if a supervisor or manager asks them to perform an unsafe task. The H.R. department must be a vocal advocate for employee safety, and the G.M. should encourage them to be just that. Other aspects of employee safety and security are included in this text in chapter 9, Safety and Property Security.

There are also a variety of health-related activities that will likely require assistance from the H.R. staff. Examples include:

- Developing and selecting programs to help employees cope with stress.
- Developing procedures that address violence in the workplace concerns.
- Communicating updated information about the human immunodeficiency virus (HIV—the virus that causes AIDS) in the workplace.
- Providing information about and helping to address concerns relative to cumulative trauma disorders, including repetitive motion injuries such as carpal tunnel syndrome.

Workforce and Work Quality Improvement

As a hotel's workforce improves in quality, the quality of its work (and service delivered to the guest) will improve also. It is an important function of the H.R. department to help make that improvement. Some technquies designed to do this include:

- Professional development. Working with line managers to implement ongoing programs so departmental employees can gain the additional job-related knowledge and skills leading to more responsible and higher paying jobs within the hotel.
- Cultural diversity. Educating managers and employees about the numerous professional, personal, and societal advantages inherent in recognizing the worth of all employees without regard to gender or race.
- Quality improvement. Helping the hotel facilitate a total quality improvement effort, including **continuous quality improvement (CQI)** to meet organizational goals by becoming more competitive.

HOTEL TERMINOLOGY AT WORK

Continuous Quality Improvement (CQI): Ongoing efforts within the hotel to better meet (or exceed) guest expectations and define ways to perform work with better, less costly, and faster methods.

■

While small, the H.R department and its director are important to a hotel's success. G.M.s that listen to the advice of a wise H.R. director will find that their legal problems related to employees and regulatory agencies are greatly reduced. Problems such as these detract from the business of the hotel and consume valuable time and resources that could be better used servicing guests.

HOTEL TERMINOLOGY AT WORK GLOSSARY

The following terms were defined within this chapter. If you are not familiar with each of them, please review the segment of the chapter that contains the term.

H.R.	Overtime	Upselling
Job description	Unemployment insurance	Role play
Job specification	Unemployment claim	Compensation
Bonified occupational	Turnover rate	Salary
qualifications	Unemployment rate	Wage
Interstate commerce	Internal recruiting	Benefits
At-will employment	External recruiting	Continuous quality
Employment agreement	Selection	improvement (CQI)
Zero tolerance	Orientation	
Minimum wage	Employee Handbook	

ISSUES AT WORK

1. A shortage of entry-level employees is a major concern of almost every G.M. today. To the extent that currently employed staff members can be retained, there will be less need to recruit new employees in today's very tight labor market. What are some specific activities that you, as a G.M., can undertake to help reduce the employee turnover rate? List at least three such activities and discuss why these would positively impact turnover. Would these same activities reduce supervisory and management turnover?

2. The concept of "Employer of Choice" was addressed in this chapter. Many jobs in a hotel are very similar to those in a competitor's hotels. Assume that the pay in your hotel and that of a nearby competitor were identical. Identify three features you could ensure existed in a hotel you manage that would help make you the Employer of Choice. How would your H.R. department be involved in your efforts?

3. Some G.M.s feel job descriptions are a waste of time. Others feel accurate job descriptions are critical to a hotel's staffing success. Think of two

jobs you have held. Did you receive a job description for either of them? Would they have been helpful? Prepare a job description and job specification, patterned after the one presented in this chapter, for the first job you ever held. Would the results of your work be helpful for the person currently holding that job?

4. Many hotels now test all employees who have accidents at work for the presence of illegal drugs. Assume this is the case in your hotel and that all employees are made aware of this during orientation. Assume also that an excellent employee in your hotel slipped and fell at work. Upon receiving medical treatment, it was confirmed that the employee tested positively for marijuana use. Because you operate a drug-free hotel, your options are to terminate the employee or to suspend the employee and mandate a thirty-day, unpaid drug treatment program that the employee must complete. The treatment program would be followed by two years of mandatory, random drug testing that the employee must pass or be automatically terminated. Your H.R. director asks you what to do. Would you terminate or mandate treatment? Why?

5. Some hotels have very different employment policies in place for their salaried and hourly workers. In addition to the fact that pay is often higher for salaried employees, what other benefits do you believe are appropriate for salaried staff, but not, perhaps, for hourly paid staff? What are three specific things a hotel G.M. can do to encourage talented hourly employees to consider supervisory or management positions in the hotel industry?

5
The Controller

This Chapter at Work

As a G.M., you are ultimately responsible for the financial performance of your property. This includes generating appropriate sales levels, a responsibility shared by all departments, as well as the appropriate management, or control, of all of your financial resources. In chapter 2, we identified "control" as one of the four major functions of management. It is not surprising, then, that the primary job of the controller is to help the G.M. "control" and analyze performance results.

In this chapter you will learn about the major responsibilities of the controller's office and how an effective controller will help you make appropriate financial management decisions by providing you with the timely and accurate accounting data you need to make those decisions.

In a large hotel, the controller's office may consist of several individuals, but in a smaller property, it may consist of only one person. In all cases, however, the tasks that are performed by the controller are critical to the success of the hotel. These tasks include forecasting hotel revenue, budgeting, preparing precise financial documents,

compiling accurate operating statistics, assisting in the development and implementation of internal control systems, and serving, along with the G.M., as a liaison with internal and external auditors.

You should know that, while it may be possible to operate an excellent hotel without an exceptional controller, experienced G.M.'s will tell you that a strong controller's office is a critical component of any truly successful hotel. Information is indeed power, and it is the controller's office that will give you the information you need to make powerful and timely decisions.

In many properties, it is the controller who will actually serve as the "acting G.M." when the G.M. is away from the property. While that is not always the case, it certainly is an indication of the value of this office and the work it performs. If the hotels you are interested in managing are too small to have a full-time controller on property, you will still find this chapter to be extremely valuable because it may very well be you, the G.M., who will perform many of the tasks traditionally assigned to the controller's office.

Chapter 5 Outline

ACCOUNTING
  Centralized Accounting Systems
  Decentralized Accounting Systems
REVENUE FORECASTING
  Rooms Revenue
  Food and Beverage Revenue

Other Revenue
BUDGETING
  Long-range Budgets
  Annual Budgets
  Monthly Budgets
FINANCIAL STATEMENTS

ACCOUNTING

The main responsibility of the **controller** is to oversee the accounting and bookkeeping functions in the hotel.

HOTEL TERMINOLOGY AT WORK

Controller: The individual responsible for recording, classifying, and summarizing the hotel's business transactions. In some hotels, this position is referred to as the comptroller.

■

While accounting and bookkeeping are similar, the purpose of book-keeping is primarily to record and summarize financial data. Accounting includes development of the systems to collect and report financial information, analyzing this same information, and making finance-related recommendations to assist in management decision making. As such, a controller who has a thorough understanding of accounting and can actually help you interpret your financial information in a way that is useful can be of tremendous assistance to you in your job as G.M.

In many regards, the controller can be considered the hotel's on-property accountant/financial advisor. Generally, a controller who is skilled in accounting techniques can be more helpful to the decision-making process of the G.M. than could an individual who is skilled only in bookkeeping. Some accountants, having successfully completed a comprehensive test given by the American Institute of Certified Public Accountants and after serving an apprenticeship under a Certified Public Accountant, receive the designation of **C.P.A.**

HOTEL TERMINOLOGY AT WORK

Certified Public Accountant C.P.A: An individual designated by the American Institute of Certified Public Accountants as competent in the field of accounting.

■

In some cases, the financial records of the hotel must be examined by a C.P.A. before owners, investors, creditors, governmental agencies, and other interested parties will accept them as accurate. In larger hotels, the controller is likely to be a C.P.A., whereas in smaller properties, it is more likely that an individual who is not a C.P.A. will be responsible for the bookkeeping and accounting functions. It would be a mistake to discount the importance of a C.P.A. to a hotel; however, it would be just as big a mistake to assume that only a person who has earned the C.P.A. designation can be an effective controller. This is true because today's accounting systems can be classified as either centralized or decentralized.

Centralized Accounting Systems

In a **centralized accounting** system, the financial data from your property is transmitted via computer (e-mail, network, Web page, etc.) to a "central" location, where it may be recorded and then analyzed by management or combined with other hotel properties for analysis.

HOTEL TERMINOLOGY AT WORK

Centralized Accounting: A financial management system that collects accounting data from an individual hotel(s), then combines and analyzes the data at a different (central) site.

■

To illustrate why some hotels operate under a centralized system, assume that you own five full-service hotels in the Southeastern United States. Assume also that your office is in the Midwest. If you wanted to know, on a daily basis, what the combined sales revenue for your five hotels was on the prior day, you would want those hotels to have reported their previous days sales to your office, where, for convenience, you would have the sales revenue of the five hotels added together to yield one number that represents your hotels' prior day's total sales. Centralized accounting is most prevalent in chain-operated or multiproperty hotel companies.

If the hotel you will manage is one of a number of hotels owned or managed by the same company, you are likely to operate under a centralized accounting system. If you do, it is also likely that the company, rather than your individual hotel, will employ a C.P.A. for data analysis. This is true because it is generally more cost-effective to employ one C.P.A. in a central location than multiple C.P.A.s in multiple locations.

Decentralized Accounting Systems

In a **decentralized accounting** system, the G.M. and the controller must take a larger role in the preparation of financial documents.

If neither the G.M. or the controller is a C.P.A., it is likely that the hotel's owners will, at least annually, employ the services of a C.P.A. to review

---

HOTEL TERMINOLOGY AT WORK

Decentralized Accounting: A financial management system that collects accounting data from an individual hotel site and combines and analyzes that data at the same site.

■

the work of the on-site controller and give a professional opinion about the reliability of the financial statements prepared by the controller's office. This review process is discussed later in this chapter in the section on **audits.**

HOTEL TERMINOLOGY AT WORK

Audit: An independent verification of financial records.

■

In this text, we will assume a decentralized accounting system is in use to illustrate all of the variety of bookkeeping and accounting functions taking place in the modern controller's office. In a property you might manage, all, some, or none of these functions may be centralized. It is essential, however, for you to understand the importance of each function.

REVENUE FORECASTING

One of the most critical managerial questions a G.M. can ask his or her staff is this, How many guests will be in the hotel today? When the future number of guests, or put another way, the future level of sales volume, is known, the proper number of staff and the supplies those staff need to do their jobs can best be predicted. At the **front desk**, knowing the number of guests coming to the hotel on a given night ensures the proper number of **guest service agents** will be available to promptly check guests in and out of the hotel.

HOTEL TERMINOLOGY AT WORK

Front Desk: The area within the hotel used for guest registration and payment.

Guest Service Agent: An employee working in the front desk area of the hotel. Also referred to by some in the industry as a "desk clerk."

■

Similarly, in the food and beverage department, sufficient wait staff, bartenders, bussers, and back-of-house staff must be available to serve the estimated number of guests. When a hotel provides other services such as parking, guest laundry, recreational activities, and the like, knowing how many people will be on the property requesting such services is a key to proper staffing. With too few staff, of course, guest service suffers. With too large a staff for the anticipated volume, excessive labor costs are incurred. An important part of the controller's job then is to estimate the number of hotel guests to be served or the revenue to be generated. For the G.M., an important indicator (but not the only one) of the economic health of the property is the anticipated sales volume in rooms, food and beverage, and other areas.

Rooms Revenue

A room revenue forecast is of great help to the G.M., and it is the role of the Controller to provide it. Because room revenues make up 50 to 75 percent of the monthly sales revenue in full-service hotels, and an even greater percentage in limited-service hotels, the dollar amount of expected revenues from the sale of guest rooms is of critical importance to the G.M. The rooms revenue forecast will likely be assembled by those employed at the front desk or in the marketing and sales department, as well as the controller. In all cases, however, it is the controller who should review these forecasts for accuracy before they are submitted to the G.M.

While a rooms revenue forecast can be very detailed or quite simple, it should, at minimum, include the following data:

- Rooms available to sell for the forecasted period
- Estimated rooms to be sold for the period
- The estimated **occupancy rate** for the period
- The estimated **ADR** for the period
- The **RevPar** for the forecasted period

HOTEL TERMINOLOGY AT WORK

Occupancy Rate: The ratio of guest rooms sold (including comps) to guest rooms available for sale in a given time period. Always expressed as a percentage, the formula for occupancy rate is

$$\frac{\text{Total Rooms Sold}}{\text{Total Rooms Available}} = \text{Occupancy Percent} \quad (\%)$$

ADR: Short for "average daily rate," the average selling price of all guest rooms for a given time period. The formula for ADR is

$$\frac{\text{Total Room Revenue}}{\text{Total Number of Rooms Sold}} = \text{ADR}$$

RevPar: Short for "revenue per available room," the average sales revenue generated by each guest room during a given time period. The formula for RevPar is

$$\text{Occupancy \% (x) ADR} = \text{RevPar}$$

■

Reasons why these three measures are the best forecasters of rooms revenue will become clearer in the chapters on The Front Office (chapter 6) and Sales and Marketing (chapter 10), but the fact remains that it is the role of the controller to provide or have available, *at all times,* accurate forecasted data on these statistics for the following periods:

- Daily
- Weekly
- Monthly
- Quarterly
- Annually

Obviously, the further into the future is the forecast, the more uncertain are the estimates. It is reasonable to expect, however, that with allowances for adjustments due to uncontrollable events, (i.e., severe weather, canceled contracts, etc.) revenue forecasts within 5 to 10 percent of actual realized revenue are realistically achievable. Excellent controllers can be even more accurate, especially in the short time frames of weekly, monthly, and quarterly forecasts. Indeed, one characteristic of an outstanding controller is that individual's ability to generate, in a timely fashion, room revenue forecasts that prove to be highly accurate.

Food and Beverage Revenue

Food and beverage (**F&B**) revenue can make up a significant portion of the sales of a full-service hotel. Even limited-service hotels are likely to generate some level of sales volume typically assigned to the F&B department.

HOTEL TERMINOLOGY AT WORK

F&B: Shortened term for "food and beverage." Used, for example as in the following:

"Please let the F&B Director know about the changes the guest has requested."

◼

In addition to the restaurant and bar areas commonly associated with F&B, the controller will forecast sales that may be generated from the following sources:

- Room service
- Banquets
- Meeting room rental revenue
- Meeting room F&B revenue
- Audio and visual equipment rental
- Service charges

Obviously, the controller would look to the F&B department head for assistance on generating revenue estimates for this area. In addition, in many cases, the number of guest rooms sold will have a direct impact on the amount of F&B sales volume that can be anticipated. If, for example, a 300-room hotel sells 250 rooms on a Tuesday night, it is likely the restaurant's breakfast areas will be busier on a Wednesday morning than on a Monday morning when the hotel has sold only 50 rooms on the prior Sunday night. Because revenue from the F&B department in a larger convention or conference center hotel can range from 10 percent to as much as 50 percent of total daily revenue, it is imperative that the controller accurately forecast the revenue that can be expected from this important hotel department.

Other Revenue

Hotel revenues that are neither room sales nor food and beverage sales are classified as **"other" revenue.**

The source of these other revenues is varied because the hotel business is varied. At a resort hotel that operates a riding stable, for example, the revenue derived from renting horses for trail rides would be considered "other" revenue. Obviously, a downtown high-rise hotel would not generate such

---

HOTEL TERMINOLOGY AT WORK

Other Revenue: Revenue derived from the sale of hotel products and services that are not classified as rooms, food, or beverages.

■

---

other income. While the tendency in the hotel business is to think of revenues as being generated primarily from the sale of rooms, food, and beverage, the sum total of all revenue derived from other revenue sources can be significant, and it is part of the controller's job to let the G.M. know what the estimated value of these revenues will be.

Typical examples of other revenue sources include:

- Pay-per-view movies
- Parking charges
- Internet access charges
- Gift shop sales of newspapers, cigarettes, candy, lotions, soft drinks, etc.
- Telephone (local and long distance calling charges)
- Guest laundry
- Coat check fees
- Golf fees
- Tennis fees

- Health club usage fees
- Pool fees

Revenue forecasting is an important part of the controller's job. An up-to-date revenue forecast, including rooms, food and beverage, and other income revenues, should always be available for the G.M.'s inspection.

We have discussed the information a revenue forecast should contain, as well as the frequency with which they should be prepared. It is important to understand why this information is so critical to the G.M. To do so, let's examine five typical questions that might well be posed to a G.M. by members of the EOC.

1. *From marketing and sales*: *"Should the budget segment devoted to winter marketing programs next year be better spent focusing on improving sales in January or February?"*

2. *From maintenance*: *"Would this July be a good time to replace carpets in one wing of the hotel (consisting of 20 percent of the guest rooms) or should the replacement be scheduled for August?"*

3. *From F&B*: *"Would September be a good time for the F&B director to take vacation?"*

4. *From housekeeping*: *"Would Tuesday or Saturday be the better day for holding the monthly departmental staff meeting?"*

5. *From safety and security*: *"Should we add an additional security person to next Friday night's schedule, or is the current staffing level appropriate?"*

Clearly, in each of these situations, as well as many more, a G.M.'s knowledge of current and future sales levels is critical to the decision-making process. Accurate revenue estimates are essential for excellent property management. In summary, an outstanding controller helps the G.M. make outstanding decisions by providing outstanding revenue forecast information.

THE INTERNET AT WORK

Revenue forecasting is a skill that can be learned. For a first-rate, yet inexpensive, guide to the forecasting process, visit

www.crisplearning.com

and use the search word "Forecast" to get information on David Bower's excellent book, *Forecasting for Control and Profit.*

BUDGETING

Budgeting for revenue, expenses, and profit is a process that consumes a significant portion of the G.M.'s time. A good controller is the G.M.'s essential partner in this budgeting process. In fact, it is the controller's office that will actually spearhead the assembly and submission of the budget to the G.M. Some hotel managers simply view a budget as an onerous, self-imposed plan for spending money that will ensure hotel revenues always exceed hotel expenses. But a G.M. does not truly need a budget simply to ensure that expenses are less than revenues. If the G.M. fails to approve necessary expenditures (funds for needed repair and maintenance of equipment, the purchase of quality guest room supplies, staffing levels that provide proper guest service, and wage increases that ensure the best staff in the hotel are not lured away by competitors), the budget may be met, but the hotel will surely suffer.

A G.M. who simply sees his or her role in the budget process as one of "never exceed the budget" does not fully understand the importance or function of the budget. Together, the controller and G.M. must develop a budget that is a crucial tool for effective management.

In a business context, a budget is much more than a plan for spending cash resources. In fact, it is a plan for utilizing resources of all kinds, including cash, tools and materials, and labor, to operate the hotel in its most effective manner.

Budgeting is sometimes described as a financial expression of the G.M.'s business strategy. This makes sense when you consider that a business strategy seeks to project where the hotel is going, how it will get there, what it will cost, and what the profit outcome will be if the strategy is implemented successfully. A well-developed budget, however, can do even more than project revenues and expense. If used properly, the budget is an important means of developing internal controls, another function that is critical to the controller's role.

The effective controller/G.M. team builds their budget, monitors it closely, modifies it when necessary, and achieves their desired results. Yet, some controller/G.M. teams do a poor job developing budgets because they feel the process is too time consuming. Developing a helpful budget does take time, however, good budgets assist the hotel in many ways, including:

1. Allowing management to anticipate and prepare for future business conditions

2. Providing a communication channel whereby the hotel's objectives are passed along to its various departments

3. Encouraging department managers who have participated in the preparation of the budget to establish their own operating objectives and evaluation techniques and tools

4. Providing the G.M. with reasonable estimates of future expense levels and serving as a tool for determining future room rates and other price structures

5. Helping the controller and G.M. to periodically carry out a self-evaluation of the hotel and its progress toward its financial objectives

In the hotel industry, operating budgets generally are one of three types:

- Long range
- Annual
- Monthly

Long-Range Budgets

A long-range budget is one that encompasses a relatively lengthy period of time, generally from two to five years, or in some cases, even longer. The G.M. and controller prepare these budgets, with input from each of the hotel's operating departments. The G.M.'s role in the process would be, in conjunction with the marketing and sales department, to forecast changes in the number of guest rooms available to sell, predicted occupancy percentage, and ADR given future market conditions, while the role of the controller (as well as the G.M.) would be to estimate expenses.

Obviously, with such a long-term outlook, these budgets are subject to changes due to unforeseen circumstances and market forces, yet they are useful for long-term planning, as well as for considering the wisdom of debt financing and refinancing and the scheduling of **capital expenditures**.

HOTEL TERMINOLOGY AT WORK

Capital Expenditure: The purchase of equipment, land, buildings, or other fixed assets necessary for the operation of the hotel.

∎

Annual Budgets

In many cases, preparation of the annual budget consumes a significant amount of the controller and G.M.'s time. This is so because, in large, multiunit hotel companies, annual budgets must be produced by the individual hotels, submitted to a central office for review, then, in some cases, revised to ensure they are in keeping with the overall financial objectives and goals of the hotel company. This process can begin as early as June or July for the following year.

As the name implies, these budgets are developed to coincide, in most cases, with the calendar year. As such, they provide more detail than a long-term budget and are subject to less fluctuation based on unforeseen events.

Monthly Budgets

The monthly budget is a natural outgrowth of the annual budget. In fact, truly outstanding controllers produce an annual budget as a result of previously producing twelve monthly budgets. With a well-developed annual budget, you might wonder why the controller should concern themselves with an accurate monthly budget. The importance of the monthly budget, however, can be seen quite clearly in the example of the annual revenue and expenses of a hotel near a ski resort. In each of the winter months, revenues will likely greatly exceed one-twelfth of the annual revenue budget, as will expenditures. In a like manner, summer month revenues and expenditures will likely fall far short of one-twelfth the annual budget. In the case of this **seasonal hotel**, to effectively reach the annual targets, great care will need to be taken with each individual month's budget. In most cases, hotels will see some variation in annual sales based on the time of year. Because that is true, monthly budgets are an excellent managerial tool for helping to determine whether the hotel is maintaining progress toward the goals developed in the annual budget.

HOTEL TERMINOLOGY AT WORK

Seasonal Hotel: A hotel whose revenue and expenditures vary greatly depending on the time (season) of the year the hotel is operating. Examples include hotels near ski resorts, beaches, theme parks, some tourist areas, sporting venues, and the like.

■

While the complete development of a hotel's operating budget is beyond the scope of this chapter, Figure 5.1 is an example of the type of detail commonly found on the expense segment of a monthly operating budget. Note how, in this case, the budget is compared with the actual results of the prior year, with a space on the document for filling in the actual expenses of the month once those numbers are known.

FIGURE 5.1 Waldo Hotel Property Operations and Maintenance Department Operating Budget for January

Waldo Hotel: Property Operations and Maintenance Budget for January			
Payroll & Related:	Actual This Year	**Budgeted This Year**	Actual Last Year
Chief Engineer	$ _____	$ 4,444	$ 4,100
Engineer Assistants	_____	9,000	8,752
Benefit Allocation	_____	3,700	3,611
Total Payroll		$ 17,144	$ 16,463
Expenses:			
Computer Equipment	_____	$ 500	$ 1,108
Equipment Rental	_____	0	400
Electrical & Mech. Equipment	_____	2,000	1,985
Elevators	_____	580	551
Elevators Repairs	_____	0	0
Engineering Supplies	_____	300	239
Floor Covering	_____	250	210
Furniture	_____	1,000	1,740
Grounds	_____	250	195
HVAC	_____	3,000	4,152
Kitchen Equipment	_____	500	481
Laundry Equipment	_____	400	310
Lightbulbs	_____	200	105
Maintenance Contracts	_____	2,500	2,500
Operating Supplies	_____	300	653

FIGURE 5.1   *(Continued)*

	Actual This Year	Budgeted This Year	Actual Last Year
Painting & Decorating	_____	500	399
Parking Lot	_____	200	110
Pest Control	_____	500	431
Plants & Interior	_____	300	274
Plumbing & Heating	_____	500	453
Refrigeration & Air Conditioning	_____	1,600	1,783
Signage Repair	_____	0	50
Snow Removal	_____	1,000	1,121
Swimming Pool	_____	3,000	3,524
Travel & Entertainment	_____	1,000	974
Telephone	_____	200	170
Trash Removal	_____	425	399
Uniforms	_____	300	271
Total Expenses	_____	$ 21,275	$ 24,588
Total Prop. Ops. & Maint.	$ _____	$ 38,419	$ 41,051

FINANCIAL STATEMENTS

In addition to producing budgets, the controller's office is also responsible for preparing, or, in a centralized accounting system, supplying the information to prepare, the financial statements that summarize the hotel's operating results. As we have seen, the budget looks to the future of the hotel's performance. There are three additional, key financial documents that look to the hotel's past accomplishments and its present financial condition. These statements, each of which should be prepared monthly for the G.M., are:

- Income statement
- Balance sheet
- Statement of cash flows

Income Statement

The income statement (more technically known as the income and expense statement) is sometimes better known as the profit and loss statement, or, even more simply, the **P&L**.

HOTEL TERMINOLOGY AT WORK

P&L: Short for the profit and loss statement, also a synonym for the income and expense statement. The P&L records total hotel revenues and expenses for a specific time period.

■

The P&L is supplied by the controller, and is one of the two or three most critical monthly documents a G.M. will receive from any department head. Essentially, this document, when properly prepared, lists the hotel's revenues, expenses, **GOP**, and **fixed charges** for a specific time period. This specific time period is typically a month, fiscal quarter, or year.

HOTEL TERMINOLOGY AT WORK

GOP: Short for gross operating profit. This popular term is taken from a pre-1990 version of the Uniform System of Accounts for Hotels (USAH) published by the New York Hotel Association. It refers to hotel revenue less those expenses typically controlled at the property level. It is generally expressed on the income statement and in the industry as both a dollar figure and percent of total revenue.

Fixed Charges: Those expenses incurred in the purchase and occupation of the hotel itself. These include rent, property taxes, insurance, interest, and depreciation and amortization.

■

While it is certainly beyond the scope of this text to fully discuss the preparation and analysis of the income statement, it should be pointed out that a competent controller will produce an accurate income statement in a time frame that the G.M. finds helpful for the proper management of the hotel. In no case should this time period exceed the middle of the next reporting period. For example, if the income statement is to be produced monthly, the January statement should be available to the G.M. no later than

FIGURE 5.2   Income Statement Information

This Period's Actual		
		Revenues
	Less	Direct operating expense
	Equals	Departmental operating income
	Less	Overhead (undistributed) expense
	Equals	Net income (GOP)
	Less	Fixed expense
	Equals	Income before taxes

February 15. Simply put, a controller who cannot achieve this time frame needs further assistance, training, or replacement. If as a G.M. you are to properly manage your hotel, a timely and accurate income statement is crucial to your success.

An Income statement that details monthly, quarterly, and/or annual revenue and expense such as that in Figure 5.2 is helpful, but is actually the bare minimum when it comes to providing the G.M. with useful information.

With the information in Figure 5.2, the G.M. can answer the question: *How did the hotel perform during this time period?*

A much more helpful format for the income statement (but one that requires more effort on the part of the Controller), is the **tricolumned statement** shown in Figure 5.3.

HOTEL TERMINOLOGY AT WORK

Tricolumned Statement: An income statement that lists (1) actual hotel operating results from a specific time period, as well as (2) budgeted operating estimates for the same time period, and, finally (3) the actual operating results from the prior year's same time period.

■

FIGURE 5.3   Tricolumned Income Statement

		This Period's Actual	This Period's Budgeted	Last Year Same Period Actual
	Revenues			
Less	Direct operating expense			
Equals	Departmental operating income			
Less	Overhead expense			
Equals	Net income (GOP)			
Less	Fixed expense			
Equals	Income before taxes			

With the income statement information shown in Figure 5.3, the G.M. can evaluate and formulate answers to the following types of questions:

1. *How did the hotel perform during this time period?*
2. *How did the hotel perform compared with our performance estimate (budget)?*
3. *Where did our estimates vary significantly?*
4. *How did the hotel perform compared with the same period last year?*
5. *Where were significant changes from last year evident?*

Clearly, the controller who can supply more information on the income statement does so to the benefit of the G.M. and, of course, their own career.

Balance Sheet

An income statement will tell the G.M. whether the month or other period in question has been a good one, but it is the balance sheet that provides a point-in-time statement of the *overall* financial position of the hotel. The balance sheet has often been described as a "snapshot" of the financial health of a hotel. This analogy is a good one because the balance sheet captures the financial condition of the hotel on the day it is produced. It does not tell how profitable the hotel was in a given accounting period, but this snapshot can be compared with previous or latter snapshots to determine the financial movement of the hotel.

The format of the balance sheet is really rather simple, listing first the hotel's assets (what the hotel owns), then its liabilities, (what it owes), and, finally, the amount owed to owners (owners' equity).

Assets owned by the hotel will typically include such items as cash, monies owed to it by others, the value of items in inventory (food, beverages, cleaning supplies, and the like), and **prepaid expenses**.

HOTEL TERMINOLOGY AT WORK

Prepaid expenses: Expenditures made for items prior to the accounting period in which the item's actual expense is incurred.

■

In addition, the asset portion of the balance sheet lists the value of the hotel's property and equipment (fixed assets), less any accumulated **depreciation**.

HOTEL TERMINOLOGY AT WORK

Depreciation: The part of a fixed asset's cost that is recognized as an expense in each accounting period because it is assumed to have been "used up" during that period.

■

The liabilities section of the balance sheet includes current liabilities. The liabilities section is generally defined as those debts that will be paid within one year and long-term liabilities, which are those debts that will be paid in a time period longer than the next twelve months. Thus, for example, an invoice for fresh produce, to be used by the food and beverage department, which is due and payable on the day the balance sheet is produced, would be considered a current liability, while the amount remaining to be paid on the hotel's twenty-year mortgage would, on the same date, be classified as a long-term liability.

The difference between what a hotel owns (assets) and what it owes (liabilities) represents the property owners' equity in the hotel. Figure 5.4 represents a sample balance sheet for the "Waldo Hotel."

The information presented by the balance sheet is important, and the controller should prepare it as often, and in as timely a manner, as the income statement is prepared. The balance sheet is especially useful when a specific time period (e.g., the end of the current year) is compared with a prior time period (e.g., the end of the prior year). The balance sheet's "point-in-time" perspective makes it a useful tool for the G.M. in the analysis of the overall financial health of the hotel.

FIGURE 5.4   Simplified Balance Sheet for the Waldo Hotel as of January 1, 200X

Assets		
Cash	$ 75,000	
Accounts receivable	50,000	
Inventories on-hand	25,000	
Prepaid expenses	10,000	
Total Assets		$ 160,000
Property and equipment	$ 7,000,000	
(Less accumulated depreciation)	500,000	
Net property and equipment		6,500,000
Total Assets		**$ 6,660,000**
Liabilities and Owners' Equity		
Current liabilities		
Accounts payable	$ 75,000	
Wages payable	25,000	
Total current liabilities	$ 100,000	
Long-term liabilities		
Mortgage payable	$ 6,300,000	
Total Liabilities		**$ 6,400,000**
Owners' equity		260,000
Total Liabilities and Owners' Equity		**$ 6,660,000**

Although little seems to be written about the limitations of the balance sheet, it is important to realize that, in the hotel industry, these limitations can be significant. A complete discussion of the balance sheet's limitations are best reviewed in a fundamental accounting text; however, of most significance is the fact that, of all the assets listed on the balance sheet, none take into account the relative value, or worth, of the staff, including the G.M., which is actually operating the hotel.

Hotel companies are fond of saying that "people (staff) are our most important asset," yet the value of experienced, well-trained staff members is not quantified on the balance sheet. To further clarify this important concept, assume you are the hotel G.M. and that you are considering a $1,000 expenditure for your marketing and sales department. Your alternatives are spending the $1,000 to replace an aging computer used by one of your sales manager's, or using the same $1,000 to send the entire five-person marketing and sales team to a one-day training class on the advanced usage of Microsoft Excel, the spreadsheet software used in your property for producing sales contracts and guest invoices.

If you decide to purchase the computer, the value of assets (property and equipment) on the balance sheet will increase, whereas if you elect to "invest" in your staff via the training program, no such increase will occur. Yet, in this case, it is highly likely that the training class, rather than a single upgraded computer, will make a much greater difference in the effectiveness, efficiency, accuracy, and "worth" of the hotel's marketing and sales department. Astute G.M.s recognize both the value and limitations of the Balance sheet when reviewing it.

Statement of Cash Flows

Traditionally, a controller has regularly provided the G.M. with an income statement and balance sheet. As we have seen, the income statement details the financial performance of the hotel during a specified time period, whereas the balance sheet shows the hotel's financial position at the end of an accounting period. These two documents are extremely useful to management, but an excellent controller provides the G.M. with a third important financial summary. That summary is the statement of cash flows. The statement of cash flows provides answers to the following types of questions that cannot be answered by either the income statement or the balance sheet:

- How much cash was provided by the hotel's operation during the accounting period?
- What was the hotel's level of capital expenditure for the period?
- How much long-term debt did the hotel commit to during the period?
- Will cash be sufficient for the next few weeks or will short-term financing be required?

In the hotel business, "Cash is King." Savvy G.M.s often make this statement because they know it is critical that a hotel not only is profitable, but also that it maintain its **solvency**.

HOTEL TERMINOLOGY AT WORK

Solvency: The ability of a hotel to pay its debts as they come due.

■

The statement of cash flows shows the effects on cash of the hotel's operating, investing, and financing activities. A simplified illustration may help to clarify the importance of the statement of cash flows. Assume that a hotel's income statement shows sales revenue of $200,000 for a given month. Assume also that the hotel shows a "profit" (income before taxes) figure of $50,000 for that month. All may seem well until it is realized that $100,000 of the sales for the month were made to a guest to whom the hotel has extended credit. Thus, the income statement may show the hotel has "made" $50,000 for the month, but those funds are not yet on deposit in the hotel's bank accounts and are not available to assist in the payment of the hotel's debts. And in fact, the hotel has been required to use $50,000 of its own cash or credit to finance the operation of the property until the $100,000 due is collected from the guest. As you can see, then, it is important for a G.M. to know how much cash debt is outstanding, as well as the likelihood of collecting on that debt. This concept, called accounts receivable aging, is discussed more fully in the section of this chapter titled 'Internal Audits'.

In addition to credit sales, the G.M. must be aware of the hotel's own short- and long-term cash needs if the hotel is to remain solvent. The cash standing of a hotel is vital, and the controller should provide the statement of cash flows detailing that standing to the G.M. just as frequently as both the income statement and balance sheet. In fact, the Financial Accounting Standards Board (FASB), which is the current accounting rule-making body, has, since 1988, required the statement of cash flows to be included with other financial statements when issued to external users.

MANAGERS AT WORK

J.D. Ojisama has recently been assigned to serve as the G.M. and oversee the renovation and expansion of a hotel that has just been purchased by the real estate investment group J.D. is employed by.

Currently, the hotel consists of 300 rooms and 8,000 square feet of meeting and banquet space.

The expansion calls for adding 150 guest rooms, as well as 8,000 additional feet of meeting space. Assume the expansion will take one year.

How is J.D. likely to begin the process of budgeting revenue for the hotel in its first year after expansion? What historical hotel data would be useful in helping J.D. complete this task? What additional information about the area in which the hotel is located would be helpful?

Where is J.D. likely to find such information? How important is the controller likely to be in this process? Why?

THE INTERNET AT WORK

To stay abreast of issues and changes in procedures in the area of accounting, periodically visit the web site of the Financial Accounting Standards Board (FASB).

You can access it by going to:

www.accounting.rutgers.edu/raw/fasb/index.html.

DAILY OPERATING STATISTICS

To effectively manage your hotel, the controller must provide you with the information you will need to make sound decisions.

Manager's Daily Sales Report

As a G.M., you will depend on the controller's office to give you a daily summary of the hotel's previous day's sales. That is, every day, in a timely manner, the controller's office should be able to provide you with an accurate recap of the prior days' rooms, F&B, and other revenues. This report is referred to as the Manager's Daily Sales Report, or more simply, the "Daily."

The Daily is prepared from data supplied nightly by the **PMS**. In some cases, the PMS may actually produce the Daily. We will examine the PMS in great detail in Chapter 6, (The Front Office), because it is the Front Office that is most responsible for its maintenance and accuracy. In fact, the PMS is the heart of the front office. The controller's office, however, uses the nightly data produced by the PMS for a variety of tasks, one of which is the preparation of the Daily.

HOTEL TERMINOLOGY AT WORK

PMS: Short for "property management system." This term refers to the computerized system used by the hotel to manage its rooms revenue, room rates, room assignments, and reservations, as well as other selected guest service functions.

■

Information that should be contained on the Daily includes the following:

For Rooms:

Number of rooms available for sale
Number of rooms sold
Occupancy rate
ADR

RevPar
Other rooms revenue information desired by the G.M.

For Food and Beverage:

Restaurant sales
Bar/lounge sales
Meeting room rentals
Banquet sales
Other F&B revenue information desired by the G.M.

For Other Income:

Telephone revenue
In-room movie revenue
No-show billings
Other income categories unique to the property

HOTEL TERMINOLOGY AT WORK

No-show: A guest who makes a confirmed room reservation but fails to cancel the reservation or arrive at the hotel on the date of the confirmed reservation.

■

Although it is called the Daily, somewhat implying that it contains only one day's information, many controllers increase the value of the Daily by including, on the report, cumulative monthly data totals, as well as individual and cumulative data from the same day in the prior year. Thus, a sample one-page daily, produced via Excel spreadsheet, might be designed in a manner similar to that shown for the Waldo Hotel in Figure 5.5.

Obviously, the more detail you desire, the longer the Daily. Some managers prefer great detail, including in their Daily information on room types sold, number of guaranteed reservations made, cash overage and shortages, or any of a variety of pieces of information the G.M. feels will be helpful in staying abreast of the hotel's business on a daily basis. It is the job of the controller to produce the daily. That job is made substantially easier when the PMS system is used to generate either all or part of the report.

Detailed Room Revenue Statistics

One very important function of the controller's office is the documentation and verification of the night auditor's report. This report, generated by the PMS, will, depending on the PMS, give management a complete and detailed breakdown of the previous day's business. Often running ten or more pages in length, the night audit report is used by the controller to ver-

FIGURE 5.5   Sample Manager's Daily Report

MANAGER'S DAILY REPORT				
THE WALDO HOTEL			January 15, 20xx	
	Today	To date	Last Year Today	Last Year To date
Rooms Available	285	4275	285	4275
Rooms Occupied	**191**	**3035**	**180**	**3011**
Occ. %	67%	71%	63%	70%
ADR	$ 105.20	$ 103.98	$ 98.99	$ 100.20
RevPar	$ 70.50	$ 73.82	$ 62.52	$ 70.57
Rooms Revenue	$ 20,093.20	$ 315,579.30	$ 17,818.20	$ 301,702.20
Food and Beverage				
Banquets	$ 4,550.00	$ 68,250.00	$ -0-	$ 71,250.00
Meeting Room Revenue	$ 1,250.00	$ 18,750.00	$ 150.00	$ 19,850.00
A/V Rental	$ 140.00	$ 2,240.00	$ 75.00	$ 2,500.00
Restaurant	$ 650.00	$ 8,450.00	$ 710.00	$ 10,650.00
Total F&B Income	**$ 6,590.00**	**$ 97,690.00**	**$ 935.00**	**$ 104,250.00**
Telephone Revenue				
Local Calls	$ 85.00	$ 1,105.00	$ 79.50	$ 1,033.50
Long Distance Calls	$ 210.00	$ 2,730.00	$ 185.00	$ 2,220.00
Other Income				
Gift Shop	$ 231.25	$ 2,312.50	$ 221.00	$ 2,210.00
In-Room Movie Sales	$ 185.00	$ 2,035.00	$ 78.00	$ 1,850.00
Guest Laundry	$ 71.50	$ 858.00	$ 61.50	$ 738.00
No-Show Revenue	$ 198.50	$ 2,580.50	$ 520.00	$ 3,200.00
Total Daily Revenue	**$ 27,664.45**	**$ 424,890.30**	**$ 19,898.20**	**$ 417,203.70**

ify credit card charges, cash on hand, revenue sales totals, detailed room revenue statistics, and **allowances and adjustments**. It is these last two categories that many G.M.s wish to have detailed to them on a regular basis.

HOTEL TERMINOLOGY AT WORK

Allowances and Adjustments: Reductions in sales revenue credited to guests because of errors in properly recording sales or to appease a guest for property shortcomings.

■

As a G.M., the Manager's Daily Report gives you much of the information you need to assess the day's operation; however, greater detail than this report generally gives on the rooms revenue picture is always important. This is true because the G.M. must be aware both of how much room revenue has been produced, but equally as important, from *whom* that revenue is being produced. The night audit report, taken from the nightly data generated by the PMS, provides a wealth of information on room sales if the controller properly uses it.

For example, the information (provided by the PMS) required to fully understand the daily sales revenue and RevPar picture on a given day includes information related to ADR, rooms sold, and market segment. Figure 5.6, titled Two Alternative Guest Profiles/Same RevPar, details exactly why a G.M. needs comprehensive information on the type of guests staying in the hotel.

As can be seen, the "makeup" of the guests in the hotel would be very different under these two scenarios. In scenario one, the hotel is filled primarily

FIGURE 5.6   Two Alternative Guest Profiles/Same RevPar

MANAGER'S ROOM REVENUE DETAIL REPORT						
THE WALDO HOTEL						
January 15, 20XX						
Rooms Available	285					
Rooms Sold	191					
Occupancy %	67.0%					
		SCENARIO 1 (285 Rooms Available)			SCENARIO 2 (285 Rooms Available)	
Market Mix	**Rooms Sold**	**ADR**	**Total Revenue**	**Rooms Sold**	**ADR**	**Total Revenue**
Transient Guests						
Corporate	25	119	$ 2,975.00	75	119	$ 8,925.00
Leisure	25	139	$ 3,475.00	5	139	$ 695.00
Government	0	0	$ 0.00	15	75	$ 1,125.00
Total Transient Guests	**50**		**$ 6,450.00**	**95**		**$ 10,745.00**
Group Guests						
Corporate	5	105	$ 525.00	60	105	$ 6,300.00
Leisure	40	118	$ 4,720.00	6	118	$ 708.00
Government	5	78	$ 390.00	30	78	$ 2,340.00
Total Group Guests	**50**		**$ 5,635.00**	**96**		**$ 9,348.00**
Tour Guests	91	88	**$ 8,008.00**	0		0
TOTAL GUESTS	**191**		**$ 20,093.00**	**191**		**$ 20,093.00**
ADR			$ 105.20			$ 105.20
RevPar			$ 70.50			$ 70.50

with people on a tour (91 rooms) and those in a group of leisure travelers (40 rooms). In the second scenario, **transient** corporate travelers make up the largest portion of guests (75 rooms), followed by corporate travelers staying in a group (60 rooms).

HOTEL TERMINOLOGY AT WORK

Transient: Guests that are neither part of a group booking or tour group. Transient guests can be further subdivided by traveler demographic to gain more detailed information about the type of guest staying in the property.

■

Assume, for a moment, that the G.M. at the Waldo Hotel knows, from past records, that the average leisure or tour room sold by the hotel houses 2.2 individuals, whereas each corporate room sold is occupied, on average, by 1.1 persons. Obviously, then, the demands placed on the hotel's restaurants and any recreational facilities, as well as housekeeping services required by these two groups, will be very different. Taking all occupied rooms into consideration, the **house count** in the first scenario is likely to be nearly twice that of the second scenario. Because this is true, it is important for the G.M. to know not only how many rooms have been sold in the hotel, and the day's RevPar, but also to what client type those rooms have been sold. It is the role of the controller to provide this information on a daily basis.

HOTEL TERMINOLOGY AT WORK

House Count: An estimate of the number of guests staying in a hotel on a given day.

■

A detailed room revenue report, which can in some cases be produced directly from the PMS, should contain, at minimum, the following information;

- Rooms available
- Total rooms occupied
- Rooms occupied by guest type
- Occupancy percent
- Total ADR
- ADR by guest type
- Total RevPar

The G.M. may, if he or she chooses, add additional decision-making rooms statistics information to the above data, which the controller should be prepared to supply.

Adjustments and Allowances

In addition to room revenue detail, the controller should, on a daily basis, provide the G.M. with a detailed listing of any adjustments or allowances made by the managers or employees of the hotel. From the perspective of the controller, the vouchers are important because they help to balance actual monies collected with monies that have been previously billed to guests. From the perspective of the G.M., however, the vouchers are important because they point out shortcomings in the hotel's operation that must be addressed and continually monitored by the G.M.

Figure 5.7 is an adjustment (and allowance) form used by a typical hotel. Note that the form has:

1. A sequence number for control purposes
2. A space for the date the voucher is used
3. A space for the name of the guest(s) for whom the adjustment was made

(1) ADJUSTMENT

№ 348685

DATE (2) 20xx

NAME (3) ROOM OR ACCT. NO. (4)

EXPLANATION (5)

X (6)

SIGNATURE

11-09-0199 (7)

FIGURE 5.7 Adjustment Voucher

4. A space for the guest's identifying room number or account
5. A space for an explanation of the event or circumstances that justified the issuing of an adjustment
6. A space for the initials or signature of the employee issuing the adjustment
7. An identification number for reordering purposes

In a small property, each of these vouchers would be tabulated and reviewed for accuracy by the controller, and then the vouchers themselves would be given to the G.M. In a larger property, the information on them might be combined and a summary of their contents would be passed on to the G.M. An effective G.M., however, insists on seeing the actual vouchers, whenever practical and not merely the total of vouchers.

The importance of daily viewing by the G.M. of these vouchers becomes clear when you understand that there are three fundamental situations that could result in the completion of an allowance and adjustment voucher.

- **Employee error in charges.** Despite appropriate training, employees can sometimes make errors in the amount they charge guests. This problem can range from charging guests the wrong room rate for their stay, to charging guest "A" for services actually used by guest "B."

When an error is discovered, the guest's bill, if previously submitted as a sale to the controller's office, must be adjusted to reflect the correct charge. Assume, for example, that Mr. and Mrs. Guild, staying in room 417 on a Saturday night, have two drinks in the hotel lounge. They sign the guest check charging their drinks to their room; however, the bartender mistakenly charges the drinks to the guest in room 471. The Guilds check out on Sunday morning. On the following Monday, the guest in 471 approaches the front desk to check out. Obviously, the guest in room 471 will, upon reviewing the bill, refuse to pay the incorrect charge. At that point, an allowance and adjustment voucher, removing the drink charges, would be prepared for the guests in 471. In such a case, it may be impossible to collect on the charges originally incurred by the Guilds (remember that they left the hotel on the previous morning).

The need for the G.M. to see this voucher is evident. Shortcomings in employee training programs, cash sales systems, or guest services techniques may become clear to the G.M. if a pattern in employee error allowance and adjustment vouchers is evident.

- **Hotel-related problems.** Despite the best efforts of the hotel's management and staff, some guests will still experience problems with the hotel's facilities or guest service. For example, an ice machine on a particular floor may, on a given day, have stopped working and, before it could be repaired by the hotel, inconvenienced a guest who found they had to walk to another section of the hotel for ice. Or, unfortunately, a hotel employee may not have been as courteous to a guest as desired, thus offending the guest. In both of these cases, and more, a guest may, upon check-out, request or demand a reduction in their bill. In these situations, an allowance or adjustment in the bill may need to be made, and the voucher would be filled out. The importance of such vouchers being seen by the hotel G.M. on a daily basis is self-evident. Changes may be required in equipment inspection programs, guest service training, or a variety of other areas where the G.M.'s intervention is critical to correct recurring problems.

- **Guest-related problems.** In some cases it is the presence of other guests, rather than the hotel, that causes a particular guest to have an unpleasant experience at the hotel. Complaints ranging from excessive noise in adjacent rooms to rowdy guest behavior in public spaces can cause a guest to feel they should be compensated for the unpleasantness of their experience. If, in the opinion of the proper hotel staff member, an allowance or adjustment to the guest's bill were warranted, the adjustment and allowance voucher would be completed. The hotel G.M. would, of course, want to be made aware of all such incidences on a daily basis. Certainly the G.M. would want to take corrective action, but also, in many cases, these same guests may contact the G.M., or the hotel's owners, or the franchise brand organization with the same complaint. If, as a G.M., you are unaware of problems on your property, curative action cannot be taken. For that reason, you should require that the controller give you, on a daily basis, the allowance and adjustment vouchers completed by the hotel staff.

The total dollar amount of allowances and adjustments compared with total overall rooms revenue can be tracked on a monthly basis using the following formula:

$$\frac{\text{Total Monthly Allowances and Adjustments}}{\text{Total Room Revenue}} = \text{Room Allowance and Adjustment \%}$$

This percentage will vary based on the age of the hotel, the quality of staff and training programs, and even the type of guest typically served. As the G.M. you should know your average monthly room allowance and adjustment percentage, but more important you should know the reason(s) for any increases in that average on a given month. Unless you know your problem areas, you will not be able to correct them. The controller's efforts to supply you with the information from the actual allowance and adjustment vouchers will always be well worth the effort.

INTERNAL CONTROLS

The position title of "controller" is derived from the word "control." It is not surprising then that one of the very most important functions of the controller's office is the development and maintenance of internal control systems. Hotels, and the restaurants they often include, routinely contain large amounts of cash, products, and equipment that can, if not carefully controlled, be the subject of fraudulent activities by guests or employees. A good controller helps the G.M. by carefully developing policies and procedures designed to ensure the safety of the hotel's assets.

Cash

Any business that routinely collects cash payments from guests must develop a system of safeguarding this important asset. Hotels are no exception. Of course, in today's hotel environment, cash assets, in addition to currency, include credit and debit card charges and personal and business checks. The potential to lose these assets to theft, fraud, or outright carelessness always exists, and it is the role of the controller as well as the G.M. and the department head of each cash handling area to develop and enforce a system of checks and balances and controls designed to ensure the security of these important assets.

In most hotels, cash is collected in a variety of locations in addition to the front desk. Restaurants, bars, lounges, parking areas, vending areas, and gift shops are just a few examples of areas within a typical hotel that routinely process cash sales. In all of these situations, at least one individual serves as a cashier/ money handler. A bartender, for example, may serve as his or her own cashier during an evening shift. Likewise, the individual responsible for replenishing soft drink vending machines will serve as a cashier of sorts when cash is removed from the machines.

In hotels, cash assets are at greater risk from internal threats than from external ones. That is, while the potential for robbery by a nonemployee certainly exists in all hotels, the greater threat to the security of the hotel's cash assets is the internal threat of employee theft or fraud.

Any time a cashier is responsible for the collection of money, several areas of potential employee theft or fraud can exist. The cashier may, for example, record a sale, collect payment from a guest, but keep the cash, or the cashier may not record the sale at all and, again, keep the cash.

The methods used by cashiers to defraud guests and/or the hotel are varied and depend to a great degree on the type of sales made. That is, the methods used by an unscrupulous bartender to defraud the hotel's food and beverage department will be different from those used by a dishonest front desk agent. In either case, management must have systems in place to verify sales and the cash receipts those sales produce. An effective, experienced controller is invaluable in designing and establishing these systems.

Even though it is fairly straightforward to consider the theft of cash by a cashier, the hotel industry affords some cashiers the opportunity to defraud guests paying by credit card as well. These, too, must be guarded against. Some common credit card–related techniques used to defraud guests include:

- Charging guest's credit cards for items not purchased, then keeping the money from the erroneous charge.
- Changing the totals on credit card charges after the guest has left or imprinting additional credit card charges and pocketing the cash difference.
- Mis-adding legitimate charges to create a higher-than-appropriate total, with the intent of keeping the overcharge. This, of course, can also be done on a cash sale.
- Charging higher-than-authorized prices for products or services, recording the proper price, and keeping the overcharge.
- Giving, or selling, the credit card numbers of guests to unauthorized individuals outside the hotel.

The G.M.'s role in asset management regarding cash is, quite simply, to monitor the quality of the cashier-related security programs designed by the controller. For example, a bartender working a shift from 5:00 P.M. to 2:00 A.M. and serving as his or her own cashier might have recorded $1,000 in beverage sales during that time period. If that were, in fact, the case, and if no errors in handling change occurred, the cash register should contain cash, checks, and bank charges equal to $1,000 (plus, of course, the amount of the beginning cash bank). If it contains less than $1,000, it is said to be **short**; if it contains more than $1,000, it is said to be **over**.

HOTEL TERMINOLOGY AT WORK

Short: A situation in which cashiers have less money in their cash drawer than the official sales records indicate. Thus, a cashier with $10 less in the cash drawer than the sales record indicates is said to be $10 "short."

Over: A situation in which cashiers have more money in their cash drawer than the official sales records indicate. Thus, a cashier with $10 more in the cash drawer than the sales record indicates is said to be $10 "over."

■

Overages and shortages should be monitored by the controller and, when excessive, brought to the immediate attention of the G.M. Cashiers rarely steal large sums of money directly from the cash drawer because such theft is easily detected, but management should make it a policy to monitor cash overages and shortages on a daily basis.

Some G.M.s believe that only cash shortages, but not overages, need to be investigated. This is not the case. Consistent cash shortages may be an indication of employee theft or carelessness and should, of course, be investigated.

It is also possible for a dishonest cashier to avoid being short, and still defraud the hotel. If, for example, the cash register or computerized cash control unit has a void key, a dishonest cashier could enter a sales amount, collect for it, and then void (erase) the sale after the guest has departed. In this way, total sales would equal the amount of the cash drawer. If the cashier then destroys records involved with this sale, the cash register total sales figure and cash drawer would all balance. To prevent this, management should insist that all cash register voids be performed by a supervisor or at least be authorized by management on an individual basis. In addition, because today's computerized cash registers records the number, individual, and time at which cashier voids are performed, these, too, should be monitored by the Controller.

Yet another method of hotel cashier theft involves the manipulation of reduced price or complimentary rooms or products. Assume, for example, that, at the Waldo Hotel, your sales and marketing department has produced and distributed a large number of guest coupons good for 50 percent off a guest's night stay. If the front desk cashier has access to these coupons, it is possible to collect the money from a guest without a coupon and then add the coupon to the cash drawer while simultaneously removing sales revenue equal to the value of the coupon. A variation on this theme is for the cashier to declare a room to be complimentary after the guest has paid the bill. In cases like this, the cashier would again remove sales revenue from the P.M.S. in an amount equal to the "comped" room.

These kinds of fraud can be prevented by denying cashiers access to unredeemed cash value coupons issued by the hotel, and by requiring special authorization from management to "comp" rooms. While the previous scenarios do not list all possible methods of revenue theft and fraud, it should be clear from this discussion that you must have a complete revenue security system if you are to ensure that all services and products sold generate sales revenue that finds its way into the hotel's bank account. It is a good idea for the controller and G.M. to regularly evaluate the cash control systems in place on the property. This includes a through evaluation of:

- Cashier training programs
- Sales revenue recording systems
- Cash overage and shortage monitoring systems
- Enforcement of employee disciplinary procedures for noncompliance

For some cashiers, the theft of cash is very tempting. Today's sophisticated cash management systems make it easier than ever to detect cashier theft, but a diligent controller and G.M. is still critical to that process.

Accounts Receivable

When a hotel elects to extend credit to a guest, it creates a **direct bill**(ing) account for that guest and then, as the guest incurs charges, an invoice is periodically prepared and sent to the guest.

HOTEL TERMINOLOGY AT WORK

Direct Bill: An arrangement whereby a guest is allowed to purchase hotel services and products on credit terms.

■

This direct guest billing may take place on the same day the guest incurs the charge, at the end of each month, quarterly, or at any mutually agreed-upon point in time. When a hotel extends credit to guests, the dollar amount of outstanding charges owed to the hotel by these guests is called the hotel's **accounts receivable (AR)**.

HOTEL TERMINOLOGY AT WORK

Accounts Receivable: Money owed to the hotel because of sales made on credit. Sometimes referred to as "AR" for short.

■

There are many reasons, including guest preference, why a hotel might elect to extend credit to some of its guests. In all cases, however, it is the controller's job to establish:

1. Which guests will be allowed to purchase good and services on credit
2. How promptly those guests will receive their bills
3. What the total amount owed to the hotel is and what the length of time is those monies have been owed

The credit worthiness of guests is one that is frequently debated between the marketing and sales area and the controller's office. In most cases, the marketing and sales office will pressure the controller to extend credit (to complete the sale), whereas the controller, in many cases, takes a more conservative view and may suggest that the hotel deny credit to potential guests who should, in fact, be extended credit terms. A good controller will work with the G.M. to establish credit policies that maximizes the number of guests electing to do business with the hotel, yet minimizes the hotel's risk of creating uncollectable accounts receivable.

To assist the controller's office in determining which groups should be allowed to enjoy the advantages of buying on credit, a Direct Bill Application (for credit) will be completed by the guest, reviewed by the controller's office, and then passed to the G.M. for final approval or denial. Figure 5.8 is an example of a Direct Bill Application that a guest seeking credit terms would complete.

To appreciate the reasons for a hotel electing to extend credit to a guest organization, consider the case of Rae Dopson, president of Dopson Construction, a midsize road construction firm. In this scenario, Rae's company has been awarded the state contract to construct two miles of new highway near your hotel. The job is a big one and will last many months. It will also involve the use of dozens of workers, each of whom will require Monday through Thursday night lodging near the work site. Since the lodging of its workers will be an expense of Dopson Construction, its managers face the alternatives of either (1) allowing each worker to stay at a hotel of their own choosing and then reimbursing each individual worker for his or her night's lodging, or (2) negotiating with a single hotel to place all of the business at that property and then request that the hotel bill the company directly for all lodging expense. Clearly, it is in the best interest of both the hotel and the guest to select the second alternative. The bookkeeping of the construction company will be simplified if it is awarded direct bill status, and the construction company will also likely be able to negotiate a better nightly rate from the hotel because it will be able to guarantee a predetermined number of room nights needed on a regular basis. The hotel benefits from simplified billing as well. Finally, it is highly likely that other hotels who desire the business from Dopson Construction will be competing for that business, in part, by granting Rea's company direct bill status.

After the determination has been made that credit terms will be extended, it is the responsibility of the controller's office to bill guests promptly. Finally, it is the controller's important job to monitor accounts receivable and to keep the G.M. informed as to their status. This is done via the **accounts receivable aging** report.

HOTEL TERMINOLOGY AT WORK

Accounts Receivable Aging: A process by which the average length of time money owed to the hotel because of sales made on credit is determined.

■

Figure 5.9 shows an example of an accounts receivable aging report for a hotel with $100,000 in outstanding accounts receivable.

Figure 5.9 shows that the total amount owed to the hotel is $100,000. This amount can be broken down into four distinct time periods. One-half

FIGURE 5.8   Direct Bill Application

Waldo Hotel

<u>*Application for Direct Billing*</u>

Date: _____   *Federal ID #* _____

Company/Organization: _____

Division/Department: _____

Mailing Address: _____

Street Address		Suite #

City	State	Zip Code

(Area Code) Phone Number	(Area Code) Fax Number

Billing Address:
(if different from above)

(Name of Invoice Recipient–Attention to)

Street (PO Box #)	Suite #

City	State	Zip Code

List of those persons entitled to authorize (call in reservation):

1. _____   _____
      FULL NAME   TITLE

2. _____   _____
      FULL NAME   TITLE

3. _____   _____
      FULL NAME   TITLE

Please circle the charges employees are authorized to bill. Circle all that apply:

Room & Tax only	*Phone*	*Restaurant Bills*
All Charges	*Movies*	*Banquet/Meeting Charges*

(continued)

FIGURE 5.8   *(Continued)*

Credit References:

1. _____
   Hotel Name

   _____
   Phone Number

2. _____
   Hotel Name

   _____
   Phone Number

3. _____
   Other

   _____
   Phone Number

Company Bank:

Bank Name: _____   Account Type: _____

Account Number: _____

At least three credit references and at least one company bank are **required** to complete this application. At least two of the references must be hotel references, while the third may be a company with whom you have a billing history.

If for some reason the application cannot be completed with the requested information, please contact the Accounts Receivable Department of the Waldo Hotel.

Please allow at least 15 days for proper processing and approvals.
*Applications must be approved **before** any direct billing may take place. You will be contacted by mail about your approval status.*

By signing this document, I allow the creditors and bank listed above to release to the Waldo Hotel all necessary information for the proper processing and approval of this application. I understand that all accumulated charges are submitted to the accounting department upon the completion of each authorized function/stay. I also understand that payment is due within 30 days from the date of the invoice. I further understand that it is my company's responsibility to keep the list of authorized personnel updated and current to avoid improper or unauthorized usage of this direct bill account, and may do so by requesting an authorization/status change form from the Accounts Receivable Department of the Waldo Hotel.

Signature of Applicant: _____   Date: _____

FIGURE 5.8 *(Continued)*

For Company Use Only:

Recommendation of Controller _____

_____

_____

_____

_____

_____

_____

_____

_____

_____

Approved By
Signature: _____   Date: _____

of the total accounts receivable ($50,000) is owed to the hotel by guests who have received their bills 30 or fewer days ago, whereas 5 percent ($5,000) is due from guests who have had over 90 days to pay their bills. As a general rule, as the age of an accounts receivable increases, its likelihood of being collected decreases. Also, as the percentage of accounts receivable 90 days or older increases, the likelihood of collecting on these receivables decreases.

FIGURE 5.9   Accounts Receivable Aging Report

Waldo Hotel: Accounts Receivable Aging Report For January, 200X

Total Amount Receivable $100,000.00

	NUMBER OF DAYS PAST DUE			
	Less than 30	**30–60**	**60–90**	**90+**
	$ 50,000			
		$ 30,000		
			$ 15,000	
	_____	_____	_____	$ 5,000
	_____	_____	_____	
Total	$ 50,000	$ 30,000	$ 15,000	$ 5,000
% of Total	50%	30%	15%	5%

As a receivable account ages, an effective controller will contact the affected guest to determine if there is a problem in billing, documentation, or some other item that is delaying payment to the hotel. In severe cases of nonpayment, the guest could have their direct billing status revoked, and the hotel would undertake collection efforts.

The extension of credit and the collection of accounts receivable is one important function of the controller's office. As a G.M., your role will be to monitor credit policies, Direct Bill applications, and the aging of accounts receivable to ensure that this cash management activity is operating properly and with the attention that it is due.

Accounts Payable

Just as a hotel will sell to some of its guests on a credit basis, many suppliers and service companies will provide goods and services to the hotel on a credit basis, with the hotel being billed by these vendors according to credit terms previously established. For example, a dairy products vendor may deliver fresh milk daily to the hotel. Obviously, it makes little sense to pay that vendor thirty times per month for the milk products delivered. Typically, a vendor such as this would establish the credit worthiness of the hotel, then send the hotel an invoice on a weekly, biweekly, or monthly basis. The charges for goods and services used by the hotel, invoiced by the vendor, but not yet paid are called a hotel's **accounts payable**, or A.P.

HOTEL TERMINOLOGY AT WORK

Accounts Payable: The sum total of all invoices owed by the hotel to its vendors for credit purchases made by the hotel. Also called A.P.

■

As a G.M. interacting with the controller's office, there are four major areas of concern you will have in regard to your own accounts payables system. These are:

- Payment of proper amounts
- Payments made in a timely manner
- Payment records properly maintained
- Payment totals assigned to the appropriate department area

Payment of Proper Amounts.   Despite the skill of any individual, mistakes can be made in paying invoices. Data entry errors can be commonplace unless the controller has established solid procedures to ensure that legitimate invoices are paid only for the amount actually due. In a well-run controller's office, invoices and payments for those invoices are checked by at least two individuals. Software developed to match invoice numbers against hotel check numbers are invaluable in this process. The intent of this type software is simply to help ensure that A.P. are processed only for the amount of the invoices due.

THE INTERNET AT WORK

To view the features of a Windows-based software program that includes modules on A.P., go to:

http://www.hallogram.com/ias/.

Scroll down and select "Accounts Payable" to review this program's features.

Payments Made in a Timely Manner.   In addition to paying the proper amount, an effective controller understands that there is a proper time to pay each invoice. Some hotels gain a reputation with their suppliers for paying invoices very promptly. This can be good, but it is important to know that cash maintained in the hotel's cash accounts is also valuable. Thus, an effective controller maintains good relations with vendors, many of which are likely to be such local businesses as plumbers, electricians, food vendors, and the like that are important for the continued successful operation of the hotel. Remember that those customers who pay bills slowly are also likely to be serviced slowly by their vendors. In fact, prompt payment of invoices is so important to many smaller businesses providing goods and services to a hotel that better purchase prices and delivery terms can often be negotiated if the hotel simply has a reputation for paying its bills on time. In addition, some vendors will actually offer the hotel the choice of paying less than the full invoice (discounts for on-time payments) if invoices are paid promptly.

In general, an effective controller should take advantage, whenever possible, of discounts offered by vendors for prompt payment. Some vendors will give a discount of 1 to 5 percent of the invoice price if a bill is paid within a specific time period. The controller should take advantage of every opportunity to build positive vendor relations and help ensure lowest costs by managing the accounts payable process professionally.

Payment Records Properly Maintained.   While it may seem fairly simple to ensure that each accounts receivable invoice to be paid is paid only once, in fact, that is not the case. Careful attention to detail is needed to make sure that invoices are paid and recorded properly. An effective controller creates a system whereby total payments to vendors match vendor billings exactly, with no overpayments or underpayments.

Payment Totals Assigned to the Appropriate Department Area.   It is not only important for the controller to pay the hotel's bills, but it is equally important to know which area within the hotel has incurred a given expense. For example, as the G.M., you may want to know how much money is being spent on plumbing repairs for a given month or year. Obviously, then, the controller must keep a record of how much money is being spent by the maintenance department for plumbing parts and labor for the time period of interest. To do so, controllers use a system of **coding** to assign actual costs to predetermined cost centers.

HOTEL TERMINOLOGY AT WORK

Coding: The process of assigning incurred costs to predetermined cost centers or categories.

■

For example, the maintenance department in a hotel will certainly be interested in its total expenditures for a month, but the expenditure breakdown in Figure 5.10 does a much better job of helping the head of maintenance, as well as the G.M., know where the money in the maintenance department is being spent and why it was somewhat over budget in the month of January. Note that each expense subcategory has been developed to help managers understand total property operations and maintenance expenditures.

An effective controller will work with those involved in the purchasing process to code the expenses incurred by the hotel to the correct departmental expense category so these expenses can be clearly analyzed by the G.M. Departmental expense categories can be developed by an individual hotel or a hotel company operating multiple hotels. In all cases, however, it is the role of the Controller's to implement a functioning expenses coding system.

Purchasing and Receiving

Perhaps the most important role the controller can play in the A.P. process is that of ensuring payment is made to vendors only for goods and services actually received. For example, a lawn service invoice may be received by the controller's office that includes charges for lawn mowing, edging, and chemical weed treatment. Obviously, the invoice should be paid if the services have been performed. However, payment should be withheld if all services have not been performed, or not completed at the agreed-upon quality level. Thus, the controller's office should pay only those vendors who have delivered the hotel's authorized goods and services at the preauthorized price and in the manner agreed upon by both the hotel and vendor.

In regard to purchasing products for the hotel, before an A.P. invoice is paid, the controller should have in place a system that verifies the terms of the sale, the product prices quoted by the vendor, and a list of the products

FIGURE 5.10   Waldo Hotel Property Operations and Maintenance Expenditures for January

	Actual	Budgeted
Payroll and Related		
Chief Engineer	$ 4,444	$ 4,444
Engineer Assistants	8,450	9,000
Benefit Allocation	3,520	3,700
Total Payroll	16,414	17,144
Expenses		
Computer Equipment	425	500
Equipment Rental	1,000	0
Electrical & Mech. Equipment	2,520	2,000
Elevators	600	580
Elevator Repairs	200	0
Engineering Supplies	250	300
Floor Covering	0	250
Furniture	0	1,000
Grounds	850	250
HVAC (heating/ventilation and air conditioning)	2,800	3,000
Kitchen Equipment	150	500
Laundry Equipment	0	400
Lightbulbs	250	200
Maintenance Contracts	2,500	2,500
Operating Supplies	185	300
Painting & Decorating	270	500
Parking Lot	1,000	200
Pest Control	350	500
Plants & Interior	280	300
Plumbing & Heating	1,585	500
Refrigeration & A/C	1,500	1,600
Signage Repair	0	0
Snow Removal	1,000	1,000
Swimming Pool	3,500	3,000
Travel & Entertainment	1,600	1,000
Telephone	150	200
Trash Removal	450	425
Uniforms	280	300
Total Expenses	$ 23,695	$ 21,275
Total Prop. Ops. & Maintenance	**$ 40,109**	**$ 38,419**

received by the hotel so these can be checked against actual vendor's invoices. In regard to services purchased by the hotel, it is the role of the controller to devise a payment system that ensures that some member(s) of the property management team has:

- Preauthorized the work to be done
- Confirmed the cost of the work to be done
- Verified that the work has been satisfactorily completed

Inventories

To properly create the income statement on a monthly basis, the controller must have a system in place to secure an accurate inventory from each department where monthly inventories are taken. This is true because the value of an inventory at the beginning of a month must be reconciled with purchases made during the month, as well as the dollar value of inventories at the end of the month. For example, if the controller is to state the dollar value of towels expense for a given month, he or she would determine the cost of providing towels for the month by using the following formula:

$$
\begin{array}{l}
\text{Beginning period value of towel inventory} \\
\underline{+ \text{ Towel Purchases}} \\
= \text{Cost of Towels Available} \\[6pt]
\underline{- \text{ Ending period value of Towel Inventory}} \\
\text{Cost of Towels used in the period}
\end{array}
$$

To illustrate, assume that the Waldo Hotel had $8,000 of towels in inventory at the beginning of the accounting period and that it purchased $1,000 worth of towels in the month. Assume also that at the end of the month, $8,300 worth of towels remained in inventory. Using the above formula, the hotel's actual cost of towels for the month would be:

$ 8,000.00	Beginning period value of towel inventory
+ 1,000.00	Towel Puchases
9,000.00	Cost of towels available
− 8,300.00	Ending period value of towel inventory
$ 700.00	Cost of towels used in the period

Accurate, timely inventories must be submitted to the controller on a monthly basis from those departments designated to do so by the G.M. It is then up to the controller to use those inventory values and the relevant accounting formulas to properly document actual expenses.

Payroll

An important function of the controller's office is the proper payment of employees' salaries and wages. This function may, if the hotel is large enough, be shared with the human resources department because, of course, accurately paying employees is a necessary part of good human resources management. From the point of view of the G.M., another important aspect of the payroll process is that of knowing exactly how property payroll dollars are being spent. This includes knowing both the total dollar amount of payroll expended by the hotel, as well as the departmental allocation of those dollars.

If, for example, the controller informs the G.M. that total payroll dollars for the month are higher than that which was budgeted, the G.M. will want to know where and why these extra dollars were expended. The controller must be prepared to promptly provide this information. Doing so will require that the controller keep detailed, department-specific payroll information. That is, the payroll dollars expended by the hotel should be segmented to allow easy viewing of each hotel department's individual payroll. This is important due to the fluid nature of labor usage in the hotel.

To illustrate, assume that you originally anticipated selling 3,000 room nights in a given month, and you planned to schedule the appropriate housekeeping staff required to clean those rooms. If you then find that your actual room sales for the month were 3,500 room nights sold, you would expect to have expended more dollars for cleaning rooms than you originally budgeted. The question for you as the G.M., of course, is whether the extra dollars spent were the proper number of extra dollars. With too many extra dollars spent, payroll resources may have been wasted; however, if too few extra dollars were spent (or if the department head elected to stay within the originally budgeted schedule regardless of the extra 500 sold rooms), guest service may suffer because the housekeeping staff would be too small to properly clean all of the rooms used. The controller should provide the data to answer questions of this type.

A competent controller plays a critical role in the evaluation of payroll dollars spent. By working with the G.M. and the appropriate department heads, the controller can provide advice to the G.M. about prevailing wage rates, worker productivity, variations from budget, and future labor needs, each of which are critical for the efficient operation of the hotel.

AUDITS

Earlier in this chapter, we defined an audit as an independent verification of financial records. While an audit includes the examination of many financial records, it is important to remember that the **auditor** will not examine every financial record produced by the controller's office since the last audit.

═══════════════════════ **MANAGERS AT WORK** ═══════════════════════

J.D. Ojisama, the G.M. of the Hotel Waldo, is convinced that the process of purchasing hotel supplies, verifying their delivery, accounting for them in inventory, and paying the invoices for those supplies is in need of a thorough review.

Assume that you are J.D. What would be clues that the process is in need of review? Which individuals within the hotel need to be involved in this review process? Who should head the review team?

What would be the likely consequence(s) if you do not institute the review process on a regular basis? What factors would influence your view of how frequently such a review should be undertaken?

Instead, the auditor will thoroughly inspect a sampling of records from a variety of areas (e.g., cash deposits, paid invoices, payroll records, restaurant sales, etc.) to determine whether consistent bookkeeping practices and standard accounting procedures are used.

HOTEL TERMINOLOGY AT WORK

Auditor: The individual(s) who conducts an independent verification of financial records.

■

If, during the sampling of records, the use of standard accounting procedures is in clear evidence, the auditor will report that, in his or her professional opinion, the financial records produced by the controller's office fairly and accurately represent the financial picture of the hotel.

If proper bookkeeping and accounting procedures are not in evidence, it is the role of auditors to describe the areas of deficiency they have found and to suggest procedures to improve the financial reporting system.

Internal Audits

An audit of records performed by accountants employed by the organization operating the hotel is known as an **internal audit**. This is a common practice that is cost-effective and quite helpful, particularly in multiunit hotel companies seeking to standardize the reporting activity of all the individual company hotels.

HOTEL TERMINOLOGY AT WORK

Internal Audit: An independent verification of financial records performed by members of the organization operating the hotel.

■

External Audits

In many cases, an independent verification of financial accuracy performed by accountants not employed by the hotel's operating company is required. Such an impartial examination of financial records is known as an **external audit**.

HOTEL TERMINOLOGY AT WORK

External Audit: An independent verification of financial records performed by accountants who are not employed by the organization operating the hotel.

■

An example of a situation that would require an external audit is that of a hotel that is owned or operated by companies who issue stock to the general public. In this case, it is important that the shareholders of the company know that an independent source is verifying the accuracy of the financial records created by the hotels. In such circumstances, an audit by a C.P.A. is likely to be required, and many privately owned companies also retain an independent C.P.A. for, at least, an annual audit. It is important to remember that, even in the external audit, the C.P.A. does not perform a detailed examination of all recorded transactions, and the objective of the assessment is the expression of an opinion about the accuracy of the hotel's financial position, in conformity with generally accepted accounting principles.

Both the internal and external audit are of great value. Often, because the internal auditors employed by a hotel company are more knowledgeable about hotel operations than are external auditors, the internal audit can detect intentional errors and theft not easily detected by the external audit.

Many of the fraudulent actions in hotels are the result of **collusion**, often so carefully planned that problems exist for a long time before they are finally discovered.

HOTEL TERMINOLOGY AT WORK

Collusion: Secret cooperation between two or more hotel employees for the purpose of committing fraud.

■

Since the external audit is not primarily designed to uncover fraud, the G.M. should truly value the work of the internal auditor, particularly as it relates to a review of internal controls.

In some cases, both the G.M. and the controller view an audit, either internal or external, with some dread. That should not be the case. Remember that an audit is performed because hotel room nights, the principle saleable product of a hotel, are an extremely perishable commodity that cannot be held and controlled in a normal manner. This is true because unsold room nights disappear at midnight on each sale day. In addition, normal service to hotel guests includes a wide variety of transactions in which fairly large amounts of cash are handled. Finally, in smaller hotel properties, there are frequently a limited number of employees among whom duties can be divided and rotated.

It is important to realize that, in nearly very case, an audit will uncover areas of financial reporting and control that can be improved. This is to be expected and should not be cause for you, as a G.M. to be alarmed. If the controller is a professional who is committed to excellence in his or her department, the audit is a tremendous opportunity for growth and improvement. An honest controller experiencing an audit will look to the G.M. for guidance as well as support. As a G.M., it is your job, for the good of the hotel and the controller's office, to provide both. Frequent and detailed auditing of hotel records is vital because of the need to establish and maintain a sound system of internal control. As the hotel G.M., an audit is a chance for you to see where the controller's office can be improved and to work with the controller to implement those improvements.

The controller's role in the hotel is complex and critical. It is imperative that the G.M. maintains a positive and professional working relationship with this essential department. Working together, a strong controller and an excellent G.M. can be a formidable competitor for any rival hotel in the market, as well as a critically valuable asset to the hotel's ownership.

THE INTERNET AT WORK

While most controllers and bookkeepers are honest, some are not. To request a free newsletter that identifies possible areas of fraud in financial reporting and records, go to the Association of Certified Fraud Examiners' Web site at:

www.cfenet.com

and register for their free antifraud newsletter.

HOTEL TERMINOLOGY AT WORK GLOSSARY

The following terms were defined within this chapter. If you are not familiar with each of them, please review the segment of the chapter that contains the term.

Controller	Audit	ADR
C.P.A.	Front desk	RevPar
Centralized accounting	Guest service agent	F&B
Decentralized accounting	Occupancy rate	Other revenue

Capital expenditure
Seasonal hotel
P&L
GOP
Fixed charges
Tricolumned statement
Prepaid expenses
Depreciation
Solvency

PMS
No-show
Allowances and adjustments
Transient
House count
Short
Over
Direct bill
Accounts Receivable

Accounts Receivable Aging
Accounts Payable
Coding
Auditor
Internal audit
External audit
Collusion

ISSUES AT WORK

1. Some G.M.s measure effectiveness using primarily ADR, while others prefer to evaluate their effectiveness by the occupancy rate generated. More recently, RevPar has become the standard by which the effectiveness of a hotel's management team is evaluated. Describe at least one strength and one weakness of each of these approaches. Are all three measures still useful? Would you, as a G.M. use RevPar as your exclusive measure of effectiveness? Why or why not?

2. The balance sheet, income statement, and statement of cash flows each yield important pieces of information. To truly understand these documents, however, it is helpful to know what they *cannot* tell you. Using this chapter and an introductory accounting text available from your library, list and consider some of the limitations of each of these three financial documents.

3. Many hotels experience difficulty when establishing credit policies. List five factors you believe would be important when determining whether to offer credit terms to a new client in your own hotel. Explain your reason for choosing each factor.

4. Improvements in technology have impacted the controller's office more than most areas within a hotel. Assume you were the G.M. of a large full-service property. What specific steps could you take to ensure that your controller stays abreast of the advances that affect his or her area? How will you evaluate that individual's efforts to maintain and improve skills? How will you keep up with the changes that will continue to revolutionize this area?

5. Often it is difficult to determine whether errors made in the financial records of a hotel, and then uncovered in an audit, represent intentional fraud or simply mistakes resulting from poor training or lack of knowledge. As the G.M., what specific criteria might you use to evaluate the controller's office if an independent audit revealed multiple areas of consistent mistakes?

6
The Front Office

This Chapter at Work

As a G.M., you will depend on the performance of an outstanding front office to help you meet your guest service and profitability goals. The front office and its manager(s) assist in, or are responsible for, a variety of important hotel functions, each of which is analyzed in detail in this chapter.

Because the rooms sold by a hotel are extremely perishable (i.e., a guest room left unsold on a given night can never again be sold on that night), it is very important that hotels do the best job possible in matching guest room availability with guest room demand. Also, since it is not possible to change the number of rooms available to sell up or down on a daily basis (because the hotel was constructed with a fixed number of rooms), an important responsibility of the front office is the sale of rooms at a rate that management feels will maximize RevPar. An aggressively managed and talented front office will do this well.

The making of guest reservations is often the first thing that comes to mind when considering the major functions of a front office, and this is indeed an important and often complex aspect of the front office's role. In addition to reservations, however, it falls upon the front office to actually assign arriving guests to specific guest rooms and respond to their special needs during their stay. These needs can include anything from transportation and information to medical assistance. In all of these situations and more, the unwavering role of the front office is to make the guest's stay as comfortable and as welcoming as possible.

An essential aspect of the front office is its responsibility for collecting the revenue charged to guests for their rooms, restaurant meals, telephone calls, and a host of other hotel services. This means that the front office manager, working with the G.M. and controller, must devise and administer revenue management systems that ensure guests are properly charged for the services they use and that the hotel fully collects all monies it has earned.

When forecasting room demand, accommodating guests, and collecting monies for services rendered, the front office generates a large quantity of data, much of which are critical for management decision making. It is the role of the front office to collect, sort, and present these data in a way that assists in management decision making. As a G.M., your daily tasks can be made much easier by the support of an effective front office. In this chapter, you will see why a well-supervised front office helps you do a better job of managing your entire hotel.

Chapter 6 Outline

OVERVIEW OF THE FRONT OFFICE

Even though the front office is sometimes referred to as the front desk, the front office controls much more than the activities occurring at the front desk. In a small, limited service hotel, the front office may consist, physically, of only that area reserved for guest registration. In a larger property, the front office may include several staff members, each responsible for a portion of the office's management or operation.

Regardless of its size, the front office must be organized to manage its key tasks and areas of responsibility. In this chapter, you will first read an

HOTEL TERMINOLOGY AT WORK

Front Office: The department within the hotel responsible for guest reservations, registration, service, and payment.

■

overview of the front office area, and then examine each of the major functional areas within the front office in greater detail.

In a typical 350-room full-service hotel, the organization of front office functions would be similar to that detailed in Figure 6.1

In most cases, the **front office manager (FOM)** reports directly to the G.M.

HOTEL TERMINOLOGY AT WORK

FOM: Short for front office manager.

■

Reporting to the FOM would be the individual(s) responsible for:

• Establishing room rates (revenue manager)
• Managing the reservation process (reservations manager)
• Providing for guest services (guest service manager) including services related to guest registration (desk staff), guest information (**concierge**), and guest assistance (**bell staff**)
• Managing the Front Office related accounting and data collection process (night auditor)

In smaller properties these duties will overlap. In fact, in a small limited service property, one person may perform all of these tasks and more. For the purpose of fully understanding these important responsibilities, however, it

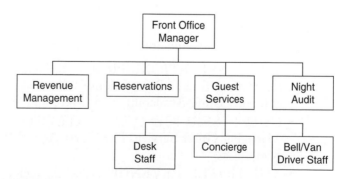

FIGURE 6.1   Front Office Functions

HOTEL TERMINOLOGY AT WORK

Concierge: The individual(s) within a full-service hotel responsible for providing guests with detailed information regarding local dining and attractions, as well as assisting with related guest needs.

Bell Staff: Those uniformed attendants responsible for guest services, including luggage handling, valet parking, airport transportation, and related guest services. The title originally arose because, in earlier years, the staff would come to the "front" (desk) to assist a guest when a bell was rung as a summons to them.

■

THE INTERNET AT WORK

Despite the industrywide use of the term, technically, only members certified by the International Association of Concierges (Les Clefs d'Or) are permitted to use the title "concierge."

Translated literally, Les Clefs d'Or is "The Order of the Keys," and its certified members proudly wear a golden crossed key lapel pin to signify their accomplishment.

To view the requirements for certification, and to learn more about this association, visit their Web site at

www. lesclefsdor.com.

will be useful to take a brief look at each, followed by a more detailed examination of how these functions interrelate in a properly managed front office.

Responsibilities of the Front Office

Complete and detailed texts have been written on the topic of "How to Manage a Hotel Front Office." The classic in the field is *Check-in Check-Out* by Vallen and Vallen. Now in its sixth edition, this text, published by Prentice Hall, covers the following areas (and more) in detail:

- THE RESERVATIONS PROCESS, including Changing Methods for Making Today's Reservations, Individual and Group Reservations, and Forecasting Availability and Overbooking
- GUEST SERVICE AND RATE STRUCTURES, including Managing Guest Service, The Guest Arrival Process, and Setting the Room Rate
- THE HOTEL REVENUE CYCLE, including Billing the Guest Folio, Cash Transactions, and Credit and the City Ledger

- ROOMS MANAGEMENT TECHNOLOGY, including The Night Audit and Property Management System and Interfaces

It is not the goal of this text to duplicate those efforts. But as a G.M., you must know what can be expected of an effectively managed front office and just as important, how you can determine if the front office is, in fact, being well managed. This task is made especially difficult today because technology has developed so quickly in this area that G.M.s who have not kept up with these technological advances, especially those in the area of the property management system (PMS), can quickly find their knowledge base inadequate for the decision making required. While it may vary somewhat based on the organizational structure of a specific size hotel, essentially the functional areas of the front office can be summarized as follows:

- The PMS and its management
- Revenue and reservations management
- Management of guest services
- Accounting for guests
- Data management

The PMS and Its Management

As described earlier in this text, the PMS is the computerized system used by the hotel to manage its rooms revenue, room rates, reservations and room assignments, guest histories, and accounting information, as well as other selected guest service and management information functions. A simple PMS will have limited features, while more extensive (and expensive) systems offer a wide range of management information features.

THE INTERNET AT WORK

Often, the specific PMS system used in a hotel is mandated by the franchisor. There are, however, many generic PMS on the market. To examine one such popular system's many features in detail, go to

www.innsystems.net/products/products_pms_features.html.

Figure 6.2 is an example of the features offered on a popular PMS system. This PMS, sold under the name "Guest Tracker," has features typical of those offered for sale today.

Essentially, the PMS records who is coming to the hotel, what they spend when they are there, and their form of payment upon departure. As a G.M., it is critical that you know all of the features that exist on your PMS.

FIGURE 6.2   Guest Tracker PMS Hotel Management Features

Guest Tracker Features

Windows 95/98/2000 True 32-Bit Application
Multi Platform Servers and Databases
  (Access, SQL, Oracle)
All Inclusive Software Package Price
Unlimited Rooms, Rates, Users, and Workstations
Room Chart Reservations
Extensive Lookup Features
Call Accounting Interface Module

Internet Reservations
Club Membership Control

Travel Agent Accounting/Commissions
Group Master Billing
Revenue Forecast Reports/Graphs
View or Print All Reports
Mailing Labels Sorted and Filtered
Export to External Files

Reservation Features

Complete Reservation System
Unlimited Rooms, Room Types, and Rates
Book by Room Type and/or Room Number
Unlimited Guest Notes
Guest Lookup by Name or Stay
Room Chart Reservations
Room Chart Color Printout by Month
Automatic Room Selection
Automatic Rate Selection
Automatic Rate Calculation By Dates
Daily, Weekend, Monthly, and Package Rates
Monthly Leases

Extended Stay Capabilities
Discount Reservations
Tax Exempt Options
Deposits Setup on the Fly
Advanced Deposits Postings
Prepost Charges at Check-in
Quick Check-in Procedures
Custom Confirmation Letters
Arrival/Departures in Detail
Arrival/Departures in Summary
Reservation History
Reservation Audit by Date/User

Group Features

Group Room Chart
Group Block Multiple Room Types
Group Master Billing

Group Confirmation Letters
Group Alpha Lookup
Group Check-in
Group Check-out

Guest Ledger — Folio Billing

Complete Folio Maintenance
Manual Folio Adjustments and Insertions
Group Master and Individual Folios
Automatic Posting of Room Charges/Taxes
Up to 3 Taxes Predefined
Rate Adjustments during Check-in
Auto Calculate Balance Due
Split Folio Payment Options
Refund Button Full or Partial by Time

Complete Expense/Income Tracking
Payment Methods Tracking by Account
Deposits Due Aging Report
Advanced Deposits
Folio Details and Summary Reporting
Folio Detail by Room or Guest Name
Room Availability and Reserved Levels
POS Register Module/Interface
Complete A/R System Interface
Billing Statements And Inquiry Screens

FIGURE 6.2 *(Continued)*

City Ledger — Direct Billing

City Ledger Accounts Setup	Adjustments, Voids, and Partial Payments
Automatic Invoice Creation at Time of Check-out	Customer Aging Reports
Assign Direct Bill Account at Time of Reservation	A/R Statements
Receipts, Invoices, and Payments Module	Fully Integrated Module

Night Audit Reporting

Automated Night Audit Procedures	Occupancy Report by Guest
Unlimited G/L Account Codes and Groupings	Housekeeping Maintenance Maids Lists
Folio Audit Report by User Shift	Room Status Updates
Complete User Shift Reporting	Auto Update Room Status
Shift Reporting By User	Auto Update Status from In-Room Phone
	Out of Service

History Reporting

History Reports by Market Code	Folio History by Guest or G/L Account
History Reports by Guest Type	Reprint Folio Invoice History
Mailing Labels by Guest Criteria	Audit History of All Transactions by Date
All History Filtered by Date/Type	Message History by Guest Pop-up Display
Guest History Detail by Room/Rate	Occupied History Statistics Reporting
Folio Billing Summary Reports by Date	History Graphs by Room Types
	Average Rate History

Often the PMS includes features that should be used, but are not currently in use by the front office. Your role as a G.M. includes ensuring that the PMS used to operate your hotel is utilized to its maximum effectiveness.

It is important to remember that the PMS, like any other piece of equipment, requires its own care and maintenance. Imagine, for example, the difficulties that would ensue if, one hour before check-in time on a sold-out night, the PMS responsible for informing the front desk staff about who was coming to the hotel, the room type these guests requested, and the room rates they were to pay for their room "crashed." It happens. In many cases it can be avoided.

A PMS consists essentially of a hardware component and a software component. Management of the hardware requires that the front office staff keep the computer equipment clean and free of dust. Cables connecting PC workstations to the main computer should be examined periodically and replaced as needed. The source of power to the system should be managed and surge-protected so that unanticipated power surges do not affect the continued operation of the system. Any installed **backup system** hardware related to the PMS should be inspected and tested on a regular basis.

HOTEL TERMINOLOGY AT WORK

Backup System: Redundant hardware and/or software operated in parallel to the system it serves. Used in times of failure or power outages, these are often operated by battery systems. For example, a backup system to the hotel's telephones would enable outside calling even if the main digital telephone system were to shut down.

■

Although hardware problems can sometimes occur, most frequently it is a software-related problem that causes PMS difficulties. Often, because the PMS is connected by a modem to the PMS's software support organization, repair can be achieved simply by calling PMS software support. In fact, one of the primary features separating outstanding PMS systems from less effective ones is the system's level and availability of software support. Software support from the PMS vendor is not typically free, thus securing service on the system's software at an affordable price is an important consideration when selecting a PMS vendor.

In relation to the management of the PMS, it is reasonable to expect that an effective FOM will provide the G.M. with:

- Proof that the hotel utilizes all appropriate PMS features
- Evidence of a regularly scheduled hardware maintenance program
- Evidence of the ability to rapidly secure software support if needed

Truly, the PMS can be considered the heart of the hotel. As such, its care and maintenance are critical to the successful operation of the front desk, as well as the entire hotel.

Revenue and Reservations Management

One of the most important roles played by the Front Office is that of maximizing the hotel's revenue per available room (RevPar). Recall that RevPar is computed as:

$$\text{Occupancy \%} \times \text{Average Daily Rate} = \text{RevPar}$$

Thus, in a hotel with an annual occupancy of 70 percent and an ADR of $95.00, RevPar would be

$$(70\ \%) \times (\$90.00) = \$63$$

Put another way, each of the hotel's rooms generate, on average, $63 each day.

Obviously, to improve RevPar, the goal must be to either increase the occupancy percent and/or the ADR. It is the job of the FOM to achieve one or both of these goals. To do so, the FOM must implement a three-step process designed to:

- Estimate (forecast) guest demand for rooms
- Practice yield management
- Control occupancy

Forecasting Guest Demand for Rooms

The daily demand for hotel rooms, even within the same geographic area, varies greatly. This is a reality and the challenge, faced by all hotel managers. Imagine, for example, the difference in demand for hotel rooms in Indianapolis, Indiana, the day before the Indianapolis 500 is run (traditionally a **sell-out** period for the entire Indianapolis area), compared with the Wednesday night before Thanksgiving (traditionally a very slow day for business travel of all types) in that same city. The point to remember is that an FOM must know when there is strong demand for the hotel's rooms. That is, what special events, group activities, holidays, or other factors will impact room demand. Recall that to maximize RevPar, the hotel's management staff must attempt to drive (increase) ADR when demand for rooms is high, and attempt to drive occupancy (by offering lower rates) when demand is low. Both these strategies, if successfully implemented, will have the effect of increasing RevPar, and both strategies depend on the ability of the management team to forecast room demand.

To illustrate the importance of forecasting demand, imagine a hotel in a college town. Five times per year, the college's football team plays a home game. Traditionally, the games cause all area hotels to sell-out at a high ADR. The importance of knowing the dates of these games as far into the future as possible so that sales related staff will not inadvertently sell rooms on those dates for a low rate is evident.

HOTEL TERMINOLOGY AT WORK

Sell-out: 1. A situation in which all rooms are sold or oversold. A hotel, area, or entire city may, if demand is strong enough, sell-out.

2. A period of time in which management attempts to maximize ADR.

■

On a less obvious scale, many hotels find that the demand for their rooms varies on a weekly basis, regardless of special events that may be held in the area. Those hotels that service primarily business travelers, for example, will generally find that Tuesday or Wednesday are the days when demand for their rooms is greatest. Those hotels that service leisure travelers will likely find that weekends generate the most business. Forecasting demand effectively requires that the front office:

- Keep accurate historical records to understand past demand
- Know about special events or circumstances that will impact future room demand

In all cases, the front office must be able to forecast the demand for rooms well enough to allow the hotel to practice the concept of yield management described in chapter 1.

Practicing Yield Management

Yield management is a concept that originated in the airline industry but is used today by the car rental, cruise line, and lodging industries as well as other industries that sell a commodity, like a hotel room, that cannot be carried over in inventory if it goes unsold on a given day. The methods utilized by FOMs, revenue managers, and automated PMS systems to use demand forecasts and thus establish yield management strategies are many and are as varied as the individuals operating their respective hotels. G.M.s must understand how they work.

To illustrate the yield management concept, assume a hotel sells its rooms for $150 per night at **rack rate.**

HOTEL TERMINOLOGY AT WORK

Rack Rate: The price at which a hotel sells its rooms when no discounts of any kind are offered to the guest. Often shortened to "rack."

■

It is appropriate to sell at "rack" when the hotel is confident that the demand for hotel rooms will be greater than the supply. That is, when it is forecast that all, or nearly all rooms will be sold, it is not necessary to discount the rooms to help ensure their sale. When demand for rooms is less than supply, discounts are typically offered.

Assume also that the hotel routinely offers discounts plans of 10 percent, 20 percent, and 30 percent off rack rate based on forecasted demand. That is, when demand is very light, discounts as high as 30 percent off rack are offered to maximize occupancy rates. When demand is stronger, the hotel offers only discounts of 20 percent, 10 percent, or, as in the case where the demand for rooms will equal or exceed supply, no discounts are offered at all.

In a high demand period, guests requesting reservations with 30 percent discounts would be told that such discounts are not available, and the hotel would not accept their reservation request. On another, lower demand date, however, that same request for a reservation at the 30 percent discount rate would indeed be accepted. The opening and closing of discounted rates is the core activity of yield management and a good revenue manager is effective in this task. Figure 6.3 is an example of a strategy that might be employed by the hotel used to "manage the yield" from the sale of rooms on a given night.

FIGURE 6.3   Yield Management Strategy Based on Room Demand

Forecasted Room Demand	Rate Strategy
90–100% occupancy	Offer no discounts
70–90% occupancy	Offer discounts up to 10%
50%–70% occupancy	Offer discounts up to 20%
Less than 50% occupancy	Offer discounts up to 30%

Sophisticated FOMs are likely to use highly advanced and often complex methods of managing yield. It is the function of the G.M. to approve such methods if they are in keeping with the long-term goals of the hotel.

Managing Occupancy

Just as it is important to use an effective yield management strategy to maximize RevPar, it is also important that the front office do a good job managing occupancy. A few examples will help to demonstrate why this is the case. Assume that a hotel with 300 rooms faces the situation in Figure 6.4 and that the weekend illustrated is one month in the future.

In this case, demand for rooms is very strong on Saturday, but weaker on Friday and much weaker on Sunday. With a goal of maximizing RevPar, but confronting this situation, an effective FOM is likely to identify Saturday as a day that is **CTA** or that has a **MLOS** attached to it.

HOTEL TERMINOLOGY AT WORK

CTA: "Closed to Arrival." In this situation, the hotel declines reservations for guests attempting to arrive on this specific date.

MLOS: "Minimum Length of Stay." In this situation, the hotel declines reservations for guests seeking to stay for fewer days than the minimum established by the hotel.

■

Identifying Saturday as a day that is CTA is logical if you realize that the demand for Saturday night reservations is likely to far exceed the hotel's number of available rooms for that night. Thus, it makes sense to deny a reservation for a guest requesting *only* a Saturday stay in favor of guests who

FIGURE 6.4   Forecasted Room Demand

	Friday	Saturday	Sunday
Rooms Left to Sell	120	25	250

request both a Friday and Saturday stay. By denying guests the opportunity to arrive on Saturday, the FOM hopes to maximize *total* weekend occupancy.

Alternatively, the FOM might identify Saturday as a day that has a MLOS of two days attached to it. In this case, only reservations from guests requesting arrival on Saturday with the intention of staying for two or more days are accepted. Those guests requesting a one-night stay with arrival on Saturday are declined. By managing the length of stay required on Saturday, the FOM again hopes to maximize total weekend occupancy.

Perhaps the most well-known, but least understood method of managing occupancy is the practice of **"overbooking"** the hotel. Any discussion on overbooking must begin with a simple truth. That truth is:

"No experienced hotel FOM would ever knowingly take a reservation for a room that is not going to be available for the guest upon arrival".

HOTEL TERMINOLOGY AT WORK

Overbooking: A situation in which the hotel has more guest reservations for rooms than it has rooms available to lodge those guests. Sometimes referred to as "oversold."

■

There are at least two reasons this is true. First, in an overbooked situation, a guest with a confirmed reservation who arrives to find that the hotel has no room available is, inevitably, and rightly so, angry. No FOM seeks to create angry guests! Second, from a financial point of view, the guest will be expensive to relocate. This is true because in most cases, the hotel that has **walked** a guest must pay for, at least:

• Transportation to/from the alternative property
• Telephone calls made by the guest to inform those that need to know about the alternative lodging accommodations
• The cost of the first night's room charges at the alternative hotel

---

HOTEL TERMINOLOGY AT WORK

Walked: A situation in which a guest with a reservation is relocated from the reserved hotel to another hotel because no room was available at the reserved hotel.

■

Why then do hotels overbook? Sometimes it is a mistake on the part of the hotel. This would be true, for example, if a guest reservation were made, but mistakenly not recorded. Sometimes, however, an experienced FOM intentionally accepts more reservations than the hotel can accommodate because the FOM wants to fill the hotel and anticipates some of the reservations for rooms will no-show.

For example, in a 100-room hotel that experiences a typical 5 percent no-show rate, the sale of 101 rooms on a given night, while technically overbooking the hotel, is not likely to result in a guest being "walked." This is true because the number of no-shows (5) will, on average, exceed the size of the reservation oversell (1).

No-shows are not unique to the hotel business. Restaurants, airlines, and rental car agencies are just a few of the businesses that must also manage their reservations while knowing that a certain percentage of those reserving will simply not show up to claim their product or service. If the hotel's total reservation management plan is too conservative (i.e., does not factor in no-shows), rooms will likely go unsold even on sell-out nights. If it is too aggressive (i.e. factors in excessively large numbers of no-shows), too many guests with confirmed reservations will arrive at the hotel. These guests will, inevitably, need to be walked and will inevitably be upset! As a G.M. it is your job to make sure that your front office has implemented the reservation policies and occupancy management strategies you believe are appropriate for your own property.

THE INTERNET AT WORK

The issuers of credit and debit cards can be a hotel manager's best friend when it comes to reducing and controlling no-shows. To see one such card company's resources that are available for free, go to:

http://www.usa.visa.com/business/merchants/industry_specific_resources.html.

Scroll down and select *"Prevent and Handle No-shows."*

Management of Guest Services

The front office is responsible for a variety of guest services. These include the welcome the guest receives at check-in, as well as services related to the stay. Some of these are:

- Airport transportation
- Parking cars
- Handling luggage
- Providing directions to attractions within the local area.
- Making restaurant reservations
- Taking guest messages
- Routing mail
- Newspaper delivery

─────────────── **MANAGERS AT WORK** ───────────────

J.D. Ojisima, G.M. of the Austin Plaza Hotel, must make a decision. It is noon on Wednesday, and the 400-room hotel managed by J.D. has 30 rooms left to sell because 170 guests currently have rooms in the hotel and another 200 guests have reservations for arrival that night. Approximately one hour ago, Tech-Mar Holdings, one of the Plaza's largest customers, called Dani Pelley, the FOM, to reserve 35 rooms for that very evening. Ms. Pelley replied that she would get "right back" to the Tech-Mar representative.

Ms. Pelley, a talented but newer FOM, has asked J.D. how the situation should be handled. After being filled in on the details of the guest's request, J.D. asks that the FOM supply the past eight weeks no-show history for the hotel. That data are presented below:

Austin Plaza No-show History

Weekday	Weeks Ago	No-show % of Total Reservations
Wednesday	1	5%
Wednesday	2	0%
Wednesday	3	2%
Wednesday	4	4%
Wednesday	5	1%
Wednesday	6	4%
Wednesday	7	0%
Wednesday	8	3%

What do you think J.D. should tell Ms. Pelley? What is your rationale for the decision? Would you advise J.D. differently if you knew that each of the Tech-Mar reservations was for a ten-night stay at full rack rate?

Assume the hotel remains oversold. What would you tell a guest that must be walked despite arriving with a confirmed reservation? What ethical issues are involved in this situation?

───

- Management of safety deposit boxes
- Supplying directions for areas within the hotel
- Setting wake-up calls
- Providing for guest security via the careful dissemination of guest-related information
- Handling guest's concerns and disputes

Depending on the location of the hotel and the services it offers, the guest service function may be attended to simply by those individuals employed as front desk agents. In a larger property with more activity, guest services may be a separate area within the front office employing a rather large staff.

Accounting for Guests

The front office is the department charged with the major responsibility of performing the accounting tasks related to the guest's stay. While the billing of guests for their night's lodging would appear to be fairly straightforward, the intricacies of the financial transactions that must be recorded by the front office can be quite complex. For example, assume that four men traveling to a hotel to attend a softball tournament share a room for two nights. Upon departure, each wants to pay their share of the **folio**'s balance. One man wishes to pay with cash, one with check, one with a credit card, and another with a debit card. As can be seen, even the simplest of transactions can get complex, but it is the job of the front office and its management staff to ensure that all guest folios are properly processed and recorded.

HOTEL TERMINOLOGY AT WORK

Folio: The detailed list of a hotel guest's room charges, as well as other charges authorized by the guest or legally imposed by the hotel.

■

Additional accounting related tasks that must be completed by the front office include maintaining an accurate list, by room number, of guest room occupants, verifying accuracy in the room rates charged to guests, and the confirmation of check-out dates.

Data Management

An extremely important front office function is that of data management. Some of these data relate to guests, and some relates to the effective management of the hotel. The amount of data processed in a hotel is large and growing larger each year.

An effective FOM in a U.S. hotel in the precomputer 1930s would, very likely, have kept a record of a specific guest's preferences for rooms, food, and the like. This information would have been written down by hand and referred to when that specific guest reserved a room or checked into the hotel. Today's FOM would have such information and much more available to them through the features of the PMS. The FOM would likely know, at the very least:

- The date of the guest's last stay
- The guest's address, telephone number, and credit card information
- The room rate paid and **room type** occupied by the guest
- A history of the guest's prior folio charges
- The form of payment used by the guest to settle his or her account with the hotel

- The guest's membership in groups receiving a discount from the hotel
- Guest's company affiliation
- Guest's room type preferences

Depending on the sophistication of the PMS, even more data may be secured (by desk staff) and maintained on an individual guest.

HOTEL TERMINOLOGY AT WORK

Room Type: The term used to designate specific configurations of guest rooms. For example, smoking versus nonsmoking, king bed versus double beds, or suite versus regular sleeping room. Commonly abbreviated (i.e., K for King, NS for Nonsmoking, etc.), the hotel's holding of the proper room type is often as important to guests as whether or not the hotel, in fact, has a room for them.

It is important to note, however, that most hotel chains guarantee only the availability of a guest's room, not room type, when a reservation is made.

■

In addition to maintaining data on individual guests, the front office collects and evaluates information related to the hotel's operation. Some guest-related examples include the tracking of guest telephone calls, including both those that are free-to-guest and those for which the hotel imposes a charge, the viewing of in-room movies, and the clean or dirty status of rooms (necessary to ensure that a guest checking into the hotel is checked into a room that has, in fact, been cleaned). Other data management tasks include monitoring the use of electronic or hard keys, maintaining safety-related data (such as daily safety inspections for hotel operated vehicles), and the record-

Roll away beds are often provided for younger children at no (or a reduced) charge to the guest.

ing of reservation-related information. As can be seen, the front office and its management staff's ability to provide good data are critical to the operation of the front office and to your success as a G.M.

Each of the functional areas discussed in this overview of the front office deserve special attention that is beyond the scope of this text. It is possible, however, to evaluate each in terms of the G.M.'s relationship to that functional area.

MANAGING GUEST RESERVATIONS

The effective management of guest reservations is, not surprisingly, one of the most complex tasks that must be achieved in a successful hotel. Because the hotel's revenue is dependent, in large measure, on the front office's ability to effectively forecast demand, establish rates, and manage occupancy, a G.M. needs a thorough understanding of the challenges faced in this area. For purposes of examining precisely how a hotel receives its guest reservations, those reservations may be segmented by type and by delivery method.

By Reservation Type

Perhaps the most important distinction that must be made in the area of reservations is that of **transient sales versus group sales.** Many people who do not understand the hotel industry believe that the great majority of rooms sold in a hotel are sold to individual travelers. This is true in some hotels, but in others, such as convention site hotels, the greatest numbers of rooms are sold to those traveling as a group or attending a group function.

HOTEL TERMINOLOGY AT WORK

Transient Sales: Rooms and services sold primarily through the efforts of the front office and its staff.

Group sales: Rooms and services sold primarily through the efforts of the hotel's sales and marketing department, and given to the front office for recording and servicing.

∎

Depending on the size of the hotel, the minimum number of rooms to be sold before the reservation will be considered a group sale might be as few as five, or as many as twenty. Regardless of when a group room sale is large enough to be serviced by the hotel's designated sales department, it is important for the G.M. to remember that an extremely effective sales department may mask the efforts of an ineffective front office sales effort. For example, assume that a hotel routinely sells 60 percent of its rooms via the front desk staff and 40 percent through the group sales department. It may well be that the hotel should, with the proper front office staff, sell even more rooms through the front desk, despite the fact that these individual sales currently make up the majority of the room nights sold. Put another way, the fact that a hotel's revenue and occupancy levels are acceptable does not, by itself, indicate that the front office is effective at selling. It is for that reason the G.M. must maintain standards levels for effectiveness through all the varied delivery methods affecting sales at the front desk.

By Delivery Method

The number of ways a hotel actually receives its reservations are varied and often not well understood. The most common form of hotel reservation delivery today is through the use of the **Global Distribution System** or GDS.

HOTEL TERMINOLOGY AT WORK

Global Distribution System: Referred to as the GDS for short, this system connects those travel professionals worldwide who reserve rooms with hotels offering rooms for sale.

■

GDS

The GDS is the system whereby a travel agent in, for example, Mexico City, uses a computer to access the room rates and availability of a hotel in Bangor, Maine. Without such a system, the travel agent would need to:

1. Find a list of hotels in Bangor, Maine
2. Identify those hotels with vacancies for the nights needed by the agent's client
3. Compare room rates and amenities offered among the various hotels
4. Select a hotel and confirm the reservation

These activities, if done by telephone, would require a great deal of time and expense on the part of the travel agent. Instead, the agent, as a GDS user, can log-on to the GDS and complete these tasks in a matter of minutes. The basic structure of the GDS is presented in Figure 6.5. Information flows from travel agent to hotel and back depending on the communication being delivered.

Essentially, the process begins when the hotel delivers its room rates and availability to one of the switches. The switches then deliver rate and availability to all four GDS sites. Travel agents as well as others with access use the GDS sites to review room rates and availability and to make their reservation selections. The GDS sites deliver reservation requests to the hotel's central reservation systems through the switches, and in turn, the hotel, uses the system to confirm the reservation to the travel agent.

FIGURE 6.5   Information Flow of the GDS

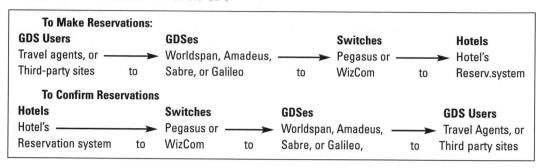

Clearly it is an important role of the FOM to make sure that all hotel information used by the GDS sites is current and accurate. On at least a quarterly basis, the G.M. should review the hotel's GDS information for accuracy.

Franchise Toll-Free Numbers

Typically, another significant source of transient room reservations is the toll-free number operated by the hotel's franchisor. In most cases, the franchisor distributes a print and/or e-directory of affiliated hotels, and then staffs one or more reservation centers with individuals who answer calls and act as reservation agents for the individual hotels within the franchisee network. Potential guests simply dial the toll-free number, make their reservation request known to the individual answering the telephone, receive information on the desired hotel(s) rates and availability, and finish their call having completed the reservation process with a **confirmation number,** or, if they are canceling a reservation, their **cancellation number.** In some cases, group rooms are also sold via the toll-free number, but these sales usually account for a fairly small amount of the total room nights sold.

HOTEL TERMINOLOGY AT WORK

Confirmation Number: A series of numbers and/or letters that serve to identify a specific hotel reservation.

Cancellation number: A series of numbers and/or letters that serve to identify the cancellation of a specific hotel reservation.

■

An effective franchise toll-free number will deliver between 5 and 40 percent of a hotel's total transient room nights sold, depending on the location of the hotel. A transient hotel near a city may receive only 10 to 20 percent of its volume from the franchisor, but a resort location will be much higher. Generally, the better known the franchisor, the larger the contribution of room nights sold by its toll-free number. Just as important, the better known franchisors typically deliver reservations sold at rates higher than those achieved by the hotel's own front office reservationists.

Because the reservation agent accepting telephone calls in a national reservation toll-free call center is not likely to be familiar with each specific hotel in the franchise system, it is critical that the information available to the agent about the hotel is 100 percent accurate. In general, a toll-free number call center will request that the hotel supply as much information as possible on a variety of topics, including:

- Room availability
- **Blackout dates**
- Room rates
- Seasonality of rates
- Room types
- Distances to local attractions
- Hotel amenities and services offered
- Directions to the property
- Ratings and ranking information

HOTEL TERMINOLOGY AT WORK

Blackout Dates: Specific days in which the hotel is "sold-out" and/or is not accepting normal reservations.

∎

Technically, a toll-free number call center is part of the GDS, and just as the information in all GDS components must be accurate, the information reported to the toll-free number must also be accurate.

It is a good idea for G.M.s to occasionally make **test calls** to their franchisor-operated call center to verify the accuracy of the information used by the center. If the information about the hotel is not accurate, the G.M., working with the FOM, must see that it is corrected.

HOTEL TERMINOLOGY AT WORK

Test Calls: Calls made to a toll-free number or other reservation system to verify the accuracy of information about a specific hotel and/or about the quality of selling done by the reservation center's staff.

∎

Internet

Increasingly, the Internet has become a popular way for individual travelers to serve as their own travel agents and book rooms with hotels without having to call the hotels directly. Hotel companies like individual consumers to use the Internet for making reservations because, unlike travel agents, these individual travelers do not charge the hotel a fee for making the reservation.

As more consumers use the Internet, and as more hotel companies see the Internet as a significant marketing tool, this source of transient reservations is likely to continue to grow from its current, industry wide, single-digit percentage of room nights sold to much larger proportions of total room sales.

THE INTERNET AT WORK

Navigating a hotel's Internet site to make reservations has become increasingly easy for consumers. To see what the traveler sees, select either of the following hotel sites:

http://www.choicehotels.com/

or

http://www.marriott.com.

Find the rates and availability of rooms for your next birthday at the hotel nearest your own hometown or school.

In addition to Web sites operated by hotel franchise companies, many independent hotels, as well as those hotels affiliated with chains, have developed their own Web sites. Often these technologically savvy hotels link their sites with those of local area attractions, businesses, nonprofit organizations, and others who are likely to need transient guest rooms on a regular basis.

THE INTERNET AT WORK

Some hotels are very creative in developing their own special Web sites. To view one such site, go to:

www.orleanscasino.com.

Note how the hotel has used the site to advertise package specials by choosing "Hotel," then "Packages" on the drop-down menu.

Increasingly, special Internet sites are developed by third parties simply to make the reservation process easier for potential guests. For example, a couple wishing to visit New York City in November for a holiday shopping trip may not know the name of a specific hotel they wish to use. Thus, they are not likely to access the site of a specific hotel company or individual hotel. By accessing a designated travel site, such as Travelocity.com, the travelers can enter the dates a room is needed and then view pricing and amenity alternatives, as well as make reservations on that Web site. While the use by hotels of such systems is primarily a marketing decision (which will be explored in chapter 10, Sales and Marketing), the accuracy of the information contained on any Web site is a matter generally monitored by the front office. This is true because the rates and availability of rooms posted on the Web must coordinate with the data in the PMS. As with the toll-free number reservation center information, it is important that any information on a hotel's Web site be accurate, and the G.M. should periodically check to ensure that it is.

Hotel Direct

In many cases, guests prefer to place a telephone call directly to the hotel when they want a transient or even group reservation. The manner in which these calls are handled by the front office staff can make a tremendous difference in the success of the hotel. Compare, for example, the two alternative telephone greetings that might be used by a front office staff member responsible for answering the telephone. Which would you prefer was in use at a hotel you are managing?

Front Desk Agent A: *"Clarion Hotel."*
Front Desk Agent B: *"It's a great day at the Clarion Hotel. This is Kimberly. How may I assist you today?"*

To check the effectiveness of the telephone sales effort, some hotels use outside parties to "shop" the hotel. These individuals call the hotel for the purpose of making a reservation. How the hotel handles the reservation request and later the cancellation process is critiqued in detail with a written summary provided to the hotel's management. These critiques can then be used to identify areas of improvement in the sales effort.

The art of selling rooms via telephone is highly developed, and there are excellent tools available to FOMs who wish to improve the effectiveness of their own staff. Critical areas that should be examined for improvement via training tools include:

- Telephone etiquette
- Qualifying the guest
- Describing the property
- Presenting the rate
- Overcoming price resistance

- Upselling
- Closing the sale
- Recapping the sale

The G.M. should know whether the individuals answering the telephone and selling rooms via telephone are effective in that task. If they are not, sales will suffer until staff training improves. A periodic review of front office telephone skills and training methods, by the G.M., is imperative if this important area is to get the attention it deserves.

Walk-In

In nearly all hotels, **walk-in**s occur on a regular basis.

HOTEL TERMINOLOGY AT WORK

Walk-In: A guest seeking a room who arrives at the hotel without an advance reservation.
■

There are many travelers who, for one reason or another, find themselves in need of a hotel room but without an advance reservation. Some travelers whose plans are variable may not, in fact, know where they will be at the end of the day. Other travelers find their plans change during the day, and still others simply prefer not to make advanced reservations. Regardless of the reason, walk-ins can very positively affect the overall profitability of a hotel. In some hotels, particularly those in highway locations, walk-ins account for as much as 30 percent or more of total room nights sold. Excellent **curb appeal,** as well as a friendly initial greeting from the front office staff, helps ensure that walk-ins are converted to guests.

HOTEL TERMINOLOGY AT WORK

Curb Appeal: The term used to indicate the initial visual impression the hotel's parking areas, grounds, and external building aesthetics create for an arriving guest.
■

As we have seen, the sources from which a guest reservation is generated vary greatly. However, in all cases the FOM, working with the G.M. and marketing and sales personnel, must ultimately ensure the hotel secures those reservations in a manner that maximizes guest satisfaction and minimizes any potential misunderstanding that may exist when the guest actually arrives at the hotel. As a G.M., you can help make sure this is the case by periodically monitoring and assisting the FOM in improving the management of all reservation sources.

MANAGING GUEST SERVICES

While the front office is not, by itself, responsible for the entire hotel guest's experience, it is an area that is especially visible to guests and, because of its responsibility for providing a large number of guest services, it is important that the front office be properly staffed and managed.

Front Desk: Arrival

When a guest arrives at a hotel, it the responsibility of the Front Office staff to greet the guest and complete the registration process as quickly and efficiently as possible. This process is, however, more complex than it may seem. Each time a guest interacts with a member of the hotel staff, the hotel makes an impression on that guest, be it a positive or a negative one. To illustrate how the front office management staff must influence the entire guest service encounter, we will examine the hypothetical experience of Mr. and Mrs. Shingi, two guests with an advanced reservation, as they arrive, register, stay, and then depart from their chosen hotel.

Prearrival

Guest services at the front desk actually begin at the time the guest makes an advance registration. This is true because, on the night before a guest's arrival date, the front desk staff will request, as part of their nightly work, that the PMS print (or hold in memory) a **registration (reg) card** for all guests scheduled to arrive the next day.

HOTEL TERMINOLOGY AT WORK

Registration (reg) Card: A document that provides details such as guest's name, arrival date, rate to be paid, departure date, and other information related to the guest's stay.

In conversation, most often shortened to "reg" card, as in: *"Who filed the reg card for room 417?"*

■

The reg card is important because it forms the basis for the legal contract that exists between the hotel and the guest. In this contract, the hotel agrees to supply a room, and the guest agrees to pay for that room. While the procedures of the hotel and the features of the hotel's PMS dictate some of the information contained on a reg card, all such cards should accurately contain;

- Guest name
- Guest address
- Guest telephone number

- E-mail Address
- Arrival date
- Departure date
- Number of adults in the room
- Rate to be paid
- Room type requested
- Form of payment used to reserve the room

When a guest arrives at the hotel, an accurate reg card should await. If it does not, the hotel's front desk staff is most likely not securing complete information at the time of reservation or, if the reservation was made by a third party, at the time the reservation was entered in the PMS. In either case, an effective FOM will ensure that the front desk has generated appropriate reg cards for all known arriving guests. In older PMS systems, the reg cards may be preprinted and held for the guest's arrival, with any changes to the reg card initialed by the guest at check-in. In modern systems, the PMS simply holds the reg card information in memory. It is revised as needed upon guest check-in, and a corrected copy is printed (if requested) for the guest.

Returning to our hypothetical guests, when the Shingis arrive, the hotel should, first and foremost, know that they are arriving! When they present themselves at the front desk and announce that they have a reservation and would like to check-in, the desk agent should be able to quickly retrieve a hard copy of their reg card. Travelers arriving at a hotel to find that their reservation has been "lost" are likely to be very upset, especially if the hotel is sold out and has no alternative available for the guest. In a similar manner, a reg card that contains a misspelled name, erroneous room rates, or incorrect room types will create negative first impressions for the guest.

Effective G.M.s will, periodically, observe the guest registration process directly. From the first greeting a guest receives upon entering the hotel to the accuracy of reg cards, the prearrival/arrival activities of the front desk make a tremendous impression on the guest. G.M.s who put themselves in a position to observe these initial impressions are in an excellent position to work with the FOM to improve the experience.

Bell Station

Depending on the size and service levels of the hotel, the Shingis may, upon arrival, have been greeted and offered assistance by a member of the bell station staff. Bell staff, originally prevalent in nearly all hotels but now limited primarily to upper-market, full-service hotels, assist guests in getting baggage into the hotel and their rooms, as well as sometimes explaining hotel services and guest room features to guests. These staff members should be friendly, knowledgeable, well groomed, and always properly in uniform.

Valet

If the Shingis arrived by car and if the hotel they have chosen is upscale or located in the downtown area of a larger city, it is likely that they will take advantage of **valet** parking, provided by the hotel either free or for a charge. This service, if offered, may be contracted to an outside company. If the hotel controls it, however, the front office manger typically manages it. As with bell staff, if valets are employed, they should be friendly, well groomed, properly uniformed, and respectful of the guest property entrusted to them.

HOTEL TERMINOLOGY AT WORK

Valet: Originally a term used to identify an individual who cared for the clothes of wealthy travelers; its most common usage now is in reference to those individuals responsible for parking guest vehicles.

■

Registration

Perhaps the most important guest service function that can be provided by a front desk agent is that of properly registering guests. This is a five-step process that consists of:

1. *Greeting the guest.* When the Shingis arrive at the front desk, a professionally dressed, well-trained staff member should greet them in a friendly way. Because most hotel guests arrive in the evening and check-in time can be very busy, it may not always be possible to avoid guests having to wait in line for registration. Proper staffing, however, should minimize the wait. When it is their turn to be registered, guests should, above all else, be made to feel welcome!

2. *Confirming the information on the reg card.* It is imperative that all the information on a reg card be accurate. This includes the spelling of the guest's name, their arrival date, departure date, and room rate (both of which should be initialed by the guest), and any other information related to that specific guest. Since the reg card will serve as the record of the guest's stay, it must be complete and precise. In addition, misunderstandings regarding room rate (one of the most frequent causes of guest dissatisfaction) can be minimized if the room rate is clearly communicated and understood by both the hotel and the guest prior to room assignment. It is critical that all information on the registration card be accurate and complete.

3. *Securing a form of payment.* In most hotels, guests must either pay for their room in advance or provide a valid alternative source of credit at registration. While many hotels accept checks, the most prevalent source of credit provided by guests is that of a credit or debit card.

These cards must be legitimate, however, before they represent an acceptable form of payment. To establish the card's legitimacy, the desk agent should **authorize** the card at the time of guest registration.

HOTEL TERMINOLOGY AT WORK

Authorize: To validate.

When used in reference to credit cards offered by guests at the time of check-in, this term refers to the desk agent's validation of the card. Validation means:

- The card is being used legally.
- The card has sufficient credit remaining to pay for the guest's estimated charges.
- A "hold" for a dollar amount determined by front office policy has been placed on the card to ensure the hotel's payment.

As in *"Lisa, Please authorize Mr. Shingi's MasterCard for $1,000."*

■

To authorize credit cards, hotels use a verification service. Typically, by telephone modem and keypad or magnetic swipe, a desk agent enters the information from the card (account number and expiration date), as well as the dollar amount to be authorized. If the card is not stolen and is, in fact, valid, the verification service issues an authorization code number that lets the hotel know it can accept the card for payment.

Effective front desk staffs always authorize the credit cards they accept as a promise of guest payment. In fact, one objective measure of how well a front office is managed is the desk's consistency in securing and authorizing valid cards.

4. *Room assignment.* Once a guest's registration information has been confirmed and an acceptable form of payment has been offered, the guest should be assigned to a specific guest room. In some hotels, all guest rooms are identical, and room assignment is of little consequence. In other hotels, the room types may vary greatly in perceived quality and/or rate based primarily on the room's:

   - Location
   - View
   - Bed type
   - Amenities

   Whenever possible, of course, guest's preferences should be accommodated. Thus, for example, if Mr. and Mrs. Shingi prefer a nonsmoking room with a king-size bed, on a lower floor, facing the hotel's courtyard, that is precisely the room they should, if possible, be assigned.

5. *Issuance of keys.* The final step in the Shingis registration process is the issuance of their room keys. The actual number of keys to be issued is a matter of hotel policy and guest preference. It is important, however, that the issuance of guest room keys be tightly controlled because the theft, loss, or unauthorized duplication of keys could seriously threaten guest safety.

   Upon receiving room keys, the Shingis would be taken or directed to their room. If bell staff were needed to provide assistance with luggage, this staff member would likely escort the Shingi's to their room. In most midsize hotels, however, the front desk agent would simply direct the guests to their room.

Concierge

The concierge is an extremely important position to hotel guests. If the Shingis find that they need assistance beyond the services typically found in their hotel, they would go to the concierge. Traditionally, the concierge in a full-service hotel is responsible for assisting guests in:

- Making dining reservations
- Securing tickets for theater and sporting events
- Arranging transportation
- Providing information on local attractions
- Language translation
- Providing hotel specific information

In hotels without a concierge staff, it is vital to remember that guests still desire many of these services. Those hotels that can provide all or most of them are in a stronger position to gain guest loyalty and repeat business. For that reason, the G.M. should be aware (as should all guests!) of the services that are provided by the front office staff.

Front Desk: Guest Privacy

Once a guest has been registered for a room, the courts have ruled that these guests enjoy many of the same constitutional rights in the room as they would in their own home. It is not simply the legal thing to do, but it is the proper thing as well, to protect the rights of guests to privacy.

Guest Information

A professionally managed front office is one in which guests are confident that their privacy is maintained by all staff members. This includes maintaining a guest's anonymity. To that end, Front Desk agents should:

- Never confirm or deny that a guest is in fact registered in the hotel without the guest's express permission
- Never give out information related to a guest's stay (arrival, departure, rate, etc.) to any third party without that guest's express permission
- Always be vigilant in informing the guest of any unusual third-party information requests regarding their stay

Room Information

Just as guests expect their own privacy to be maintained, they should also feel confident that information regarding their actual room is kept confidential. This is both a safety and a privacy issue. To that end, front desk agents should:

- Never give out a guest's room number to any third party without that guest's express permission
- Never perform registration tasks in such a way as to allow guest room information to be overheard by others in the front office area
- Never mark room numbers directly onto keys
- Never issue a duplicate room key to anyone without confirming the positive identification of that person as the room's properly registered guest

The Shingis, and all guests, upon check in, should be confident that personal details of their stay will remain confidential; that information the hotel may have about them, including their address, telephone number, and credit card is secure; and that no unauthorized person can gain access to their room. An effective front office can perform no more important task than ensuring guest privacy, and it is the FOM's job to make certain this is the case.

Front Desk: Stay and Departure

During their stay, including the point at which they check out, guests will constantly interact with the front office. Its staff may be called upon to supply a variety of services or information at any time during the guest's stay.

Guest Satisfaction Issues

One of the most challenging aspects of providing guest service at the front desk relates to ensuring that guests are satisfied during their stay. When guests experience difficulties in the hotel, they will most likely turn to the front desk and its staff for assistance. As noted in the previous chapter, there are a variety of reasons guest may have special needs or experience dissatisfaction during their stay. During their stay, and at time of checkout, guests are likely to bring up any issues they find that detracted from their experience. Routine items such as requesting room repairs, additional in-room amenities, or information can, if handled professionally, actually enhance the guest's experience. As a G.M., it is a good idea to monitor the efforts of the front desk staff to ensure that guests, especially those who have legitimate complaints, are treated courteously and with empathy.

The Walked Guest

One of the most difficult situations that can be confronted by a front desk agent is that of walking a guest. Recall that a guest who must be walked is one that has a confirmed reservation but cannot be accommodated by the hotel. When this occurs, it is imperative that the front desk agent carefully follows the hotel's established policies for walking a guest. As a G.M., it is your responsibility to work with the FOM to establish those policies and see that they are implemented when needed. In all cases, when confronted with the task of walking a guest, the front office staff should be observed to:

- Apologize to the guest for the inconvenience
- Clearly explain the hotel's walk policy to the guest
- Offer any reasonable assistance possible to the guest to minimize the difficulties of the situation

ACCOUNTING FOR GUESTS

Accounting for guests, while less visible than providing guest services, is another critical responsibility of the front office. During their stay, the Shingis are likely to have purchased a variety of hotel goods and services in addition to having rented their room. Accounting for guests simply means that all charges incurred by a guest's use of the hotel are charged for properly. Depending on the services and amenities offered by the hotel, the source of guest charges can be numerous. The following product and services list is not inclusive, but does represent some of the many possible guest charges that must be accurately collected and **posted** to the guest's folio.

- Guest room charges including appropriate taxes
- In-room minibar purchases
- In-room safe charges
- Pay-per-view movies/games
- Internet access charges
- Restaurant charges
- Bar charges
- Room service charges
- Telephone tolls

- Gift shop purchases
- Laundry charges
- Valet parking charges
- Meeting room charges
- Audiovisual equipment rental
- Banquet charges
- Service charges

HOTEL TERMINOLOGY AT WORK

Post: To enter a guest's charges into the PMS, thus creating a permanent record of the sale, as in *"Please post this meeting room charge to Mr. Walker's folio."*

■

Rooms Management/Assignment

Perhaps no job performed by the front office is more important than the seemingly straightforward task of assigning guests to the right room, at the right room rate, with the right required form of payment. In reality, this process, despite the use of a sophisticated PMS, can be quite complex. Essentially, there are two methods employed for the registration of guests. These are front desk check-in and self check-in.

Front Desk Check-In

Guests arriving at a hotel to check-in want to be quickly assigned to a room. In the typical case, guests present themselves at a front desk area to begin the registration process. Depending on the level of service provided and priority of the guest, special check-in areas may be established within the hotel. Regardless, however, of where the check-in area is, it is important that the front desk agent confirm the status of the selected room prior to room assignment. Clearly a guest should not be assigned to a room that has not been cleaned or that is occupied by another guest. While each hotel may use its own abbreviations, typically, a vacant room is identified in the PMS with a "V" (for vacant) or an "O" (for occupied). Further, the room must be designated as "C" (for cleaned) and ready to rent. As can be seen, it is important that those individuals responsible for cleaning and inspecting rooms are in close contact with the front desk so the status of guest rooms can be updated continuously throughout the day.

Self Check-In

While automated self checkout systems are currently in greater use than self check-in systems, the technology exists to create a kiosk that allows guests to enter personal information such as that found on their credit card or smart card, choose from a display of available rooms, and receive a key to the selected room. There are, perhaps, two reasons why this self check-in option has not been widely adopted, despite the advantage of speeding up the check-in process. The first is the lack of personal contact. The second is the obvious legal liability that could exist for the hotel should a malfunction of the self-operated system allow a guest to check-in to an already occupied room.

In either check-in situation, it is important that the FOM has systems in place that allow the front desk staff to:

- Verify and document personal information positively identifying the guest to whom the room is rented
- Assign guests, whenever possible, to the room type they have requested
- Assure the status of the room assigned to the guest is "Clean and Vacant"
- Confirm the rate to be paid by the guest prior to the issuance of room keys
- Confirm the guest's departure date prior to the issuance of room keys
- Secure an acceptable form of payment from the guest

The G.M. wishing to minimize accounting difficulties resulting from guest misunderstandings and billing errors will work with the controller and FOM to confirm that systems are in place to achieve the above objectives.

Bucket Check

Errors in recording the information related to a guest's stay make the hotel's accounting records inaccurate. In addition, room rate adjustments made at checkout are both annoying and time consuming to guests. To help eliminate these problems, professional FOMs develop and implement an effective **bucket check** program for all front desk shifts. The "bucket" is the industry term for the location of the actual registration cards signed by guests at check-in. The bucket check is simply a manual procedure for assuring the accuracy of information related to the guest's actual room assignment, rate to be paid, departure date, form of payment, and any other accounting-related information deemed important by the FOM.

HOTEL TERMINOLOGY AT WORK

Bucket Check: A procedure used to verify, for each guest, the accuracy of that guest's registration information.

■

When performing the bucket check, the desk agent physically verifies that the information on the guest's registration card is complete and matches that in the PMS.

When an appropriate bucket check is performed at each shift, the number of errors related to billing guests' folios is greatly reduced. As a G.M., if you detect excessive room rate adjustments, numerous guest complaints due to erroneous billing, or uncollectable guest charges due to insufficient documentation of form of payment, the FOM is likely not enforcing bucket check procedures.

Billing the Folio

Busy hotels process hundreds of guest-related billing transactions daily. Depending on the type of PMS in use, some of these charges will be posted automatically by the PMS while others must be posted manually. In all cases, the controller's office will want to verify the accuracy of the charge and to have a transactional trail for each charge. That is, the front desk should be able to produce independent supporting documentation for each charge posted to a guest's folio. For example, assume that a guest has ordered a bottle of wine from the hotel's room service department. The guest has asked that the cost of the bottle of wine and an appropriate gratuity for the room service waitperson bringing the wine to the room be added to the guest's folio. Upon checkout, the guest may wish to review these charges. The front desk agent responsible for checking the guest out may need to produce some documentation of the charge. In this case, the documentation would likely be the actual room service ticket signed by the guest when the wine was delivered. It is the responsibility of each shift of the front desk to ensure that all appropriate guest charges incurred are posted to the appropriate guest's folio and that the documentation supporting such charges has been thoroughly reviewed prior to posting. The **night auditor** depends on appropriate documentation provided by each shift of the front desk to support the charges that will be finalized and posted to the guest's folio during the night audit.

HOTEL TERMINOLOGY AT WORK

Night Auditor: The individual who performs the daily review of guest transactions recorded by the front office.

■

Night Audit

Because hotels are open seven days a week, twenty-four hours a day, an interesting accounting issue arises: When does one day's hotel sales end and another's begin?

To illustrate the issue, assume that, on a winter night, due to inclement weather, a hotel on an interstate highway checks different guests into the hotel at the following times: 11:00 P.M., midnight, 1:00 A.M., 2:00 A.M., 3:00 A.M., 4:00 A.M., 5:00 A.M., and so on.

At what point are these guests considered Monday night guests, and at what point should they be considered Tuesday guests?

Traditionally, the "end" of the day (and, therefore, the beginning of the next day) is not a fixed time period at all, but rather is designated as the time at which the night auditor concludes (closes) the **night audit.** Even though the night audit could, theoretically, be performed at any time during the day or night, traditionally it has been performed in the late evening/early morning hours when the hotel's overall activity is at its slowest because most guests have, at that point, checked in for the night.

HOTEL TERMINOLOGY AT WORK

Night Audit: The process of reviewing for accuracy and completeness the accounting transactions from one day to conclude or "close" that day's sales information in preparation for posting the transactions of the next day.

■

The night audit function is important for many departments in the hotel. Essentially, completing it consists of the following eight key items:

1. Posting the appropriate room and tax rates to folios of the guests currently in the hotel
2. Verification of an accurate room status (in the PMS) of all rooms
3. Posting any necessary adjustments or allowances to guest folios
4. Verification that all legitimate, nonroom charges have been posted, throughout the day, to the proper guest folio
5. Monitoring guest account balances to determine whether any are over the guest's credit limit
6. Balancing and reconciling the front desk's cash bank
7. Updating and backing up the electronic data maintained by the front office
8. Producing, duplicating, and distributing all management mandated reports, such as those related to ADR, occupancy percentage, source of business, in-house guest lists, and the like

With a computerized PMS, some of the above tasks may be completed automatically. In most hotels, the night auditor completes the audit between 1:00 A.M. and 4:00 A.M. It is important that this task is completed correctly and on time because some guests will begin to check out of the hotel very early in the morning and their folios must be as up-to-date as possible at that time.

Checkout

Increasingly, hotels provide guests the option of using express or self-checkout systems when they conclude their stay. These are popular and appropriate for some guests. In the normal case, however, when guests check out, the front desk should perform two important tasks.

The first, of course, is the settlement of the guest's bill. This consists of a several step process, including:

- Confirmation of the guest's identity
- Checking for, and giving to the guest, any late faxes or guest messages that have not been delivered
- Inquiring about and returning any guest belongings in the hotel's safety deposit boxes
- Posting of any final charges
- Producing a copy of the folio for the guest's inspection
- Processing the guest's payment
- Revising the room's status in the PMS to designate the room as vacant

In most cases, guest checkout is a relatively straightforward process. This is especially true if the guest's form of payment has been confirmed at check-in and if bucket checks have been performed throughout the guest's stay to verify that the appropriate room rate has been charged.

In some cases, guests will have experienced a difficulty with their stay and an adjustment of their bill may be in order. It is important that the FOM and each desk agent know the limits to their authority to make adjustments. That is, the desk agent may be authorized by the FOM to make folio adjustments up to a predetermined dollar amount, but only a supervisor or manager could authorize adjustments exceeding that amount. In a like manner, the FOM may be authorized to make adjustments subject to the level of authority delegated by the hotel's G.M.

The second essential task that can be accomplished by the desk agent when a guest checks out is the rebooking of the guest for a future stay. If the guest's stay has been a positive one, it is proper, as well as good front office management, to ask the guest if future reservations can be made for them at the hotel or, if appropriate, at another hotel within the chain. This is an often overlooked selling opportunity. In addition, a G.M. can frequently determine the selling focus of an FOM by the presence or absence of this front office activity.

DATA MANAGEMENT

The front office is the center for the hotel's data management systems. At the front office, the PMS, as well as other accounting systems, maintain the financial and operational records of the hotel. In most cases, these systems are extensive as well as complex. Their management requires a talented and technologically savvy FOM because an increasing number of important data generating systems are, or should be, **interfaced** with the hotel's PMS.

HOTEL TERMINOLOGY AT WORK

Interfaced: The term used to describe the process in which one data generating system shares its data electronically with another system.

■

The process of interfacing two data management systems can be challenging because, in most cases, different companies manufacture the systems. For example, the company that produces the hotel's PMS will not be the same as the company providing the hotel with its electronic guest room door lock system. Clearly, however, it is ideal that a guest, who is checked in to room 101 by the PMS, automatically is issued a key for room 101 (not room 102!) by the electronic locking system. When the PMS and lock system are interfaced, this happens immediately. When they are not, the key maker must produce the key separately, which introduces the possibility of an error.

To complicate matters further, in many cases multiple system interfaces are required, not all of which are completely under the control of the hotel. For example, a hotel that wishes to upgrade its **call accounting** system will find that the new system must be interfaced with the existing telephone system, the local telephone call provider's system, the long distance call provider's system, and the hotel's PMS. The challenges of implementing such an integrated system are many and fall primarily to the FOM.

HOTEL TERMINOLOGY AT WORK

Call Accounting: The system within the hotel used to document and charge guests for their use of the telephone.

■

Credit Cards

Credit cards are the most common form of guest payment used in most hotels. Properly processing charges to credit (and, increasingly, debit) cards is an important responsibility of the front office. Accuracy and a commitment to security when processing guest credit card charges are two characteristics every G.M. should seek from the FOM. Today, credit cards are issued with three-dimensional designs, magnetic strips, encoded numbers,

The number of telephone lines required for a modern hotel is extremely large.

smart chips, and other features to reduce consumer fraud. In addition, electronic credit card verification systems are fast, accurate, and designed to reduce loss. While these verification systems, which are currently in use in most hotels, cut down on the number processing errors, security and fraud prevention remain significant considerations. Federal laws prohibit the fraudulent use of credit cards, yet many times hotels are the victims of such fraud. An effective FOM implements systems to minimize credit card fraud while, at the same time, protecting the security of the guest's credit card number and the integrity of the hotel's credit card database.

In some cases, hotels face the challenge of credit card holders who pay their full bill with their card but later protest all or part of that bill. Unless the dispute can be settled between the hotel and guest, the FOM may have to defend the hotel's card processing procedures. Each major credit card issuer has its own preferred procedures, and FOMs should be familiar with those required by the cards they accept.

Credit card issuers have a responsibility to both the hotel and the cardholder. To be fair, the card issuer will require the hotel to have followed the issuer's procedures for accepting cards and billing for products and services. Then, if guests have a legitimate complaint, these guests will be treated fairly, while at the same time, the hotel is protected from fraud. As a G.M., you should monitor the credit card procedures used at the front desk. Credit card acceptance and processing guidelines that should exist in written form for ease in training front desk agents include:

- Confirmation procedures ensure that the name on the card is the same as that of the individual presenting the card for payment. (Driver's license or other acceptable forms of identification can be used.)
- Examination of the card for obvious signs of alteration.

- Confirmation that the card has not expired.
- Comparison of the signature on the card with the one made by the guest paying with the card.
- Documentation (usually by initialing) of the employee who processed the charge.
- The balancing and reconciling of credit card charges at the conclusion of each front office shift.

Locking/Security Systems

An extensive discussion of hotel key and locking systems and their role in guest safety and security is included in this book (chapter 9, Safety and Property Security). However, because the front office is responsible for issuing guest room keys, it is appropriate to examine the FOM's role in maintaining the data and the security systems related to the issuing of room keys.

Modern hotels increasingly utilize a **recodable locking system** to ensure guest safety. The typical installed cost of such a system is approximately $300–$500 per guest room. Whether keys are lost, stolen, or accidentally thrown away, the challenge for you as a G.M. becomes how to cost-effectively protect your guests, your property, and your bottom line. Recodable locking systems help you do just that.

HOTEL TERMINOLOGY AT WORK

Recodable Locking System: A hotel guest room locking system designed such that when a guest inserts their "key" (typically an electromagnetic card) into the guest room lock for the first time, the lock is immediately recoded, canceling entry authorization for the previous guest's key and thus enhancing guest safety.

■

Most recodable locking systems in use today are independent and standalone. That is, no wiring back to a central computer or PMS is required. Except in life-threatening emergencies, only standard magnetic strip cards issued to hotel staff as well as guests open the lock. This means that the hotel's entire room security system is controlled by software programmed into the individual locks, activated by cards coded on a card-issuing computer. **Keycards** are time sensitive and can be issued up to twelve months in advance, meaning that individuals or groups can be sent room keys when reservations are confirmed to speed registration.

HOTEL TERMINOLOGY AT WORK

Keycards: The electromagnetic card used in a recodable locking system.

■

The advantages of recodable locks are so great that no hotelier would seriously consider building a hotel today without including such a system.

The data management challenge for the FOM managing a recodable lock system is to ensure that front desk agents do not issue keys to individuals not properly registered in the guest room. For example, assume the (very common) situation where a guest approaches the front desk and states, "I have misplaced my room key." Clearly the staff member must:

1. Be trained to issue duplicate keys only to confirmed registered guests
2. Maintain an accurate data system that actually identifies registered guests and their assigned room numbers

The advantages of an interfaced recodable locking system and PMS are clear in this case. As a G.M., you must ensure that the required security training is in place to handle the above situation. As well, data systems must be maintained well enough to avoid issuing guest room keys to unauthorized individuals.

Telephones

One of the most complex data and equipment management areas within the hotel is that of telephones and telephone-related services. Even the smallest of hotels is large enough to have its own private branch exchange, or **PBX.**

HOTEL TERMINOLOGY AT WORK

PBX: The system within the hotel used to process incoming, internal, and outgoing telephone calls.

■

Today's hotel PBX is highly automated, as it must be because of the tremendous use made of telephones within the typical hotel. The PBX is typically maintained by the front office. Therefore the FOM is responsible for the proper operation of the following areas.

Call Accounting

When guests make telephone calls outside the hotel, it is in the best interest of the hotel to route those calls in a way that minimizes the hotel's cost. For example, if a registered guest directly dials a person in another state from his or her hotel room, it is the hotel that will actually be billed for the call. Of course, the hotel would want its cost of providing the call to be as low as possible while still assuring that guests have quality long-distance service. The hotel will, depending on the distance and length of the long distance call, add a charge to the guest's folio to offset the cost of the call. For those hotels providing in-room fax machines, these calls, like all others, can be charged to the guest's folio with a call accounting system interfaced with the PMS.

The call accounting system records the time, length, and number called of each telephone call made within each guest room (as well as those made from administrative phones). These call records must be accurate if guests are to be expected to pay for the calls they have initiated. The hotel's management determines which of these made calls will be billed to guests and which will not. Some hotels use the call accounting system to charge guests for local calls as well as long distance, whereas other hotels routinely allow guests to make free local calls. The call accounting system, when interfaced with the PMS, posts these charges directly to the guest's folio. It is important to remember that even local calls are not "free" to the hotel. Proper operation of the call accounting system is important because telephone calls, for many hotels, are a significant source of revenue. Telephone revenue, as a percentage of total hotel revenue, has been declining in recent years due to the increased use of cell phones and pagers; however, a properly managed call accounting system is still a vital part of any effective front office operation because telephone revenue that goes uncollected due to an improperly managed system is damaging to the hotel's bottom line.

Wake-up Calls

Traditionally, guests who wish to wake up at a given time have called the front desk to request a "wake-up" call. A member of the front office staff would then call the guest at the requested time. Today's telephone systems automate these calls, and they can be programmed into the PBX either by guests in their own rooms or by staff at the front desk.

Voice Mail

Voice mail is a feature that may be interfaced with the PBX but is, in fact, a separate telephone component. A properly operating voice mail system is nearly mandatory for those hotels seeking to attract business travelers, and hotels increasingly provide this service to guests. In a modern PBX system interfaced with voice mail, the voice mailbox for the guest is activated by the PMS at check-in and then deactivated by the PMS when the guest checks out. Voice mail is also critical for administrative staff that must have telephone contact with guests or potential guests. This is especially true of the sales and marketing department.

Message on Hold

This telephone feature allows the hotel to play a "message" on the line when a caller is placed on hold. For example, a caller attempting to make a room reservation may be placed on hold for a short period of time until the next reservationist is available. During this time, the hotel may play a recorded message that can include features of the hotel, unique services offered, and a general "apology" for placing the caller on hold, while, at the same time, assuring the call will be answered shortly. Typically a message on hold apparatus interfaces the PBX with a combination of pleasant music and well-written marketing script.

Additional use of hotel telephones includes those calls made by guests to other guests within the hotel (room-to-room); calls made to the front desk from **house phones;** emergency phones such as those located in elevators, at the pool, or fitness areas; and the hotel staff's own interoffice calls.

HOTEL TERMINOLOGY AT WORK

House Phone: A publicly located telephone within the hotel used to call the front desk, or, in some cases, the front desk and guest rooms.

■

The telephone system in a hotel is a critical service to guests, as well as an effective management tool. Its uninterrupted operation is important, and it is the FOM in conjunction with affected departments that must ensure its smooth operation.

THE INTERNET AT WORK

For an overview of the many features and capabilities provided by today's telephone systems, review the site of one of the industry's leading providers of telephone systems for smaller properties. You can do so at:

http://www.innphones.com/.

Point of Sale (POS)

In most cases the hotel's PMS will be interfaced with one or more **point of sale** systems. Any sales recording system not located at the front desk is technically considered to be a **POS** system. In a larger hotel, there are multiple POS systems in operation. Some examples include:

- Restaurants
- Room service
- Lounges
- Laundry
- Valet
- Shops

- Fitness centers
- Business centers

It is the role of the front office to ensure that all legitimate purchases made at a POS and charged to an account are posted to the proper guest or nonguest folio.

HOTEL TERMINOLOGY AT WORK

Point of Sale (POS): A location, excluding the front desk, at which hotel goods and services are purchased. In many hotels, the POS(s) is interfaced with the PMS.

■

In-Room Services

Increasingly, guests can use the televisions, telephones, and/or hotel-provided keyboards in their rooms to access products and services provided by the hotel. As the traveling public becomes even more computer sophisticated, look for this trend to continue and expand. Currently some of the most popular products and services guests can access from their rooms include movies, games, minibars, safes, and Internet connections.

Movies

Pay-per-view movie systems have long been a popular feature offered to hotel guests. Essentially, these systems offer guests the opportunity to view movies that are currently, or that have just recently finished, showing in movie theaters. In addition, most pay-per-view providers offer a variety of adult-oriented movies as well. The demand for these current and popular movies can be quite strong. Guests pay the hotel for viewing the movies. Then, at month's end, the movie provider charges the hotel based on the number of movies viewed, as well as for any equipment charges included in the hotel's pay-per-view contract. If a movie shown on the system is defective (e.g., poor audio or color quality), the provider typically allows the hotel to not bill the guest, and in turn does not bill the hotel. Some guests, often those who view the adult movies offered by the pay-per-view system, dispute that they have watched the movies. A good FOM has systems in place that distinguish between those guests who truly have had problems with their movie quality while at the same time minimizing the number of guests who might attempt to defraud the hotel. As a G.M., it is important to monitor the number of movies viewed per month versus the number of movies actually billed to guests. If the difference between these two numbers is excessive, a review of front office policy in this area is needed.

Originally devised as videotape-based systems, today's in-room movie services are more likely to be delivered by satellite and to include enhanced features that allow guests to review their folios on their television screens,

---

THE INTERNET AT WORK

For a sample of the type of movies shown to guests on a pay-per-view system, review the offerings of Lodgenet, one of the largest pay-per-view movie and services providers. You can do so at:

www.lodgenet.com/guests/index.html.

---

and even to check out of the hotel using a PMS interfaced pay-per-view system.

Games

Guests are increasingly offered the chance to play "video" games on the television screens in their rooms. The games are typically accessed in the same manner as pay-per-view movies. While these game services are very similar to pay-per-view movies (they are pay-per-play), the significant difference is the requirement for an in-room joystick, mouse, or keyboard to actually play the game. This means that the hotel must provide these electronic devices and keep them secure in the rooms. The logistics and difficulty of doing so has made some G.M.s reluctant to actively offer games as an in-room amenity. The FOM is not responsible for the security of the in-room devices, but is responsible for maintaining an effective interface so that all games played are, in fact, charged to the proper guest folio.

In-Room Minibars

Hotels have long provided in-room minibars that allowed guests the convenience of selecting alcoholic beverages, soft drinks, and snacks from in-room storage units (minibars). Only recently, however, have advances in bar coding technology created a situation in which in-room minibars can be interfaced with the PMS so that, as a guest removes an item from the minibar, the time of the transaction as well as the selling price of the item removed is automatically posted to the guest's folio.

HOTEL TERMINOLOGY AT WORK

Minibars: Small, in-room refrigerated or unrefrigerated cabinets used to store beverages, snacks, and other items the hotel wishes to offer for sale to guests.

■

Safes

Recently more hotels have begun offering in-room safes for guests' use. These safes are electronic and can be opened only by the guest and the hotel's own staff. Charges, if any for the use of the safe are typically posted to the guest's folio.

Beginning in the mid-1800s and continuing today, each state has developed its own view of how liable hotels should be for the possessions of their guests. The laws in each state vary considerably, however, so it is extremely important that hotel managers familiarize themselves with applicable laws before implementing an in-room safe service. In most states, if a hotel wishes to take advantage of their state's laws limiting liability for the theft or loss of a guest's possessions, the guest must be made aware of the existence and content of that law. Also, in most states, if the hotel is to provide in-room safes under the control of the guest, the hotel must also offer, and publicize the fact that it offers, a safe at "no-charge" where guests can keep their valuables during their stay.

A hotel is not required to accept for safekeeping an unlimited amount of personal property. A hotel is not a bank, and it is not reasonable to assume that it would be as secure as a bank. However, guest demand for in-room safes is increasing, and, in nearly all states, a hotel is fully responsible for theft by its employees. Just as important, the hotel becomes liable for the full amount of any property loss resulting from the actions of the hotel's staff. For that reason and others, many hotels have been slower to implement this guest service. G.M.s interested in providing in-room safes for a fee are well advised to consult their property's attorney prior to implementation of the service.

Internet Connections

In the late 1990s, some hotels began to aggressively market in-room Internet services. The intent was to capitalize on the increasing use of the Internet by travelers of all types. Some of these efforts met with success, while others, the victim of the famous "dot.com" bust of 2001, were canceled or delayed when companies offering the services failed to deliver because of defective business models.

Certainly, the use of the Internet has exploded. In many ways (e.g., the marketing of hotel properties and the ability of guests to make reservations directly using the Internet), the impact of the Internet on hotels has been very positive. The ability of hotels to profitably harness the Internet on a pay-to-connect basis in a guest's room, however, is still undetermined. This is especially the case when the guest's own personal computer is used to make the connection. Nevertheless, some hotels do profitably charge for Internet usage, and, for those that do, their interface to the PMS must be maintained and controlled by the FOM.

Back Office Systems

As we saw in the previous chapter, the financial data from the PMS must ultimately be transferred to the controller's office. The **back office system** used by the controller to prepare the hotel's financial documents will get a large portion of its data from the PMS; therefore, it is important that the data in the PMS be accurate.

HOTEL TERMINOLOGY AT WORK

Back Office System: The accounting system used by the controller to prepare the hotel's financial documents such as the balance sheet, income statement, and so on.

■

It is somewhat surprising that few makers of PMSs develop their products with the capability of interfacing directly with the most popular back office systems on the market today. As a result, the data collected and maintained by the FOM are sometimes inconsistent with that needed by the controller. The advantages of a seamless integration are many and, when the software required for such integration is fully developed and functional, will be anxiously awaited by G.M.s as well as controllers and FOMs.

Although it is not mandatory that the back office system used by a hotel is computerized, few hotels today would attempt to operate a back office system that does not rely on the most advanced accounting software available. There are hundreds of accounting software packages available in the marketplace today. Nearly all of these packages offer unique features and capabilities that are to be commended, admired, and sometimes applauded. However, the majority of these products also suffer from glaring weaknesses and shortcomings. Assuming that the back office system is not interfaced directly to the PMS or manufactured by the PMS maker, G.M.s will find that the FOM and controller will co-exist best when the back office accounting system selected for use in the hotel offers:

- A good underlying technology
- A strong company behind the product, including good leadership
- Compatibility with popular hardware products
- A sizable customer base
- Good customization capabilities
- Expandability
- Ease of use by nontechnology-based employees
- Excellent support via telephone
- Excellent on-line support
- The potential for PMS interface

In the future, more PMS developers will likely include back office accounting systems as part of their package. It is also probable that call accounting and POS systems will soon make their way to become part of the standard PMSs from which G.M.s can choose.

THE INTERNET AT WORK

For an example of an excellent back office system that could be even better were it interfaced with the most popular property management systems in use, review "Great Plains Dynamics," Microsoft's entry into hospitality back office systems software. You will find information about the software at:

http://www.greatplains.com/.

The FOM is often the hotel's guest service expert and, increasingly, the hotel's technological leader. Few other hotel departments have been, nor likely will be, as impacted by the changing capabilities of equipment and of guest expectations. As a G.M., the need for a talented front office staff that can maximize revenue, provide outstanding guest service, and record the data needed for the smooth operation of the property is unquestionable.

MANAGERS AT WORK

J.D. Ojisima, the hotel G.M., has been approached by a salesperson from Lucid Technologies. Essentially, Lucid is proposing, for a fee, to install the high-speed co-axial cable required to provide rapid Internet access to each guest room in J.D.'s hotel. The Lucid representative maintains that the cost of the installation will be recouped via the fees the hotel can charge Internet users for the high-speed service. Guests can use their own computers or, for a higher fee, Lucid will provide the hotel keyboards so that guests can use the in-room TV for their monitor.

The clientele the hotel serves is 80 percent business traveler and 20 percent leisure traveler through the week, with the reverse true on the weekends. The Internet service is touted by Lucid as a critical need of the business traveler.

In addition to the financial cost/benefits of the service, what specific front office interface issues must J.D. consider before committing to the purchase? Which other areas of the hotel would be affected by the decision to implement or not implement the service?

How can J.D. obtain the technology-related information needed to make a wise decision? Identify at least three specific sources of such information.

HOTEL TERMINOLOGY AT WORK GLOSSARY

The following terms were defined within this chapter. If you are not familiar with each of them, please review the segment of the chapter that contains the term.

Front office	Backup systems	MLOS
FOM	Sell-out	Overbooking
Concierge	Rack rate	Walked
Bell staff	CTA	Folio

Room type	Walk-in	Interfaced
Transient sales	Curb Appeal	Call accounting
Group sales	Registration (reg) card	Recodable locking system
Global Distribution System	Valet	Keycards
(GDS)	Authorize	PBX
Confirmation number	Post	House phone
Cancellation number	Bucket check	Point of sale (POS)
Blackout dates	Night auditor	Minibars
Test calls	Night audit	Back office system

ISSUES AT WORK

1. In some hotels, the position of revenue manager reports to a sales and marketing director, whereas in others it reports to the FOM. Why do you think this is so? As a G.M., how would these two alternative arrangements affect the way you would manage the property?

2. Rapid advances in technology create a situation where, often, the FOM has greater technical expertise in using the PMS than does the G.M. What difficulties do you see in such a situation? As a G.M., what techniques and resources can you use to overcome these difficulties?

3. CTA and MLOS are often used to control occupancy levels. Assume a weekend where the demand for Saturday is strong but the demand for Friday and Sunday is weak. Under what specific circumstances would it be best to employ CTA to maximize occupancy? When is the MLOS strategy the better choice? Give an example of each.

4. As advances in technology make the self-registration of guests more easily achievable, some hotel companies have moved aggressively to implement such technologies. Those who have not cite the diminished role personal service plays in the process and the potential long-term negative affects to consumer loyalty that may result. Do you think the average business traveler prefers the speed of self-check in or the human interaction of a front desk agent? How about the average leisure traveler? Please explain your positions in detail.

5. The increased use of personal cell phones and the consumer's perception that hotel telephone charges are excessive have led to industrywide reduced revenue derived from telephone services supplied by the hotel. List three specific methods you would employ to encourage in-room telephone use in a hotel you would manage. Describe how you would use the front office staff to help implement each of these plans.

7
Housekeeping

This Chapter at Work

G.M.s are sometimes asked by those outside the hotel business to identify the "most important" department in their hotels. While it is not really possible for a G.M. to answer that question because all departments are important, from the point of view of the hotel's guests the answer would be simple. It is the housekeeping department. Hotel industry surveys consistently confirm this fact. Guests want, first and foremost, a clean room. It is the role of the housekeeping department to provide that clean room, as well as to clean most other areas within the hotel.

There are three primary areas within the hotel that are the responsibility of the housekeeping department. These are (1) public spaces such as public restrooms, exercise areas, pools, lobbies, corridors and the like, (2) guestrooms, and (3) the hotel's laundry area. To manage the care and cleaning of the hotel, a G.M. will employ the services of an excellent executive housekeeper. This individual will direct the inspectors (those who review the work of the housekeeping staff); the public area cleaners, the room attendants who actually clean guest rooms, and the laundry attendants who wash, dry, and fold towels and linen.

The job of the executive housekeeper is complex and growing more so every day. Properly cleaning a hotel requires knowledge of the available tools and chemicals that make cleaning jobs easier. Just as important as the selection of the best cleaning aids is the training of staff in the safe and proper use of these aids. This can be especially challenging if, as is often the case, the staff of the department is multinational and thus multilingual. Increasingly, hotel managers are aware that training housekeeping staff to work safely, and to perform their work in a way that ensures the safety of guests is just as important as making sure the hotel is clean.

As a G.M. you will count on the expertise and professional standards of an excellent executive housekeeper to select employees who understand the importance of cleaning, to train those employees to meet the standards for cleanliness you have established, and to manage the inventories of cleaning supplies and guest service products needed to efficiently operate the housekeeping department.

In this chapter you will see how the work of the housekeeping department affects the work of other departments in the hotel and learn about the specific tasks that are involved in cleaning public spaces and guest rooms. It is critical that guests as well as hotel staff feel that the housekeeping department does an excellent job. As a G.M., it is an important part of your job to ensure that they do.

Chapter 7 Outline

THE ROLE OF THE HOUSEKEEPING DEPARTMENT

The housekeeping department in a hotel is responsible for the hotel's cleanliness. Because that is true, every guest or visitor to the hotel will be able to readily see the results of the housekeeper's work. When a hotel's housekeeping staff is effective, guest satisfaction is high, employee morale is good, and ultimately the hotel is profitable. When the housekeeping staff's work is below par, guest complaints soar, employees at the front desk and in other areas of the hotel become disillusioned about management's commitment to quality service, and profits suffer due to increased allowances and adjustments made at the front desk to compensate guests for poor experiences. In addition, guests who feel the hotel was not clean simply do not return.

The number of areas within a hotel that must be kept clean are so many that the housekeeping department will nearly always be the hotel's largest department in terms of the number of employees. Depending on the type and size of hotel, the housekeeping department will generally be responsible for cleaning and maintaining all of the following:

Public Spaces
Lobby areas
Public restrooms

Front desk areas
Management offices
Game rooms

Public Spaces *(cont.)*
Exercise areas
Pool and spa areas
Employee break rooms
   and locker rooms
Selected meeting and food
   service areas

Guest Room Areas
Elevators

Corridors
Stairwells
Guest rooms

Laundry
Laundry preparation areas
Laundry supply closets
Guest linen and supplies storage areas

Public Space

The **public space** in a hotel is among the first seen by the guests. In a larger hotel, these areas require the efforts of one or more full-time **house persons** to maintain proper cleanliness levels.

HOTEL TERMINOLOGY AT WORK

Public Space: Those areas within the hotel that can be freely accessed by guests and visitors. Examples include lobby areas, public rest rooms, corridors, and stairwells.

House Person: The individual responsible for the cleaning of public spaces (the house). Also sometimes referred to as a PA (public area cleaner) or porter.
■

The decisions made about the number of employees required to clean these areas, as well as the frequency of cleaning, are the responsibility of the **executive housekeeper**.

HOTEL TERMINOLOGY AT WORK

Executive Housekeeper: The individual responsible for the management and operation of the housekeeping department.
■

It can sometimes be unclear whether a space in a hotel is public and thus the responsibility of the housekeeping department or if the space is department specific to another department. A good example is the dining area in a full-service hotel. In some hotels, it may be the decision of the G.M. that housekeeping staff clean the dining room, whereas in other hotels the G.M. may decide it would be the responsibility of the F&B department to do the cleaning. The important rule is that every department knows its cleaning responsibilities and completes them.

MANAGERS AT WORK

"It isn't fair," Jenna Walbert, the executive housekeeper, said to J.D. Ojisima, the hotel G.M. "My staff clean the men's employee locker room every day, but just look at this!"

J.D. carefully inspected the area. Ashtrays overflowed, food was left on benches, dirty uniforms littered the ground, and newspapers were strewn about the floor. It was a mess.

"The guys in food and beverage and maintenance do this every day," continued Jenna angrily. "Our house person is too busy trying to keep the lobby carpets sharp to spend an hour a day down here cleaning up after our own staff. I think you should make the food and beverage and maintenance departments keep this clean. <u>They</u> are the ones who are messing it up."

Assume that housekeeping has been charged with the responsibility of cleaning employee locker rooms. What should J.D. tell Jenna Walbert? What should be done to solve her problem? What should be communicated to the other departments involved in the problem?

There will always be areas within a hotel where management judgments must be made about who should clean them. The G.M., in conjunction with the executive housekeeper, must make these decisions so that the cleaning of every area within the hotel is the responsibility of a specific department. To facilitate this process, many hotels use a color-coded map of the entire property. Areas of cleaning responsibility are then assigned to each department by color code. Each department is responsible for cleaning and maintaining the areas that match its assigned color code. The responsibility for the cleaning of every area within the hotel is then known by the department head assigned to the area, and accountability can be ensured.

Guest Rooms

Providing perfectly cleaned guest rooms is a top priority for any well-run hotel. The cleaning of guest rooms is always the responsibility of the housekeeping department and must be executed flawlessly. The specifics of guest room cleaning are examined later in this chapter; however, what is less well-known, but of utmost importance, is the communication role the housekeeping department must play in relaying **room status** information to the front desk staff and room maintenance issues to the engineering and maintenance department.

HOTEL TERMINOLOGY AT WORK

Room Status: The up-to-date (actual) condition (occupied, vacant, dirty, etc.) of the hotel's individual guest rooms.

■

In most hotels, it is a strict policy not to assign a guest to a room unless that room has been:

1. Properly cleaned by the housekeeping department
2. Verified as clean by a second member of housekeeping
3. The room's status has been reported to the front desk

While this might, at first glance, appear to be a simple process, it is quite complex and contains the potential for a variety of miscommunications if the process is not managed properly.

To examine the importance of maintaining accurate guest room status, let's examine the hypothetical stay of Mr. and Mrs. Flood. This couple checks into a room at the Waldo Hotel at 4:00 P.M. on Monday afternoon and are assigned to a room that the housekeeping staff has reported to the front desk is "Clean and Vacant." That is, housekeeping has communicated that the room has been cleaned and inspected for cleanliness and that no other guest is occupying the room. If, in fact, the room is clean and no other guest is assigned to it, the Floods, upon arriving at the room, should have no housekeeping-related complaints about it.

Consider, however, the problems that could occur if the room, instead of being clean, was scheduled for cleaning but the cleaning had not yet occurred. In this case, the couple would have been checked into a dirty room and, of course, will return to the front desk area unhappy and concerned about the overall quality of their stay. In a similar manner, if the room is cleaned but the Floods discover someone's possessions (or someone!) in the room upon their arrival, they will again be upset and return to the front desk area unhappy and concerned about the quality of the hotel's management staff.

As a G.M., it is critical that your housekeeping staff continuously and accurately maintain the room status of all guest rooms in the hotel that are subject to rental. Figure 7.1 below lists the room status definitions commonly used in U.S. hotels. Specific companies or areas of the country may vary the terms (and the abbreviations used to designate them) somewhat; however, these terms or their equivalents must be used in the hotel if housekeeping is to accurately represent room status to the front desk.

It is easy to see that the housekeeping department must carefully report the status of rooms. The process of communicating room status between housekeeping and the front desk begins each morning when the housekeeping department receives, from the front desk, an occupancy report that has been produced as part of the night audit. This occupancy report will detail, for each room, the room status the PMS is displaying for front desk agents. If there are no discrepancies, the report will accurately show those rooms that are **stay-overs**, occupied, vacant, on-change, out of order, and so forth. It is up to the housekeeping department to take this report and, as room status

FIGURE 7.1   Room Status Terminology

Term	Meaning
Clean and Vacant	The room is vacant, has been cleaned, and can be assigned to a guest.
Occupied	The room is registered to a current guest.
On-Change	The room is vacant but not yet cleaned.
Do Not Disturb	The room is occupied but has not been cleaned due to the guest's request not to be disturbed.
Sleep-out (Sleeper)	The room is reported as occupied, but the room was not used (bed not used, no personal belongings in room) and the guest is not present.
Stay-over	The guest will stay in the room at least one more night.
Due Out	The guest(s) have indicated this is the last day they will use the room.
Checkout	The guest(s) have departed.
Out of Order	The room is unrentable and thus unassignable at this time.
Lock Out	The guest has items in the room, but will be denied access until approved to reenter by management.
Late Checkout	The guests have requested and been given an extension of the regular checkout time.

changes are made, report those changes to the front desk, just as the front desk should communicate its known room status changes to housekeeping.

HOTEL TERMINOLOGY AT WORK

Stay-over: A guest that is *not* scheduled to check out of the hotel on the day his or her room status is assessed. That is, the guest will be staying at least one more day.

■

If both of these departments perform their jobs well, an accurate, up-to-date room status is maintained in the PMS throughout the day. Generally, the front desk notifies the housekeeping department of room status changes, such as checkouts, throughout the day by calling the executive housekeeper or a housekeeping supervisor, updating the PMS (when the housekeeping department has easy access to it), or using another communication device such as a two-way radio. Changes in room status made by housekeeping can be communicated to the front desk in a variety of ways also, including having a housekeeping supervisor contact the front desk by telephone (from each room as that room's status changes), via radio or handheld computer, or by using the telephone's interface with the PMS to make the changes via codes entered into the telephone in the affected room.

At the end of the housekeeping shift, the housekeeping department will prepare a final room status report based on a physical check of each room.

This report is then compared with the updated PMS occupancy report to identify any discrepancies. If any exist, the front office manager would then investigate these discrepancies. As a G.M., it is important that you ensure this cross-checking is completed daily. If, for example, a front desk agent is fraudulently selling rooms to guests (assigning the guests to a room but not posting the income to the hotel's PMS), the discrepancy report would uncover this activity because the guest room, reported as "vacant" in the PMS, would show as "occupied" on the housekeeping room status report.

An additional and absolutely critical communication line must exist between housekeeping and the engineering and maintenance departments. As guests use guest rooms, repair and replacement issues occur. For example, when lightbulbs burn out in a guest room, they must be replaced. This simple task may be assigned to housekeeping. If, however, a guest accidentally breaks the leg off of a chair in the room, or if a toilet is running constantly, a repair must be requested by housekeeping. It will always be the case that the ability of the housekeeping department to aggressively identify and then quickly report needed room repairs makes a significant difference in the satisfaction level of guests subsequently using the rooms. The actual method used by housekeeping to report room issues to the engineering and maintenance department is detailed in chapter 11 (Facility Engineering and Maintenance). The important point to remember is that the housekeeping department, because its staff members are in the rooms most frequently, plays a critical role in maintaining room quality by reporting room defects quickly and accurately to those individuals responsible for eliminating those defects. Engineering and maintenance makes the repairs, cleans up their work, or, if appropriate, contacts housekeeping to retidy the room prior to renting it to a guest.

Laundry

Hotels generate a tremendous amount of laundry. Some hotels, especially smaller ones, may not actually do their laundry on-site. Most hotels, however, do their own laundry. When you consider the time, equipment, and expertise required to properly wash, dry, and fold the large amount of **linen** and **terry** generated by a hotel, as well as employee uniforms and other laundry items, it is not surprising that laundry represents one of the hotel's largest expenses and that an **OPL** must be properly managed if the hotel is to control this important cost.

A hotel's laundry needs will vary with its size and product offerings. A smaller (less than 100 rooms) extended stay or limited service property may find that it does less than 500,000 pounds of laundry per year. At this volume level, the hotel may use linens that are wrinkle free, and thus the OPL may consist simply of washers and dryers. Larger, full-service hotels with extensive food and beverage volume will find their OPL needs expanded due

---

HOTEL TERMINOLOGY AT WORK

Linen: A generic term for the guest room sheets and pillowcases and tablecloths and napkins washed and dried in the laundry area.

Terry: A generic term for the bath towels, hand towels, and washcloths washed and dried in the laundry area.

OPL: Short for "On Premise Laundry."

■

---

to the tablecloths and napkins that are processed in the laundry, as well as the increased linen and terry needs when there are more guest rooms. In hotels of this type, additional laundry equipment required to press and fold the laundered items may be required. In very large hotels, the OPL may process well over 1 million pounds of laundry per year and will likely employ dozens of staff, as well as maintain a substantial number of pieces of high-volume laundry-related equipment. Regardless of its size, the OPL and its effective operation is a major responsibility of the housekeeping department and the executive housekeeper.

THE INTERNET AT WORK

Large volume OPLs require large volume equipment. One of the hotel industry's leading suppliers of large volume laundry equipment is the Pellerin Milnor Corporation. To review some features of their "tunnel washer" designed specifically for OPLs that process laundry for hotels of 500 rooms or more, go to:

http://www.milnor.com/CBWwhatis.asp?model=36.

STAFFING THE DEPARTMENT

Traditionally the housekeeping department has been one of the most difficult to staff in the entire hotel. This is true because of the large number of housekeeping staff needed, the difficulty of the work, and, unfortunately in some cases, a wage structure that does not ensure that the best potential employees seek careers in this department of the hotel. Properly approached and fairly treated, however, this department can be well staffed with stabile, highly professional employees who add tremendously to the success of the hotel.

Executive Housekeeper

Those G.M.s whose staff includes a highly trained, motivated, professional executive housekeeper have a tremendous advantage over those who do not. An effective executive housekeeper is not only a valuable member of the

EOC, he or she is also an effective administrator, department motivator, and team player.

At many hotels, the executive housekeeper is an individual that worked his or her way up from an entry-level housekeeping position. In other hotels, the executive housekeeper may not have held any entry-level housekeeping positions. In either case, the skills required to be an effective executive housekeeper, like the skills needed by all managers, include those related to planning, organizing, directing, and controlling the activities of the department. The executive housekeeper's commitment to cleanliness must be unquestioned, their standards must be impeccable, their dedication to their area unflinching, and their human resources–related skills well above average for managers. It is only with these characteristics that the hotel's executive housekeeper will provide the departmental leadership required in today's competitive hotel environment.

THE INTERNET AT WORK

Those G.M.s that want to stay abreast of the rapidly changing health, safety, and technology issues involved in housekeeping would do well to join, or encourage the hotel's executive housekeeper to join, the International Executive Housekeeper's Association (IEHA). With over 6,000 members, the IEHA offers educational programs and certification and publishes a monthly magazine. To view their Web site, go to:

http://www.ieha.org/

Room Inspectors

In most hotels, one or more individuals hold the position of **inspector (inspectress)** in the Housekeeping department. These individuals report directly to the executive housekeeper.

HOTEL TERMINOLOGY AT WORK

Inspector (Inspectress): The individual(s) responsible for physically checking the room status of guest rooms, as well as other tasks as assigned by the executive housekeeper.
∎

Regardless of a hotel's size, it is important that someone verify the actual readiness of guest rooms before they are listed in the PMS as clean, vacant, and available to sell. This job falls to the inspectors. An inspector is the individual who physically enters, and checks, a guest room after it has been cleaned to determine whether any areas that should have been cleaned have been missed or if there are other defects in the room that require further attention.

In a large hotel, there may be several inspectors working at the same time. The primary responsibility of the inspector is to assess the quality of room cleanliness, but more important, it is to point out deficiencies to **room attendants**, get those deficiencies corrected, and report revisions to room status to the executive housekeeper or the front desk.

HOTEL TERMINOLOGY AT WORK

Room Attendants: The individual(s) responsible for cleaning guest rooms. Sometimes referred to as "housekeepers."

Also sometimes called "maids," by guests, but this term is not used by members of an enlightened management team.

■

An effective inspector is one with high standards of cleanliness and the ability to point out deficiencies in rooms reportedly cleaned by room attendants in a way that motivates those attendants to do their very best work without appearing overly critical of sincere efforts to do a good job. Inspectors are truly a hotel guest's best friend because it is this sharp-eyed individual who will enforce the standards of cleanliness established by the executive housekeeper and the G.M.

Each executive housekeeper creates an appropriate inspection checklist for guest rooms based upon the contents and the physical layout of the room. As a G.M., you should review this checklist on a regular basis with the executive housekeeper and compare it with your own checklist (presented later in this chapter). The executive housekeeper's checklist should be revised as needed to ensure appropriate attention is paid to potential problem areas that may be frequently overlooked by room attendants (who may have their own room checklists), as well as to institute additional staff training when consistent deficiencies become apparent.

Room Attendants

Highly skilled and motivated room attendants are incredibly vital to a hotel's success. Yet in many hotels recruiting, selecting, and retaining a sufficient number of room attendants to adequately clean the number of rooms sold is a difficult process. Hotels operate shorthanded in the room attendant area and room cleanliness suffers, managers end up cleaning rooms, and inspectors sometimes are not able to inspect because they are too busy helping clean rooms to do their jobs properly. When G.M.s inquire about the difficulty of retaining quality room attendants and the problems that result, they are often told things like:

• We don't pay enough to attract the right people.
• The work is too hard.

- There is a labor shortage.
- Today's workers simply won't work.
- Workers don't care about doing a good job anymore.

As a G.M., it is sometimes tempting to accept statements such as these as truth. You should not because they are simply not true. It is interesting to note that the best executive housekeepers and G.M.s not only have adequate numbers of room attendants on staff, but they also have a waiting list of room attendants from other area hotels hoping to join their staff. Strategies designed to properly recruit and retain room attendants must be put in place if your hotel is to be perceived as the employer of choice for your area's best room attendants.

Properly cleaning guest rooms can be hard, physically demanding work, and it is also true that entry-level room attendant wages are often among the lowest in the hotel. Despite these facts, it is possible and critical that you build a highly motivated, dedicated staff of room attendants. The approaches to doing so are many but, at minimum, include:

- Treating room attendants with the respect they deserve at all times
- Ensuring that room attendants are supervised only by excellent supervisors
- Maintaining room cleaning assignment policies that are perceived as fair by the room attendants
- Providing excellent, ongoing training
- Providing a realistic career ladder for room attendants
- Enforcing housekeeping department policies that affect room attendants consistently and without favoritism
- Ensuring room attendant safety through training and appropriate hotel policies
- Providing benefit packages that are competitive for the area
- Paying fair wages

Many hotel G.M.s disagree about what it means to pay "fair wages" to room attendants. Some hotels simply pay room attendants an hourly wage. Others add, to the hourly wage, incentives for extra effort, such as meeting established quality levels. Still others pay room attendants a designated dollar amount for each room cleaned. Regardless of the payment approach used, it is important that room attendants are treated fairly. Some hoteliers treat room attendants as if they are not important. Hotels that do this will, inevitably, lose their best room attendants to those hotels that demonstrate real concern for these crucial staff members.

Additional Housekeeping Staff

In addition to the executive housekeeper, inspectors, and room attendants required, the housekeeping department will, depending on its size, employ one or more house persons for the cleaning of public spaces and records or payroll clerks who serve as administrative assistants to the executive house-keeper and OPL workers.

The OPL in a hotel is often a hot and physically demanding place to work. Employees needed in this area include those actually moving linen and terry from the guest rooms to the laundry area, those loading and unloading washers and dryers, and those responsible for folding and storing the cleaned items, as well as transporting them back to carts or storage areas located near guest rooms. In some special cases, seamstresses are even employed to care for uniforms and guest clothes.

Some G.M.s believe that these OPL jobs are easily filled. In fact, maintaining quality workers in the OPL is as difficult as any other area of the hotel. The same employee approaches previously identified as assisting in the recruitment and retention of room attendants, however, will be extremely helpful in maintaining a quality OPL staff. A hotel's financial investment in linen, terry, and the machines used to clean and maintain them is significant. Without a quality OPL workforce, and proper supervision, the value of these investments can quickly be reduced.

MANAGING HOUSEKEEPING

The executive housekeeper in a hotel must be a very knowledgeable individual. He or she must know about personnel administration, budgeting, laundry sanitation, fabrics and uniforms, room cleaning chemicals and routines, and, of course, be guest-service oriented. Only the G.M. has more responsibility for the cleanliness of the facility. Because this is true, the partnership between the executive housekeeper and the G.M. must be a strong one, based upon mutual respect for the ability of each.

MANAGERS AT WORK

"The problem, I'm afraid, is just age," Jenna Walbert, the executive housekeeper, said to J.D. Ojisima, the hotel G.M.

"What do you mean?" replied J.D.

"Well, Penny Cooper has worked as a housekeeper in this hotel for over twenty-five years and has always done an excellent job. But recently she has had more trouble doing her share of the rooms in the time allowed. Some of the other room attendants are complaining because, after they finish their own rooms, they are assigned to help Penny finish hers."

"She tries," continued Jenna, "but as you know, room cleaning is a tough, physically demanding job. Lots of the younger room attendants are challenged until they get the hang of things. In Penny's case, she knows what to do; it's just that she can't do it as fast as she used to. The room inspectors are finding the quality of her work acceptable; it's the quantity that is the problem. I wonder how long we can keep her?"

Assume you are J.D. What would you advise Jenna to do about Penny's situation? What would you advise her to say to the other room attendants? What human resources–related issues and laws might come into play in this situation?

Managers in the housekeeping department must be among a hotel's most talented. The challenges of keeping a hotel clean are many, and the special issues faced by the executive housekeeper and the housekeeping staff requires that, as a G.M., you are especially encouraging and supportive of this area. Some of the unique issues faced by the department include those related to safety, employee scheduling, and inventory management.

Safety

Employee accident rates in the housekeeping department are generally among the highest in the hotel. There are two reasons this is true. The first is the simple fact that the housekeeping department is usually one of the hotel's largest in terms of the number of workers it employs. The second reason, however, relates to the physical nature of the job. Housekeepers often work with equipment and supplies that must be very carefully handled if accidents are to be avoided. Proper housekeeping equipment and supplies help improve productivity and safety as well as reduce accidents and therefore should be provided to each housekeeper and placed, where appropriate, on every **room attendant cart**. If they are not, unnecessary on-the-job injuries will result and medical-related costs for the hotel will increase.

HOTEL TERMINOLOGY AT WORK

Room Attendant Cart: A wheeled cart that contains all of the items needed to properly and safely clean and restock a guest room.

■

Training the housekeeping staff properly is just as important as providing them with the tools to do their jobs. Employee training is always a crucial aspect of the executive housekeeper's job, and safety training is the most essential type that can be provided. As the hotel's G.M., it is part of your job to ensure that this department has the necessary equipment, supplies, and training programs in place to minimize threats to worker safety.

Equipment and Supplies

Housekeeper's jobs often require the use of machines such as vacuum cleaners, washers, dryers, high-capacity linen ironing and folding apparatus, and other equipment. Workers should never be allowed to operate these until they are fully trained. Supplies used by housekeepers in the completion of their daily tasks include powerful cleaners and chemicals that, properly used, make these worker's jobs easier. Improperly used, the same chemicals and cleaners can cause nausea, skin rashes, vomiting, blindness, and even death. A good rule to follow is that all housekeeping employees handle only those pieces of machinery and supplies that they have been properly and thoroughly trained to handle.

Training

All hotel employees require both general and department-specific training, and the housekeeping department is no exception. In housekeeping, particular areas of training concern include:

- Chemical handling
- Cleaning procedures
- Correct lifting techniques
- Properly entering guest rooms
- Contending with guest rooms containing:
  - Firearms
  - Uncaged pets/animals
  - Individuals perceived to be threatening
  - Guests who are ill/unconscious

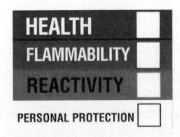

Chemical warning labels should include information related to a product's health, flammability, reactivity, and personal protection.

- Drugs and drug paraphernalia
- Blood and potential **blood-borne pathogens**
- Guest service
- Guest room security
- Lost and found procedures

HOTEL TERMINOLOGY AT WORK

Blood-Borne Pathogen: Any microorganism or virus, carried by blood, that can cause a disease.

■

Of the special training required by housekeeping staff, blood-borne pathogens and lost and found training deserve the special attention of the G.M.

Blood-borne pathogen training is especially important for room attendants because they can readily come into contact with body fluids and/or bloody sheets, towels, or tissues as they clean guest rooms. If employees are not trained in the proper procedures for such situations, they could become infected. In addition, needles from intravenous drug users or those with medical conditions requiring the use of hypodermic needles can result in threats to the safety of room attendants. Human immundeficiency virus (HIV) is a serious disease spread by blood-borne pathogens. This and other health threats must be addressed through proper training, and it is the responsibility of the executive housekeeper and G.M. to see that such training takes place.

Executive housekeepers should provide room attendants with required safety equipment, including those related to blood borne pathogens.

THE INTERNET AT WORK

The federal government is very involved in the development of standards, education, and training materials for workers who could be exposed to blood-borne pathogens. To view a Web site devoted exclusively to this topic, go to:

www.osha-slc.gov/SLTC/bloodbornepathogens/index.html.

THE INTERNET AT WORK

Because housekeepers often come from a variety of backgrounds, language barriers in the housekeeping department can make training difficult. To view an innovative, dialogue-free video training program for room attendants developed for the Educational Institute of the American Hotel and Lodging Association (E.I.), with the vison and support of then Executive Director E. Ray Swan, and now marketed extensively by them, go to:

http://www.ei-ahla.org/ei1/product_display2.asp.

Employee Scheduling

Properly scheduling employees in the housekeeping department requires skill on the part of the manager creating the schedule and, often, flexibility on the part of the staff. Depending on the size and occupancy rate of the hotel, it is not unusual to find housekeeping staff working at any time of the day or night. Public space cleaners may find that late night or early morning hours are best for completing their work, and laundry workers, to complete the number of loads needed to support the hotel's occupancy levels, may also work very late or early.

Room attendants' work schedules are generally less flexible with regard to when they can work. That is, guests in stay-over rooms will expect that their rooms be cleaned between the time they leave and the time they are reasonably likely to return to their room after their day's activities. Therefore, unless the guest requests alternative times, stay-over rooms in the typical hotel should be cleaned between 8:00 A.M. and 3:00 P.M. In addition, the housekeeping staff must have cleaned enough rooms to allow front desk staff to check guests in at the check-in time established by the hotel. Thus, if check-in is at 3:00 P.M., sufficient rooms must be ready to allow guests to be assigned a room promptly upon their 3:00 P.M. arrival. If this is not done, and if arriving guests are told by front desk staff, *"Your room is not ready yet, Housekeeping is working on cleaning rooms now!"* guest dissatisfaction will likely result.

The number of room attendants that should be scheduled on any given day depends on several factors, including the size of the guest rooms, amenities in the rooms, the number of rooms to be cleaned, and the amount, if any, of **deep cleaning**, taking place.

HOTEL TERMINOLOGY AT WORK

Deep Cleaning: The intensive cleaning of a guest room, typically including the thorough cleaning of items such as drapes, lamp shades, carpets, furniture, walls, and the like.

Regularly scheduled deep cleaning of guest rooms is one mark of an effective housekeeping department.

■

Larger guests rooms take more time to properly clean than smaller ones, and rooms with special amenities such as refrigerators, microwaves, stoves, and dining areas require more attendant time than those without these features.

The actual number of rooms to be cleaned is the variable that is most critical to effective scheduling, and it is important to realize that this number is subject to normal, but rapid, fluctuation. Assume, for example, that an executive housekeeper wishes to inform employees one week ahead of time about that week's work schedule. That is, if Monday were the first day of the month, the executive housekeeper would like to post, on that day, the room attendant work schedule for the week of the 8th through the 15th. Based upon the room sales forecast provided by the G.M. or front office manager, the executive housekeeper determines the proper number of room attendants needed, and then posts the schedule. If, however, on the 5th of that same month the sales department makes a large (75 rooms per night) but last minute sale to guests arriving on the 7th and staying through the 10th, the number of room attendants needed will vary greatly from the original schedule. Alternatively, if significant numbers of guest reservation cancellations occur, the number of room attendants originally scheduled may be too great. This can be the case when inclement weather, airport closings, or other unusual events cause major disruptions in typical travel patterns.

Some inexperienced executive housekeepers, in an attempt to firmly quantify the number of workers needed on a given day, rely exclusively on a **minutes per room** target to establish the room attendants' schedule.

HOTEL TERMINOLOGY AT WORK

Minutes per Room: The average number of minutes required to clean a guest room. Determined by the following computation:

$$\frac{\text{Total number of minutes worked by room attendants}}{\text{Total number of guest rooms cleaned}} = \text{Minutes per room}$$

■

For example, if the number of minutes typically required per room in a hotel is 30, and if it is estimated that 200 rooms are to be sold, the two-step formula used to compute the number of room attendant's hours that should be scheduled would be:

$$30 \text{ minutes per room} \times 200 \text{ rooms} = 6,000 \text{ minutes}$$

$$\frac{6,000 \text{ minutes}}{60 \text{ minutes per hour}} = 100 \text{ hours of room attendant time}$$

The actual number of room attendants scheduled would depend on the number of full- and part-time housekeepers placed on the schedule.

Experienced housekeepers rely both on rooms per minute computations *and* knowledge of the guests themselves to determine the actual number of room attendant hours that should be scheduled on a given day. For example, executive housekeepers know it takes more minutes to clean a room in which the guest has checked out than one in which the guest is a stay-over. As a result, when the percentage of guest rooms that are stay-overs increases, the number of room attendant minutes (and, therefore, total hours) required to clean those rooms declines. Likewise, when a room has multiple occupants, it is more likely to require additional cleaning time than does a room housing only a single guest. With experience, executive housekeepers and G.M.s can agree upon a formula that uses both minutes per room and the unique characteristics of the hotel's guests and sales patterns to determine achievable productivity levels and thus scheduling levels for room attendants.

Inventory Management

The housekeeping department maintains a large number of products used in the cleaning and servicing of rooms. The following partial list gives some indication of the number of inventory items that must be maintained by the executive housekeeper:

Sheets (all sizes)
Pillowcases
Bedspreads
Bath towels
Hand towels
Washcloths
Soaps
Shampoos
Conditioners
Sewing kits
Glass cleaners

Furniture polish
Acid-based cleaners
Glassware
Cups
Coffee/coffee filters
In-room literature
Telephone books
Pens
Paper pads

If too many units of any item are kept in storage, the hotel may have committed money to housekeeping inventory levels that could be better put to use elsewhere in the hotel. Alternatively, if too few items are kept on hand, housekeepers may not have the products they need to properly clean and service rooms. Therefore, the executive housekeeper must know how much of each item is in use, in storage, and/or on order. Purchasing and receiving replacements for some items such as custom bedspreads, drapes, or logo items may take weeks or even months. Because that is true, an actual monthly count of all significant housekeeping supplies is strongly recommended and, as a G.M., these counts should be submitted to you to ensure that they have in fact been taken.

A second value of monthly inventories is that they allow the executive housekeeper to compute monthly **product usage reports**.

HOTEL TERMINOLOGY AT WORK

Product Usage Report: A report detailing the amount of an inventoried item used by a hotel in a specified time period (i.e., week, month, quarter, year).

■

Figure 7.2 is an example of a monthly product usage report for king-size bedsheets. It is completed using actual product counts taken at the beginning

FIGURE 7.2   Waldo Hotel Product Usage Report

Department: Housekeeping	Item: King-size Sheets
Prepared By:	Date:
For Period:	to

Count on: January 1		850 units
	Plus	
Purchased in month		144 units
Total in service		994 units
	Less	
Count on: February 1		877 units
Total Monthly Usage		**117**

of each month by the housekeeping staff. Note that this format can be used to compute product usage in any department and for any product in the hotel, as well as for any housekeeping product.

When determining the count of products in housekeeping, it is important to remember to count the entire product on hand, whether it is in use, in storage, or in reserve. In the example of king-size bedsheets, to accurately determine the total number of these actually on hand, physical counts would need to be taken in:

- Guest rooms
- Room attendant carts
- Soiled linen areas (including washers and dryers)
- Clean linen storage areas
- New product (unopened) product storage areas

Note that in Figure 7.2, 117 bedsheets were "used" in the month. This may mean the sheets were taken out of service because they were too badly stained to continue using, that the sheets had become torn or frayed beyond use, or that they were stolen. Regardless of the reason, if the physical count of the king-size bed sheets is accurate, management knows the number and can easily compute the cost of king-size sheets taken out of service in January. The executive housekeeper, assisted by the housekeeping staff, should compute monthly usage rates on all significant housekeeping items.

Lost and Found

Often, guests either intentionally or accidentally leave valuable items in their rooms when they check out. As a result, the housekeeping department must have specific, written lost and found procedures in place.

Sometimes it is hard to know what to do with property whose ownership is unknown. In most states, the law makes a distinction between three types of property whose ownership is in doubt. Each of the three types of unclaimed property requires that your housekeeping staff respond differently. The three property types are:

- *Mislaid property:* The owner has unintentionally left the item(s) behind.
- *Lost property:* The owner has unintentionally left the item(s) behind, then forgotten them.
- *Abandoned property:* The owner has intentionally left the item(s) behind.

The law requires that hotels safeguard mislaid property until the rightful owner returns. For example, a laptop computer left in a guest room is to be protected by the hotel until its owner returns. To throw or give the computer away on the same day it was discovered in the room would be illegal. In fact, if the hotel were to give it away to someone other than its rightful owner, the hotel itself would be responsible to the actual owner for the value of the computer. As the G.M., you should make sure a policy is in place requiring that employees discovering mislaid property turn it over to their supervisor.

In the case of a laptop computer, it is highly likely that the guest, upon discovering that the computer has been mislaid, will contact the hotel to arrange for the computer's return. If that does not happen in a reasonable amount of time (in most states sixty to ninety days) the mislaid property would now, from a legal perspective, be considered lost property (property that the owner has forgotten).

A hotel must hold lost property until the rightful owner returns to claim it. Also, in many states, the item's finder must make a good faith effort to return the lost item to its owner. For example, if a leather jacket is left in a guest room, the hotel, upon discovering the owner's name and telephone number sewn into the jacket's lining, must attempt to reach the jacket's owner. As with mislaid property, employees who find lost property in the course of their work should be required to give the property to their employer.

The length of time a hotel must hold lost property depends on the value of the property. The greater the value, the more reasonable it is to hold it for an extended period of time. The G.M. should, in conjunction with the executive housekeeper, establish the length of time mislaid and lost property should be held before the hotel disposes it of. In most cases, ninety days is a reasonable time to hold items found in a hotel.

In the case of abandoned property, the owner has no intention of returning to retrieve the item(s). Interestingly, the law does not require a hotel to attempt to find an abandoned property's owner. It is also true that the majority of guest items left in hotel rooms fall into this category. Magazines, worn-out clothing, personal toiletry items such as combs and razors, and a variety of grocery items are often abandoned.

It can be difficult for a hotel manager to know when an item has been abandoned rather than misplaced or lost. Therefore, when in doubt, property left behind in a room or found in a lobby area should be treated as either mislaid or lost. After it is held for a reasonable period of time, the hotel should dispose of the property. Some hotels give such items to local charities; others give the items to the hotel employee that found them.

Regardless of the hotel's abandoned property policy, it is the job of the executive housekeeper to have a written lost and found procedure in place that protects guest property until it is, in fact, declared abandoned. In those hotels with designated safety and security departments, the head of that department may develop this policy and may even be responsible for the security of any misplaced, lost, or abandonded items.

In all cases, preprinted forms for keeping information related to lost and found items are readily available from a variety of business forms sources and can be useful. Regardless of the form(s) used, the executive housekeeper should, to protect the hotel, have a written record of:

- The date the item was found
- A description of the item
- Location where the item was found (room number, if applicable)
- Name of the finder
- Supervisor who received the item

When returned to the rightful owner, or disposed of, the written record should include:

- The date the item was returned to the owner
- Owner's name/address/telephone number
- Housekeeping manager returning the item
- Method of return (mail, in person, etc.)
- Date the property was declared to be abandoned
- Name of hotel employee receiving the abandoned property

THE INTERNET AT WORK

There are a variety of companies that sell complete "Lost and Found" documentation packages that include forms and log books.

The American Hotel Registry company is a full-service hotel products supplier. To view this innovative company's lost and found (and other) product offerings, go to:

http://www.americanhotel.com/.

FACILITY CARE AND CLEANING

While it is beyond the scope of this book to detail the specific how-to's of public space cleaning, guest room cleaning, and laundry operations, it is important that G.M.s know what to look for when inspecting these areas. G.M.s often see and work in the public spaces of the hotel in the course of their daily activities, and, therefore, it is common for G.M.s to identify public space areas that need further attention from housekeeping to maintain desired cleanliness standards.

What is less common is for the G.M., working with the executive housekeeper, to participate in consistent, physical guest room and laundry room inspections. G.M.s simply must inspect these areas on a regular (weekly) basis. It is only through this process that executive housekeepers and inspectors will have a good idea about the cleanliness standards that the G.M. expects to be in place. Also, it is often the G.M. who knows, because of interaction with the front desk, those cleanliness deficiencies within guest rooms that have generated the most guest complaints.

Inspection sheets developed to identify areas to be evaluated during routine inspections of public spaces, guest bathroom and sleeping room areas, and the laundry are a good idea. They focus attention on every area affecting guest satisfaction. Of course, the actual property inspection sheets used by a hotel must be built upon the specific needs and characteristics of that hotel. Inspection checklists, however, can provide an excellent starting point for the inspection process and are presented next in this chapter.

Public Space Cleaning

A consistent theme in this chapter is the importance of guestroom cleanliness because it is very critical to the long-term success of the hotel. Public spaces, however, are equally important because they form the basis for a guest's initial impression of the property. It is essential, therefore, that goals for all public space areas include excellent appearance and impeccable cleanliness. Each hotel will have its own requirements for public space cleaning based on its size and product offerings. Figure 7.3 is an inspection checklist designed to help the G.M. (and managers on duty) examine some public spaces common to many hotels. It should be modified to reflect the needs of the hotel using it.

Guest Room Cleaning

Effective guestroom cleaning is the heart of the housekeeping department, as well as the entire hotel. In most hotels, this activity, more than any other, will determine the long-term success or failure of the property. It must be done extremely well. A motivated executive housekeeper and well-trained staff are required, but so, too, is the interest of the G.M. Routine inspections that identify areas for improvement and reinforce good practices are a tremendous help in keeping the housekeeping department operating at its best. Too often, G.M.s seek to evaluate the effectiveness of their housekeeping departments only through the computation of labor, cleaning, or guest supplies **costs per occupied room**.

It is wrong to think that lower costs per occupied room or fewer minutes spent cleaning each room is always "better." In fact, spending too few dollars or too few minutes cleaning each guest room is as bad, or worse, than spending too many dollars or minutes. The proper approach for a G.M. is to inspect guest rooms and then determine whether the hotel is maximizing the effectiveness of the housekeeping department. If it is not, additional staff

FIGURE 7.3   Sample Public Space Inspection Sheet

G.M.'s Public Space Inspection				
Date: _____	Inspection assisted by: _____			
Item/Area	**Outstanding**	**Acceptable**	**Unacceptable**	**Comments**
Lobby/Front Desk				
Entrance door/glass clean	✓	✓	✓	
Ashtrays clean	✓	✓	✓	
Front desk counter area clean	✓	✓	✓	
Drapes/window treatments clean	✓	✓	✓	
Decorative pieces dust-free	✓	✓	✓	
Carpets, floors clean	✓	✓	✓	
Furniture straight/clean	✓	✓	✓	
Pictures straight/dusted	✓	✓	✓	
Lobby telephones clean	✓	✓	✓	
Ceiling/wall vents clean	✓	✓	✓	
Pool/ Spa/ Exercise Areas				
Wet terry collected	✓	✓	✓	
Terry supplies adequate/ properly placed	✓	✓	✓	
Carpet unspotted/clean	✓	✓	✓	
Floors clean	✓	✓	✓	
Windows/ledges clean	✓	✓	✓	
Exercise equipment clean	✓	✓	✓	
Wall coverings clean	✓	✓	✓	
Public rest rooms clean	✓	✓	✓	
Air vents dusted	✓	✓	✓	
Safety equipment clean/in place	✓	✓	✓	
Administrative Areas				
Lightbulbs/lamps clean and functioning	✓	✓	✓	
Telephones clean	✓	✓	✓	
Carpet unspotted	✓	✓	✓	
Windows clean	✓	✓	✓	
Upholstered furniture clean	✓	✓	✓	
Furniture/desks dusted	✓	✓	✓	
Waste containers clean/ in place	✓	✓	✓	
Pictures, wall hangings straight/dusted	✓	✓	✓	
Air vents dusted	✓	✓	✓	
Wall coverings clean	✓	✓	✓	

HOTEL TERMINOLOGY AT WORK

Cost per Occupied Room: Total costs incurred for an item or area, divided by the number of rooms occupied in the hotel for the time period examined.

For example, in a hotel that spent $7,000 on room attendant wages in a week that the hotel sold, 1,000 rooms, the cost per occupied room for room attendants would be computed as

$$\frac{\$\,7,000 \text{ room attendant cost}}{1,000 \text{ rooms sold}} = \$\,7 \text{ room attendant cost per occupied room}$$

■

training in procedures or staff additions or replacements may be required, and the G.M. should implement these changes.

Sleeping Area

The sleeping area of a guestroom is typically the first part seen by the guest when entering the room. It must be absolutely clean. Figure 7.4 is an example of an inspection sheet a G.M. could use to inspect the sleeping area of a guest room. The actual inspection sheet used would be tailored specifically for the hotel inspected.

Bathroom Area

The bathroom area of a guest room is one that is very closely inspected by guests for cleanliness. Inadequate cleaning of this area by the housekeeping staff will inevitably result in guest dissatisfaction and complaints. Like the sleeping area of the guest room, the bathroom area must be absolutely clean. Figure 7.5 is an example of an inspection sheet a G.M. would use to inspect the bathroom area of a guest room. The actual inspection sheet used would be tailored specifically for the hotel inspected.

LAUNDRY

When most people think of a laundry, they think of clothes washers and dryers. In an OPL, the process is more complex, involves more equipment, and actually begins not in the laundry area but in the guest rooms, pool area, dining rooms, and meeting spaces. It is in these areas that room attendants will collect the dirty linen and terry that must be cleaned by the OPL. Operating an effective OPL is a multistep process that includes:

- Collecting
- Sorting/repairing
- Washing

FIGURE 7.4   Sample Guest room Sleeping Area Inspection Sheet

G.M.'s Guestroom Sleeping Area Inspection				
Date: _____ Inspection assisted by: _____				
Room Number: _____				
Item/Area	**Outstanding**	**Acceptable**	**Unacceptable**	**Comments**
All lightbulbs functioning	✓	✓	✓	
Lamps clean/functioning	✓	✓	✓	
Carpet unspotted	✓	✓	✓	
Drapes/cords/hooks in place	✓	✓	✓	
Outside windows/ledges clean	✓	✓	✓	
Bedspread clean	✓	✓	✓	
Pillows in good condition	✓	✓	✓	
Pictures straight/dusted	✓	✓	✓	
Air vents dusted	✓	✓	✓	
Mirrors clean	✓	✓	✓	
TV clean/dusted	✓	✓	✓	
Counters/furniture dusted	✓	✓	✓	
Guest amenities (iron/boards, etc.) in place	✓	✓	✓	
Guest literature in place	✓	✓	✓	
Telephone clean	✓	✓	✓	
Telephone handset clean	✓	✓	✓	
Night stand clean	✓	✓	✓	
Furniture dusted	✓	✓	✓	
Closet doors clean	✓	✓	✓	
Closet shelf clean	✓	✓	✓	
Proper number/type hangers	✓	✓	✓	
Laundry bags in place	✓	✓	✓	
Extra pillows/blankets in place	✓	✓	✓	
Refrigerators/microwaves clean	✓	✓	✓	
Dresser top clean	✓	✓	✓	
Dresser drawers clean	✓	✓	✓	
Area under bed or bed box clean	✓	✓	✓	
Coffeepot clean	✓	✓	✓	
Coffee items stocked	✓	✓	✓	
Waste basket in place	✓	✓	✓	
Logo items in place	✓	✓	✓	
Inside of corridor door clean	✓	✓	✓	
Print material posted on door	✓	✓	✓	
Evacuation sign in place	✓	✓	✓	
Do Not Disturb sign in place	✓	✓	✓	

FIGURE 7.4   *(Continued)*

Other	✓	✓	✓	
Other	✓	✓	✓	
Other	✓	✓	✓	
Other	✓	✓	✓	
Other	✓	✓	✓	

- Drying
- Finishing/folding
- Storing
- Delivering

Collecting

Room attendants collect dirty linen from guest room sleeping areas, and dirty terry products from guestroom bath areas, spa areas, and pools. In the guest rooms, room attendants strip beds and place dirty linens directly into laundry bags attached to their cleaning carts. When full, these laundry bags are either hand carried or carted to the OPL. Dirty linen and terry should never be used as rags to actually clean a guest room because doing so could damage these items. In some cases, laundry is presorted in the guest room before it ever reaches the OPL. This is the case when linen or terry is blood-stained and must be placed separately into a **biohazard waste bag** to help OPL workers avoid unneeded exposure to blood-borne pathogens. Bags of this type should be placed on every housekeeping cart, and room attendants should be required to use them.

HOTEL TERMINOLOGY AT WORK

Biohazard Waste Bag: A specially marked plastic bag used in hotels. Laundry items that are blood or bodily fluid stained and thus need special handling in the OPL are placed into these bags for transporting to the OPL.

■

The food service department will generate tablecloths and napkins that must be cleaned, and, in larger hotels, employee uniforms may be processed in the OPL. As a result, the executive housekeeper must have efficient methods in place to collect these items from their various locations and deliver them to the OPL.

FIGURE 7.5 Sample Guestroom Bath Area Inspection Sheet

G.M.'s Guestroom Bath Area Inspection				
Date: _____ Inspection assisted by: _____				
Room Number: _____				
Item/Area	**Outstanding**	**Acceptable**	**Unacceptable**	**Comments**
Lights working	✓	✓	✓	
Light fixtures clean	✓	✓	✓	
Fans working	✓	✓	✓	
Air vents clean	✓	✓	✓	
Telephone clean/functioning	✓	✓	✓	
Shower head clean	✓	✓	✓	
Bathtub fixtures clean	✓	✓	✓	
Tile and tub clean	✓	✓	✓	
Safety handles clean	✓	✓	✓	
Shower rod clean/all hooks in place	✓	✓	✓	
Shower curtain clean	✓	✓	✓	
Toilet free of water stains inside	✓	✓	✓	
Toilet exterior and back clean	✓	✓	✓	
Sink fixtures clean	✓	✓	✓	
Sink and stopper clean	✓	✓	✓	
Mirror(s) clean	✓	✓	✓	
Countertops clean	✓	✓	✓	
Hair dryers/other amenities clean	✓	✓	✓	
Floor tiles clean	✓	✓	✓	
Soaps/amenities in place	✓	✓	✓	
Electrical switches/outlets clean	✓	✓	✓	
Towel bars clean	✓	✓	✓	
Proper terry in place	✓	✓	✓	
Tissues in place	✓	✓	✓	
Toilet paper holder clean	✓	✓	✓	
Toilet paper in place	✓	✓	✓	
Wall coverings clean	✓	✓	✓	
Inside door clean	✓	✓	✓	
Locks polished/working	✓	✓	✓	
Exterior of bath door clean	✓	✓	✓	
Other	✓	✓	✓	
Other	✓	✓	✓	
Other	✓	✓	✓	
Other	✓	✓	✓	
Other	✓	✓	✓	

Sorting/Repairing

Once in the OPL, laundry is sorted both in terms of its fabric type and degree of staining. Different fibers and colors require different cleaning chemicals in the wash and, in many cases, different water temperatures or length of washing. Linens made of 100 percent cotton, for example, are washed in a different manner than an employee uniform that has a high polyester content. In a similar manner, a white terry washcloth used by a guest to polish black shoes would not be washed in the same load as the regular terry collected in the hotel because the heavily soiled cloth would need special prewash stain removal treatment to come completely clean, or, in some hotels, it may be laundered in a special washer designated only for heavily stained laundry. In some cases, a tear or rip in a cloth item can be repaired. When this is the case, these repairs are typically made prior to washing.

Washing

Washing is the most complex part of the laundering process. Despite the fact that today's laundry items are made from very durable fabrics and that washers can be preset to dispense cleaning products into the water at the right time and in the right amounts, the executive housekeeper must still teach laundry workers to monitor washing times, wash temperatures, chemicals, and **agitation** when actually washing laundry.

HOTEL TERMINOLOGY AT WORK

Agitation: Movement of the washing machine resulting in friction as fabrics rub against each other.

■

Length of washing time is a key factor because heavily stained items will need to be washed longer than lightly soiled items. Too long a washing cycle may waste time, water, energy, and chemicals. If the washing cycle selected is too short, the laundry may not come clean. Wash water temperature is important because some fabrics can handle exposure to very hot water while others cannot. Generally, hot water cleans better than cold, but fabrics washed in overly hot water for their fiber type can be damaged.

The chemicals used to wash items are determined by the type of fabric to be cleaned. Typically, chemicals used in the laundry area include detergents, bleaches, heavy stain removers, and fabric softeners. The amount of each that should be used is important both to maximize the cleanliness of the fabric washed and to control the cost of chemical usage. Lastly, agitation length and strength must be determined for each fabric type. Agitation is the friction of the laundry against itself during the wash cycle. With too little agitation (caused when the washer is packed too full), the items washed will not be cleaned properly. With excessive agitation, the fabrics washed will wear out too rapidly because of the damage done to the fibers in them.

The next step in the wash cycle is water extraction. By removing the most water possible, washed laundry is lighter and easier for laundry workers to handle. In addition, those items that require drying will dry more quickly. When the water has been extracted from the cleaned fabrics, the wash cycle is complete.

In today's modern washing machines, the time, temperature, chemical, and agitation levels can be preset. These must first be determined, however, by a knowledgeable executive housekeeper in consultation with the washing equipment manufacturer and the chemical supplier if wash results are to be maximized and if OPL costs are to be controlled to the greatest degree possible.

THE INTERNET AT WORK

The number of possible setting combinations on a commercial washer/water extractor is extremely large. To review one manufacturer's options utilizing microchip technology to preselect settings, go to:

http://www. speedqueen.com/opl/products/prod_micromaster_features.htm.

Drying

Some fabrics are not dried after they are washed. This is the case with some linens that are removed from the washer and then immediately ironed. Terry, however, as well as most other fabrics, must be properly dried before folding or ironing. Drying is simply a process of moving hot air (140–145 degrees F.) through the fabrics to vaporize and remove moisture. Fabrics that are dried must go through a cool-down period in the dryer before they are removed from it. This minimizes any damage done to the fabric and helps prevent wrinkling. Once removed from the dryer, however, these items should be immediately finished.

Finishing/Folding

The finishing of fabrics is important because washers and dryers should not produce more clean laundry than workers can readily process by ironing and/or folding it. Since more and more hotels use wrinkle-free fabrics, more finishing work today involves folding than it does ironing. Regardless of how much ironing is done, the space required for finishing laundry must be adequate. In larger hotels, the folding of linens and terry may be done by machine, while in smaller properties it is generally done by hand. The finishing area must be very clean so that the finishing process itself does not soil the laundry. Once the laundry has been finished, it moves to the storage area(s) of the housekeeping department.

Storing

The storage of linens is important because many fabrics must "rest" after washing and drying if the damage to them is to be minimized. Most laundry experts suggest a rest time of twenty-four hours for cleaned laundry. Therefore, the housekeeping department should strive to maintain **laundry par levels** of three times normal usage. For example, in a 350-room hotel, the G.M. should provide the laundry area with enough linen and terry to have:

- One set in the rooms
- One set in the laundry (being washed and dried)
- One set in storage

In this manner, the hotel will have adequate products for guests and enough reserve to permit the laundry to rest before being placed back into rooms.

HOTEL TERMINOLOGY AT WORK

Laundry Par Levels: The amount of laundry in use, in process, and in storage.

■

If laundry par levels are too high, storage may be difficult, and excessive dollars will have been committed to laundry inventories. If laundry par levels are too low, guests may not get the items they need, and room attendants may not be able to complete their work in a timely manner because they must wait for cleaned laundry products to finish cleaning rooms. In addition, fabrics may not be allowed to rest properly if they are needed immediately to make up rooms that must be sold.

Delivering

In smaller hotels, room attendants may go to laundry storage areas in the OPL to pick up linen and terry items. In larger properties, these items may be delivered to housekeeping storage areas located in various parts of the hotel. Because these linens and terry are frequent targets of theft by hotel guests and staff, the storage areas containing these items should be kept locked, and the housekeeping staff should inventory them on a regular basis.

Although G.M.s will not generally need to inspect laundry areas as often as guest rooms, a periodic inspection of these areas is a good idea both for

FIGURE 7.6 Sample Laundry Area Inspection Sheet

G.M.'S Laundry Area Inspection				
Date: _____	Inspection assisted by: _____			
Item/Area	**Outstanding**	**Acceptable**	**Unacceptable**	**Comments**
Bags and carts used to collect laundry are clean and in good condition	✓	✓	✓	
Area used to sort laundry is clean/uncluttered	✓	✓	✓	
Washers clean inside and out	✓	✓	✓	
Washing instruction signs easily read	✓	✓	✓	
Area around washers clean/free of clutter	✓	✓	✓	
Chemicals properly labeled and stored	✓	✓	✓	
Material Safety Data Sheets available	✓	✓	✓	
Dryer temperatures controlled, posted	✓	✓	✓	
Folding area adequate, clean of all debris	✓	✓	✓	
Storage areas clean, labeled	✓	✓	✓	
Other	✓	✓	✓	
Other	✓	✓	✓	
Other	✓	✓	✓	
Other	✓	✓	✓	
Other	✓	✓	✓	

the safety and morale of laundry workers. Figure 7.6 is an example of an inspection sheet that can be modified and used.

HOTEL TERMINOLOGY AT WORK GLOSSARY

The following terms were defined within this chapter. If you are not familiar with each of them, please review the segment of the chapter that contains the term.

Public space	Room Status	Terry
House person	Stay-over	OPL
Executive housekeeper	Linen	Inspector (inspectress)

Room attendants

Room attendant cart

Blood-borne pathogen

Deep cleaning

Minutes per room

Product usage report

Cost per occupied room

Biohazard waste bag

Agitation

Laundry par levels

ISSUES AT WORK

1. Some executive housekeepers like to allow room attendants to work independently, with only one attendant assigned to each room to be cleaned. Others prefer a system that teams two or more attendants together for each room assigned to be cleaned. Those preferring the single attendant system cite the tendency of the team system members to "talk" too much to each other and thus not complete their tasks in a timely manner. Those favoring teams point to the increased security provided by having two attendants work together, as well as the advantages of "two sets of eyes" on each room. Discuss at least three additional advantages and disadvantages of each approach. Which do you believe is the best for guests? For the hotel? For the hotel's room attendants? Which would you use in your hotel? Why?

2. Housekeeping is one of the departments in the hotel that must work every holiday because the hotel is open and often very busy. Assume you have a housekeeping department with twenty-four employees and your hotel recognizes New Year's Day, Memorial Day, Fourth of July, Labor Day, Thanksgiving, and Christmas as paid holidays. Also assume that at least one-quarter (six) of your housekeeping employees need to work each holiday to clean the stay-over rooms. Design a scheduling system that fairly assigns these holidays to the employees. What factors would you take into consideration in developing the system?

3. Some G.M.s feel that room attendants must be able to fluently speak the language of the majority of the hotel's guests to do their jobs effectively. Essentially, these G.M.s feel that guest contact is an important role of the room attendant's job and to converse with the guests they must have strong language skills. Other G.M.s feel that a command of the principal language used by guests is not required. How important do you feel it is that room attendants and public space cleaners can speak fluently to guests? List three challenges you may encounter if you make a command of the guest's language a job requirement for housekeepers, and three challenges you may face if you do not. How would you encourage your executive housekeeper to overcome these challenges?

4. Nearly all hotels experience "peak" and "slow" occupancy times. For those hotels catering to the business traveler, the Christmas holidays often represent slow periods. In some hotels, the result is a temporary layoff or

reduction in work hours of some hourly housekeeping employees. What specific strategies can you and your executive housekeeper employ to reduce the chances of negatively impacting the income of your lower paid housekeeping employees during these times? How important is it for you to do so? Why?

5. In some hotels, the G.M. allows, and even encourages, tipping of room attendants. This is typically done through the placement of a "tip envelope" in the room. Should there be tip envelopes in guest rooms? Defend your position in a memo that you, as a G.M., will direct to your housekeeping staff.

8
Food and Beverage

This Chapter at Work

A hotel is considered "full-service" when it provides guests with extensive food and beverage products and services. G.M.s at full service hotels are, routinely, paid better than their limited service G.M. counterparts. This is so because, in nearly every situation, operating a full-service hotel is more complex and requires greater G.M. skill than managing a limited-service hotel. If you seek to manage a full-service hotel, you will find the supervision of the food and beverage (F&B) department to be both challenging and rewarding. You will also find that operating a hotel F&B department is vastly more complex than simply operating a restaurant.

In this chapter you will explore some of the features that make hotel F&B so complex. This chapter is not designed to teach you how to operate an F&B department, but rather its focus is on features of F&B that are unique to hotel management. These unique features include room service, banquets and catering, and the service of alcoholic beverages.

Full-service hotels can offer guests a variety of F&B options. A large, 1000+ room property may operate several restaurants, each with its own theme or cuisine style, as well as several lounges or bars. A smaller, 150-room hotel may operate a single dining room and lounge, but both hotels will likely provide room service, a unique style of F&B that you, as a G.M., must understand well and that is explained in detail in this chapter. In addition to restaurants and room service, the F&B department is responsible for the hotel's banquet and catering efforts. In most full-service hotels, the revenue from these will far exceed that of its restaurants. Profits, too, are higher in the banquet and catering area. As a result, it is important for you to fully understand this major responsibility of the F&B department.

In the majority of full-service hotels, the sale of food is accompanied by the sale of alcoholic beverages. Hoteliers, like restaurateurs, have a professional responsibility, as well as a legal obligation, to serve alcohol responsibly. This special concern of full-service hotel G.M.s is important, and concludes the chapter's discussion of the F&B department.

In recent years, full-service hotels have, in many areas, lost market share to newer and smaller limited-service properties. There will continue, however, to be a need for full-service hotels. As a result, there will be a need for hotel G.M.s who understand F&B. This chapter begins a serious student's study of this essential and intricate area.

Chapter 8 Outline

OVERVIEW OF HOTEL FOOD AND BEVERAGE OPERATIONS

Similarities: Hotel and Restaurant Food Services

OVERVIEW OF HOTEL FOOD AND BEVERAGE OPERATIONS

Some hotel managers believe that managing a hotel with a food and beverage (F&B) department means that they are in the restaurant business. They are not. Operating a profitable hotel F&B department is much more complex than operating a profitable restaurant. In fact, some hotel F&B departments lose money for their hotels. As a result, it requires a G.M who understands how hotel F&B is similar, and dissimilar, to managing a traditional restaurant if the hotel is to maximize the effectiveness and profitability of this important department.

Hotel F&B is complicated for many reasons, one of which is the variety of offerings. A typical restaurant generally offers one type of cuisine and serves that offering for one or two meal periods per day (i.e., lunch and dinner). Consider popular priced or fine dining restaurants you are familiar with. Do these offer breakfast and are they open seven days per week? In most cases, the answer to these two questions is likely "no." While it is true that many quick service restaurants serve breakfast, lunch, and dinner and are open seven days a week, these restaurants also serve their food on self-serve trays or, more recently, "deliver" their food in paper bags to the driver's side window of the customer's car. A hotel restaurant, however, must offer, at least, breakfast, lunch, and dinner on a daily basis, and it must offer these meals in a manner that is in keeping with the quality of the hotel.

In addition, an effective F&B department may offer multiple, additional restaurant operations, twenty-four-hour room service, banquet operations, and a wide range of other food/beverage alternatives, including snack bars, coffee break, and meal services as part of convention/meeting operations, take-out and off-site catering, vending and alcoholic beverage outlets in lounges, show bars, and lobby areas. The individual responsible for the effective operation of the F&B department is the **food and beverage director.** The F&B director is a critical component in the management of the F&B department and hotel and, as a result, should report directly to the G.M.

HOTEL TERMINOLOGY AT WORK

Food and Beverage Director: The individual responsible for the operation of a hotel's F&B program(s).

■

Experienced G.M.s know that the F&B department will generate less revenue, more complaints, and fewer profits than will the rental of the hotel's guest rooms. In general, full-service hotels will get 60 to 75 percent of their revenue from the sale of guest rooms. The F&B department will generate 20 to 35 percent (the balance of hotel revenue is generated from telephone and other income). The F&B department, however, will not often, if ever, generate this same proportion of profit. In fact, even when they are run extremely well, some hotel F&B departments will be profitable whereas others will have a difficult time contributing any significant profits.

It is critical for full-service G.M.s to remember, however, that in many cases it is only because of the F&B department that guests come to the hotel. To fully understand this concept, consider a hotel's swimming pool. Swimming pools attract guests. A G.M. would not expect the swimming pool to make a "profit," yet the appearance of the pool, the temperature and clarity of the water, and the cleanliness of the pool area are all important to the hotel's profitability. In a similar manner, F&B products are important, regardless of their contribution to profitability. This is true because, some guests (especially those planning conventions, conferences, and other group meetings) select a hotel, in part, because of the quality and value of the F&B services that are offered. Second, other travelers and those within the community will choose to spend discretionary dining dollars in hotels with a reputation for providing quality dining services at fair prices. Third, hotels may generate their own profits from F&B services, but in all cases, F&B can strongly support the sale of other, more profitable hotel features.

Similarities: Hotel and Restaurant Food Services

There are many similarities between hotel and restaurant food services. Basic principles for planning, for managing financial resources, for sanitation and food preparation, and for controlling costs, among many other factors, are the same. G.M.s will find that they need not be experts in the culinary arts to understand how these concepts relate to food quality and departmental efficiency. Unfortunately, some G.M.s tend to avoid the F&B area because of its complexity. This is a mistake because, improperly managed, the F&B

department can be a tremendous drain on a hotel's financial resources. This area of the hotel deserves the very best of management attention, and it is up to the G.M. and F&B director to provide it.

Some aspects of managing F&B operations in hotels are identical to those needed to manage these services in other venues. In fact, the basics of managing a **commercial food service operation,** including those in hotels and restaurants, are almost identical to those used to successfully operate an **institutional (noncommercial) food service operation.** Commercial businesses such as hotels, which seek to make a profit from F&B operations (and from the sale of guest rooms), must address financial, human resources, product control, and marketing issues.

HOTEL TERMINOLOGY AT WORK

Commercial Food Service Operations: Food services offered in hotels and restaurants and other organizations whose primary purpose for existence involves generation of profits from the sale of food and beverage products.

■

HOTEL TERMINOLOGY AT WORK

Institutional (Noncommercial) Food Service Operations: Those food services provided by health care, educational, military, religious, and numerous other organizations whose primary reason for existence is *not* to generate a profit from the sale of food/beverage products but rather is to support another organizational purpose.

■

These same general concerns confront their institutional counterparts such as hospitals and schools that must offer food services to support their primary purpose (e.g., health care for hospitals and education for schools). In fact, for those G.M.s who believe the primary function of an F&B department is to promote hotel guest room and **function room** sales, the operation of this department is, philosophically, very much like that of an institutional (support) food service.

HOTEL TERMINOLOGY AT WORK

Function Room: Public space such as meeting rooms, conference areas, and ballrooms (which can frequently be subdivided into smaller spaces) that are available in the hotel for banquet, meeting, or other group rental purposes.

■

Operational Similarities

Hotel food service operations are similar to other food service operations in numerous ways, including:

- *Planning issues.* The need to begin planning by focusing on a menu, which is driven by the wants, needs, and/or preferences of those who will be served, is critical. The menu, in turn, impacts the design, facility layout, and equipment needs of the operation, as well as the labor required to produce and serve the menu items.

- *Financial concerns.* Economic issues are important regardless of whether the food service operation desires to generate profit (commercial operations) or to minimize expenses (noncommercial facilities). Operating budgets are required to estimate revenues and plan for expenses.

- *Emphasis on the consumer.* When an F&B department is well managed, guests return. The **repeat business** generated by a properly managed F&B department is important to the hotel's overall financial success.

HOTEL TERMINOLOGY AT WORK

Repeat Business: Revenues generated from guests returning to a commercial operation such as a hotel as a result of positive experiences on previous visits.

■

Consider, for example, the full-service hotel that successfully books a city's annual Chamber of Commerce holiday party. Attendees will represent significant business leaders in the community. If the event is a success, the attendees will experience the ten components of a successful F&B event. These are:

1. An attractive parking, reception area for arriving guests
2. An event that began at the scheduled time
3. A clean, well-lighted, and attractive function room
4. Properly attired staff
5. The proper number of attentive staff
6. Quality food, served at the proper temperature
7. Clean rest room facilities
8. A visibly present F&B manager or "contact person"
9. Fair pricing
10. Accurate billing

If these components are experienced, the local business leaders will likely come back to the hotel for future events, as well as for the purchase of more profitable guest rooms to serve their business needs. If one or more of the above components is not in place, not only will the Chamber of Commerce be less likely to rebook their event at the hotel, the attendees are less likely to use it also. G.M.s should regularly use the above ten components as a checklist to ensure quality F&B events and to work with the F&B director to take corrective action if needed.

• *Cost control procedures.* Food service operations of all types provide numerous cost control challenges when managing all available **resources.**

HOTEL TERMINOLOGY AT WORK

Resources: Something of value to the organization. Typical resources include money, labor, time, equipment, food/beverage products, supplies, and energy.

■

Consider, for example, the food and beverage products used in the hotel's F&B department. Standard operating procedures are needed to manage these products during each step in the control cycle, and as a G.M., you should ensure that procedures such as these are visibly in place. Figure 8.1 (Cycle of Food and Beverage Product Control) details examples of procedures that can be used to control food/beverage products.

The examples of applicable control concerns at each control step noted in Figure 8.1 represent just a few of the hundreds (or more!) of procedures that must be carefully thought out and, where appropriate, incorporated into operating procedures designed to effectively manage product costs. Each of these, as well as management concerns related to all other resources used in the F&B department, should be addressed in every type of food service operation, including hotels.

Personnel Requirement Similarities

The number of staff needed in an F&B department is dependent on the size of the hotel and the complexity of its F&B offerings. As a result, an F&B department can range from the less complicated (one dining room and limited function space) to the extremely complicated (multiple restaurants, bars, lounges, extensive function space, and associated F&B outlets).

THE INTERNET AT WORK

One of the largest and most extensive F&B programs in the United States is operated at the Opryland Hotel in Nashville, Tennessee. To view their F&B choices, go to:

http://www.gaylordopryland.com.

Just as quality restaurants depend on selecting and keeping trained F&B professionals, so, too, do those hotels that seek to do an excellent job operating their F&B departments. In addition to the F&B director, the F&B department is likely to employ:

FIGURE 8.1   Cycle of Food and Beverage Product Control

Control Step	Examples of Applicable Control Concerns
Purchasing	• Development of purchase specifications indicating quality requirements for all products to be purchased. (Beverages are often purchased by brand, and guest preferences must be known.) • Supplier selection, which assures that product prices and vendor service/information are optimized. • Purchasing correct quantities ranging from just-in-time (JIT; daily or more frequent) purchases to purchases for longer-term needs. • Use of practices to help reduce the possibilities of collusion between property and supplier staff. • Evaluation of manual and computerized aspects of the purchasing process.
Receiving	• Development of receiving procedures, including incoming product inspections, weighing and counting, and other tactics to ensure that the hotel "gets what it pays for." • Completion of necessary receiving reports, which address financial and security concerns.
Storing	• Effective use of an appropriate inventory system. • Control of product quality during storage. • Tactics to reduce theft while products are in storage. • Predetermined location of products within storage areas.
Issuing	• Product rotation concerns to assure that products in storage the longest are issued and used first. • Matching quantities of products issued with quantities of products needed/used. • Procedures to trigger purchase procedures as issuing depletes product inventories.
Prepreparation	• Mise-en-place (a French word meaning everything in its place), which results from accurate production planning to determine quantities of items to be prepared. • Careful prepreparation of food products to minimize food waste and to assure maximum nutrient retention.
Preparation	• Use of standardized recipes to control ingredient costs and preparation times and to better assure that the quality of food/beverage products produced meet the hotel's standards. • Use of portion control (e.g., scoops, scales, and ladles) to help assure that product costs and guest goals about value (price relative to quality) are attained. • Requirements for food safety (sanitation) and employee safety standards to reduce burns, slips, falls, and numerous other injuries that can occur from working in fast-paced, hot, and potentially dangerous conditions.

FIGURE 8.1 *(Continued)*

Serving	*(Note: Serving involves moving products [food and beverage] from production personnel [cooks and bartenders] to service personnel [food and beverage servers]).* • Timing of food delivery. • Portion control. • Revenue management concerns relating to items, which servers must order from production personnel versus those, that servers may obtain for themselves (e.g., soups, salads, beverages, and desserts).
Service	*(Note: Service involves moving products [food and beverage] from service personnel [food and beverage servers] to the guests.)* • Revenue control concerns. • Serving alcoholic beverages responsibly (beverage operations). • Sanitation and cleanliness. • Food and beverage server attentiveness.

HOTEL TERMINOLOGY AT WORK

Serving: The process of moving food and beverage products from production personnel (cooks and bartenders) to food and beverage servers who will serve them to guests.

■

HOTEL TERMINOLOGY AT WORK

Service: The process of moving food and beverage products from service staff to the guests.

■

- Culinarians: These individuals are highly trained in food preparation and kitchen management.

THE INTERNET AT WORK

The best culinarians are members of the American Culinary Federation. Their emphasis on training is very strong, and the group promotes professionalism among its members. To view their Web site, go to:

http://www.acfchefs.org.

- Restaurant and dining room managers: These individuals operate the "open to the public" restaurant facilities within the hotel.
- Catering managers: These individuals supervise the banquets, meetings, catering, and special events held at the hotel.

THE INTERNET AT WORK

The National Association of Catering Executives (NACE) is the professional association for those managers who specialize in catering. To view their Web site, go to:

http://www.nace.net/.

- Beverage managers and bartenders: These individuals manage and operate the hotel's alcoholic beverage outlets.

THE INTERNET AT WORK

Skilled bartenders are extremely valuable to a hotel. To view the Web site of this group's professional association, go to:

www.americanbartenders.org.

- Kitchen staff: These maintain the kitchen spaces, wash dishes, and assist the hotel's food production personnel.
- Service staff: These individuals actually serve the guests in the restaurants, bars, lounge, room service, and banquet areas of the hotel.

Hotel F&B managers seek, to a great degree, the same type of individuals as their restaurant counterparts. As can be seen, depending on its extensiveness, the F&B department can be very large. As a result, it can be costly to operate. In addition, it is one in which guest difficulties often arise.

Many observers believe that the vast majority of all problems in any hotel operation (including the F&B department!) are actually caused by managers. Sometimes this is true. As a G.M., it is part of your job to help the F&B (as well as all other) departments perform at their very best. From a staffing perspective, operating an effective F&B department consists of at least three mandatory steps. First, F&B staff must receive the necessary training to learn the knowledge and skills required to work according to standardized procedures. Second, managers must provide direction to employees by telling them about the wants, needs, and expectations of the guests being served. Third, managers must provide the necessary resources required to perform the work properly. As a G.M., if you experience repeated F&B-related difficulties, a review of the existence, or absence of, these three steps can help you pinpoint operation difficulties so they can be resolved quickly.

Differences: Hotel and Restaurant Food Services

The above section has suggested many similarities between F&B operations in lodging and restaurant properties in operations and personnel needs.

There are, however, significant differences between the F&B operation within the hotel and the operation of a restaurant. A restaurant seeks to financially support itself through sales. A properly managed hotel F&B program seeks to financially support the hotel through sales. The philosophic and practical differences between these two approaches are immense.

The service of food and beverages in the guest rooms provides an example of one way that hotel food service operations differ from their restaurant counterparts. Many full-service hotels offer "room service," the delivery of food to the guest's room. Significant planning by room service managers is required to determine how quality goals can be attained when food must be transported over long distances involving long time periods between plating and guest service. Imagine, for example, the challenges faced by a 500-room corporate traveler–oriented hotel if 100 guests have requested room service breakfast to be served to their rooms between 7:00 A.M. and 7:30 A.M.! There are, sometimes, guest complaints about room service. Typically these involve cold and/or low-quality food—both of which usually result from timing problems as food moves from the kitchen to the guest room. Most restaurants do not face these same issues.

Of course, room service menus can be planned to incorporate these quality concerns. As well, careful communication between the guest placing the order, the employee taking the order, the production person(s) producing the order, and, of course, the room server delivering the order is required. If communication is not effective, the guest will be dissatisfied, and the hotel will suffer from guest perceptions that room service standards were low.

The extent of banquet operations is another way that hotel F&B operations differ from restaurants. Some hotels generate significant revenue from the sale of food and beverages at group functions. In fact, in nearly every full-service hotel, the main focus of the F&B department is on banquets and in-house catered events, and *not* on its open-to-the-public restaurants and bars. In banquets, as in room service, attention to detail is absolutely critical. There is a need for coordination between departments as marketing/sales personnel interact with the guests and communicate their needs to F&B production staff and as service personnel within the F&B department set up and service the group function. In large hotels with staff members designated to service conventions and large meetings, another communication and coordination challenge occurs, as representatives from this area must also interact with the guests and staff members within the hotel to make the group function successful.

Well-planned and executed banquets are very profitable. It is for this reason that the G.M. should evaluate the quality of these events so frequently. This can be done by inspecting such events with the F&B director before the event begins, reviewing guest comments regarding the functions, and discussing problems and solutions with the F&B director and his or her staff of professionals.

Banquets, apart from their own profitability, are important because, when they are held, guests and potential guests will experience what the hotel can offer. This provides opportunities for repeat business in the sale of guest rooms, public dining alternatives, and future banquet events. There are many things that hotels can do to set their banquet events apart from their competitors. Utilizing a variety of service styles, serving food that is of the proper quality, and paying attention to the many details that address guest preferences and needs are among these.

Unlike most restaurants, a hotel F&B department is responsible for fulfilling guest requests for **audiovisual (AV) equipment.** Increasingly, the requests guests make for AV equipment requires that these items be sophisticated and, of course, always kept in good working order.

HOTEL TERMINOLOGY AT WORK

Audiovisual (AV) Equipment: Those items including DVD players, laptops, LCD projectors, microphones, sound systems, flip charts, overhead projectors, slide projectors, TVs, and VCRs that are used to communicate information to meeting attendees during their meetings.

■

In addition to room service, an emphasis on banquets, and AV equipment, there are other fundamental differences between hotel F&B and restaurants about which hotel G.M.s should be aware. One of the most important relates to profitability.

Profitability Differences

Profitability relates to the extent to which the revenues generated by an F&B operation exceed assigned expenses.

HOTEL TERMINOLOGY AT WORK

Profitability: Revenue − Expenses = Profit.

The G.M.'s assignment of specific revenues and expenses to a given department will, in great measure, dictate profit levels in that department.

■

The amount of profit generated by a traditional restaurant is relatively easy to calculate. All revenue is generated from the sale of food and/or beverage products in the restaurant. As well, all **expenses** normally will be clearly identified in the accounting records of the establishment.

HOTEL TERMINOLOGY AT WORK

Expenses: The amount of money spent to generate revenues.

■

By contrast, the process of assigning revenues and expenses applicable to the F&B department in a hotel is more difficult. Consider, for example, a holiday weekend package plan that includes one night's stay, dinner, and breakfast and is sold to guests for one price. How should the revenue generated from the guests be split between room revenue and the F&B department? Consider also expenses. How much (if any) of the salary paid to the hotel's G.M. and controller, along with other expenses such as utilities, landscaping, and marketing, be allocated between departments (including F&B) within the hotel?

It can then be difficult to compare the profitability of a restaurant with that of its F&B counterpart in a lodging property. With this as a caution, let's review Figure 8.2 (Profitability of Food and Beverage Operations in Hotels and Restaurants). Although the financial data provided are from the most current and reputable sources, the issue of assigning expenses noted earlier does make generalization about the data more difficult.

Upon initial review, it appears that F&B operations in hotels are much more profitable than their restaurant counterparts (29.2% departmental income [profit] in hotels versus only 6% in restaurants). Note, first, however, that hotels generate almost 18 percent of their revenue from two sources (room rental and other income) not available to restaurants. "Other income" includes charges for audio/video rental, and **service charges** initially collected for subsequent distribution to employees as additional compensation.

FIGURE 8.2 Profitability of Food and Beverage Operations in Hotels and Restaurants[1]

	Hotel F&B		Restaurant F&B	
Net Revenue	100.0%		100.0%	
Cost of F/B Sales	(28.4%)		(34.0%)	
Gross Profit (from combined sales)		71.6%		66.0%
Room Rentals	7.1%		—	
Other Income	10.8%		—	
Gross Profit/Other Income		89.5%		66.0%
Departmental Expenses				
Salaries/Wages	36.8%		31.0%	
Payroll Taxes/Benefits	12.2%		4.0%	
	49.0%		35.0%	
Other Allocated Expenses	11.3%		25.0%[2]	
Total Expenses		(60.3%)		(60.0%)
Departmental Income (Profit)		29.2%		6.0%[3]

[1]Lodging data from *Trends in the Hotel Industry,* USA edition—2000. PKF Consulting, 2000. Restaurant data from *Restaurant Industry Operations Report.* National Restaurant Association and Deloitte & Touche, 2000. (All data are from 1999.)
[2]Includes occupancy costs of 6 percent.
[3]Before income taxes.

HOTEL TERMINOLOGY AT WORK

Service Charges: A mandatory amount added to a guest's bill for services performed by a hotel staff member(s).

■

Without these revenue sources, the hotel's departmental income (profit) from F&B operations would be 11.3 percent (29.2% − 17.9%). Additionally, there are a wide range of expenses directly incurred by the restaurant, which are not allocated to the F&B operation in the hotel. For example, restaurant occupancy costs are 6 percent of revenue; these expenses include leasehold payments, interest on leasehold improvements, real estate taxes, and others, that are not allocated (assigned) to the F&B department in the typical hotel. If all costs were accurately allocated between the F&B and other hotel departments, it is likely that the hotel's "bottom line" profit from food/beverage sales would be, at best, equal to and perhaps less than that generated by a restaurant.

In an effort to contrast the profit levels of hotel food/beverage departments and restaurants, it is also possible to study just the two highest costs: those for products and labor. These two costs (costs of food/beverage sales and payroll [salaries/wages and payroll taxes/benefits]) are relatively easy to identify and are likely to be (relatively) carefully allocated to the F&B department within the hotel. Note, in Figure 8.2, for example, that the cost of food/beverage sales in a restaurant is 5.6 percent higher in the restaurant than in the hotel (34.0% − 28.4%). This may be because a hotel can more effectively control food/beverage costs; it may also be because many hotels charge more for their meals. (Many hotels position their F&B operations to be "special occasion" dining outlets for the local community and do not, therefore, compete with lower guest check average properties in the marketplace.)

Payroll costs are much higher in the hotel F&B department than in the restaurant (49% of revenue versus 35% of revenue). Wages for a specific position within a community are likely to be similar, so salary/wage rates are not likely to account for this significant difference. There are several factors that likely influence the higher payroll costs in hotel F&B operations. For example, restaurants are open at the times when the majority of guests want to be served. (For example, a dinner steak house is not likely to be open for breakfast; a breakfast diner will not be open for an evening meal.) By contrast, a hotel restaurant will most likely remain open for three meal periods daily to serve hotel guests. In extreme cases, for example, a hotel restaurant may remain open for several hours after the "normal" dinner business subsides to provide food services for guests arriving on late night airline flights. As a second example, restaurants may close for a day or more during weather emergencies; hotel restaurants will likely remain open to provide food services to its guests. **Fixed labor costs** (the labor hours and dollars associated with keeping a restaurant open for minimum business) can, therefore, be excessive as business slows in a hotel F&B operation, and yet it remains open.

HOTEL TERMINOLOGY AT WORK

Fixed Labor Costs: The minimum number of labor hours and associated labor costs that are required to operate the food service operation whenever it is open regardless of the number, if any, of guests that are served.

■

Marketing-Related Differences

As already noted, the rental of guest rooms in a hotel generate higher levels of income (profit) than does the sale of food and beverage products. For this reason, many hotels emphasize guest room rentals—not restaurant operations—in their marketing efforts. There are, of course, some lodging properties in some communities that compete with freestanding restaurants and aggressively advertise in local news media to retain (or, hopefully, increase) their market share. Other hotels recognize that guests select a hotel, in part, because of the dining alternatives within it. With these exceptions, it is generally true that restaurants more effectively market their food/beverage products and services than do hotel F&B operations.

Several other marketing-related differences between F&B operations in hotels and restaurants can be noted. These include:

- *Location within the community.* Successful restaurant operators know that location is a very significant factor in operating success. They want to place their restaurant properties in locations that are easily accessible to potential guests. By contrast, hotels are placed in locations that are, hopefully, most accessible to those guests desiring lodging accommodations. These sites may differ from those convenient to guests desiring food and beverage services. Historically, F&B operations in large urban hotels were often seen as the preferred dining location in the community. Holiday and special occasion events were held at these facilities. Over time, in part because of an increase in upscale restaurant alternatives, the position of hotel restaurants in the dining hierarchy of many communities was reduced. In addition, as popular national chains spread across the country, hotels were seen as less attractive purveyors of "quality" dining experiences.

  To pursue local banquet and catering business, hotels routinely advertise, participate in local community service-based organizations, and otherwise promote their F&B alternatives to the community. The property's location is, however, still a factor in guest preference decisions. Consider, for example, a hotel in a downtown location attracting weekday business travelers. On weekends, when this business is absent, it may be hard to attract diners from the distant suburbs who are a potential market for the hotel's restaurant.

- *Location within a hotel.* Ideally, hotels catering to local ("walk-in") guests have outdoor signage and outdoor entrances to attract local diners. Sometimes, however, this is not possible. Immediate parking, building access, and the remote location of a restaurant within a hotel can be major obstacles to overcome, which hinder the popularity of a hotel's restaurant operation.

- *Menu.* Often a hotel restaurant is designed to cater to the traveling guests it desires to attract. It may need, for example, to offer an upscale menu or, perhaps, one in concert with a local theme, which may be of less interest to potential guests in the community.

Many of the differences between hotel and restaurant food services relate primarily to the fact that offering F&B services is not the primary business purpose of a hotel. (The sale of guest rooms is, of course, its primary objective.) Rather, food service is viewed as an amenity to attract guests and to provide food and beverage alternatives to increase the hotel's revenues from the base established by guest room rentals. To some extent, then, the role of the F&B department is, appropriately, secondary to that of those departments providing and servicing guest rooms. Experienced G.M.s understand this and resist the temptation (often advocated by managers in the F&B department) to endeavor to be "in the restaurant business."

In summary, there are two major, and many additional ways in which the hotel's F&B operations differ from those in restaurants. The two major areas of difference that a G.M. must understand are the availability of room service and the significant amount of business generated by banquet and convention services. These special dining services provide unique challenges to managers in a hotel's F&B departments and deserve additional attention.[1]

ROOM SERVICE OPERATIONS

Luxury and first-class hotels typically offer room service; many provide this amenity to guests 24/7 (24 hours per day, 7 days per week). Smaller full-service hotels generally will offer room service also, but on a more limited basis. Guests of all types utilize room service, ranging from the business traveler wanting a quick breakfast to small groups desiring a lunch while meeting in guest room suites, to couples desiring a romantic meal alone in the evening.

In large hotels, a room service manager with total responsibility for this service will be employed. In these operations, there may be a separate food

[1]Many books have been written about the field of quantity food production management and food service operations in sit-down dining operations. See, for example, Jack Ninemeier and David Hayes, *Restaurant Operations Management: Principles and Practices* (New York: Prentice-Hall, Incorporated), in production.

preparation area staffed by one or more cooks whose primary responsibilities involve preparation of room service orders. Likewise, room service orders from guests will be taken and delivered by, respectively, order takers and room service attendants whose primary responsibilities involve these tasks. In smaller properties, the F&B director may plan the room service menu, which is prepared by the same cook who produces restaurant meals. The meal would then be delivered to the guest room by a restaurant server according to the order written up by a server or dining room receptionist who serves as the order taker.

Profitability Concerns

Guests and others who look at room service menus may think, "With these high prices, hotels must make a lot of profit on room service." In fact, relatively few properties generate profits from room service.[2]

If room service is not profitable for the hotel, why then is it offered? First, it is a service to guests. Some may select properties on the basis of room service availability. Examples include those arriving on late airline flights, guests wanting food and beverage services for small business meetings in their guest rooms, or simply the individuals who wish to enjoy the luxury of "breakfast in bed." Also, hotel rating services such as American Automobile Association (AAA) and Mobil assign their highest ratings to properties that offer room service, as well as numerous other amenities.

Why does room service frequently lose money? One reason is that labor costs are very high. It can take a significant amount of time to transport food from the kitchen to guest room areas. Vertical (elevator) transportation required in high-rise hotels and travel to remote locations when rooms are located in cottages or condominium units in resort properties require time and experienced delivery staff who know the fastest way to guest room locations.

Expenses incurred for capital costs such as delivery carts and warming devices can be significant also. Likewise, if costs were assigned to the F&B department for elevators needed to transport room service items and for "staging" areas needed to store room service carts and to prepare them for deliveries and other associated room service costs, true F&B expenses would even be greater. Finally, items such as glasses, cups, flatware, and service ware increase room service costs still further. The need to return soiled room service items to kitchen areas often creates operating, as well as financial, problems. Even when quality food products are delivered quickly, and guest

[2]Recall difficulties with allocating expenses between departments and within the food and beverage department noted earlier. Without careful allocation, the financial status of one activity—restaurant, bar, room service, or banquets—will be difficult to accurately assess. It is unlikely that many hotels allocate costs other than direct food and labor costs to the room service profit center although costs for equipment, supplies, menus, utilities, and other costs may be significant.

satisfaction is high, dirty trays and dishes placed outside the room in hallways must be picked up and returned to the F&B department. Housekeeping personnel, maintenance and security staff, and even managers who encounter these items often notice but do not pick up and return these to the F&B area, thus necessitating even more F&B labor for pickup.

Some hotels utilize the room service department to provide F&B service in **hospitality suites** and for other group functions within a guest room.

HOTEL TERMINOLOGY AT WORK

Hospitality Suites: A guest room usually rented during conventions/conferences to provide complimentary food and/or beverages to invited guests.

■

For example, in convention properties, vendors and other exhibitors may invite current and prospective customers to visit hotel rooms for **hosted events** (such as complimentary food and beverages).

HOTEL TERMINOLOGY AT WORK

Hosted Events: Functions served by a hotel, which are complimentary to invited guests because costs are borne by the event's sponsor.

For example, a hosted bar may offer free beverages to guests of a wedding party, or a corporate sponsor may pay for a hosted reception with appetizers in a banquet room.

■

In hotels where this service is provided by room service rather than by banquet service the likelihood that room service is profitable on those specific events does increase. As a G.M., it is important to understand the challenges of room service offerings and determine the proper resources to give this essential, but less profitable, area of F&B.

Menu Planning Factors

Special concerns must be addressed when planning room service menus. First, as with any other food service alternative, quality is an important concern. Therefore, room service menus should offer only those products that can be transported relatively long distances from food preparation areas without decreases in quality. As distance increases, so does the time required to transport items. We have already noted that many guests perceive that room service prices are excessively high. They will certainly demand that food quality requirements be maintained to help justify the perceived high prices. Unfortunately, some popular items (e.g., omelets and french fries) are not ideal room service menu items because of the quality deterioration that occurs because these products are held at serving temperature for long periods of time as they are transported to guest rooms. It is relatively easy for you, as the G.M., to check food quality in a hotel restaurant or even in a banquet setting. Food and beverage items in these areas can (and should) be sampled. However, you are less likely to easily access the products served in room service. A proactive effort to solicit feedback from guests is critical to help assure that quality requirements are consistently attained.

Cross-selling on room service menus is one possible way to help improve F&B profitability. For example, a room service breakfast menu might indicate that the hotel's Sunday brunch in the dining room is very popular for guests staying through the weekend. An invitation on the room service breakfast menu to call about daily dinner specials available through room service or in the dining room can also be of interest to guests "thinking ahead" about evening plans.

HOTEL TERMINOLOGY AT WORK

Cross-selling: Messages designed to advertise the availability of other hotel services. For example, a dinner menu may provide information about the hotel's Sunday brunch.

■

Hotels in airports, urban, and other locations housing international guests may experience language barriers, another room service challenge. A guest who does not speak English and who is alone in a guest room with a menu written in English may have great difficulty in ordering. Alternatives such as pictures and menu item descriptions written in the languages most used by international guests visiting the specific hotel may be among the solutions. If there are minimum order charges, mandatory tipping policies, and/or other requirements for guest room orders, these should be clearly indicated on the menu and, perhaps, should also be stated by the order taker if applicable. Increasingly, hotels are using their in-room movie services to display room service menus in a variety of languages, as well as an opportunity for guests to evaluate the hotel (including F&B) from their own television screens using the TV's remote control.

THE INTERNET AT WORK

Pay-per-view (in-room) movie companies offer a variety of services to hotels, including those related to F&B. To view one such company's Web site, go to

www.oncommand.com

and review their F&B, as well as related product offerings.

Operating Issues

G.M.s must be assured that numerous room service operating issues are satisfactorily addressed within their property. For example, it is important that highly trained order takers be available regardless of whether this is a full-time position or only part of their responsibility. "Communication" problems occur all too frequently in room service. If complete orders are not taken, guest dissatisfaction is likely. The same types of questions asked in an à la carte restaurant must be asked by the room service order taker:

- How would you like your steak prepared?
- Would you like sour cream with your baked potato?
- Would you like tartar sauce with your fish fillet?
- Would you like a glass of wine to complete your dinner? (Tonight's special wines would go well with your entrée, and they are a great value.)

It is sometimes difficult to correct errors in any food service operation. However, an inaccurate order in the dining room can sometimes be quickly corrected. For example, catsup for french fries can be immediately retrieved from the kitchen or servers' station for guest service in the dining room. However, the catsup or other condiment omitted from the room service tray will require a relatively long and time-consuming trip back to the kitchen. Should the guest wait with lowered food quality as a result? Alternatively, should the guest consume the meal without the desired condiments? Either way, guest dissatisfaction will result, and the negative impressions that occur may carry over to other experiences within the hotel. At the same time, servers who must spend additional time on this re-work task will be unavailable to serve other guests. These guests, in turn, may become dissatisfied as the wait for their own room service order increases. A "minor" problem, then, can create a ripple effect that significantly impacts the guests' perceptions about the entire lodging experience.

Opportunities for upselling are also very useful for room service but, unfortunately, are often overlooked. The room service **guest check average** can be increased if guests are informed about items they may not have initially ordered because they didn't know or think about them (e.g., appetizers, cocktails, desserts, and à la carte entrée accompaniments).

HOTEL TERMINOLOGY AT WORK

Guest Check Average: The average amount spent by a guest in a room service or dining room order. The guest check average typically includes the food and alcoholic beverage sales.

Guest check average = total revenue ÷ total number of guests served.

■

If effective communication is very important between the guest ordering room service and the order taker who receives the order (and it is!), then communication between the room service food production staff and service staff is likewise critical. Room service orders may be handwritten or, increasingly more frequently, may be entered into a **point-of-sale (POS) terminal.** Orders can then be printed on hard copy tickets that are given to the room service cook(s). In this case, a copy is also given to the server when the order is transported to the guestroom. Alternatively, the POS system can be used to transmit orders to the cook(s) via a **remote printer.** Either way, it is important that any abbreviations (does "sp" stand for shrimp plate or seafood platter?) be clearly understood by both the order taker and food production personnel. It is also important for the room service attendant to carefully note that the items ordered are, in fact, the exact items that have been plated and placed on the cart for delivery.

HOTEL TERMINOLOGY AT WORK

Point-of-Sale (POS) Terminal: A computerized device that contains its own input and output components and, perhaps, some memory capacity but without a central processing unit.

HOTEL TERMINOLOGY AT WORK

Remote Printer: A unit in the kitchen preparation area that receives and prints orders entered through a point-of-sale terminal located in the dining room, room service order taker's workstation, or other area.

Touch screens in Food and Beverage operations increase speed and accuracy.

Technology has improved the accuracy of room service orders. For example, today's systems typically indicate the room number and the name of the guest registered in the room from which the order is placed. Using the guest's name is an effective selling and communication tactic, and it then becomes easy for the order taker to do this. Also, when the order is placed, information about the ability of the guest to charge a room service meal becomes available. For example, guests who pay cash for a room at time of check-in are usually not permitted to charge room service or other product/services purchases to their room. Likewise, as guests using a credit card near a preestablished credit limit, this information is also readily available when the room service area is interfaced with the property management system (PMS). It is important, however, that G.M.s enforce security precautions by not allowing the food and beverage department to print an unsecured document (which could threaten guest safety) that includes the guest's room number and name to appear on the same printed ticket.

Within-Room Service

From the perspective of guests, room service does not "end" when the order reaches the guest room. In fact, that is only the beginning. Room service attendants must be adequately trained in service procedures, including:

- Asking guests where the room service meal should be set up
- Explaining procedures for retrieval of room service items
- Presenting the guest check and securing payment
- Opening bottles of wine, if applicable
- Providing an attitude of genuine hospitality (as opposed to being rushed to return to the kitchen for another room service delivery)

G.M.s must be aware of how room service in their hotel can be maintained and improved. In some properties, a section relating to room service is included in a general guest rating form used to evaluate the entire property which may be left by housekeeping staff in all guest rooms. Alternately, a specific evaluation form provided when room service is delivered is used by some properties. The results of all guest feedback should be randomly requested from the F&B director and should be personally reviewed by the G.M. When results are favorable, affected personnel should be complimented. If challenges arise, the G.M. should work with affected staff to resolve guest service issues.

MANAGERS AT WORK

"Ya see, J.D., your problem is you have no 'Wow' factor," said Robert Fooley. "That's why you aren't packin 'em in like me and the Outback Steakhouse."

J.D. Ojisima, the hotel G.M., and David Berger, the hotel's F&B director, were having lunch with Robert Fooley, the owner of a successful Italian restaurant located near the hotel.

David had met Robert at a Chamber of Commerce meeting, invited him to lunch at Seville's, the hotel's main dining area, and asked the G.M. to join them because David knew Fooley's restaurant was one of J.D.'s favorites.

"If this were my place", continued Robert, "I'd put in an Italian menu, because that's popular with everyone. You could call it Gardino's or something Italian. Create some specialty items that are really good. Then advertise it all over the city. That's how you get business. And I'd close at breakfast. There's too little volume then anyway because everybody wants fast food in the morning. Drive-ups are too popular . . . ya know? Let me tell you, I know from experience, focus on what you do best and eliminate the rest. That's my motto, and it saves on labor costs!"

J.D. listened politely. "Interesting ideas, Bob," said J.D. "I'll discuss them with David after lunch."

If you were J.D., how would you react to Mr. Fooley's ideas? Why? What does the average restaurateur not understand about hotel food service? If you were J.D., and David left his employment at your hotel, would you hire Mr. Fooley as a replacement? Why or Why not?

BANQUET OPERATIONS

The ability to plan and deliver a wide variety of types and sizes of **banquet** events sold by a **catering** salesperson is an important factor that separates F&B departments in hotels from many of their counterparts in other segments of the hospitality industry.

HOTEL TERMINOLOGY AT WORK

Banquet: A food and/or beverage event held in a function room.

■

HOTEL TERMINOLOGY AT WORK

Catering: The process of selling and carrying out the details of a banquet event.

In a large hotel, there may be a separate catering department, or it may be a unit within the marketing and sales department. Often catering responsibilities are shared between the F&B and the sales and marketing departments.

■

The volume of banquet business helps determine whether banquet operations are the responsibility of food production and service staff or, alternatively, whether persons with specialized banquet duties are utilized. The hotel's sales and marketing staff will normally be responsible for generating banquet business in negotiating contracts and details for specific banquet events. (Chapter 10, Sales and Marketing discusses these activities in depth.) However, there is an old saying in the hotel business: "You are only as good as your last banquet." Repeat business generated from guests who have enjoyed previous banquets can be very helpful in "selling" future ones. By contrast, the negative **"word-of-mouth" advertising** created by dissatisfied banquet guests can significantly increase (and undo) the work of the sales and marketing staff. It is just as important to satisfy banquet guests as it is to please guests being served in the hotel's restaurants, bars, lounges, and in-room service.

HOTEL TERMINOLOGY AT WORK

Word-of-Mouth Advertising: Informal conversations between persons as they "discuss" their positive or negative experiences at a hotel.

■

Hotels that attract extensive convention and meeting business will have additional banquet needs. Large properties will likely have a separate convention services department whose personnel plan and coordinate all activities (including those that are F&B related) for the groups visiting the hotel. Planning a banquet for a group staying at the hotel is similar to planning a function for someone who is hosting an event for guests who are not staying at the hotel. There are, however, some differences, including:

- The need for numerous coffee and refreshment breaks for attendees during intermissions in business meetings
- The provision of hospitality suites and other functions within guest rooms
- The potential setup of receptions, breaks, and even dinner/buffet food services in public spaces within the hotel that may not normally used for these purposes

G.M.s of smaller hotels in which the F&B director administers the banquet function and their counterparts in larger properties with specialized banquet managers reporting to the F&B director have something in common: they must both know and understand how banquet functions "work," how they can be evaluated, and how the banquets provided can better meet the hotel's profitability and guest-related goals.

Profit Opportunities

Banquet events are generally more profitable than restaurant (dining room) operations in hotels for several reasons:

- Banquets are frequently used to celebrate special events. This provides the opportunity for menu items that are more expensive and, therefore, higher in **contribution margin**.

HOTEL TERMINOLOGY AT WORK

Contribution Margin: The amount that remains after the product (food) cost of a menu item is subtracted from its selling price.

■

- The number of meals to be served at a banquet is known in advance; in fact, there is a formal **guarantee**. It is, therefore, easier to schedule food production staff to reduce the "peaks and valleys" in labor that often occur during, respectively, busy and slow periods in dining room operations. Often some parts of a banquet's food production can be done several days prior to the event. There is also less likelihood of overproduction of food with subsequent waste because guest counts are known.

HOTEL TERMINOLOGY AT WORK

Guarantee: A contractual agreement about the number of meals to be provided at a banquet event. Typically, a guarantee must be made several days in advance of the event. At that time, the entity contracting with the hotel for the event agrees to pay for the larger of the actual number of guests served or the number of guests guaranteed.

■

- Banquet planners are frequently able to sell **hosted bars** or **cash bars**, which enable increased sales of alcoholic beverages to guests desiring them.

HOTEL TERMINOLOGY AT WORK

Hosted Bar: A beverage service alternative in which the host of a function pays for beverages during all or part of the banquet event; also called an "open" bar.

■

HOTEL TERMINOLOGY AT WORK

Cash Bars: A beverage service alternative where guests desiring beverages during a banquet function pay for them personally.

■

- Banquet service is performed within a relatively short time frame with known starting and ending times that make service labor planning easier. In addition, servers find working these events attractive because, in most cases, mandatory service charges result in significant increases in their income.
- Often charges for the actual function space in which the banquet is held will represent significant additions to food and beverage product sales. For example, a hotel's ballroom, on a Saturday night in December, may command a significant rental fee in addition to the meal(s) and beverages purchased, because of the increased demand for such space around the December holidays.

For these reasons, banquet business is very desirable, and G.M.s should assure that the property is receiving its reasonable portion of the market's available banquet business. It is a good idea to collect, review, and evaluate banquet revenue separately from other sources of revenue within F&B.

Menu Planning

Most of the factors involved in planning a menu for the hotel's restaurant(s) and other dining outlets are important when planning banquet menus. These include concerns about:

- Guest preferences
- The ability to consistently produce items of the desired quality
- The availability of ingredients required to produce the menu items
- Production/service staff with appropriate skills
- Equipment/layout/facility design issues
- Nutritional issues
- Sanitation concerns
- Peak volume production and operating concerns
- The ability to generate required profit levels at the selling prices charged

There are additional, special concerns applicable to planning banquet menus. For example, the menu planner must be confident that the items to be offered can be produced in the appropriate quantity at the appropriate level of quality and within the required time schedule. The old saying, "The guest (host) is always right," must be tempered when banquet menus are planned. "Cooked-to-order" steaks, for example, are not practical when 500 guests must be served in thirty minutes. The menu planner must recognize that the hotel, not the host, will likely be criticized if there is a failure to deliver according to anticipated standards. For example, consider an overzealous host desiring a flambéed entrée, tableside Caesar salad, and handmade pastries for hundreds of guests. These items are very labor-intensive, and a large amount of specialized service/equipment is needed. Personnel in the sales and marketing department are setting up a "no-win" situation for the hotel if they book this event when the hotel is not able to adequately execute it. If the hotel accepts the business and is unable to effectively deliver the promised banquet event, all or many of the guests may be upset. If the host cannot be "sold" on a more practical menu at the time the event is planned, future business may be lost because the hotel will not perform well. As a result, it is certainly in the hotel's best long-term interests to refuse banquet business that cannot be delivered according to quality standards.

Because of the potential complexity of banquet menus, many hotels offering banquets have preestablished banquet menus. Carefully developed to consider the hotel's production limitations and to incorporate the property's desired contribution margin, these menus are an excellent starting point for negotiations with prospective clients. Often these menus can be used without change, or relatively minor changes such as a substitution of a specific dessert or vegetable item can be made.

On other occasions a menu designed specifically for the host and his/her special event is needed or desired. A talented banquet planner working in close conjunction with the property's culinarians can develop a menu, that meets the guests' expectations and the hotel's financial requirements. By contrast, when there is not close cooperation between the sales and marketing department and food preparation personnel, concerns to generate short-term business (e.g., to meet revenue goals) may overshadow longer-term goals of consistently pleasing guests to generate repeat business. Alternatively, if F&B departments put excessive restrictions on sales personnel (e.g., by overly restricting what food items can be produced), sales revenue will suffer. G.M.s must continually monitor this relationship to assure that neither the sales and marketing nor the F&B department are operating in ways that are detrimental to the hotel's success.

Successful catering is a matter of paying attention to numerous details. To help in the planning process, most hotels utilize a customized **banquet event order (BEO)**. A sample BEO is shown in Figure 8.3. Properties doing extensive business in certain events, for example, weddings or bar mitzfahs, may have specialized BEOs for these occasions. Figure 8.4 shows a Sample Wedding Banquet Event Order Checklist. Banquet event orders can be very simple (all details might be included on a single BEO); alternatively, they can be much more extensive.

HOTEL TERMINOLOGY AT WORK

Banquet Event Order (BEO): A form used by the sales, catering, and food production areas to detail all requirements for a banquet. Information provided by the banquet client is summarized on the form, and it becomes the basis for the formal contract between the client and the hotel.

■

FIGURE 8.3 Sample Banquet Event Order (BEO)

EVENT DATE:	**BANQUET EVENT ORDER (BEO) #:**
Organization:	
Billing Address:	**Business Phone #:**
	Business Fax #:
Contact Name:	**Business E-Mail:**
Account Executive:	**Room Rental: $**
Guaranteed: ( ) persons	

BEVERAGES

- Full   • Limited
- Hosted bar   • Non-hosted bar
- With bartender   (   ) bars
- Cash bar   (   ) cashiers
- Premium   • Call   • House
( ) per drink   (   ) bar package
( ) hours of operation

Time: **Room:**

_____

Bar Opening/Closing Instructions:

Bar to close at: _____ A.M. / P.M.

Bar to reopen at: _____ A.M. / P.M.

Wine with Lunch / Dinner

_____ with entrée,

_____ servers

Time: Location:

_____

Additional Instructions:

_____

FOOD MENU
_____

_____ baseplates

_____ waterglasses

_____ butter rosettes on lemon leaves

- Introduction   • Invocation
- Nothing before meal _____

First Course Served at: _____ A.M. / P.M.

Meal Served at: _____ A.M. / P.M.

ROOM SET UP
_____

- Classroom   • Theater
- Other: _____

_____

- Diagram below

Need:

- Registration table / chairs: _____
- Wastebasket
- Easels
- Podium: • standing   • tabletop
- Pads / pencils / pens / mints
- Water / glasses

Diagram:

Linen:
- White   • Other:
_____

Skirting:
_____

Napkin:
- White   • Other:
_____

Music:
_____

AUDIO/VISUAL
- Microphone: _____
- Slide Projector - package: _____

FIGURE 8.3 *(Continued)*

BEVERAGE MENU	• Overhead Projector - package: _____
	• VHS / monitor / package: _____
	• Mixer, _____ channel • AV—cart
	• White board / markers • Screen
	• Flipchart/pads/tape/pens
	• LCD projector _____
	COAT CHECK
	• Hosted • Cash: _____
	( ) Attendant(s) ( ) Coat Racks
	PARKING
	• Hosted • Cash: $ _____
	• Fee per car: $ _____
	BILLING (METHOD OF PAYMENT)
	• Deposit received: $ _____

Service Styles

Banquet events can involve numerous ways to serve food and beverage products to guests. In fact, frequently more than one service style is used in a single event. Examples include:

- Butler service. appetizers and prepoured champagne, for example, can be passed by service personnel as they circulate among guests standing at a reception.
- Buffet service. Quantities of food are prearranged on a self-service line; guests pass through the line and help themselves. Sometimes items such as roast beef or ham are carved or omelets are prepared at the guests' request by production staff.
- Family style. Also called "English" style, platters and bowls of food are filled in the kitchen and are brought to the guests' tables. Guests help themselves to the food and pass platters to each other just as they might do at home.
- French service. This most elegant of service involves table-side preparation or finishing of food items such as tossing a Caesar salad or flambéing an entrée, beverage, or a sauce for dessert.
- Platter service. Also called "Russian" service, this style involves the plating of food in the kitchen onto large serving trays. These trays are then brought to the table where the server places individual portions on guest plates that have been preset.

FIGURE 8.4 Sample Wedding Banquet Event Order Checklist

REHEARSAL	Time: _____	Room: _____

- Skirted Table: _____
- Theater Style facing: _____
- Water Station: _____
- Coat Rack
- Juice—Charge to: • Client   • A&P
- Soft Drinks—Charge to: • Client   • A&P
- Coffee/Tea—Charge to: • Client   • A&P

PICTURES	Time: _____	Room: _____

- Finger Sandwiches: _____
- Assorted Juices: _____
- Assorted Soft Drinks: _____
- Cabaret Style Seating: _____
- Water Station: _____

PRE-CEREMONY RECEPTION	Time: _____	Room: _____

- Beverage:
- Food:
- Placecard Table
- Other Information:

CEREMONY	Time: _____	Room: _____

Doors Open: _____
Invitation Time: _____
Wedding Ceremony: _____
- Theater Style facing: _____
- Skirted Table: _____
- Placecard Table
- Linen:
- Skirt: _____
- Musicians   • Piano
- Florist   • Coat Check
- A/V—1 standing mike

RECEPTION	Time: _____	Room: _____

- Postceremony Beverage Service: _____

- Hosted Bar: _____

- Closing Instructions: _____

- Champagne Toast: _____

- Wine Toast with Dinner: _____

- After Dinner Beverage Service: _____

See reverse side for additional bar information

FIGURE 8.4 *(Continued)*

HORS D'OEUVRES

- Butler Style (see reverse)
- Buffet Style (see reverse)
- Station Style (see reverse)

RECEPTION INSTRUCTIONS

- Set _____ Bars: _____
- Seating: _____
- Votives: _____
- Hurricanes: _____
- Receiving line on _____ wall
- Piano on _____ wall
- See diagram for buffet station location(s):
Smoking: • Allowed   • Not-Allowed

DINNER/DANCE   Time: _____   Room: _____

ANNOUNCE/TOAST/DANCE INSTRUCTIONS

- Bride & Groom to be announced   • Bridal Dance
- Blessing Before the Meal
- Wedding Toast: _____
- Dance Sets: _____
- Cake Cutting: _____

WEDDING SPECIAL INSTRUCTIONS

- Base Plates
- Water Glasses

MENU

- Entrée (see reverse)
- Meal Substitutions (see reverse)

CAKE/SWEET/TABLE/COFFEE

- Wedding Cake   • Client's Own (see reverse)
- Sweet Table   • Client's Own (see reverse)
- Sweet Table Server(s): _____
- Wedding Coffee Service: _____ gallons

DINNER/DANCE INSTRUCTIONS

- Rounds per floor plan to be numbered: _____
- Table numbers provided by: • Client   • Hotel
- Dance Floor: _____
- Cake Table set per diagram
- Sweet Table set per diagram
- Extra Cabaret Tables set: _____
Smoking: • Allowed   • Not Allowed
- Linen: _____
- Skirting: _____
- Napkin Fold: _____
- Entertainment   • Florist
- Photographer   • Videographer

(continued)

FIGURE 8.4 *(Continued)*

- Parking Valet: $_____ /car
- Hosted   • Guests to handle own charges

- Consultant: _____

Hors D'oeuvres

Dinner

Wedding Cake

Coffee Service

Sweets Table

Other Information

- Plated service. Also called "American" service, this style involves the preportioning of food on plates that are then brought to the table for service to the guests.

Service styles can be a way to differentiate an elegant and often higher-priced banquet from less-elegant and lower-priced counterparts. For example, a Caesar salad might be prepared as a "demonstration" for those seated at a **head table,** and then preportioned servings of the Caesar salad could then be brought to the remaining guest tables for service.

HOTEL TERMINOLOGY AT WORK

Head Table: Special seating at a banquet reserved for guests of honor.

■

Alternatively, vegetables for a soup course could be brought to the guest table in a bowl (American service); service staff could pour broth from a sterling pitcher into each guest's bowl (modified Russian service). These are examples of simple ways to make a banquet appear more elegant.

Contrast these examples with a more traditional banquet service style where salads are preset when guests arrive, and the entrée with accompanying vegetables is served American-style after salad plates are removed. G.M.s should be aware of the impact that elegance can have on banquet events and should encourage catering and banquet staff to sell, produce, and deliver high-quality and creative banquet services that are within their capabilities. Guests will think, "Wow; what a great surprise," and the first steps toward repeat banquet business will have been taken.

Beverage Functions

Banquets often feature the service of alcoholic beverages. This can involve receptions before an event and wine service during the function, as well as continuing service of beverages during and after the meal service has concluded.

Keeping in mind that banquets often celebrate special occasions, there may be increased opportunities to offer **"call brand"** or **"premium brand" beverages** in addition to or in place of the property's **"house brand" beverages**.

HOTEL TERMINOLOGY AT WORK

Call Brand Beverages: High-priced and higher-quality alcoholic beverages that are sold by name (such as Johnny Walker Red Scotch or Bombay Gin) rather than sold by type of liquor (scotch or gin) only.

■

HOTEL TERMINOLOGY AT WORK

Premium Brand Beverages: The highest-priced and highest-quality beverages generally available. Examples include Johnny Walker Black Scotch and Bombay Sapphire Gin; these brands are sometimes referred to as "Super Call" brands.

■

HOTEL TERMINOLOGY AT WORK

House Brand Beverages: Alcoholic beverages that are sold by type (scotch, gin, etc.) rather than by brand name and that are served when a call brand beverage is not requested. Sometimes referred to as "Well" brands.

■

There are several common ways that beverages sold at banquet events can be charged for and priced. For example, beverages can be sold at a cash bar where guests desiring beverages pay for them personally. By contrast, some events may offer a "Host" (open) in which beverages are paid for by the host. Still other events have a combination cash and host bar where, for example, drink tickets are issued for complimentary drinks and the guest can then purchase additional beverages. Another variation of this arrangement occurs when drinks are complimentary for a specified time period (e.g., before dinner) and are then paid for on a cash basis by guests desiring them after that time (e.g., during and after dinner).

There are several ways that charges for beverages can be assessed. These include:

- *Individual drink price.* With this method, cash or a ticket sold for cash is collected when each drink is sold. Alternatively, with a host bar, a tally is made of the number of each type of drink sold, and the host is charged an agreed-upon price per drink basis at the end of the banquet event.
- *Bottle charge.* With this method, commonly used with a Host bar, beverages are charged for on a by-bottle basis for each bottle consumed/ opened. Normally, any bottle opened is charged at a full, agreed-upon rate. Guests are not allowed to take open bottles away from the hotel.
- *Per-person charge.* This method involves charging a specific price for beverages based upon attendance at the event. For example, the same number of guests used for the meal guarantee (discussed earlier) may be used as the basis for the per-person charge for alcoholic beverages. A deduction from the guarantee is made for minors attending the event who will not be permitted to consume alcoholic beverages.
- *Hourly charge.* This method involved charging the host a specific price for each hour of beverage service. Properties using this pricing method must first determine the number of guests to be present (the

food guarantee can be used with adjustment for guests who will not consume alcoholic beverages) along with the estimated number of drinks to be consumed per hour to arrive at a proper price.

Labor and Other Charges

Costs for labor required to produce and serve banquet food is normally included in the price charged for the banquet. However, sometimes, especially when the estimated number of guests is small and the variety of services requested is large, additional charges for the following types of labor are assessed:

- Bartenders and barbacks (bartender assistants)
- Beverage servers
- Beverage cashiers
- Security personnel
- Valet (parking) staff
- Coat room employees

Some hotels charge a **corkage fee** for alcoholic beverages brought into the property for use during the event.

HOTEL TERMINOLOGY AT WORK

Corkage Fee: A charge levied by a hotel when a guest brings a bottle (e.g., of a special wine) to the hotel for consumption at a banquet function or in the hotel's dining room.

■

Often misunderstood by banquet guests, hotels *do* incur fees when guests bring in prepurchased beverages. For example, the beverages must be served, and the bar and dining areas must be clean; glasses are subject to breakage and must be used and washed; stir sticks, cocktail napkins along with appropriate garnishes, if applicable, and, perhaps, other supplies will also still be necessary.

Hotels charge for meeting space and function room space. Most frequently, this occurs when the number of guests to be served, and, therefore, the amount of revenue to be generated, is small. These charges may be waived or reduced when a specified minimum amount of revenue will be generated by a banquet event.

Banquet Room Setup

In large hotels, banquet rooms may be setup by housekeeping (public space) staff. In other facilities, especially properties such as those that are being discussed in this text, this activity may be the responsibility of staff members within the F&B department. Regardless of the department responsible, the required activities are the same.

The function space assigned for a banquet is normally determined when the banquet event is booked and will be specified on the banquet event order. Unfortunately, hoteliers are sometimes confronted with ethical, financial, and/or legal issues when, for example, space originally committed to one event is reallocated for the retention of another event. This often occurs when larger (and more profitable) events are brought to the attention of the personnel in the sales and marketing department after commitments with groups hosting smaller events have been made.

Numerous details are involved in setting up a banquet room. Size is, obviously, determined by the number of guests expected although local fire safety codes and ordinances may also impact this decision. In addition to the number of guests, the type of dining room tables (round, rectangular, etc.) along with their size and the number of seats per table and required space for aisles, dance floors, band stands, other entertainment, head tables, and reception/buffet tables, if applicable, will impact requirements. Timing also becomes critical as when, for example, the same space is to be used for different functions throughout the same day or when a very large evening event precedes a very large breakfast event in the same space on the following day.

Banquet Contracts and Billing Policies

G.M.s must confirm that plans, procedures, and policies are in effect to help assure that there are "no surprises" as banquets are being planned and served. A banquet contract is an excellent tool in this effort. It is wise to have the hotel's standard banquet contract reviewed by an experienced attorney to assure that the best interests of the hotel are legally protected. Topics to be addressed by banquet contracts typically include:

- Guest contact information.
- Agreed-upon charges and prices.
- Specific function room assignment.
- Last date that function space will be held without a signed contract.
- Time by when a guarantee of attendance must be received.
- Cancellation policies, including an explanation of fees to be assessed if the banquet contract is canceled. For example, if the contract date is 180 or more days in advance of the event, the fee for canceling may be 50 percent of the anticipated billing; if the contract is voided from 61–179 days before the event, there may be a cancellation fee of 75 percent; a 100 percent fee may apply if a cancellation occurs 60 days or less from the date of the event.
- Guarantee reduction policy. If, for example, the final guarantee is less than a specified percentage of the initial guarantee, an additional charge (often equal to the meeting room charge) may be assessed.

- Billing. Information about the amount and schedule for guest payment is frequently included. Typically, the full remaining payment is due at the beginning or end of the event.

- Information about the service of alcoholic beverages (if applicable).

- Other information applicable to the specific event.

A sample copy of a banquet contract is shown in Figure 8.5.

Accurate and timely billing of banquets when they have been completed is critical. It is the final step in the catering process and must be handled well. As a hotel G.M., it is important to remember that a banquet that was properly executed will still become a negative experience for the client if the billing is not appropriately handled, as well as a negative experience for the hotel if the billings are not accurately made and monies collected in a timely manner. Working with the F&B department and the controller, the G.M. must assure that proper procedures are in place to achieve these goals.

MANAGERS AT WORK

The DOSM was very excited and couldn't wait to tell J.D. Ojisima, the hotel's G.M.

"You won't believe who I just talked to, J.D." said Michele Austin. "I just got off the phone with the meeting planner for the Accidental Insurance group. They want to book us for four days of meetings here. Basically, they want all the function space we have available, plus a large block of overnight rooms."

"That's great," replied J.D. "Nice job, Michele. You rock! I know your sales team has worked hard to get them to give us a try. This could be really big for us. I would estimate they buy 2,000 to 3,000 room nights per year, every year, in this city."

"That's not all," continued Michele "The big news for us now is that they want to have a gala reception and banquet at the end of their meeting to honor their new incoming president . . . who's best friend happens to be the governor! So the governor will be attending! I might be overstating it a little bit, J.D., but, basically, my contact said that for this event, money is no problem. They want it nice and they understand the costs."

"How many people at the Gala?" asked J.D.

"They want to hold a function for about 450 people with pre-dinner cocktails, ice carvings, live entertainment, a four-course meal, and just about anything else we want to suggest for them," replied Michele.

"Well," said J.D., "this is great, but it will also be a challenge! Everyone will really have to be on top of things that night. Let's go see the F&B director and give him the news."

"You have got to be kidding!" exclaimed the F&B director when he heard about the sale, "I requested that weekend off three months ago for an Alaskan cruise, and I already bought nonrefundable tickets for my wife and myself. You approved my request, J.D. Remember? Now what do we do?"

If you were J.D., would you ask the F&B director to cancel his vacation? What types of F&B related concerns might you have about the event as it has been described? How much of a role should J.D. play as this event is being planned? In which departments? How important is it that this event makes a profit for the hotel? What level of food production skill must J.D. have to be able to lead the department heads in the successful execution of this event? Why?

FIGURE 8.5   Sample Copy of a Banquet Contract

Date _____

Address

Dear, _____

It was a great pleasure speaking with you today, and I would like to thank you for selecting the new Waldo Hotel & Conference Center for your meeting location. We are extremely pleased to do business with you and your group. Based on our discussion the following arrangements have been made.

Schedule of Events:

Room Rental:
Your events will be held in our _____ room at a rate of $_____/day plus applicable tax. Meeting rooms are reserved on the basis of anticipated attendance. Setup style and times are required. The hotel reserves the right to change the room accommodations to best suit your needs and actual final guest count guarantee. A request to change the contracted set-up of a meeting room (once the room has been set) will result in a $____ reset fee.

Audiovisual:
Should you require any audiovisual equipment, please let me know as soon as possible as I may need to order the equipment in advance.

Food and Beverage:
The hotel must supply all food and beverage. Menu arrangements should be concluded at least 14 days prior to each function and a guarantee of the number of guests is needed 7 business days in advance, with final adjustment of guarantee at least 72 hours prior to your scheduled function date. The Waldo Hotel will allow for a variance of 5 percent over the number of guests guaranteed in preparation of food and table settings.

Billing:
All meeting room and food charges will be the responsibility of _____.

Form of Payment:
A deposit in full, valid credit card number, or completed direct bill application must be returned with this signed contract for guarantee purposes.

General Liability:
The Waldo Hotel reserves the right to inspect and control all functions. The Waldo Hotel is not responsible for loss or damages no matter how caused, to any samples, displays, properties, or personal effects, brought into the hotel.

FIGURE 8.5   *(Continued)*

Cancellation Policy:

This agreement may be canceled by either party, without penalty, or liability, in the event of Acts of Nature, government regulations, disaster, strikes, labor strife, civil disorder, construction activities, fire, flood, earthquake, or other emergency or event making it inadvisable, illegal, or impossible to provide facilities or to hold the function upon written notice to the other party specifying such cause.

Should it be necessary to cancel your function less than 14 business days prior to your arrival a cancellation fee of $ _____ will be billed to _____.

No Show Policy:

In the event of a no-show on your behalf, we will bill your company for the cancellation fee and any food, audiovisual, or setup fees that your group would have accrued.

The above outlined arrangements are currently being held on:

A tentative first-option basis for _____ days

To confirm these arrangements, please sign and return one copy of this Letter of Agreement by _____. After this date, we reserve the right to release the space you have requested.

Our entire hotel is looking forward to working with you and your group. If you have any questions, please feel free to call me on my direct line at (xxx) xxx-xxxxx.

Sincerely;

Signature

Agreed To:

By the Hotel   _____   By the Client   _____

Title   _____   Title   _____

Date   _____   Date   _____

ALCOHOLIC BEVERAGE SERVICE IN HOTELS

Those hotels that serve alcoholic beverages face even greater responsibilities in the operation of their F&B department than do hotels that do not have a license to serve these products. The consumption of alcoholic beverages is, of course, common with meal service, at premeal receptions, and in a hotel's bars and lounges. Alcohol has, for centuries, been enjoyed, in moderation, before, during, and after meals. Today, moderate (not excessive) consumption of alcohol is obligatory for those who serve and those who consume alcohol because, in part, of the expansion of **third-party liability (Dram shop)** legislation.

HOTEL TERMINOLOGY AT WORK

Third-Party Liability: A legal concept that holds the second party (the hotel serving alcohol) responsible for acts caused by the first party (the drinker), if the drinker subsequently causes harm to a third party (the victim of an accident).

This is often referred to as Dram shop liability.

■

Like restaurants, all hotels selling alcoholic beverages must comply with numerous state and local laws and regulations as a condition to do so. As a result, the need to develop procedures and to provide employee training designed to help assure the responsible service and consumption of alcoholic beverages is an integral part of the responsibility of the F&B director's job and is an area the G.M.s should personally monitor for compliance. Simply put, as the hotel's G.M., you must assure that every individual who will serve alcoholic beverages has been trained in proper service procedures and that this training is well documented. You owe this duty to your hotel owners, your franchise affiliation, your guests, your own staff, and of course, the community in which you live.

The effects of a highly publicized case in which your hotel illegally served alcohol to a guest that results in injury to another is reason enough for you to absolutely ensure that training in alcohol service is mandatory in your hotel. Fortunately, materials to conduct such training are readily available.

THE INTERNET AT WORK

One of the most popular alcohol server programs is TIPS (Training for Intervention Procedures). To view their Web site go to:

http://www.gettips.com.

In fact, many G.M.s require that every employee (even those not in F&B) be trained in some aspect of alcohol awareness. Such training is important for many reasons. Some examples include:

- Hotel personnel in non-F&B positions can be trained to recognize and respond to obvious and visible signs of guests' (and nonguests') intoxication and report these to management.
- Any employee may observe guests consuming alcohol within the hotel but in locations where such consumption is not allowed.
- Front desk, housekeeping, maintenance, and/or security staff may observe guests appearing to be underage bringing alcoholic beverages on to the property and into guest rooms.
- Employees of any department may observe guests who are legally able to consume alcohol supplying that alcohol to underage guests.

Controlling the sale of alcoholic beverages is difficult enough in dining rooms, bars, and lounges, but is even more difficult in banquet rooms where guests do not have a designated server, but rather go to a portable bar area and then return to their tables. In cases such as this, it can be difficult to monitor the number of drinks consumed by each guests. The service of alcoholic beverages during banquets is just another example of why managing a hotel F&B department is more difficult than managing a traditional restaurant or bar.

Recognizing the seriousness of the alcoholic beverage service issue, the Educational Institute of the American Hotel and Lodging Association has developed an extensive array of hotel-specific training materials designed to assist F&B directors and G.M.s in providing the proper alcohol related training for all hotel staff members. As the hotel's G.M., you must assure that this training occurs as part of your property's efforts to protect guests, the public, and the hotel itself from tragedies and lawsuits that can arise when this training is not provided.

THE INTERNET AT WORK

The Educational Institute of AH&LA continually improves "CARE," its alcohol-related training program. To download clips from their most recent CARE training videos; go to:

http://www.ei-ahla.org.

Under "Products" select; "E.I. Products."

Under "Choose by Product" select "CARE," then select "Care for Servers."

Finally, select "See sample video" to see a segment of Alcohol Server training videos.

Food and beverage service is the defining characteristic of full-service hotels. This department may be large or small, but it is always a complex and fascinating area of hotel administration. The serious G.M. is advised to become as knowledgeable as possible in the intricacies of F&B management to ensure that this important department contributes to, rather than detracts from, the hotel's guest service and financial performance goals.

HOTEL TERMINOLOGY AT WORK GLOSSARY

The following terms were defined within this chapter. If you are not familiar with each of them, please review the segment of the chapter that contains the term.

Food and beverage director
Commercial food service operation
Institutional (noncommercial) food service operation
Function room
Repeat business
Resources
Serving
Service
Audiovisual (AV) equipment
Profitability
Expenses

Service charges
Fixed labor costs
Hospitality suites
Hosted events
Cross-selling
Guest check average
Point-of-sale (POS) terminal
Remote printer
Banquet
Catering
"Word-of-mouth" advertising
Contribution margin

Guarantee
Hosted bars
Cash bars
Banquet event order (BEO)
Head table
Call brand beverages
Premium brand beverages
House brand beverages
Corkage fee
Third-party liability (Dram shop)

ISSUES AT WORK

1. This chapter has identified some similarities and differences between F&B operations in hotels and restaurants. If you were interested in a food and beverage management position, how would you decide the segment in which you would initially seek employment? What are some advantages and disadvantages to an F&B career in hotels versus restaurants?

2. How does the extent to which revenues and expenses are assigned (allocated) between hotel departments impact the ability of an F&B department to show a profit? As a G.M., what guidelines could you establish to help assure that all F&B expense allocation procedures are practical and fair?

3. One ongoing source of potential hotel conflict involves the F&B department and the sales and marketing department. As a future G.M., do you

feel that catering event coordination management should be a part of the sales and marketing department or the F&B department? Identify at least three advantages and disadvantages of each organizational placement.

4. Some hotels use dining room servers and room service attendants interchangeably. What kind of special training would a room service attendant need to become an efficient dining room server? What types of additional training would a dining room server require to be an effective room service attendant? What are the advantages and disadvantages to utilizing the same persons to work in both of these positions during the same shift?

5. This chapter has stated that *all* personnel in the hotel require training in the responsible service of alcoholic beverages. How would you explain the need for this training to a new room service attendant, front desk clerk, and maintenance department employee? How would you incorporate this training into the new employee orientation of each?

9

Safety and Property Security

This Chapter at Work

As a G.M., your guests depend on you to provide an atmosphere that assures their safety to the greatest degree possible. Your guests, however, are not the only individuals concerned with your safety efforts. Your employees also count upon you to provide a working environment that allows them to do their jobs free from the concern of unnecessary risks.

The owners of a hotel also depend on the G.M. to develop practices and procedures that will safeguard the hotel's assets and minimize the owner's legal liability. In addition, there are governmental agencies at all levels that are charged with monitoring the safety related efforts of hotels. One of the most important of these is the Occupational Health and Safety Administration (OSHA), a federal agency charged with the responsibility of ensuring a safe workplace for employees. In this chapter, you will learn about the important role OSHA plays in the hospitality industry and how documenting your safety efforts will help you stay in compliance with their requirements.

A primary focus in this chapter is the issue of legal liability. You will learn about your safety- and security-related legal responsibilities to your guests, employees, and owners. You will also discover the importance of security as a department within the hotel and as the shared responsibility of each employee.

The hotel industry is committed to safety. Because that is true, the industry offers concerned G.M.s a variety of security-oriented tools, including recodable locks, alarm systems, surveillance systems, and emergency plans that can be used to reduce safety and security risks. In this chapter, you will learn about all of these.

Depending on their location and the services offered, some hotels have unique safety and security issues. These include protecting guests in swimming pool areas, spas, and, in nearly all cases, parking lots. While hotels are not the insurers of guest safety, hotels do have a responsibility to exercise reasonable care in protecting the welfare of guests. In this chapter, you will learn how to meet the reasonable care standard.

Threats to the security of hotel assets can come from both internal and external sources. To protect assets adequately, programs must be in place to guard against these threats. In this chapter, you will learn how to develop programs that reduce the chances of incurring loss due to dishonest guests and employees. In some cases, safety and security threats are unique to specific hotel departments. For example, in the front office, cash is routinely kept on hand and must be safeguarded, while in the housekeeping department this is not the case. In this chapter, the important department-specific security concerns of the front office, housekeeping, food and beverage, sales and marketing, and maintenance and engineering are examined in detail.

Chapter 9 Outline

PERSONAL SAFETY

Regardless of the size of the hotel, all G.M.s must be concerned about **safety** and **security**. This concern for the safety of guests and the security of their possessions is not merely good business; it is also a legal responsibility of the hotel's ownership and becomes an important responsibility of each staff member in the hotel. Employees and other nonguests visiting the hotel also have a legal right to expect that management be interested in assuring, to the greatest degree possible, their health and well-being.

HOTEL TERMINOLOGY AT WORK

Safety: Protection of an individual's physical well-being and health.

Security: Protection of an individual or business's property or assets.

■

Legal Liability and Guest Safety

Since the earliest days of travel, guests have been rightfully concerned about their safety when they sleep. Innkeepers and hoteliers have responded to these concerns by striving to provide a safe haven for travelers. In addition to the good intentions of hotel managers, however, there are laws that require those who operate hotels to provide the traveling public with an environment that is safe and secure. These laws do not hold hotels responsible for everything that could happen to guests during their stay. Hotels are not required to ensure guest safety. For example, a guest may slip and fall in a bathtub. The hotel will not be held responsible for any resulting injuries if it is determined that the hotel has exercised **reasonable care** in the manner in which it provides and maintains its bathtubs.

HOTEL TERMINOLOGY AT WORK

Reasonable Care: A legal concept identifying the amount of care a reasonably prudent person would exercise in a specific situation.

■

As a G.M., it is important to remember that the legal standard of reasonable care means you must operate your hotel with a degree of care equal to that of other reasonable persons (general managers). For example, if you know, or should know about a threat to the safety of your guests, it is reasonable to assume that you would either immediately eliminate the threat or clearly inform your guests of it. Not to do so would likely indicate that you exhibited an absence of reasonable care for the safety of your guests. If there is a threat to guest safety that results in loss or injury and if it is determined that the hotel did not exercise reasonable care in regard to that threat, it is possible that the hotel will be held wholly or partially **liable** for the resulting loss or injury.

HOTEL TERMINOLOGY AT WORK

Liable: Legally bound to compensate for loss or injury.

■

If a hotel is found to be liable for injuries to a guest or employee, the hotel will likely bear the cost of that liability. For example, assume that a hotel manager knew about a defective lock on a guest room door yet did not authorize an immediate repair of the lock. Subsequently a guest named Ms. Stevens rented the room with the defective lock and was robbed and assaulted by an assailant who obtained unlawful entry to the room via the door with the defective lock. In this case, it is highly likely that an attorney hired by the guest to seek **damages** against the hotel would be successful. In this hypothetical case, the damages would likely include **compensatory damages** and possibly even **punitive damages.** These damages could amount to extremely large amounts of money the hotel would be required to pay to Ms. Stevens. These would be costs that could have been avoided by the hotel had the guest room lock been repaired, as it should have been, in a timely manner.

It is important to note that good managers do not manage well simply to avoid paying damages. A demonstrated concern for guest safety is not

---

HOTEL TERMINOLOGY AT WORK

Damages: The actual amount of losses or costs incurred due to the wrongful act of a liable party.

Compensatory Damages: Also known as actual damages, this monetary amount is intended to compensate injured parties for actual losses or damage they have incurred. This typically includes items such as medical bills and lost wages.

Punitive Damages: This monetary amount is assessed to punish liable parties and to serve as an example to the liable party as well as others not to commit the wrongful act in the future.

■

---

merely a good business practice, it is also the right thing to do. Guest safety is an important part of every manager's job. Indeed, the emphasis placed upon safety by a G.M. and his or her management team is a good indication of the true professionalism of the G.M. and that team.

Staffing for Security

Even when management is truly committed to guest safety, it takes the effort of every employee in the hotel to eliminate, to the greatest degree possible, threats to the safety and security of guests and the hotel. In larger hotels, there may be a full-time director of safety and security as well as departmental staff that routinely patrol the hotel's grounds, make safety and security checks, and direct the hotel's safety programs. In other cases, the hotel may contract with a private security firm to provide some security services. In still other cases, off-duty police may be hired to assist the hotel's security efforts. In many hotels of the size considered in this text, safety and security would not likely be a completely separate department, but rather, safety and security programs would be administered within each hotel department and overseen by the G.M. or a designated **safety and security committee.**

HOTEL TERMINOLOGY AT WORK

Safety and Security Committee: An interdepartmental task force consisting of hotel managers, supervisors, and hourly employees charged with the responsibility of monitoring and refining a hotel's safety and security efforts.

■

Many G.M.s find that maintaining an effectively operating safety and security committee is actually preferable to a separate safety and security department simply because the operation of such a committee reinforces the fact that guest safety and hotel security is the responsibility of every manager, supervisor, and employee of the hotel. Regardless of the organizational structure of the hotel's safety and security efforts, the training of hotel staff is a key component of any effective program. In addition, local law enforcement officials can be of great assistance to you in your efforts to help ensure guest safety. The combined activities of your own well-trained staff along with those of your local police will go a long way toward demonstrating reasonable care on the part of your management team should the need ever arise.

Employee Safety Training

Training employees to help ensure guest safety, to work safely, and to assist the hotel's security efforts is an ongoing process. One way to view the safety training needs of employees is in terms of that training required by all employees and that training that is essential only to members of a specific department. For example, teaching all employees to promptly report any unauthorized or suspicious person found lurking in the hotel's parking lot would be appropriate, while providing training about the safe handling of food would be appropriate only for those employees involved in the food and beverage department.

Individual hotels or hotel companies develop and implement many fine safety-training programs. In addition, many excellent safety and security related training materials are developed and continually updated by the Educational Institute of the American Hotel and Lodging Association (E.I.). These materials are made available to hotels at a very reasonable cost.

THE INTERNET AT WORK

The Educational Institute (E.I.) offers a variety of safety and security related training products developed for all employees within a hotel in addition to programs that are departmental specific. E.I. also offers a self-paced training program leading to the Certified Lodging Security Officer designation (CLSO). To view that program as well as others, go to:

www.ei-ahla.org

and enter "Safety and Security" in the search field.

Local Law Enforcement

Your employees can and should be well trained, but their safety and security efforts will be helped tremendously when you establish and maintain an excellent relationship with your own local law enforcement professionals. As an effective G.M., you should personally know the individual responsible for law enforcement in the area in which your hotel is located. Local law enforcement officials can advise and assist you and, in many cases, provide no-cost safety and security training for your employees. For example, you can request a property safety and security review from your local police. This will likely result in the identification of specific steps your hotel can take to reduce safety and security threats, as well as actions you can take to make improvements. Good G.M.s make it a point to meet frequently with local police, an important source of information and assistance.

Safety Resources

In addition to the staff training resources that can assist in your guest safety efforts, there are other hotel industry resources at your disposal that can help you achieve your guest safety and security goals. The appropriate selection and use of these tools depends on the safety and security needs of each hotel.

Recodable Locks

At one time, a hotel's purchase and use of a recodable locking system was such a significant event that the hotel could actually market its use of such locks to its potential guests. Today, recodable locks are the industry standard and, simply put, no hotel should operate without them.

Recodable lock systems are sold by a variety of companies. Essentially, however, a quality system, regardless of manufacturer, consists of electronic door locks that "stand-alone." That is, there's no need to wire the locks back to a central computer. Except in life-threatening emergencies, only a standard magnetic stripe card issued by the front desk or management opens the door lock. Thus, the hotel's entire guestroom security system is controlled by software contained in the locks themselves and activated by cards coded on a keycard-issuing computer.

Each lock contains a card reader and electronic lock control module connected to a motor-actuated lock mechanism. Standard AA alkaline batteries power the entire lock. A warning light visible only to staff warns when the batteries are within three months of needing replacing. When a guest inserts the keycard into the lock for the first time, the lock is immediately recoded, which cancels entry authorization for the previous guest. In a quality system, multiple keycards can be issued to the same guest. In addition to guest rooms and exterior doors, recodable locks can be used to limit guest access to designated hotel areas such as special elevator floors, swimming pools, spas, exercise rooms, and reserved breakfast or bar areas and can limit employee access to specified storage areas within the hotel.

Because guest rooms must be regularly cleaned and maintained, management issues master keycards to those hotel staff that need them. With today's recodable lock systems, an electronic record is kept of all keycards used in the lock for a specific period of time. As a result, should the need arise, management can determine whose keycard was used to open a lock and at what day and time the key was used.

Unlike nonrecodable locks, the use of recodable locks severely reduces the chance for guests to be victimized in their room by someone who had

Individual electronic keys add to guest safety and security.

rented the same room on a prior night. In addition, recodable locks help reduce the incident of employee theft from rooms. They should be used by all hotel managers truly concerned for guest safety and asset security.

THE INTERNET AT WORK

To view the operational features of one of the most popular recodable locking systems, go to:

www.tesalocks.com

and click on "Hotels and Resorts."

Alarm Systems

Alarms of many types are used within the hotel industry. They can be either audible or silent. Audible alarms typically consist of high-pitched buzzers, bells, or alternative noises. Alarm devices, whether audible or silent, normally consist of electrical connections, photoelectric light beams, seismic detectors, infrared beams, magnetic contacts, or radio frequency (RF) fields that, when activated, create the alarm.

Alarms many be classified as either **internal alarms** or **contact alarms.**

HOTEL TERMINOLOGY AT WORK

Internal Alarm: A warning system that notifies an area within the hotel if the alarm is activated.

Contact Alarm: A warning system that notifies (contacts) an external entity such as the fire or police department if the alarm is activated.

■

Internal alarms generally are designed to serve as a deterrent to criminal or mischief activity. For example, a warning buzzer on a hotel's fire exit door would typically be wired only to notify hotel personnel if the door was used. In a like manner, an alarm on a liquor storeroom door might serve to notify a manager or the food and beverage director. Conversely, an alarm that would be activated by a front desk agent during or after an armed robbery would most likely be wired directly to the local police department for the purpose of contacting them immediately.

Some important areas that may be protected by internal alarms include:

• Storage areas
• Hotel facilities such as pools, spa, and exercise areas
• Hotel grounds and perimeter

Some important areas that are more likely to be protected by contact alarms include:

• Front desk
• Food and beverage cashier stations
• Controller's office

Hotel fire alarms are so important that federal law, as well as local building codes, mandate them. Good hotels will have these devices wired as both internal and contact alarms. Remember that, in case of a fire, hotel staff, guests, and the fire department would all need to be made aware of the danger. Thus, heat or smoke detectors in a guest room may set off an internal alarm that would be heard by the guest in the room, and should be checked immediately by the appropriate hotel staff, whereas a fire alarm that is activated in a public area may result in an automatic contact and summons of firefighters because the alarm was wired directly to the local fire department.

First and foremost, effective G.M.s, have reviewed their alarm systems needs to determine which areas of the hotel need to be part of the overall alarm program. Second, they are responsible for ensuring that, periodically and frequently, all alarms are checked for proper operation. This is necessary because a hotel with a nonfunctioning alarm system will have great difficulty demonstrating that it exercised reasonable care toward employee and guest safety should the need ever arise. An effective and comprehensive alarm system is an invaluable tool in every hotel's complete safety and security effort.

Surveillance Systems

Properly implemented, electronic surveillance can play a big role in a hotel's safety and security programs. This surveillance generally is one of two types. The first involves simply recording, via a VCR, the activity within an area of the hotel. Thus, for example, a hotel could set up a VCR that records the activity outside a liquor storeroom. Then if, on a given night, the storeroom was broken into, a videotaped record of the break-in would exist that could be useful in identifying the thieves. Recording activity at the front desk, in parking areas, and near cashiers are among the most frequent use of the VCR surveillance system.

Some hotels use **closed-circuit television (CCTV)** as a tool in their safety and security systems programs.

HOTEL TERMINOLOGY AT WORK

Closed-Circuit television (CCTV): A Camera and monitor system that displays, in real time, the activity within a camera's field of vision. A CCTV consisting of several cameras and screens showing the camera's field of vision may be monitored in a single hotel location.

The potential uses of CCTV within a hotel are many. CCTV can be used, for example, in a multiple-entry property where management desires to monitor activity outside each entrance. It is important to remember that, to be most effective, a CCTV system must be monitored. Viewing monitors are typically placed in a central location and viewed by an assigned employee who is trained to respond appropriately to activities seen on the monitor. For example, if an outside entrance is being monitored, and the monitor shows that a break-in is being attempted, the employee may have been trained to summon the local police. Some hotels add an intercom to the area being monitored, thus "extending" the effectiveness of the individual monitoring the system. Within casino hotels, states typically mandate the use of CCTV to improve security.

Some hotel managers attempt to give the illusion of having a CCTV system in place, when in fact the "cameras" are not truly cameras or the monitors are not constantly monitored. This is typically done in an effort to save money on the cost of operating the CCTV system. The rationale for this has been that the mere presence of the cameras would be sufficient to deter criminals, who would not realize that they were not actually being observed. The courts and juries have found, however, that this approach may not establish reasonable security care by the hotel because victims may think that help is on the way (because they believe their situation is being monitored) and they may base their behavior on that belief.

If fact, since the monitors are not being viewed, no such help is likely to arrive. Hotel managers wishing to operate a CCTV that is not monitored should consult with both their insurers and their legal counsel before implementing such an approach.

When considering the use of either the VCR or CCTV system, the issues for management involve balancing guest and employee privacy with safety and assessing whether visible cameras increase or detract from a guest's sense of security in the hotel.

Emergency Plans

Despite your best efforts, safety and security emergencies will occur in your hotel. When they do, the hotel must be ready to respond appropriately. Preplanning is perhaps the very best tool available to managers concerned with safety and security. In cases of unforeseen emergencies, it may not be possible to determine the proper response until the actual event occurs. In the case of crises that are foreseeable (such as severe weather storms or power outages), some of the things your hotel must be prepared to do will be quite similar, if not routine, in each crisis.

To prepare the hotel for a crisis, the G.M. should develop and implement an **emergency plan**.

HOTEL TERMINOLOGY AT WORK

Emergency Plan: A document describing a hotel's predetermined, intended response to a safety/security threat encountered by the hotel.

■

An emergency plan is, quite simply, the identification of a threat to the safety and/or security of the hotel, as well as the hotel's planned response to the threat. For example, an emergency plan for a hotel near a heavily wooded area might include an evacuation plan that should be implemented in case of a forest fire. Alternatively, a hotel on a Florida coast might include in its emergency plan a method of evacuating the hotel in the event of an impending hurricane.

Responses to events such as the following are included in most hotels' emergency plans:

- Fire
- Power outages
- Severely inclement weather
- Robbery
- Death or injury to a guest or employee

- Bomb threat
- Intense negative publicity by the media

In all of these cases, the hotel's management and employees may be called upon to react quickly in the crises. The emergency plan prepares them to do so. This can be accomplished because many crises share similar characteristics that can, to some degree, be controlled by preplanning: These characteristics include:

- Extreme importance
- Disruption of normal business
- Potential for human suffering
- Financial loss
- Potential scrutiny by the media
- Threat to the reputation or health of the business

An emergency plan must be a written document. This is important because you must identify precisely what is expected of management and employees in times of crisis. In addition, if the hotel becomes subject to a lawsuit as a result of the crisis, a written emergency plan can help show that your hotel exercised reasonable care in preparing for the crisis.

An emergency plan should be kept simple because it will likely be implemented only in a time of heightened stress. For each crisis identified, a clearly developed emergency plan would include:

- Type of crisis
- Who should be told when the crisis occurs (include telephone or pager numbers)
- What should be done and who should do it in the event the crisis occurs
- Who should be informed of the results or impact of the crisis when it is over

The actual plan should be reviewed frequently by management and shared with employees so they know what they should do during the emergency. Where practical, hotels should practice the implementation of their plan. By doing so, they demonstrate strongly their commitment to ensuring the safety and security of the hotel and all who are in it.

Special Safety Issues

Hotels are unique places of business that have unique guest safety concerns. G.M.s wishing to reduce their legal liability would do well to monitor the staff's efforts in any area deemed to require extra caution or effort. For many hotels, three of the most important of these special areas of concern are swimming pools, spas, and parking lots.

Swimming Pools

Hotel swimming pools are exceptionally popular despite the fact that they are typically used by only a small percentage of hotel guests. Consistently, in opinion polls regarding desirable services, travelers rank the mere presence of a swimming pool near the top of hotel amenities that influence their hotel selection. The potential legal liability resulting from accidental slipping, diving, or even drowning, however, requires that the individual responsible for taking care of the pool area, as well as the G.M., be extraordinarily vigilant in enforcing pool safety procedures.

It is not possible to avoid all potential accidents in a pool area. It is possible, however, to minimize the chances for such an accident. Figure 9.1 lists ten key practices that affect swimming pool safety and legal liability. The G.M. should review them on a monthly basis with affected employees to ensure consistent compliance.

Spas

Hotels that have common area spas or hot tubs face special safety and liability concerns. While the spas are popular, they can be dangerous to young children, the elderly, intoxicated individuals, and those on special medications. Like pools, it may be impossible to prevent all possible accidents, however, the practices listed in Figure 9.2 can go long way toward improving

FIGURE 9.1 Swimming Pool Safety

1. Post the pool's operational hours and open the pool only during those hours.
2. Clearly mark the depths of pools accurately and in both metric measure and in feet/inches.
3. Make sure the pool and pool area is properly illuminated and that any electrical components are regularly inspected and maintained to meet local electrical codes.
4. Install self-closing and self-latching and/or locking gates to prevent unauthorized access to the pool area. If possible, lock the entrance to the pool with a recodable lock.
5. Have appropriate lifesaving equipment on hand and easily accessible, as well as at least one cardiopulmonary resuscitation (CPR) certified employee on duty at all times the pool is opened.
6. Allow pool use only by registered guests and specifically authorized others.
7. Contact the hotel's insurer to determine the number, placement, and content of necessary pool warning signs.
8. Post all pool policy and information signs in the language(s) of guests. Enforce the policies at all times.
9. Provide an emergency telephone in the pool area that rings directly either to the Front Desk or to 911 depending on the preference of the hotel's insurer.
10. Carefully document all activities related to pool maintenance, local ordinance compliance, and operational policy enforcement.

FIGURE 9.2   Spa Safety

1. Inspect and document the inspection of spa drain covers on a daily basis.
2. Post all spa policies signs in the language(s) of guests.
3. Install a thermometer and check the spa temperature frequently; record your readings. (A range not to exceed 102–105 degrees Fahrenheit is recommended.)
4. Display spa temperatures in a manner that is easily readable by guests.
5. Clearly mark the depths of the spa in both metric measures and feet/inches.
6. Do not allow the consumption of alcohol while using the spa.
7. Install nonslip flooring surfaces around the spa and provide stairs/ ladders for entry.
8. Prohibit spa use by young children and nonguests.
9. Provide an emergency telephone in the spa area that rings directly either to the front desk or to 911 depending on the preference of the hotel's insurer.
10. Carefully document all activities related to spa maintenance, local ordinance compliance, and operational policy enforcement.

guest safety and minimizing the legal liability of the hotel. As with pools, the G.M. should review these practices on a monthly basis to ensure compliance.

Parking Lots

Most hotels have parking areas for guest vehicles. Although hotels are not the insurers of vehicles parked in their lots, they are responsible for providing reasonable care in the protection of vehicles and guests using the lots. Figure 9.3 lists ten key practices that affect the safety of parking areas. Again, the G.M. should review them with affected personnel on a monthly basis to ensure compliance.

────────── **MANAGERS AT WORK** ──────────

J.D. Ojisima, the G.M. of the hotel, walked quickly to the hotel's pool area.

"There are an awfully lot of kids . . . and only one adult . . . down at the pool" was the statement made a few minutes earlier to the front office manager by the housekeeper who had gone to the pool area to replenish the towel supply. All housekeepers in the hotel had been trained to report any activity that could possibly be considered dangerous,

and this housekeeper had performed well.

Because she could not leave the front desk area unattended, Jodi Guild, the front office manager, had called J.D. in the G.M.'s office to ask for assistance.

"What's the problem?" stated the guest when J.D. arrived in the pool area. " I rented a room at this hotel to hold my son's eleventh birthday party. These are his friends. Are you saying we are not allowed to invite guests to visit us

when we are registered in your hotel?"

J.D. quickly counted over 20 young people attending the "party."

If you were J.D., would you impose limits on the number of "guests of guests" allowed to use hotel facilities? Who do you believe is responsible for the safety of the young people attending the party? Why? What would you say to the guest you are now speaking with?

FIGURE 9.3 Parking Lot Safety

1. Inspect parking lot lighting on a daily basis. Arrange for replacement of burned-out lights immediately.
2. Inspect parking lot surfaces daily and arrange for pavement patches immediately if they threaten guest safety. Keep surfaces free of ice and snow in inclement weather.
3. Ensure parking lot stripes and directional signs are easily seen to avoid pedestrian/vehicle accidents.
4. Post easily readable signs in the parking lot reminding guests not to leave valuables in their vehicles.
5. If valet parking is provided, document the training of all drivers you employ.
6. Require guests to identify their vehicles by license number or make/color upon check-in.
7. Keep landscaping around parking lots well trimmed to avoid dangerous areas that may provide hiding places for individuals that could threaten guest safety or property security.
8. If possible, arrange for regular and frequent parking lot "drive-through" patrols by local law enforcement officials.
9. Arrange for daily daytime and nighttime "walk-through" patrols by hotel staff.
10. Use a manager's daily log to document your parking lot maintenance procedures.

Documenting Safety Efforts

All hotels should carefully document their safety and security related efforts. This is true because, if it were ever needed, this documentation could be powerful evidence that the hotel took its safety and security responsibilities very seriously. Thus, if the duties of the evening **MOD** include a "walk around" the property as part of the safety and security program, these checklists or documents should be maintained.

HOTEL TERMINOLOGY AT WORK

MOD: Manager on Duty. The individual on the hotel property responsible for making any management decisions required during the period he or she is MOD.

■

MOD checklists that demonstrate a consistent effort on the part of the hotel to maintain safety and security standards are excellent. Each hotel must determine the frequency, content and number of checklists that are appropriate. These should be prepared and completed for each area of the hotel. Figure 9.4 is an example of an MOD checklist related to parking areas in a hotel.

FIGURE 9.4 MOD Checklist for Parking Areas

Waldo Hotel
MOD Checklist for Parking Areas

Performed by: _____

Date of Inspection: _____

Time of Inspection: _____

To ensure the integrity of your walk-through, this checklist should be completed in sequence as it appears.

As appropriate, a check must be placed in the "yes" or "no" column to the right of this paper. If a "no" is required, please indicate the problem in the "comments" section. If a work order is submitted, note the work order number in the "comments" section.

Item	Yes	No	Comments
Outdoor parking lot is well lit.	✓	✓	
Outdoor parking lot is free of trash and debris.	✓	✓	
Painted stripes are in good condition, i.e., yellow, white, and red stripes.	✓	✓	
Directional signs are posted in conspicuous location.	✓	✓	
Lot patrolled at irregular intervals.	✓	✓	
All entrance gates locked after 8:00 P.M. with the exception of the main entrance.	✓	✓	
Emergency call boxes are located throughout the parking lot and functioning properly.	✓	✓	
Closed circuit cameras function properly and send clear images to security.	✓	✓	
Gangs or vagrants are noticed.	✓	✓	
Cars are checked for length of stay, i.e., cars covered with tarp, excessive dirt.	✓	✓	
Security is aware of long-term stay automobiles.	✓	✓	
Correct percentage of ADA parking is available and well marked.	✓	✓	
Grass areas and bushes are well maintained.	✓	✓	
Bushes and plants are trimmed and away from entrance doors.	✓	✓	
Walkways are well lit.	✓	✓	

(continued)

FIGURE 9.4 *(Continued)*

Outside entrances are free of trash and debris.	✓	✓	
All external doors leading to the inside are closed, locked and card accessible.	✓	✓	
Keycard readers work properly at each entrance.	✓	✓	
All entrances are well lit.	✓	✓	
All entrances are secured.	✓	✓	
Directional signage at each entrance is compatible with ADA requirements.	✓	✓	
Outdoor ADA requirements are met regarding wheelchair ramps.	✓	✓	
Other: _____	✓	✓	
Other: _____	✓	✓	
Other: _____	✓	✓	

Accidents can and will happen. When **incident reports** are prepared that list the "who, what, where, how," and the hotel's response to an accident or injury, these should also be filed and maintained.

HOTEL TERMINOLOGY AT WORK

Incident Report: A document prepared to record the details of an accident, injury, or disturbance, and the hotel's response to it.

THE INTERNET AT WORK

For an excellent and free example of a hotel incident report, go to:

www.hospitalitylawyer.com.

Then use the Search field and enter the words "Incident Report."

This site charges no fee and is an exceptional source of up-to-date safety and security related information.

Other examples of documentation that should be maintained by the hotel include minutes from safety and security committee meetings, general staff meeting notes relevant to safety issues, records of employee training related to safety and security, and safety seminars attended or certifications acquired by employees.

In summary, any and all efforts of the hotel related to the safety and security needs of guests should be documented. Reasonable care can sometimes be a difficult concept to prove, and any documentation the hotel has that can help establish its presence will be useful.

The Occupational Safety and Health Administration (OSHA)

Guest safety is important, but the safety of employees when they work is equally important. Because this is true, the federal government in 1970 passed the Occupational Safety and Health Act, which created, within the Department of Labor, the Occupational Safety and Health Administration **(OSHA)**

HOTEL TERMINOLOGY AT WORK

OSHA: The Occupational Safety and Health Administration. A federal agency established in 1970 that is responsible for developing and enforcing regulations related to assuring safe and healthful working conditions.

■

The purpose of the Occupational Safety and Health Act is to help assure safe and healthful working conditions. OSHA is very aggressive in enforcing the rights of workers. Your hotel is legally required to comply with the extensive safety practices, equipment specifications, and employee communication procedures mandated by OSHA. As the hotel's G.M., your interaction with OSHA can be an adversarial one or, preferably, one in which this agency is viewed as a partner in your safety efforts. In either case, OSHA will perform its main tasks related to worker safety. These include ensuring that businesses:

- Provide a safe workplace for employees by complying with OSHA safety and health standards
- Provide workers only with tools and equipment to do their jobs that meet OSHA specifications for health and safety
- Establish training programs for employees who operate dangerous equipment
- Report to OSHA within forty-eight hours any work site accident that results in a fatality or requires the hospitalization of five or more employees
- Maintain the "OSHA Log 200" (an on-site record of work-related injuries or illnesses) and submit it to OSHA once per year

- Display OSHA notices regarding employee rights and safety in prominent places within the hotel
- Provide all employees access to the **Material Safety Data Sheets (MSDS)** that provide information about the dangerous chemicals they may be handling during work
- Offer no-cost hepatitis B vaccinations for employees who may have come into contact with blood or body fluids

---

HOTEL TERMINOLOGY AT WORK

Material Safety Data Sheet (MSDS). A written statement describing the potential hazards of, and best ways to handle, a chemical or toxic substance. An MSDS is provided by the manufacturer of the chemical or toxic substance to the buyer of the product and must be posted and/or made available in a place where it is easily accessible to those who will actually use the product.

■

OSHA has inspectors that monitor the safety related efforts of businesses. These inspectors are allowed to visit your hotel to ensure your compliance with their regulations. When initially developed, few businesses viewed OSHA as a partner in their worker safety efforts. Today, astute G.M.s recognize that compliance with OSHA standards results in fewer accidents, lower insurance costs, and a healthier workforce.

THE INTERNET AT WORK

OSHA maintains an active Web site with valuable information that can be easily accessed. To stay current on OSHA regulations and enforcement programs visit and bookmark:

www.osha.gov/

PROPERTY SECURITY

As stated earlier in this chapter, safety-related hotel programs are designed to keep people safe from harm, whereas security related efforts are directed toward protecting property from theft or damage. While the safety of people is always more important than the security of property, good hotel managers know that they must use sound judgment and establish effective programs to protect the personal assets of guests while they travel, as well as the assets of the hotel itself. Not to do so would be a disservice to the traveler and the hotel's owners.

Threats to Asset Security

Threats to the security of assets can come from individuals inside the hotel itself or from people outside the hotel. In both cases, these individuals seek to steal or damage property that rightfully belongs to the hotel's guests, employees, or owners. Effective G.M.s and department heads design, implement, and monitor security programs that reduce, to the greatest extent possible, these internal and external threats to asset security.

Internal threats

Sometimes employees steal assets owned by guests or the hotel. When it is clear that an employee is involved in such activity, the response of the G.M. should be appropriate and, above all else, consistent. Some hotels include in their employee handbook a phrase that indicates theft will be considered grounds for dismissal. When the theft or loss of property involves significant amounts of money, the hotel may elect to file charges against the individual employee. Regardless of the approach used, it should be applied equally to all employees at all levels.

Consider, for example, a supervisor or manager involved in criminal activity that is caught, but then allowed to resign, while in the same hotel an hourly employee caught in the same activity is fired and/or prosecuted. If this occurred, the hotel leaves itself open to charges of discrimination or unfair labor practices against which it may be difficult to defend. It also sends, to others still employed at the hotel, a mixed message about management's view of theft.

If the hotel wishes to communicate to employees that theft of all types will be dealt with swiftly and severely, it must pursue the internal threat to security just as aggressively as threats posed by nonemployees.

Cash.   In many cases, when hotel managers think of employee theft, they think of employees stealing money. **Embezzlement** is a potential problem in hotels, but using procedures and policies designed to prevent it can minimize its likelihood.

HOTEL TERMINOLOGY AT WORK

Embezzlement: The theft of a company's financial assets by an employee.

■

Some hotels are so concerned about employee theft that they **bond** those employees who are in a position to embezzle funds.

HOTEL TERMINOLOGY AT WORK

Bond(ing): Purchasing an insurance policy against the possibility that an employee will steal.

■

The methods used by employees to defraud their employers of cash are numerous, and a good G.M. will stay current in the areas of cost and revenue control systems. Good financial controls, based on solid control principles, will go a long way toward reducing employee theft. Of particular importance are controls related to cashiering positions because cashiers can, in a variety of ways, attempt to defraud the hotel. Typical methods of fraud related to cashiering include:

- Charging guests for items not purchased, then keeping the overcharge
- Changing the totals on credit card charges after the guest has left or imprinting additional credit card charges and pocketing the cash difference
- Misadding legitimate charges to create a higher-than-appropriate total with the intent of keeping the overcharge
- Purposely shortchanging guests when giving back change, then removing the extra change from the cash drawer
- Voiding legitimate sales as "mistakes" and keeping the cash amount of the legitimate sale.
- Charging higher-than-appropriate prices for hotel goods or services, recording the proper price, then keeping the overcharge

In addition to cashier theft that can affect the hotel or hotel guests, the theft of cash by employees can occur in the accounts payable area (by paying the hotel's bills in such a way as to funnel money to the embezzling employee) or the accounts receivable area (by fraudulently diverting funds intended for the hotel to the embezzling employee). The responsibility for preventing the theft of hotel funds falls to the controller and each hotel department head involved in the handling of cash. Effective G.M.s will oversee these efforts with diligence.

Other Assets.   Cash is not the only hotel asset that can be stolen by employees. In fact, the number and type of assets that can be unlawfully taken by employees is large. As a G.M., you must be aware of all the threats to your assets and implement programs to reduce or eliminate employee theft. When considering such programs, many G.M.s find it helpful to create programs designed to protect the three noncash assets most subject to employee theft. These three loss areas involve the stealing of time, company property, or services.

It may seem strange to consider time a hotel asset, yet it is the asset most easily taken by employees. In nearly all cases, employees are paid for their work by the hour or, as in the case of salaried individuals, by the week or month. In effect, the hotel is exchanging one asset (cash) for another (employee time). When an employee takes a hotel's cash but does not reciprocate by giving the hotel back the time agreed upon, the hotel loses. The theft of time can consist of employees fraudulently filling out time sheets or punching time cards. In some large hotels, particularly those with weak supervision programs, theft of time may result from employees simply "disappearing" for hours at a time with the result that work they should have performed is not completed.

The best way to prevent theft of time by employees is to have strong controls in place with regard to time cards. To help in this area, more and more hotels are issuing individual employee swipe cards to reduce the chances of one employee fraudulently punching another employee in or out.

When considering plans to reduce employee theft that involves lack of productivity, managers must be vigilant. This can be challenging, especially in large properties. Good supervision, however, and a realistic workload for each employee on the schedule that is reviewed on a daily basis will go a long way toward improving the hotel's ability to detect such theft.

Company property can disappear through the actions of employees as easily as through those of guests. In fact, employees usually know best which assets management has neglected to protect as well as they could. From apples in the food and beverage department to zippered laundry bags in housekeeping, employees often find that the physical assets of a hotel are the type they could use at home. That makes these items very susceptible to employee theft. The best approach to preventing the theft of company property is to:

- Carefully screen employees prior to hiring
- Reduce the chances for theft through the use of effective recodeable locks, inventory systems, and other security measures
- Ensure that managers, as well as employees, are aware of the penalty for theft
- Treat all proven cases of similar theft in a similar manner

It is unlikely, even with the best controls, that all employee theft in a hotel can be eliminated. There are simply too many opportunities for dishonest employees to take advantage of their access to the hotel's physical resources. Effective employee screening, however, and the creation of an environment that discourages stealing, which consistently disciplines, terminates, or prosecutes employees for known cases of theft, will go a long way toward reducing employee-related pilfering.

Some employees steal company property while others steal services provided by the hotel. In many ways, this type of theft is even harder to detect than the theft of company property. For example, assume that a front office supervisor, working late at night, spends an hour or more per day making a long-distance call to his girlfriend who lives several states away. That inappropriate use of hotel assets will result in the hotel incurring a larger than necessary long-distance telephone bill for the month (as well as experiencing the theft of time discussed earlier). This theft of services may go undetected unless someone at the property is effectively monitoring long-distance telephone bills generated by each administrative telephone extension number. In-room movies and games, telephone tolls, copy and faxing services, and the like are all susceptible to employee theft. Again, proper management controls must be in place to minimize, to the greatest degree possible, the chances for loss of hotel services.

External Threats

Because hotels are open 24/7, they are susceptible to asset threats any time of day or night. Guests or nonguests can pose these threats. As is the case when protecting assets from threats posed by employees, managers protecting hotel assets from the illegal activities of nonemployees must guard both cash and noncash assets.

Cash.   Nearly all hotels keep some money on the property at all times. Because that is true, and because some hotels offer thieves the chance to make rapid getaways by automobile, hotel staff members can sometimes be confronted by armed or unarmed robbers. Preventing such robberies is best achieved by management working with the hotel staff and local law enforcement officials to identify and eliminate opportunities thieves may have to rob the hotel.

It is important for managers to understand that a robbery is *not* an occasion to attempt the protection of cash assets. A robbery is a time to protect staff! In the event of a robbery, the hotel staff member(s) involved should obey the robber's demands and make no movements that might be perceived by the robber as an attempt to stop the crime. Employees should do nothing to risk or jeopardize their lives. Employees can, of course, be trained to observe the robber carefully for the purpose of later recalling physical characteristics such as height, weight, color and length of hair, color of eyes, mustaches or beards, tattoos, accents, or other identifying characteristics. During a robbery, complying with the robber's demands and observation of the robber should be the employee's only concern.

To help apprehend robbers, many managers install a contact alarm system in their cashier's cash drawers. This alarm is activated when a predetermined bill or packet of bills is removed from the cash drawer. The alarm is wired to summons local law enforcement officers trained to deal with robbery-in-progress situations. If no such alarm is in place, an employee who is robbed should, at the earliest safe opportunity, contact local law enforcement officials, as well as others indicated in the robbery section of the hotel's emergency plan.

Other Assets.   Robbers steal from hotels, but so do guests. In fact, guests are much greater threats to the noncash assets of hotels than are robbers. Most often, the targets of guests are not cash but rather the products and services hotels offer for sale. Every experienced hotel manager has a "humorous" story about a guest who removed (or tried to remove!) a significant asset from a hotel illegally. From furniture and artwork to minor items such as towels, robes, and ashtrays, guest theft costs hotels millions of dollars annually in lost assets.

The reality for most guest theft, however, is that it is simply recognized as a cost of doing business. It makes little sense, for example, to accuse a guest of stealing a wooden clothes hanger (even if the hanger was, in fact, stolen by the guest) and then attempt to charge the guest for the item. Some hotel managers place small signs in guest rooms offering to "sell" guests those items that frequently disappear. Other managers, in an effort to deter theft, word guest room signs in such a way as to imply that a room attendant will be held financially responsible for any loss of guest room items. Whether managers use these in-room sign approaches (neither of which is recommended by the authors) or other less obtrusive ones, guests and visitors to a hotel represent a significant threat to asset security. Therefore, it is good business practice to take precautions designed to reduce theft. To that end, security-conscious managers:

- Hang all artwork in lobbies and guest rooms with lock-down style hangers
- Avoid placing valuable decorations and décor pieces in areas where they can be easily taken by guests
- Train room attendants to alert management if excessive amounts of terry cloth products or in-room items are missing from stay-over rooms
- Bolt televisions securely to guest room furniture
- Train all employees to be alert regarding the loss of hotel property and to report any suspicious activity they encounter

It is important to remember that theft of services by guests can happen just as easily as the theft of physical assets, and proper controls must be in place to prevent these occurrences.

Just as retail stores endure losses due to shoplifters, hotels will lose items to guest pilferage. However, retail stores and their hotel counterparts must be diligent to limit losses caused by shoplifters through the implementation of policies and procedures designed to reduce such losses.

Departmental-Specific Threats to Asset Security

Threats to a hotel's assets can occur at any time and in any department. Some departments, however, by the nature of their operation, are subject to specific security threats of which the G.M. should be aware.

Front Office.   In addition to the threats to cash posed by employee theft or robbery, the largest area of concern within the front desk is that of the fraudulent selling of rooms. Consider, for example, the night auditor who checks a guest into the hotel very late at night. The guest states they only need the room for a few hours to get some sleep and continue on their travel. The auditor collects the guest's payment in cash at the time of check-in, but later reduces the day's room revenue by that same amount stating that the guest was unhappy with the room, left early, and that the auditor refunded the guest's cash. Obviously, this could have happened. On the other hand, it is also possible that the guest stayed as they indicated upon check-in and the auditor has simply defrauded the hotel of one night's room revenue.

Alternatively, assume that a member of the front office staff simply gives the key to a vacant guest room to a friend or relative and collects no room revenue from that individual. The room, of course, must be cleaned the next day by the housekeeping staff. Again, in this case, the hotel has been defrauded of its rightful room revenue.

G.M.s, and front office managers must have systems in place that minimize the chances for employee fraud. In regard to room revenue fraud, one significant detection tool that managers can use is the housekeeping **discrepancy report.** This report compares the room status of rooms as listed by the PMS with the room status the housekeeping department determines during their daily inspection of all rooms.

HOTEL TERMINOLOGY AT WORK

Discrepancy Report: A daily comparison between the status of rooms as listed by the PMS at the front office, and the status of rooms as listed by the housekeeping department.

■

Each discrepancy should be investigated. That is, if the PMS lists room 417 as "clean and vacant" yet upon physical inspection housekeeping staff report the status of the same room as "on-change," it is the joint responsibility of the front office and housekeeping departments to determine the cause of the discrepancy. If discrepancy reports are not generated and the findings resolved on a daily basis, there will be many opportunities for employees to commit fraud by the inappropriate selling of rooms.

Housekeeping.   In the housekeeping department, managers must be aware of two distinctly different security issues. The first is the theft of the housekeeping supplies such as in-room amenities, towels, sheets, and the like. Thefts such as these can, of course, be committed either by guests or employees. Although it is virtually impossible to stop all theft of minor amenities and in-room items, proper controls and systems should be in place to detect and respond to significant thefts of this type.

Hotels are required to offer guests safety deposit boxes to be in compliance with most state liability laws.

The second, and much more sensitive housekeeping issue involves theft from guest rooms by room attendants or other employees. When guests travel, they often keep valuables in their rooms. This is true despite the recommended use of safety deposit boxes for such items. When a guest claims that there has been a room theft, there are at least four possible scenarios:

1. The guest actually is mistaken, and the item(s) reported stolen have been misplaced.
2. The guest is attempting to defraud the hotel.
3. The theft was committed but by another guest.
4. A hotel employee, in fact, committed the theft.

Obviously, the management of the hotel must be very careful in a situation such as this. If, upon inquiry, the G.M. believes a theft by anyone has, in fact, occurred, it is the best policy to report the incident to local law enforcement officials who are trained to investigate the actual existence of a crime.

Food and Beverage.   Because food and beverage items can be consumed by virtually everyone, they are a common target for theft. Guests may take silverware and glassware as mementos of their stay, and employees may pilfer the same items for their own homes. More significantly, however, employees who purchase products for the food and beverage department may defraud the hotel by accepting kickbacks from vendors or by purchasing,

─────────────────── **MANAGERS AT WORK** ───────────────────

J.D. Ojisima, the G.M., asked Ms. Cooper, the guest in room 117, to carefully explain what had happened.

"What happened," stated the guest, "is that I found your employees are thieves!"

The guest then related to J.D. that she had left her room in the hotel that day at 7:00 A.M. and at that time placed a valuable gold necklace, given to her by her grandmother, in her room on the nightstand near the bed. When she returned at 6:00 P.M. that same day, stated Ms. Cooper, the necklace was gone.

"What I want to know now," said the guest, "is what are you going to do about this!"

Assume that J.D. performs an electronic lock audit and finds that only one housekeeper (9:00 A.M.) and the inspectress (2:00 P.M.) were in the room between 7:00 A.M. and 5:00 P.M. that day. Assume further that neither individual had ever previously been identified as having been inside a room where a guest reported a theft. What would you advise J.D. to do?

Would you change your advice to J.D. if it were discovered that the specific room attendant who cleaned Ms. Cooper's room had, on three previous occasions over a six-month period, been revealed by lock audit to have been in a room where a guest reported a theft?

───────────────────

then stealing, food and beverage items intended for the hotel. It is in the development of systems and procedures to reduce the threat of this type of fraud about which the G.M. and controller must be extremely vigilant.

Sales and Marketing.   Sales and marketing staff are responsible for preventing fraudulent behavior directed at the hotel by unscrupulous individuals. Very often this takes the form of outside parties billing the hotel for services that were not rendered or were not requested. Typically, this scam takes the form of an official-looking invoice arriving in the sales and marketing department via mail or fax. The invoice states the hotel owes money for its listing in a published directory of hotels targeted toward a specific group such as government employees. The invoice further states that the hotel must pay promptly to avoid being dropped from the directory. In fact, however, the directory does not even exist. Those responsible for sending the invoice hope that the hotel will, without investigation, pay the invoice. This scam and others of a similar nature are common, and hotels that do not have sufficient control of their accounts payable system may fall prey to it.

It may seem unusual to consider sales and marketing employees themselves as a source of fraud; however, due to the nature of their interaction with clients, potential threats to asset security do exist. Some of these threats take the form of irregularities with expense accounts. Misstating mileage traveled, clients entertained, or sales trips taken can cause the expense account expenditures of sales staff to be overstated, and, as a result, their reimbursements to be too high. To combat such potential problems, G.M.s must have a good check and balance system that requires documentation of sales expenses and routine audits of reimbursements.

Maintenance and Engineering.   A unique problem in the maintenance and engineering department relates to the loss of small, but sometimes expensive, hand tools and supplies. It is important to remember that the types of items typically used in a hotel's repair shop are the same items employees and guests would use to do repairs in their own homes. Thus, portable hand drills, electric saws, wrenches, and the like can easily turn up missing if they are not carefully controlled.

It might seem as if this would be an easy problem to alleviate. In fact, taking an inventory of small hand tools like a set of pliers or screwdriver on a monthly basis is time consuming and thus is often not done. When that is the case, dishonest employees know that they can take small items without much fear of detection. In addition, tools left at the work site within the hotel during lunch or other breaks can, if unsecured, be stolen by guests or others in the hotel. To prevent either of these sources of fraud, small hand tools should always be inventoried monthly to determine losses, if any. In addition, hand tools should never be left unattended in a public area within the hotel. The temptation for theft and potential for loss is too great. While it may inconvenience the department, if regular inventories indicate that theft is a significant problem, the G.M. may consider requiring that this area implement a **sign-in/sign-out program** for all tools.

HOTEL TERMINOLOGY AT WORK

Sign-In, Sign-Out Program: An arrangement in which individuals taking responsibility for hotel assets (such as hand tools, power equipment, or keys to secured areas) must document their responsibility by placing their signature as well as the date and time on a form developed to identify who last had possession of, and thus responsibility for, the asset.

■

HOTEL TERMINOLOGY AT WORK GLOSSARY

The following terms were defined within this chapter. If you are not familiar with each of them, please review the segment of the chapter that contains the term.

Safety	Liable	Punitive damages
Security	Damages	Safety and security committee
Reasonable care	Compensatory damages	

Internal alarms

Contact alarms

Closed-Circuit Television (CCTV)

Emergency plan

MOD

Incident Report

OSHA

Material Safety Data Sheet (MSDS)

Embezzlement

Bond(ing)

Discrepancy report

Sign-in/Sign-out program

ISSUES AT WORK

1. Some hotel managers believe that uniformed security personnel within the hotel increase the comfort level of guests in the same manner as uniformed police officers. Other managers feel such uniformed security personnel serve to increase a guest's concern about security and their own safety and thus have a net negative affect. Assume you were required to make a decision about the issue at your hotel. Would you put your security force in "police-style" uniforms or uniforms that "blend" with your clientele. What factors would influence your decision making?

2. Guest safety is a primary concern of all effective hotel managers. What specific steps can you take to ensure that all of the hotel's employees share your concern for guest safety? Identify at least three general and three departmental-specific activities. Who, on the hotel property, do you believe should be responsible for ensuring that these types of steps and activities are implemented? Consider both a larger property with a designated security department and a smaller property without one.

3. Every hotel location faces unique threats to the safety of its guests and the security of its assets. Hotels near the ocean may face threats related to storms and water damage whereas those in cold climates face threats related to winter storms. Regardless of the threats, G.M.s must be prepared to deal with emergency situations. Outline a plan for creating a program you would implement to prepare your hotel for the potential outbreak of a serious fire. What hotel departments should be involved in the plan's development? What external entities should be involved? Where would you go for resources that could help your efforts? Would your plan include "fire drills" that involve clearing the hotel of all guests as a way of practicing the final plan's implementation? Why or why not?

4. Material Safety Data Sheets are a valuable source of safety-related information to workers. In most cases, however, these documents are provided only in English and Spanish. Increasingly, the hotel industry employs individuals whose native language is neither of these. What obligation do you believe a hotel has to provide an MSDS in the language of every employee? Assume that your hotel employs twenty-five such individuals speaking five different languages. How would you help ensure the safety of these workers with regard to handling chemicals and other toxic materials?

5. Assume that your hotel's food and beverage department is experiencing periodic losses of products that you believe are due to employee theft. What specific steps would you, as the G.M., want to see your food and beverage director take to address this issue? How would you monitor the success of the director's efforts? How would you ensure it was not the director that was involved?

10
Sales and Marketing

This Chapter at Work

The economic health of a hotel is dependent on it securing its proper share of the available market. If a hotel does not have an effective sales and marketing department, it will not capture the amount of the business it should. An excellent sales and marketing department ensures that the hotel gets its fair share of the business, and more!

As a G.M., the interaction you will have with sales and marketing is extensive. In addition, your working relationship with the director of this department will play a large role in your own success. Ultimately, a well-run hotel must attract, maintain, and expand a strong customer base. This is the job of the sales and marketing department.

The sales and marketing department does its work both inside and outside the hotel. Within the hotel, the sales and marketing department initiates and manages the sales effort. Externally, the department effectively markets and promotes the products and services offered by the hotel.

In very small hotels, the G.M. may serve as the director of sales and marketing. In larger hotels, the department may be segmented among many departmental members based on the hotel service sold, the type of customer buying the service, or by the way the service is purchased. In this chapter you will learn about alternative ways hotels segment their sales and marketing efforts to improve effectiveness.

Good G.M.s are very aware of the relationship between effort and success in a sales and marketing department. This is a challenging task because a strong effort in a weak market may actually yield less business than a weak effort in a strong market. Because this is true, G.M.s must understand the tools available to properly and impartially evaluate the sales and marketing department's internal and external efforts. In this chapter, you will learn about those tools.

You will also learn how technology has changed and is changing the way sales and Marketing departments operate. As a G.M., you must stay abreast of technological advances affecting the way your hotel is marketed and sold so that you will continually grow and expand your business and so that you can fairly evaluate the quality of your sales and marketing department and help them improve.

Chapter 10 Outline

THE ROLE OF SALES AND MARKETING

Very few hotels operate in a noncompetitive environment. In most cases, a guest who elects to use a hotel does so after evaluating several alternative properties. Also, not all hotels will appeal equally to all guests. For example, a couple with children looking for a nearby weekend getaway may want to stay only at a hotel with a swimming pool their children can use. In a similar manner, a large business group that meets weekly for breakfast in a city will require that the hotel site it chooses for its meeting can accommodate its average of hundred attendees. Hotels that cannot accommodate this number will not meet their needs. In both of these cases, the guest has needs, and the hotel has facilities that may, or may not, meet those needs. It is the job of the sales and marketing department to find and cultivate those potential guests whose needs match the product offerings of the hotel. This effort is led by the hotel's **DOSM.**

HOTEL TERMINOLOGY AT WORK

DOSM: Short for "Director of Sales and Marketing." Variations include DOS (Director of Sales) and DOM (Director of Marketing).

■

The DOSM not only identifies and cultivates clients, he or she effectively manages the hotel's marketing efforts, sets rates to maximize RevPar, negotiates sales contracts on behalf of the hotel, and serves as a leader to the hotel's sales and marketing team.

Entire books and magazines are devoted to the topic of hotel sales and marketing. In fact, because of its immediate impact on the hotel profits, in most cases no department within the hotel gets more attention from the G.M. than does sales and marketing. Nor is any area of hotel management subject to more debate regarding how it is best done. There are nearly as many unique approaches to the sales and marketing of hotels as there are hotel sales and marketing staffs. Even definitions of the terms "sales" and "marketing" are often debated within the hotel industry. In fact, there is no universally accepted definition for these terms as they relate to the hotel business. For purposes of this text, we will consider "marketing" as all those activities designed to increase consumer awareness and demand by promoting and advertising the hotel and "sales" as those activities related directly to servicing consumer demand and **booking** clients.

HOTEL TERMINOLOGY AT WORK

Booking: Hotel jargon for making a confirmed sale. As in, "What is the current booking volume for the month in the Food and Beverage department?" or "How many out-of-state tour buses were booked into the hotel last month?"

■

The distinction between sales and marketing activities is sometimes clear-cut but more often is somewhat uncertain. For example, conceiving an advertisement and placing it in the local Yellow Pages telephone directory is clearly a marketing activity. Typing a final sales contract for a group reserving one hundred sleeping rooms is clearly a sales activity. If, however, the DOSM is representing the hotel at a trade show whose attendees are professional meeting planners, that activity could be considered marketing (an activity related to increasing demand), or sales (activities related to meeting demand), or both. For the G.M., a distinct definition of sales or marketing is less important than knowing that those sales and marketing activities that must be implemented inside and outside of the hotel are implemented effectively.

THE INTERNET AT WORK

The professional association for those individuals interested in hotel, travel, and tourism sales and marketing is called the Hotel Sales and Marketing Association International (HSMAI). To read this group's mission statement and to view a calendar of their activities, go to:

http://www.hsmai.org

In the Hotel

In many hotels, the majority of a sales and marketing staff's time is spent inside the property. The type of hotel, its size, and the structure of the sales and marketing staff will determine the actual amount of the staff's on-property time. In all cases, however, the DOSM will be an important member of the executive operating committee and thus will heavily influence the hotel's internal operational decisions. When new hotel policies, procedures, and product and service offerings are considered, they must always be evaluated for their potential positive or negative impact on sales.

The marketing efforts of the sales and marketing department affect the entire hotel. Although the front office is a major selling force for transient rooms and the sales and marketing department actively works to develop sales of this type, an additional effort of most sales departments involves **group sales.**

HOTEL TERMINOLOGY AT WORK

Group Sale: A large sale (in number of rooms or dollar volume) of the hotel's rooms or services. The sales and marketing department, not the front desk, books sales of this type.

■

With their group sales focus, the sales and marketing staff will be active in a large number of in-hotel tasks, including:

MANAGERS AT WORK

"What's wrong with being first? We should be proactive, not reactive," said Jenna Walbert, executive housekeeper at the Waldo Hotel.

"I'm telling you, it's simply a bad idea . . . at this time . . . in this market," replied Michele Austin, the hotel's DOSM. "No one else is doing it."

"It" was the idea of converting all of the guest rooms that currently permitted smoking to a nonsmoking status. It was being proposed by the executive housekeeper and maintenance chief, both of whom pointed out the operational cost savings involved with prohibiting smoking in the guest rooms.

"We'll save thousands of dollars just in not having to replace burn holes in carpets!" said the maintenance chief.

"We have over 85 percent of the rooms as nonsmoking now," replied Michele. "I need some rooms to stay as smoking rooms or we will lose group sales to other hotels who are not as restrictive."

J.D. Ojisima, the hotel's G.M. listened to the discussion carefully. Ultimately, it would be the G.M.'s decision to change the number of nonsmoking rooms, or to keep the current number.

If you were J.D., what non-sales-related factors would influence your decision? Would it be important to know how other hotels in your market area were thinking about this issue? How would you find out? What are the sales-related factors that would influence your final decision? How, if at all, should your own views on smoking influence your decision?

- Planning the hotel's sales and marketing strategy
- Preparing and issuing sales contracts in a timely manner
- Maintaining accurate sales records, forecasts, and histories
- Coordinating and communicating special client requests with the affected hotel departments
- Hosting clients during their stay
- Conducting **site tours**

HOTEL TERMINOLOGY AT WORK

Site Tour: A physical trip (tour) around the hotel, usually hosted by a sales and marketing staff member, for the purpose of introducing potential clients and other interested parties to the hotel's features.

■

G.M.s seeking to evaluate the effectiveness of their sales and marketing staff will, as part of that evaluation, examine the staff's ability to successfully complete their important in-hotel duties, as well as those performed in the community.

In the Community

A hotel's perceived and actual presence in its own business community is critical to its success. In a smaller city, a major full-service hotel will be a focal point for important community events, gatherings, and celebrations. In larger cities a hotel plays all of these roles and should also play a significant role in representing the city as a business or tourism destination to its own state, the country, or even internationally. Regardless of the size of the business community the hotel impacts, its DOSM and the entire sales team should have a noticeable, positive impact on the lodging-related business community.

Opportunities to impact the business community are many and always yield two significant sales opportunities for the hotel. The first is that of informing those in the community about the hotel and the services it offers. Occasions that allow for disseminating information can be pursued if the DOSM and sales team (including the G.M.) are active members of the business community. This involves taking a leadership role in service organizations, business organizations, and the local **Chamber of Commerce.**

HOTEL TERMINOLOGY AT WORK

Chamber of Commerce: An organization whose goal is the advancement of business interests within a community or larger business region.

■

As a G.M., the memberships, activities, and appointed or elected offices your sales team hold in appropriate community organizations is a good indicator of their stature, visibility, and promotion efforts in the business community.

THE INTERNET AT WORK

Chambers of Commerce exist in nearly every community. There are also regional, state, and national chambers. Also called "The Chamber" for short.

Go to: http://www.chamberofcommerce.com/

and utilize the site's Search Engine to find and explore the chamber nearest you.

In addition to promotion opportunities, sales efforts in the community include innumerable **networking** opportunities.

HOTEL TERMINOLOGY AT WORK

Networking: The development of personal relationships for a business-related purpose. For example, a Chamber of Commerce–sponsored breakfast open to all community business leaders interested in improving local traffic conditions would be an excellent example of a networking opportunity for a member of a hotel's sales team.

■

Perhaps no organization provides hotel sales staff with better promotion and networking opportunities than does the local **Convention and Visitor Bureau (CVB).**

HOTEL TERMINOLOGY AT WORK

Convention and Visitors Bureau: An organization, generally funded by taxes levied on overnight hotel guests, that seeks to increase the number of visitors to the area it represents. Also called the "CVB" for short.

■

Good G.M.s are active members of their CVBs. In addition, these G.M.s encourage significant CVB participation at the DOSM and sales team level. DOSMs who are not considered by the CVB to be active leaders in their community will have fewer chances to influence the CVB in ways that increase business opportunities for their hotels.

The ability of a DOSM and individual sales team members to seek out and take advantage of the networking opportunities available to them is an excellent indicator of the effectiveness of the sales team. These opportunities

---

THE INTERNET AT WORK

Convention and Visitors Bureaus work hard to promote the areas they represent. One of the very best is the CVB of New York City. To view their Web site and explore the ways a CVB can help promote tourism-related and other visitors to a business community, go to:

http://www.nycvisit.com.

---

will result in increased numbers of **sales calls,** and as experienced DOSMs will attest, as sales calls increase, hotel sales levels increase.

HOTEL TERMINOLOGY AT WORK

Sales Call: A meeting arranged for the purpose of selling the hotel's products and services.

■

As a G.M., you should be aware of and evaluate the impact your own sales team makes in your community. A sales team that is not active and visible will, undoubtedly, lose opportunities to improve the sales volume of the hotel because it will miss promotional and networking opportunities that could be capitalized upon by the team if it were aggressively seeking such opportunities.

A hotel sales staff that is performing well will do an excellent job inside the hotel, as well as in the business community it impacts. Exactly how it will do that job is determined in large part by how the G.M. and DOSM decide to structure the department.

SEGMENTATION OF THE SALES AND MARKETING DEPARTMENT

The type of hotel, its clients, and the services it offers often determine the structure and number of staff in the sales and marketing department. Traditionally, this department is organized or segmented based upon:

- The product(s) sold by the sales and marketing staff member
- The market (client) type served
- The method by which the product is distributed (sold)

We will examine these three alternative approaches to departmental organization because, in your career, you will likely encounter variations of each.

By Product Sold

Some DOSMs organize their departments based on what their sales persons sell best. For example, the skills required to effectively sell a banquet require greater knowledge about food production and service than does the sale of a group of guest rooms. When hotels find that the variety of products they sell is great, segmentation of the sales and marketing staff by product sold makes good sense. Typical product designations that can become sales specialty areas include:

- Group guest rooms
- Conferences
- Catered events
- Meetings
- Conventions
- Weddings and special events

Thus, for example, a DOSM may assign a specific salesperson to sell one or more of the above products. In this way, that individual can become very skilled at selling the product (or service) involved.

By Market

In some cases, the DOSM will decide that the department is best organized by considering not the product sold, but, rather, the type of guest who buys the product. Guests with a common characteristic are referred to as a market or market segment. The market segment approach to departmental organization is a traditional one in the hotel industry, and it is frequently used. Market segments commonly identified include the following.

Corporate

This segment consists of the business traveler. It is a very important segment because the room rates paid by business travelers are among the highest the hotel will be able to achieve. Business travelers have special needs, and those in the sales and marketing staff that sell to them must be keenly aware of both the source of these travelers and the hotel services they desire. As seen in chapter 1, the business traveler makes up a large portion of the traveling public. Its makeup is increasingly changing from one that was dominated by male travelers to one divided almost evenly between male and female travelers. Business travelers are a demanding group, but one that pays well for what it wants. It is for this reason that many hotels assign their very best salespersons to this market segment.

Leisure

Leisure travelers come to the hotel for a variety of reasons. These include vacations, weddings, the visiting of friends and family in the area, or any of a number of other non-work-related reasons. Unlike the corporate traveler who may return to the same geographic area frequently, leisure travelers tend to visit a specific area or hotel less often. Because that is true, leisure travelers have traditionally relied heavily on the advice of **travel agents (T.A.)** and other travel advisory groups to recommend hotels. When travel agents book their clients in a hotel, the hotel, in most cases, pays a commission to the T.A. for the booking.

HOTEL TERMINOLOGY AT WORK

Travel Agent: A hospitality professional that assists clients in planning travel. Also known as a T.A.

■

One of the largest and most popular travel advisory groups is the American Automobile Association (AAA). AAA is a not-for-profit membership organization of over eighty motor clubs, with more than 1,000 agency offices serving over 44 million people in the United States and Canada.

AAA publishes a tour book that rates hotels for leisure travelers. Without announcing that they are coming, but at the hotel's specific request, AAA evaluators visit a hotel and rate it on the following six characteristics:

* Exterior, grounds, and public areas
* Guest rooms and bathrooms
* Housekeeping and maintenance
* Room décor, ambiance, and amenities
* Management
* Guest services

Based on the evaluator's assessment, the hotel is assigned an overall property rating consisting of one to five diamonds, with five diamonds being the highest possible score. Of all hotels rated in 2001, the AAA rating book listed the following results:

* 0.2% were 5 Diamond properties
* 2.8% were 4 Diamond properties
* 53.2% were 3 Diamond properties
* 34.5% were 2 Diamond properties
* 6.8% were 1 Diamond properties
* 2.5% Failed 1 Diamond rating

Figure 10.1 describes the rating system used by AAA. It is similar to other rating systems in use (Stars, Class, etc.) but is gererally recognized in the United States as the rating system of greatest importance.

FIGURE 10.1   What the AAA Diamond Ratings Represent

One Diamond: Essential, no-frills accommodations. These hotels meet basic requirements related to comfort, cleanliness, and hospitality.

Two Diamonds: Modest enhancements to the one-diamond type property are required. Moderate prices prevail, and amenities and design elements are modest as well.

Three Diamonds: These properties appeal to the travelers with greater needs than those provided by Two Diamond hotels. Marked improvements in physical attributes, amenities, and level of service above the two diamond properties are evident in these hotels.

Four Diamonds: These hotels are upscale in all areas. Accommodations are refined and stylish. The hallmark of a Four Diamond hotel is its extensive array of amenities and a high degree of hospitality, service, and attention to detail.

Five Diamonds: This highest level reflects a hotel of the first class. The physical facilities are extraordinary in every manner. The fundamental hallmarks at this level are meticulous service and the ability to exceed all guest expectations while maintaining an impeccable standard of excellence and personalized service.

THE INTERNET AT WORK

AAA ratings are important to leisure travelers as well as to G.M.s. To learn more about this membership travel organization, go to their Web site at:

http://www.aaa.com.

The leisure market is significant and, in some resort and tourist areas, represents an extremely large proportion of all rooms booked in the area hotels.

Long-Term Stay

In some cases, when guests check in to a hotel they plan to stay for a very long time. These long-term or extended-stay guests are an emerging market segment. In fact, some entire hotel brands have been designed to appeal specifically to them. Not all hotels appeal to the long-term stay guest but most hotels have some clients who fit this category. At the less expensive end of the room charge scale, some properties that attract extended stay guests do so by providing larger rooms (or suites), cooking facilities, and refrigerators. At the higher end of the room charge scale, hotels have always appealed to some wealthy clients who prefer to live in an environment that provides food, security, and cleaning services rather than in an apartment.

Long-term stay guests come to hotels for a wide variety of reasons and include individuals working on construction projects, those seeking permanent housing in the area, or those whose homes are temporarily uninhabitable. This is a highly desirable market segment for several reasons, including the guaranteed occupancy such guests bring to the hotel, the ease of cleaning their rooms, and their relatively uncomplicated billing. A disadvantage is that these rooms are often sold at very low daily rates. Despite that fact, some DOSMs assign specific sales managers to this segment and have great success with it.

THE INTERNET AT WORK

To view the features offered by one of the very best managed extended-stay brands, visit the Hawthorn Suites Web site at:

http://www.hawthorn.com/.

SMERF and Others

Groups consisting of social, military, educational, religious, or fraternal organizations are known by the acronym **SMERF.**

HOTEL TERMINOLOGY AT WORK

SMERF: Short for social, military, educational, religious, or fraternal organizations as in, "We should assign Vernon to work the SMERF market next year because he has extensive contacts with these groups."

■

This market segment can also be of significant size. Group members hold organizational meetings, may travel as a group and frequently hold conferences and conventions. Additional market groups that, depending on the hotel, may require a dedicated sales staff include sports teams, government workers, tour bus, or any other defined group large enough that, in the opinion of the DOSM, a designated salesperson should be assigned to it.

By Distribution Network

Increasingly, DOSMs structure their departments based on "how" the hotel's sales are made. The specific **distribution channels** that are important to a hotel will vary based on the hotel's type and its market; however, the following are important distribution channels that should be addressed by the sales and marketing department regardless of whether they influence departmental structure.

HOTEL TERMINOLOGY AT WORK

Distribution Channel: A distinct and definable source of hotel rooms or services sales. For example, the Internet is one distribution channel, and meeting planners are another.

■

Drop Ins

Sometimes overlooked, the importance of the **drop in** cannot be overstated.

HOTEL TERMINOLOGY AT WORK

Drop In: A potential buyer (guest) who arrives at the hotel without an appointment.

■

This potential guest simply arrives on the property and requests a site tour that may include sleeping rooms, meeting rooms, or banquet facilities. If a member of the hotel's staff is not available to meet with this prospect when they arrive, the sales opportunity may be lost. Drop ins are a reminder to management that some member of the hotel's sales staff should be available the maximum number of reasonable hours per day to conduct site tours.

Meeting Planners

Professional meeting planners annually buy large numbers of sleeping rooms, as well as reserve significant amounts of meeting and catering space. These individuals may represent a variety of corporations, groups, and organizations. They are sophisticated buyers of hotel products who often use comparison-shopping techniques, and who can heavily influence a hotel's reputation based on their experience with it. It is not unusual for a DOSM to designate one (or more) experienced staff members to deal exclusively with this group of professionals.

THE INTERNET AT WORK

Meeting Professionals International (MPI) is the world's largest association of meeting planning professionals with more than 19,000 members in sixty-four countries. To visit their Web site, go to:

http://www.mpiweb.org

Note the large number of member educational services they offer.

Travel Agents

As discussed earlier, travel agents (T.A.s), are a significant factor in the hotel industry. T.A.s may be retailers, wholesalers, or both. Retail travel agencies and their agents sell directly to the public. For example, if a couple wished to reserve a room at the Waldo Hotel described in this book, they could simply contact a local travel agency in their city (or anywhere in the world), and the agent, using the Global Distribution System (GDS), would make the reservation. In return, the hotel would pay the travel agency a commission for the sale. Depending on the agency and its arrangement with the hotel this commission can range from 5 to 20 percent of the room rate paid by the guest.

Wholesale travel agencies purchase hotel, airline, and other services in bulk from hotels and other businesses, and then offer them for resale through retail T.A.s. In many cases, the wholesaler will **package** the hospitality services they have purchased before offering them for resale.

HOTEL TERMINOLOGY AT WORK

Package: A group of hospitality services (such as hotel rooms, meals, and airfare) sold for one price. For example, a Valentine's Day getaway package to Las Vegas offered by a T.A. might include airfare, lodging, meals, and show tickets for two people at one inclusive price.

■

In addition to individual packages, group tours are often packaged and sold. For example, individual travelers from many different geographic areas purchase a tour package developed by a wholesaler and marketed through retail T.A.s. When travel wholesalers work with travel retailers, the commission paid by the hotel is split, in a prearranged manner, between the wholesale and retail T.A.

In some cases, larger retail T.A.s put together their own packages. In all cases, the T.A. market is an important one for the hotel, and many DOSMs feel it is deserving of a designated sales manager.

THE INTERNET AT WORK

While many people know them as a credit card company, American Express is also a large wholesale and retail travel agency. To view their travel site and investigate the types of services such a T.A. offers, go to:

http://travel.americanexpress.com/travel/personal/.

THE INTERNET AT WORK

ASTA, short for the American Society of Travel Agents, is the world's largest association of travel professionals. Its 26,000 members include travel agents and the companies whose products they sell such as tours, cruises, hotels, and car rentals. As professionals, they are held to high ethical standards. To review their code of ethics, go to:

http://www.astanet.com/about/codeofethics.asp.

Consortia

Consortia are the largest customers of many hotels. Consortia are simply multiple large buyers of hotel (or other hospitality) services who affiliate for

---

HOTEL TERMINOLOGY AT WORK

Consortia: Groups of hotel service buyers organized for the purpose of reducing their client's travel-related costs. A single such group is a consortium.

■

---

the purpose of obtaining lower prices for their members. For example, a consortium representing dozens of large corporate travel departments may request that a hotel offer significant discounts if any of the corporate travelers represented by the consortium stay at the hotel. If the hotel agrees to work with the consortium, it is the job of the DOSM or other member of the sales team to evaluate the potential volume level of this client, establish a **negotiated rate**, identify any blackout dates, and then monitor the consortium's **pickup.**

HOTEL TERMINOLOGY AT WORK

Negotiated Rate: A special room rate, offered for a fixed period of time, to a specific client of the hotel. As in, "What is the negotiated rate we should offer the Travelsavers consortium next year?"

Pickup: The actual number of rooms used by a client in a defined time period. As in "What was Travelsavers' pickup last year?"

■

Internet

The Internet is a fairly recent but extremely significant new distribution channel. In addition, it is a channel that many DOSMs who are not technologically up-to-date have not used to its fullest capacity. Technically, the Internet is both its own distribution channel and a way for other channels to communicate with the hotel. Consider, for example, that drop-ins, meeting planners, travel agents, and consortium members may all have learned about a specific hotel by surfing hotel Web sites on the Internet. In addition, individual buyers can purchase via the net, and meeting planners can view a hotel's rooms and meeting space through the hotel's on-line brochure or, more recently, streaming video tours. In addition, many travel wholesalers sell on the Internet, and technology savvy hotel DOSMs can link their own hotel Web sites to those sites likely to draw potential customers from any distribution channel. The total percentage of room nights booked exclusively over the Internet make it the fastest growing distribution channel in the hotel industry today. Accordingly, some DOSMs designate a qualified sales staff member exclusively to this growing area.

THE INTERNET AT WORK

For an example of how a hotel can effectively link its own Internet site to that of a site that may bring it additional business, visit the site of the Atlanta Convention and Visitor's Bureau at:

http://www.acvb.com.

When you arrive at the site, click on "Accommodations"; then choose "All Hotels"; then choose "Hyatt Regency Atlanta"; and note how easy it is for potential clients to both "see" and "book" a hotel using today's Internet technology.

SALES AND MARKETING ACTIVITIES

The pressure to increase sales placed upon the DOSM by the G.M. and the hotel's owners is often intense. But for a G.M. without a strong background in sales and marketing, the productivity and quality of work performed in this department can be difficult to evaluate.

As a good G.M., you should strive to stay current with the most recent trends in hotel sales techniques. You should also know that all individuals responsible for the sales and marketing of the hotel must accomplish some tasks that can, indeed, be evaluated. These tasks include a variety of important activities in the areas of selling and marketing. By examining the presence and quality of key sales and marketing areas, the G.M. can more fairly and effectively evaluate the work of the DOSM and the sales and marketing department's staff.

Sales Efforts

When G.M.s are asked about who is responsible for the sales and marketing effort at their hotels, their answer should be "everyone." Every staff member in the hotel should be a salesperson. That is, every employee of the hotel, doing his or her job properly, helps the sales and marketing department to better "sell" the hotel. It falls to the DOSM and his or her staff, however, to perform the tasks required to identify potential clients, to maintain records of the department's interactions with them, and to undertake activities to ensure that clients know they are appreciated.

The Sales and Marketing Committee

Well-managed hotels have a designated DOSM. Those properties that are best managed, however, will also have a **sales and marketing committee** chaired by the hotel's G.M.

Many areas within the hotel are affected by the sales effort. If, for example, the DOSM wishes to create and promote an **inclusive** weekend getaway

HOTEL TERMINOLOGY AT WORK

Sales and Marketing Committee: The group of individuals responsible for coordinating the hotel's sales and marketing effort.

■

package for couples that includes a room at the hotel, a complimentary pay-per-view movie, dinner buffet, and late checkout the next morning, the impact on the hotel's operations will be significant.

HOTEL TERMINOLOGY AT WORK

Inclusive: A single price that includes all charges.

■

In this example, the staff required to service and the food production cost required to prepare the dinner buffet affect the food and beverage department. The FOM is affected because the front office staff must be instructed that the package price includes the free movie and thus movie charges, as they occur, should not be posted (charged) to the guest's folio, because the guest has in fact already paid for the movie as part of the inclusive package. The controller must assign prorated portions of the inclusive revenue to the appropriate department, and the housekeeping staff must be informed that rooms reserved for this package will have to be cleaned later than usual (because of the late checkout). In this example, a coordination of efforts is clearly required. It is the role of the sales and marketing committee to provide that coordination.

The sales and marketing committee will generally consist of the G.M., the DOSM, all members of the sales and marketing staff, the controller, the food and beverage director, the FOM, and the executive housekeeper (or **rooms division manager**).

HOTEL TERMINOLOGY AT WORK

Rooms Division Manager: An individual in a hotel responsible for the management of both the front office and the housekeeping departments. (This position does not exist in every hotel.)

■

Additional members may be added depending on the needs of the hotel and the talents of the management staff. This committee harmonizes efforts across departmental lines, engages in long-term planning, and ensures the cooperation of all involved in the sales and marketing process. The G.M.'s participation is important in two ways. First, the mere presence of the G.M. demonstrates the significance of the group. Second, when departments must be encouraged (or instructed) to modify their current activities or procedures to assist in new sales or marketing initiatives, the G.M. is on hand to confirm that the modifications should be undertaken and that they have the G.M.'s support.

The Sales Cycle

One beneficial way to examine the sales activities of the sales and marketing department is to consider the activities involved before, during, and after a hypothetical sale. Of course, not all sales involve each of the activities we will examine, but each does exist in the sales cycle. At each phase in the sales cycle, hotel employees must perform well or risk losing the sale to another property. As a G.M., if you continually find client dissatisfaction at any one of these phases, immediate corrective action is required to help ensure that your sales and marketing department maintains its reputation for quality and competency. In addition, uncorrected problems in the sales and marketing department will ultimately be damaging to the long-term economic health of the hotel so it is a good idea to regularly monitor and correct sales-related problems as they are identified.

The following events are typically encountered in the sales cycle.

- **Presale Phase**
  - Aleshia M., a Waldo Hotel sales manager, meets, for the first time, Mr. Jodi at a golf outing held to raise funds for the American Cancer Society. Mr. Jodi mentions that he is this year's president of the Society of Antique Furniture Appraisers.
  - At dinner following the golf outing, Aleshia inquires about any meetings held in the city by the society. Mr. Jodi replies that they annually meet in the area, for three days, and that the Society's board of directors votes each year on which hotel the group will select. In the past, states Mr. Jodi, the group has stayed exclusively at the Altoona Hotel (a competitor) and that they are relatively happy with that hotel.
  - After dinner, Aleshia invites Mr. Jodi to the Waldo Hotel for lunch and a site tour. Based primarily on the friendship established on the golf course, Mr. Jodi agrees to the meeting.
  - At the lunch, Aleshia determines that the Waldo has meeting space and sleeping rooms sufficient to meet the needs of the society and that the hotel could accommodate the dates of the society's next meeting. On the site tour, Aleshia points out the Waldo Hotel's best features, subtly contrasting them to the Altoona Hotel, but without disparaging that competitor. At the conclusion of the lunch, Aleshia asks Mr. Jodi if he could arrange to include the Waldo on the list of hotels allowed to submit a **bid** on the Society's next meeting. Mr. Jodi agrees to do so.

HOTEL TERMINOLOGY AT WORK

Bid: An offer by the hotel to supply sleeping rooms, meeting space, food and beverages, or other services to a potential client at a stated price. If the bid is accepted, the hotel will issue the client a contract detailing the agreement made between the hotel and the client.

■

- **Sales Phase**
  - With the help of Mr. Jodi, Aleshia receives an **RFP** from the society.

HOTEL TERMINOLOGY AT WORK

RFP: Short for "Request for Proposal." An RFP is a request from a potential client for the hotel to submit its pricing offer (proposal) to the client in writing. An RFP may include questions about the hotel's features and services in addition to the prices it is offering.

■

- In conjunction with the DOSM, the RFP is completed and submitted on time. Room rates are established based on the hotel's estimate of the group's sleeping room pickup, as well as the food and beverage and meeting room revenue the group will generate.
- Based on the RFPs received, the society's board narrows its choice of hotels to two, one of which is the Waldo Hotel. The society, following a site tour by the entire board, a complimentary lunch served by the F&B department (and attended by the G.M.), and with the visible support of Mr. Jodi, selects the Waldo Hotel as the site for its next meeting.
- Aleshia, in conjunction with the DOSM, prepares a **group contract** for the society detailing the agreement with the hotel that specifically addresses any **attrition** and cancellation penalties.

HOTEL TERMINOLOGY AT WORK

Group Contract: A legal document used to summarize the agreement between a hotel and its group client.

Attrition: The difference between the original request and the actual purchases of a group. For example, a group might reserve one hundred rooms, but actually use only fifty. The hotel's standard group contract may, in such a case, stipulate that the group pay a penalty for "over-reserving."

■

- Aleshia arranges with the controller's office to forward a direct bill application to the society. The society's bank references are reviewed by the controller's office, and a credit line is established.

- Aleshia establishes a group **block** for the society to ensure they have sleeping rooms reserved for their meeting.

HOTEL TERMINOLOGY AT WORK

Block: Rooms reserved exclusively for members of a specific group. As in, "We need to create a block of fifty rooms for May 10 and 11 for the Society of Antique Furniture Appraisers."
∎

- Aleshia, or another member of the sales and marketing team, details the client's contracted requirements, in writing, to those hotel departments (food and beverage, controller, front office, housekeeping, etc.) needing this information.
- Aleshia, or some member of the Sales and Marketing team, monitors the client's block to ensure that the hotel meets contractual terms regarding the block. That is, it holds, for the group's purchase only, the required number of rooms for the length of time stipulated in the contract.
- Aleshia attends a preevent sales meeting of hotel staff. The staff reviews the needs and special requests of the groups that will be coming to the hotel in the next week. One such group is the society, and Aleshia reviews the contract terms with the staff.
- Aleshia is present on the first day of the society's meeting to welcome the client. Periodically throughout the meeting, she checks in on the group's main contact person to ensure the meeting is going well and to solve any problems that may arise.
- Aleshia is on hand at the society's closing cocktail party/dinner event to personally thank Mr. Jodi and the board for selecting the Waldo.
- **Postsale Phase**
  - Aleshia writes to each member of the society's board thanking them for choosing the Waldo Hotel. The letter is cosigned by the DOSM or G.M. Aleshia hand delivers a special token of appreciation to Mr. Jodi and thanks him for his assistance with the society.
  - Aleshia reviews with the accounts receivable clerk in the controller's office the society's final bill to ensure that it is accurate.
  - The society is added to the preferred client list, ensuring that it will be contacted and recognized, in some manner, by the hotel on a regular basis.
  - An entry is made in the sales activity calendar ensuring that the hotel sales team will begin the bid process with the society next year in ample time to retain the business.
  - All written records related to the society's event are properly filed.

As can be seen, there are many activities that must be performed flawlessly in the competitive hotel sales process. People skills, organizational skills, and conflict management abilities are essential characteristics of sales and marketing department staff members. Many of the sales activities identified earlier (and more) are complex and vitally important. Errors could be made in any of the processes required for a successful sale, and these errors could cause as much client dissatisfaction as would errors in any of the hotel's operating departments.

The marketing activities of a hotel typically draw a great deal of attention from the G.M., however, it is a wise G.M. who recognizes that sales execution is equally as, or more, important than marketing activities. While it is somewhat of an oversimplification, it can be said that sales is the process of servicing business currently identified while marketing seeks to generate new business. It makes little sense to expend tremendous effort attracting new clients if the sales processes involving the hotel's current clients are not properly managed. In fact, until the hotel's sales process is a smooth and efficient one, it is probably best not to risk permanently alienating new clients by serving them poorly also.

Trace Systems

All sales and marketing departments must have a way to keep a record of the hotel's clients. This record includes those who have used the hotel in the past, those currently using the hotel, and those **prospects** that might use the hotel in the future. In addition, records of guest rooms and meeting space that (a) have been sold, (b) is currently reserved, and (c) that will be sold in the future, as well as the rates at which these are sold, must be accurately maintained.

HOTEL TERMINOLOGY AT WORK

Prospect: An individual or group who, while not currently using the hotel, are considered potential clients with a good likelihood of using the hotel in the future.

Note: "Prospecting" is the verb used to indicate the process of finding "Prospects."

■

When you consider that a sales and marketing department makes hundreds or thousands of client contacts and sales per year, it is not surprising that a system must be in place to keep track of all these contacts. A good DOSM has a **trace system** to help the department maintain its sales records, meet deadlines, and plan future activities.

By examining a simple sales call, you can see the importance of an effective trace system. Assume that a member of the Waldo Hotel's sales team visits the office of the president of a local environmental group that holds quarterly meetings of its membership. The prospect states that they could be interested in moving their meeting business to the Waldo Hotel, but have a

HOTEL TERMINOLOGY AT WORK

Trace System: A methodical process used to record what has been done in the past and what must be done in the future to maximize sales effectiveness. An effective trace system includes a "contact management" component that allows records to be kept for each individual client (contact).

■

current contract with a competing hotel that will not expire for eight months. The following are activities that should, at minimum, happen following the sales call:

- A thank-you note or letter is written to the prospect thanking them for the meeting.
- A calendar notation is made of when to contact the client in the future so that a sales proposal can be submitted for the client's review.
- A site-tour should be scheduled, if possible.
- The client's demographic data should be added to the hotel's group database.

Without an effective trace system, deadlines will be missed, follow-up calls will not be made, important client information will be misplaced, over-bookings or underbookings will occur, and business will ultimately be lost. In today's competitive environment, it is imperative that the DOSM use an automated trace system. As a G.M., you should review the features of the system in use at your hotel to ensure that it is being utilized to its fullest potential.

THE INTERNET AT WORK

One of the most popular computerized contact management systems available is the "ACT" program developed by the Interact Commerce Corp. You can view their Web site at:

www.act.com.

To download a free trial of the system that will familiarize you with its many features, go to:

http://www.act.com/home/index.php3?cellid=207000011011.

Sales Leads/Cold Calling

The majority of guests who visit a hotel are not return guests. While some guests do return week after week or year after year, most guests do not. Because that is true, a hotel must continually seek new clients. Prospecting for new clients is, arguably, the single most important task of the DOSM's staff. A sales **lead** can come from many sources.

HOTEL TERMINOLOGY AT WORK

Lead: Information about a prospect who is likely to buy from the hotel.

■

Networking can create leads. Leads can come from a CVB, from a referral by a current guest, by employees, or simply by a prospect's telephone call to the hotel. A DOSM's ability to seek out and cultivate quality leads is critical to his or her own success as well as that of the hotel. In fact, one good way for a G.M. to evaluate the quality of a DOSM's skills is to meet and discuss on a regular basis:

- New leads that have been uncovered since the last meeting
- The realistic sales potential of these leads
- Who in the department is following up on the leads
- How the leads will be pursued
- What, if anything, the G.M. can do to help cultivate the prospect
- Any sales that have resulted from the leads discussed at previous meetings

An effective DOSM structures the sales and marketing department in a way that provides for plenty of time to adequately follow-up leads with a sales call, and even more important, reserves adequate time for **cold calling.**

HOTEL TERMINOLOGY AT WORK

Cold Calling: Making a sales visit/presentation to a potential client without having previously set an appointment to do so.

■

Good sales people seek opportunities to cold call whenever they can. The objective of such sales calls is to qualify prospective clients by identifying those that have a high likelihood of using the hotel's rooms or services. Of course, those that are likely prospects are further cultivated until a sale is made. While an in-depth discussion of the techniques good hotel sales people use to identify and qualify prospects is beyond the scope of this book, it is important for you, as a G.M., to be able to identify an active prospective client solicitation program. That is, sales and marketing staff should not simply "answer the phone" and take an order for a sale. Rather, they should actively go out to seek and create sales opportunities by following up on sales leads and by making an appropriate number of cold calls each week.

There is not a significant amount of regularly published, hotel-specific sales information available to DOSMs. Because of that, HSMAI memberships, as well as subscriptions to hotel magazines and journals that do publish articles and in-depth features related to hotel sales techniques, are a worthwhile investment for G.M.s to make in a sales and marketing staff.

Client Appreciation Activities

Experienced DOSMs know that making a sale is the beginning, not the end, of the client/hotel relationship. Too many hotels lose clients simply because they did not let the client know how much their business was appreciated. Client appreciation activities are designed to allow the hotel to express its gratitude to clients for their current business. These activities can include anything from inviting a client or group of clients to join the DOSM or G.M. for dinner or drinks, to organizing an elaborate, once or twice a year gala client appreciation event. Golfing and other sporting events, concerts and theater tickets are all common ways to express a genuine appreciation for business that has been received. Gift giving is another traditional way to express appreciation to a hotel's best clients. Gifts given to clients as tokens of appreciation can range from the simple to the elaborate. It is, of course, important to first determine whether his or her employer allows the client to accept such gifts. In all cases, the goal of a successful client appreciation event or activity is to both solidify the business relationship with current clients and to communicate to potential clients the seriousness with which the hotel views the hotel/client relationship.

As a G.M., you should be able to objectively review and evaluate the quality of client appreciation activities designed and executed by your sales and marketing department. In addition, simply talking to current clients will give you a good idea of what, if any, client appreciation activities are actually being implemented and how well these are received.

Marketing Efforts

Earlier in this chapter we noted that the definitions of "sales" and "marketing" vary widely. Add to the confusion the terms "publicity," "promotion," "public relations," and "advertising," and one can readily see why so many involved in sales and marketing view these activities differently.

For purposes of this book, marketing is considered to involve all the activities designed to improve the hotel's profitability by increasing ADR, occupancy percentage, or both. These activities include market research to discover, for example, what groups of potential clients exist, what their needs are, and which of those needs you can meet. It also includes communicating your abilities to meet needs to those potential clients you identify so that they can, in time, become clients to whom you sell regularly.

Marketing Plan Development

Effective marketing begins with the development of a **marketing plan.**

HOTEL TERMINOLOGY AT WORK

Marketing Plan: A calendar of specific activities designed to meet the hotel's sales goals.

■

The marketing plan is simply a compilation of activities designed to meet the goals of the sales and marketing department. Marketing plans are typically prepared on an annual basis. In a hotel, the DOSM, in conjunction with the G.M., is responsible for developing the marketing plan. Activities often included in a marketing plan involve analysis of your competition, an analysis of your own hotel, establishing your prices, and publicizing your offerings through continued advertising, promotions, and public relations activities.

The format of marketing plans can vary greatly, but most include the following:

- A review of the market in which you compete, including historical
  - Occupancy trends
  - ADR trends
  - Performance of your hotel in the market

- Competitive analysis, including a review of your competitor's
  - Strengths
  - Weaknesses
  - Price structure

- Competitive analysis of your own hotel, including a review of your hotel's
  - Strengths
  - Weaknesses
  - Price structure

- Forecast of future market conditions, including
  - Estimates of market growth or contraction
  - Performance goals and objectives for your hotel
  - Timeline for achieving these goals and objectives

- The determination of specific marketing strategies and activities designed to meet your goals and objectives, including those related to
  - Advertising
  - Public Relations
  - Promotions

- Preparation of a marketing budget

- The development of measurement and evaluation tools to help assess the marketing plan's effectiveness and allow for needed modifications

When completed, the marketing plan is submitted to the G.M. and, often, the hotel's owners for approval and funding. A marketing plan is essentially a blueprint for the sales and marketing effort. As a G.M., you will want to carefully review marketing plans submitted to you for approval and monitor those that are currently in place to ensure that they are being implemented by the DOSM and the sales and marketing department staff.

Advertising

While a thorough discussion of advertising principles and philosophies is beyond the scope of this book, hotel managers should become familiar enough with them to assist the DOSM in decision making. Essentially, hotel advertising involves bringing the hotel's products and services to the attention of potential and current customers. Hotel advertising is typically done using one or more of the following:

- Exterior signage
- In-hotel and in-room signage and materials
- Brochures
- Radio or television commercials
- Direct mailings
- Internet banners
- E-mail messages
- Yellow Pages
- Franchisor-supplied advertising vehicles (directories, co-ops, etc.)
- Billboards
- Personal contact

Effective advertising can be costly and thus its effectiveness must be constantly evaluated. While there is a great deal of variability in successful advertising pieces and campaigns, the best of these:

- Are eye or ear catching
- Are memorable
- Sell the hotel's features
- Are cost-effective
- Do not become quickly outdated
- Reflect positively on the hotel's image
- Can be easily directed to the hotel's core client groups

An effective marketing plan will include the advertising activities (and their costs) that are to be undertaken by the sales and marketing department in the period covered by the marketing plan, as well as a way in which to measure the advertising's value to the hotel.

Promotions, Publicity, and Public Relations

In addition to advertising, an effective sales and marketing department includes promotion, publicity, and public relations activities. These three terms are closely related, sometimes overlap, and are often confused; however, each plays a part in the successful sales and marketing of a hotel.

- *Promotions.* In the hotel industry, the term "promotion" most often refers to a "special" packaging of products or services. For example, a hotel in a cold climate may create a "Summer Getaway" promotion to be marketed in the winter. The inclusive package might include a sleeping room, the use of the hotel's pool, a special "Beach Theme" dinner party, and complimentary rum-based drinks reminiscent of those consumed on the beach. Specially priced, this promotion would be "promoted" through advertising and publicity. Similarly, a franchise company may offer, as a special promotion, triple airline (frequent flier) miles for all stays completed between two fixed dates. Again, information about this promotion would be disseminated through advertising and, possibly, through publicity.

- *Publicity.* Publicity refers to information about the hotel that is distributed, free of charge, by the media. The good news is that publicity costs the hotel nothing. The bad news is that the publicity may be either good or bad. The news media is, of necessity, an independent force in the shaping of public opinion. Cultivating good relationships with the media is an important job of the G.M. When such a relationship exists, it may be easier for the hotel to achieve positive publicity. If, for example, the governor of the state is visiting your hotel and that fact is mentioned in the newspaper, the publicity value is good. However, even with good media relationships established, a highly publicized drug-related shooting in a nearby hotel carrying the same brand affiliation as your hotel will likely reflect poorly on your own property. In situations such as this, it is important that the hotel have an active public relations program in place.

- *Public Relations (PR).* PR includes those activities designed to ensure that the hotel has a positive public image. PR activities help the hotel let potential clients know that it is (as it should be) a good citizen of the community. PR efforts can include, among many other activities, hosting charity events, contributing cash or in-kind services, or the donation of the hotel's staff time for a worthy cause. It is important to remember that the hotel's community can, depending on the hotel, be viewed as affecting local, state, national, and even international inhabitants. In all cases, it is the intent of the hotel that its PR activities positively reflect the values of the hotel and those of its ownership and that, if necessary, the hotel can rely on positive PR to help counter any unwarranted negative publicity.

In the hotel business, the terms "marketing," "advertising," "promotion," "publicity," "public relations," and "sales" are intertwined. They become more clear-cut, however, when evaluating a single event. For example, if the city in which your hotel is located is hosting the annual convention of Rodeo Cowboys, if you are the **headquarter hotel** and if your hotel decides to offering an evening of free country western dance lessons on your outdoor patio during that same period, you could certainly create a sign saying you are offering the free lessons. If you do, that's "advertising."

HOTEL TERMINOLOGY AT WORK

Headquarter Hotel: The hotel that hosts the main group of attendees during an event in which there are multiple host hotels.

■

If you place a copy of that sign in 100 locations in town, that's "promotion." If, as part of the patio décor, you lease the use of a live bull for the night and the bull escapes and tramples the head of the City Council's flower bed, that's "publicity." If you can get the head of the City Council to laugh about it because you are known as a big supporter of community beautification efforts, that's "public relations." If some of the people in your city who purchase significant numbers of hotel rooms and meeting spaces each year attend the free dance lessons, see the hotel's features, discuss the costs and benefits with your sales staff, and ultimately become clients who spend money at your hotel, that's "sales."

An effective DOSM and sales and marketing department must be adept at all aspects of marketing because marketing, properly executed, produces profitable sales. As a G.M., it is sales volume, in addition to other important hotel goals, that will ultimately be used to gauge your own effectiveness.

Internet Sales and Marketing

While the Internet is, in many respects, simply another marketing tool used by a hotel, its significance, growth, and potential requires special attention. When properly utilized and managed, the Internet is an excellent vehicle for communicating with current and potential clients. An important point for the G.M. to remember is that the Internet allows smaller hotels to compete, on an equal footing, with larger ones. The Internet, at this point in its development, delivers just three media components. These are audio, text, and images, all of which can be just as good as (or better) on your site(s) than on your competitor's site.

Effective use of the Web allows your hotel to take advantage of an inexpensive direct line to consumers. This is a situation that hotel sales and marketing departments have never before experienced and may not know how to manage properly. Prior to the widespread use of the Internet, if you wanted the individual consumer or T.A. to "see" and experience your hotel, you were required to do costly direct mail pieces or site visits. Both these strategies are expensive. On the Web, you can sell directly to your potential clients for a few hundred dollars a month.

While there are many sales and marketing uses of the Internet, three that are of growing importance to hotels are:

- On-line reservation systems
- Web sites
- E-mail systems

On-Line Reservation Systems

The teaming of the GDS with the Internet has been one of the most significant technological advancements in the hotel industry in the past fifty years. T.A.s have, for many years, been able to check availability, compare prices, and book a hotel on-line. Now, virtually any traveler can do the same. Simply typing the words "Discount Hotel Reservations" into the search bar of a typical Web server produces hundreds of alternative sites to review. On many of these sites, consumers can book hotels on-line if the hotel has given the site authority to do so. Some on-line sites, such as Travelocity.com (American Airline's site), and Expedia.com (Microsoft's site) are very popular and well known because they service virtually all the hotels found on the GDS. Other, smaller sites, such as A1-discount-hotels.com, specialize in specific larger cities.

THE INTERNET AT WORK

One of the most popular international booking sites since its inception in 1971, as well as one of the best managed, is the German site: HRS. To view this multilingual site, go to:

www.hrs.com.

Note that the site has been translated into twenty-two languages.

In all cases, placing your hotel's room inventory on line and allowing consumers the ability to book rooms in real time is clearly a critical part of a hotel's overall marketing strategy. Those on-line reservation sites selected should be in keeping with the hotel's desired image, and the booking results of the sites should be measurable.

Like all consumer advertising and communication mediums, on-line booking sites vary in quality and popularity. They are, however, the fastest growing source of reservations in the hotel industry and deserve the special attention of the DOSM. As a G.M., it is important that the sites you use accurately reflect the products and services you offer at the prices at which you wish to sell.

Web Sites

As the popularity of the Internet has grown, many large hotels have created their own Web sites. In addition, smaller hotels affiliated with a brand often share Web sites with other brand franchisees. In this way, even small hotels can achieve some level of visibility on their own Web page.

The appearance of a hotel's Web site has become increasingly important and will continue to become even more so. The placement of text, images, and other media, and white space, on a Web page makes a strong statement about the quality of a hotel's products and services. Despite that fact, most hoteliers simply do not have the ability to create an effective Web page, nor do they have the technical skill required to evaluate the site's effectiveness.

THE INTERNET AT WORK

Some companies specialize in providing Web site design and other technology application solutions to hotels. To view one such company's product offerings, go to:

www.acromarketing.com.

Even evaluating the work of a Web site designer can be complex for a DOSM and G.M. There are, however, some facts that are true about all effective hotel Web sites.

- The site is easy to navigate.
- The site has some level of interactivity.
- The site is connected (linked) to appropriate companion sites.
- The site allows for on-line booking.
- The site balances guest privacy needs with the hotel's desire to build a customer database.
- Updating and revising room rates on the site is easy.
- The site includes a virtual tour of the property (with at least enough pictures or streaming video to ensure that potential guests get an accurate image of the hotel).
- The site complements your other marketing efforts.

- The site is in the language(s) of your clients.
- The site address is easy to remember.

Too often, DOSMs evaluate the quality of their site based on the number of visits (hits) the site receives per day or week. It is important to remember that the end goal of a Web site is not simply hits. The goal is sales. Site traffic is important, but the quality of that traffic in terms of potential sales is much more important. Measures of Web site effectiveness must be tied to sales production, not to hits. This, of course, is no different than the normal procedure of evaluating a salesperson on their actual sales production (sales made), rather than sales calls (hits).

Some hotels fail to produce the results they seek from their Web sites because they do not **link** their sites properly nor do they take full advantage of Internet search engines to identify those sites.

HOTEL TERMINOLOGY AT WORK

Link: A relationship between two Web sites. When Web site users select a link at one site, they are taken to another Web site address. An external link leads to a Web page other than the current one; an internal link leads elsewhere on the current page.

■

Effective DOSMs ensure that their Web sites are linked in a manner designed to maximize the sales potential of the site. For example, assume your hotel is located near the stadium of a professional sports team. Those Internet users who enter the name of the sports team in an Internet search engine (e.g., Excite or Yahoo) are likely looking for information about the team, such as its roster, won/lost record, schedule, and the like. These are not necessarily consumers seeking hotel rooms. Thus, linking with sites that appear on a search for the team "name" may not be effective, even though the number of hits to these sites may be high.

Alternatively, however, those consumers who search for "driving directions to the stadium" are likely to be:

- Attending one or more of the games
- Unfamiliar with the area
- Potentially seeking a place to dine or stay overnight

In this example, Web sites that appear when "stadium," "stadium driving directions," and similar entries are entered into search engines are likely to produce the consumers the hotel truly seeks, even though the number of hits from such related sites may be smaller. Of course, this is no different from the experience of retail stores who have long recognized that there is a big difference between those who are "just looking" and those who are "buying."

Which sites should you link with? The answer is easier when you put yourself in your guest's position. If your hotel is near a museum, search for "museum." The sites to which you will be sent are the same ones to which your clients will be sent, so those are where an effective DOSM will seek reciprocal links. As a G.M., it is relatively easy to use the same search engines as your potential clients to see if your DOSM has linked you with the **demand generators** you have identified for your hotel.

HOTEL TERMINOLOGY AT WORK

Demand Generator: An organization, entity, or location that creates a significant need for hotel services. Examples in a community include large businesses, tourist sites, sports teams, educational facilities, and manufacturing plants.

∎

Another misunderstood aspect of hotel Internet sites relates to offering discounts on packages or guest rooms when those items are purchased on the hotel's Web site. One of the best ways to spend money promoting your Web site is to reduce the selling prices on the products you feature on it. Spending money on regular advertising means you must pay for everyone who sees (and doesn't see) the ad, whether or not they ever make a purchase. When, however, you spend advertising money by charging less for your products booked on-line, you only have to pay for the people who actually place orders. As a result you only pay for this form of advertising when it works! Web shoppers are often looking for the best quality of hotel they can select at the lowest price available, and Web advertising makes it easy for them to identify which hotel offers it. Selling rooms on the Web for a reduced price makes economic sense in the long run. Because it is less expensive to sell on the Web, if you split your savings with your guests, you and your guests will both benefit.

There is little question that hotel Web sites will play an increasingly large role in every hotel's sales and marketing efforts. Therefore, a good DOSM will always promote the Web site to current clients and contacts by including the hotel's site address on business cards, as well as in all promotional materials.

E-mail Systems

Hotels have long communicated with guests through direct mailings, the telephone, and more recently, by fax. Today, e-mail systems are a newer method of mass communication that is increasingly used. The number of DOSMs and sales managers putting e-mail addresses on their own business cards is rapidly increasing. This practice is no longer unique, but rather has become quite commonplace. The same is true of the hotel's clients. Therefore an effective, up-to-date e-mail list is today's equivalent of traditional systems of manually filing business cards. Unlike direct mail, e-mails can be inexpensively sent to virtually hundreds of clients and potential clients in a matter of seconds.

In addition to their usefulness in quickly moving documents via their attachment feature, most e-mail systems also automatically update the user's database whenever an e-mail is received. Properly used, this database can be accessed whenever the hotel wishes to innovatively communicate a special rate, promotion, or new hotel feature to its client list. E-mail systems play an increasingly important communications role in hotel sales and marketing and should be utilized to their fullest potential.

Evaluating the Sales and Marketing Department

One of the most difficult tasks faced by the G.M. is that of evaluating the effort of the sales and marketing staff. Reduced sales and guest counts, for example, are not always the result of ineffective sales and marketing department efforts. Consider, for example, that a hotel facing stagnate or declining sales may not provide good service. This could be the case when the housekeeping, maintenance, or food and beverage staffs do not perform well. In other cases, the hotel may face lowered sales levels if the property is older or if newer competitors are capturing market share. Also, if the total market size declines, it is reasonable to expect that sales levels, at least in the short run, will decline also. Despite the difficulties of isolating the impact of the efforts of the sales and marketing staff, it is a task that must be done. Fortunately, there are a variety of tools available to make this job easier.

Certainly G.M.s can subjectively evaluate the professionalism and appearance of the staff, their diligence at work, and their creativity in presenting the hotel's best features. Also, in some cases, increasing occupancies may indicate good effort by the sales and marketing department, as may an increase in ADR. It is important to remember, however, that both of these increases could be the result of an increase in guest demand and thus could actually mask a decline in the quality of sales and marketing efforts. Fortunately, there are also quantitative reports designed to measure the actual end result of the DOSM's efforts. Two of the most widely used and most closely watched of these are the Pace and the STAR reports.

The Pace Report

With the proper marketing plan in place and with the DOSM's staff trained in effective selling techniques, a hotel sales and marketing department will sell, at some volume level (pace), the hotel's group rooms and services. As a G.M., it is important for you to know and monitor the group rooms sales pace set by the DOSM and the sales and marketing staff.

Confirmed group sales made by the sales and marketing department during the month should be recorded. Some of these sales may be made during the month, for that month, but most will be made for a future date that will likely be months or even years in the future. Of course, in a given month, the hotel may also experience some group cancellations. In addition, during the month some clients will have requested that a contract be sent to them for review before signing. These tentative pieces of business may represent significant work on the part of the sales and marketing staff and will likely yield sales in the future.

To determine the pace at which actual group sales take place, G.M.s should rely on a monthly, (or more frequently prepared) group **Pace Report.** Figure 10.2 is an example of a monthly group rooms pace report.

HOTEL TERMINOLOGY AT WORK

Pace Report: A document summarizing confirmed (group) sales made by the sales and marketing department.

■

Note that the Pace Report details sales made in a given month (January, in this example) that will be realized in future months. A review of the data in Figure 10.2 reveals that the selling pace of the hotel for January (8,550 rooms) is up a total of 21 percent over last year (7,055 rooms). This percentage change is computed as:

$$\frac{\text{Total Sales This January} - \text{Total Sales Last January}}{\text{Total Sales Last January}} = \text{Percentage Change}$$

FIGURE 10.2   Sample Pace Report

Waldo Hotel Group Rooms Pace Report for JANUARY, 200X			
	Sold This Month	Total Sold YTD	Sold Same Month Last Year	Total Sold Last YTD
Jan	25		150	
Feb	450	750	250	550
Mar	550	1,550	330	1,250
Apr	650	1,550	550	1,350
May	875	1,175	650	1,050
June	1,100	1,400	800	1,700
July	1,350	2,250	1,100	2,150
Aug	1,700	2,900	1,500	1,900
Sept	500	700	750	1,750
Oct	300	800	550	1,050
Nov	850	1,150	300	600
Dec	200	550	125	225
Total	8,550	14,775	7,055	13,575

In this example, using January sales data:

$$\frac{8{,}550 - 7{,}055}{7{,}055} = 21.1\%$$

Using the same formula, for year to date (**YTD**) data:

$$\frac{14{,}775 - 13{,}575}{13{,}575} = 8.1\%$$

HOTEL TERMINOLOGY AT WORK

YTD: Short for "year to date." Used when comparing performance from the beginning of the year up through, and including, the present period.

■

In this example, it appears that sales in the month of January were very good (up 21%) compared with January of last year, and that the YTD sales productivity of the DOSM's staff is good (up 8%) compared with the same period last year.

A Pace Report can be prepared based on the number of rooms sold, the sales value (in dollars) of the sales made, or both. It can also be produced to include any period of time in the future. In this example, the Pace Report was prepared based on the number of group rooms sold in January for a twelve-month period that ends in December of the same year.

Traditionally, cancellations are tracked separately and reported in the month they are canceled, not when the group was slated to arrive. That is, if a group of one hundred rooms canceled, in January, their contract for rooms in the coming June, that value would be noted in the January cancellation total. Tentative contracts, which may also be monitored, are not counted as a sale until a signed contract has been returned.

Note that the Pace Report tells management where future occupancy problems may exist. For example, in Figure 10.2 it is possible that a potential problem exists in September because, compared with last year, much less business was booked (700 rooms this YTD vs. 1,750 YTD at this same time last year). Corrective management action in this case may consist of increased sales efforts and attention devoted now to sales in September.

Of course, the number of rooms reserved by a guest is only an estimate of the rooms sold until those rooms are actually occupied. Therefore, it is important that the group contracts signed by the hotel and its group guests are realistic in regard to the number of rooms that will actually be sold. If the sales department overestimates the pick up on a contract, the Pace Report will be artificially inflated. Many G.M.s also request that the DOSM prepare a catering Pace Report detailing the monthly food or meeting room sales made by the sales and marketing staff. A Pace Report should be prepared for any identifiable segment of business that the G.M. would like to monitor.

A strong Pace Report would show that sales made by the sales and marketing department are increasing on a monthly and/or annual basis. A weaker report would show they are level or declining. By comparing the Pace Report in any given month with the Pace Report of the same month in the prior year, a G.M. can evaluate the bottom-line effectiveness of the sales and marketing department's efforts. Of course, unusual circumstances can cause a Pace Report to fluctuate. An exceptionally large sale or cancellation can materially affect the Pace Report in a given month. In addition, market conditions will affect sales results. In any of these situations, however, the joint evaluation of Pace Reports by the G.M. and the DOSM gives them the opportunity to discuss the hotel's selling environment and plan reactive strategies. Preparing accurate Pace Reports is the job of the DOSM. The DOSM and G.M. should review them at least once a month.

The Star Report

The Pace Report tells the hotel's owner and management the actual sales volume generated by the sales and marketing department. It does not, however, indicate what the actual sales volume *should* be. That is, if the hotel is experiencing a 60 percent occupancy rate, it is difficult to know whether that level of occupancy is good or bad unless the occupancy level of competing hotels is also known. If, for example, your hotel is averaging a 60 percent occupancy and your competitors are averaging 50 percent, you may be pleased with the performance of your sales and marketing team. If, on the other hand, your direct competitors are averaging a 70 percent occupancy, it is clear that you are not achieving your fair share of the business available in your market. In a similar manner, if your ADR is $100 and your competitors' ADR is $80, your sales team is showing success in selling at a good rate. If your competitors' ADR is $120, you are comparatively less successful. As a G.M., you want to know the comparative strength of your hotel and the sales and marketing staff. The Smith Travel Accommodations Report **(STAR Report)** is the recognized measure of comparative performance in the hotel industry.

HOTEL TERMINOLOGY AT WORK

STAR Report: Short for the Smith Travel Accommodations Report. Produced by Smith Travel Research, this report is used to compare a hotel's sales results with those of its selected competitors.

■

Unbiased occupancy rate, ADR, RevPar, and market share comparisons are important to a wide range of interest groups. These include:

- *Hotel Owners:* Hotel owners and investors want to know if the management team they have put in place is effective in competing in the marketplace. Managing the asset (hotel) to maximize its financial potential is an important goal, and the STAR report indicates how well this goal is being achieved.

- *Management Companies:* These companies know that their effectiveness as managing consultants will be based, to some degree, on how well they perform on the STAR Report. Good results are used to demonstrate the value of these companies to owners.

- *Property Managers:* G.M.s and DOSMs want to know the effectiveness of their marketing plans and sales abilities, as well as those of their competitors.

- *Franchisors:* Brand managers want a measure of how well their brands compete in the marketplace. Strong brand performance helps sell additional franchises. Weak performance by the brand helps indicate where brand managers can better assist current franchisees.

- *Appraisers:* These professionals interpret STAR Report results to assist in establishing the financial value of a hotel.

- *The Financial Community:* Those asked to invest or lend money to buy or renovate hotels want to know about the sales strength of the hotel seeking funding. Good relative performance (a strong STAR Report) helps persuade lenders to lend, whereas a weak STAR Report indicates potential problems and will make it more difficult to secure funding.

While a variety of groups may be interested in the STAR Report for a specific hotel or a specific geographic area, for many G.M.s and DOSMs, the STAR Report is the primary measure used to judge their own performance.

STAR Reports can provide a wealth of information to those sophisticated enough to read and analyze the data they contain. Fortunately, Smith Travel Research produces excellent materials that teach managers how to fully interpret their STAR Reports.

THE INTERNET AT WORK

STAR Report interpretation and analysis is an important, but not often recognized, part of a G.M.'s job. To request instructional information on interpreting STAR reports, and to see the wide variety of benchmarking products Smith Travel Research produces, go to:

www.str-online.com.

Smith Travel Research (Smith) actually produces a variety of comparative reports on a daily, weekly, monthly, and annual basis. Hotels voluntarily submit financial data to Smith. In return, Smith maintains the confidentiality of all individual hotel data it receives. By combining the operating data submitted by selected competitors, an individual hotel's operating performance can be compared with that of its **competitive set.**

HOTEL TERMINOLOGY AT WORK

Competitive Set: The group of competing hotels to which an individual hotel's operating performance is compared.

■

Understanding the competitive set is a key component of understanding the STAR Report. Essentially, a competitive set is a group of hotels used to establish a performance benchmark. To illustrate, assume that you manage a 300-room full-service property in a large city. You compete for most of your customers with five other hotels in your area, each of which has approximately the same number of rooms, services, and quality as your own property. Assume also that you have identified these five properties to Smith Travel as the group you wish to consider as your competitive set. In most cases, each of these hotels will, as will you, voluntarily submit monthly (or more frequent) actual sales data to Smith. These data are then tabulated and returned to your hotel in the form of a STAR Report. Smith will only report the aggregate results of the competitive set. They never release or divulge information on an individual property or brand.

Operating comparisons produced by Smith can be customized but popular comparisons include those related to:

- Occupancy
- ADR
- RevPar
- Market share
- Historical trends
- To-date performances
- State or region

The segment of a STAR Report related to hotel occupancy helps illustrate how the STAR performance Report is used to assess hotel performance. To interpret Figure 10.3, assume that your hotel (property) is the 300-room property referred to earlier. Your competitive set is the five similar hotels that you have identified as your competition.

In Figure 10.3, the Property column refers to the hotel under examination (your hotel). The Comp. Set column refers to the five hotels you have chosen as your competitive set (as well as your own hotel). The monthly occupancy percentages listed represent the occupancy rates, respectively, of your hotel and the combined (average) occupancy of your competitors. The

FIGURE 10.3   STAR Report: Occupancy Trend Segment

YEAR	Month	Occupancy Property	% Change	Comp. Set	% Change	Index	Index % Change
Last	Jan	55.2		52.2		105.7	
Last	Feb	59.7		58.2		102.6	
Last	Mar	63.1		63.6		99.2	
Last	Apr	64.2		64.4		99.7	
Last	May	63.9		61.7		103.6	
Last	June	67.6		66.1		102.3	
Last	July	68.9		63.5		108.5	
Last	Aug	72.7		58.8		123.6	
Last	Sept	81.8		82.9		98.7	
Last	Oct	83.1		85.5		97.2	
Last	Nov	65.6		67.1		97.8	
Last	Dec	60.2		57.6		104.5	
This	Jan	57.5	4.2	51.3	−1.7	112.1	6.0
This	Feb	61.3	2.7	59.6	2.4	102.9	0.3
This	Mar	63.5	0.6	66.9	5.2	94.9	−4.3
This	Apr	66.7	3.9	64.6	0.3	103.3	3.6
This	May	65.2	2.0	60.5	−1.9	107.8	4.1
This	June	67.5	−0.1	63.8	−3.5	105.8	3.5
This	July	70.2	1.9	64.1	0.9	109.5	0.9

Index column is computed as property performance divided by competitive set performance. Thus, for example, last year, in February, your hotel's (Occupancy) Index was 102.6 percent.

$$\frac{\text{Last February Property Occupancy}}{\text{Last February Competitive Set Occupancy}} = \text{Last February Occupancy Index}$$

$$\frac{59.7\%}{58.2\%} = 102.6$$

Stated another way, your hotel was able to achieve an occupancy rate 2.6 percent higher than that of your competitors. When the index is less than 100, your property is not achieving an occupancy rate equal to or higher than its competitors (see, e.g., March, Last Year in Figure 10.3). As a G.M., in all but the most unusual of circumstances, you will want to achieve an occupancy rate higher than that of your competitors and an occupancy index higher than 100.

The % Change column represents the performance change from the previous year's same time period. For example, the occupancy change for your property this January versus last January was 4.2 percent.

$$\frac{\text{Occupancy \% This Year} - \text{Occupancy \% Last Year}}{\text{Occupancy \% Last Year}} = \% \text{ Change}$$

$$\frac{57.5 - 55.2}{55.2} = 4.2$$

Therefore, your property increased its occupancy 4.2 percent from the prior January. Note that the competitive set, in the same time period, actually showed a decrease (-1.7) in their occupancy percentage during this period. Note also that your property's index does not always exceed 100. In fact, in March, April, September, October, and November of Last Year, your property was outperformed by its competitors.

It is important to remember that occupancy rate is, of course, related to ADR. Thus, a complete analysis of the STAR Report for this property would need to include, at the minimum, a review of its ADR and RevPar indices. Occupancy reviews, however, can be helpful. For example, several things can be learned from an analysis of this segment of the STAR Report, including:

- In most months, the property outperforms its competitive set.
- This year, the occupancy trend for the property, as well as its competitors, is an upward one.
- The property's occupancy performance last year was weakest in September, October, and November and strongest in August.
- While occupancy rate for the property was down in June of this year, compared with June of last year, the hotel's competitors experienced an even greater decline.
- The hotel may want to consider yield managing ADR more aggressively in August this year based on its strong occupancy performance in August last year.

To accurately gauge the effectiveness of a hotel's management, a property's STAR Report must be viewed in its entirety. It is always the case, however, that achieving performance indexes of less than 100 percent means the hotel is performing at a rate below its competition, while obtaining performance indexes above 100 percent means the hotel is outperforming its competitive set.

STAR performance goals can be established for any operating criteria, including occupancy rate, ADR, RevPar, market penetration, or growth.

When STAR performance does not reach the goals set by the hotel's owners or managers, there can be a variety of problems, not all of which can be solved by the G.M. or the sales and marketing department. Some of these include:

- Poor franchise (brand) name
- Poor signage
- Poor **room mix** for the market
- Substandard furnishings or décor
- Marketing/advertising budget too small
- Marketing staff too small
- Marketing staff ineffective

HOTEL TERMINOLOGY AT WORK

Room Mix: The ratio of room types contained in a hotel. For example, the number of double-bedded rooms compared with king-bedded rooms, the number of smoking permitted rooms to no smoking permitted rooms, and the number of suites compared with standard rooms.

■

Some managers dislike STAR Reports because they view them as an objective measure (indexes) of a subjective activity (management). Despite their limitations, STAR Reports are perceived by many as the best indicator of sales and marketing, and thus managerial, effectiveness. STAR Reports, properly interpreted, are indeed a valuable tool for assessing the performance of a sales and marketing department, as well as the entire property. The G.M. and DOSM should learn to analyze them and to then review them on a monthly or more frequent, basis.

HOTEL TERMINOLOGY AT WORK GLOSSARY

The following terms were defined within this chapter. If you are not familiar with each of them, please review the segment of the chapter that contains the term.

DOSM	Sales call	Pickup
Booking	Travel agent	Sales and marketing committee
Group sale	SMERF	
Site tour	Distribution channel	Inclusive
Chamber of Commerce	Drop in	Rooms division manager
Networking	Package	Bid
Convention and Visitors	Consortia	RFP
Bureau (CVB)	Negotiated rate	Group contract

─────────────────── **MANAGERS AT WORK** ───────────────────

"Well, Michele, how does it look?," asked J.D. Ojisima, the hotel's G.M.

"About like last month," replied Michele Austin, the hotel's DOSM as she glanced up from the document she was intently studying. "This month's Pace Report for future group room sales is about 4 percent below last year's level."

This was not good news, as J.D. well knew. The drop-off in sales was now in its third consecutive month. The same was true, to a smaller degree, in the food and beverage department's catering bookings also, and while the hotel was not experiencing an occupancy decline or occupancy index decline evident in the monthly STAR Report, it was clear that future business bookings, which would be measured by future STAR Reports, were declining.

"Well," replied J.D. "What do you think is causing the drop-off?"

"I'm not positive," stated Michelle, "but it could be several things. Citywide bookings may be down, the new sales manager we hired for corporate groups may not be up-to-speed yet, or perhaps we are being too rate aggressive in our bidding. I know that unless things turn around quickly we will have real difficulty meeting our revenue goals next quarter. What would you like me to do?"

What are some additional possible reasons for the decline revealed by the PACE Report? If you were J.D., how would you go about assessing the sales difficulties experienced by the hotel and the DOSM? What tools would you use to help understand and solve the revenue problem? How responsible should the G.M. be held for the sales level of a hotel?

───

Attrition	Cold calling	Pace Report
Block	Marketing plan	YTD
Prospect	Headquarter hotel	STAR Report
Trace system	Link	Competitive Set
Lead	Demand generator	Room mix

ISSUES AT WORK

1. The distinctions between the terms "sales" and "marketing" are as many as there are authors writing about the topics. Find at least three books devoted to the sales and marketing area and compare the definitions of these two terms in each book. What similarities did you find? What differences? How would you define the difference between sales and marketing? Why do you think HSMAI is titled as it is, rather than titled as "HMSAI"?

2. Effectively networking in a room full of strangers is a crucial skill but one that is often lacking in younger, less experienced sales team members. As a G.M., discuss five specific steps you (or your DOSM) could take to ensure that the least experienced of your sales team rapidly develops this important skill. How important is it that the G.M. be good at networking? Why? How does this skill affect cold calling ability?

3. Technology has impacted the sales and marketing departments of hotels more than any other department. Assume you were the G.M. for a very large (over 1,000 room) hotel. What technological advances do you see in the near future that you believe will most affect your hotel? What could you and your DOSM do to foresee these changes and prepare your hotel for them?

4. Departmental structure is important to the success of a sales and marketing department. Of the three approaches to departmental structure described in this chapter (product, market, and distribution method), which do you believe would be most effective in the hotel you hope to manage? Why? What influence do you believe the G.M. should have on the DOSM's decision on this matter? How do you think the size of the sales and marketing department will influence the decisions made by the G.M. and the DOSM in regard to departmental structure?

5. Some in the hotel industry believe that too heavy a reliance on the STAR Report to evaluate a hotel's sales effort has a negative effect. Others defend the STAR as the only independent way to evaluate a sales staff's effectiveness. Discuss three positive and three negative factors involved in an analysis of a hotel's monthly STAR Report. What alternative performance indicators of a hotel would you choose to evaluate? Why?

11
Facility Engineering and Maintenance

This Chapter at Work

As a G.M., you will find that your guests have expectations about your hotel that you simply must meet. These include such basic items as ample hot water for baths and showers, guest room lights that work, and comfortable temperatures in the hotel's public space and guest rooms. In addition, the owners of the hotel will have expectations. These include ensuring that the routine repair and maintenance of the building required to protect the value of their asset is diligently performed. The expectations of both of these audiences will be met if you create and support a dynamic engineering and maintenance (E&M) department within your property.

The hotel's E&M department head is called the chief engineer. This individual, along with the department's staff, ensures that the hotel's grounds and physical plant are well maintained. A well-run department assists the hotel's sales effort by providing guests with the very best experience possible as it relates to the appearance and maintenance of the exterior and interior of the building, thus making the hotel easier to sell.

It is easy to see why, for example, it is critical to change a burned out lightbulb in a hotel's parking lot. Guests need to be able to see in the parking lot at night, guest safety is affected, and the entire hotel will look better if the lightbulb is promptly replaced. In a similar manner, a guest room television that does not work properly should be promptly identified, repaired, or replaced or guest satisfaction will be adversely affected. It is less easy to see, yet just as important, for someone to be responsible for maintaining all of the hotel's equipment and facilities in the public areas, guest rooms, and food service and laundry areas. If this is not done, guest complaints and a reduction in the hotel's value are the inevitable result.

The general condition of public space, including exterior grounds, lobbies, and corridors, make a big impression on guests who stay in your hotel. In this chapter the maintenance needs of these visible areas, as well as important areas within guest rooms and the hotel's food service and laundry facilities, are examined in detail. This will help you gain the knowledge you need to implement procedures designed to ensure that guests enjoy their stay at your hotel.

In addition to affecting guests, the way a hotel's physical plant is maintained has a tremendous impact on the hotel's profitability. When utilities such as water, gas, and electricity are not well managed, and the equipment that utilizes these resources are not well maintained, the hotel's operating costs will be higher than they should be and, just as importantly, valuable natural resources will be wasted by the hotel. In this chapter, you will learn how to effectively oversee this important area of your hotel.

Chapter 11 Outline

ROLE OF THE ENGINEERING AND
MAINTENANCE DEPARTMENT
   Engineering
   Maintenance
   Design and Renovation
STAFFING THE DEPARTMENT
   Chief Engineer
   Maintenance Assistants
MANAGING MAINTENANCE
   Routine Maintenance
     Exterior
     Interior
   Preventative Maintenance
     Public Space
     Guest rooms

   Food service
   Laundry
   Other equipment
   Emergency Maintenance
MANAGING UTILITIES
   Electricity
   Lighting
   HVAC
   Natural Gas
   Water
   Waste
HOTEL TERMINOLOGY AT WORK
GLOSSARY
ISSUES AT WORK

Every hotel has a variety of valuable assets. These include the hotel's staff, its cash in the bank, its customer base, and its reputation. The hotel's grounds, buildings, and equipment, which comprise the hotel's most visible and usually its most expensive asset, directly affect the value of the hotel's other assets. How guests perceive the hotel's facilities makes a tremendous impact on a hotel's profitability. It is important then, that the hotel's owners, its G.M., and its other managers protect and maintain the value of the hotel's facilities.

THE ROLE OF THE ENGINEERING AND MAINTENANCE DEPARTMENT

When a hotel's building, equipment, and grounds are properly maintained, guests will be more likely to receive a positive experience during their stay, and the hotel's ability to increase sales is enhanced. This is the primary job of the E&M department. When guests experience poor facilities such as potholes in parking areas, leaking faucets, burned-out lightbulbs, poor heating/cooling capacity, or insufficient hot water, guest dissatisfaction increases, and the hotel's sales potential is diminished. In addition to guest satisfaction, however, an effective E&M department will achieve many other important goals, including:

- Protecting and enhancing the financial value of the building and grounds for the hotel's owners
- Supporting the efforts of all other hotel departments through the timely attention to their E&M needs

- Controlling maintenance and repair costs
- Controlling energy usage
- Increasing the pride and morale of the hotel's staff
- Ensuring the safety of those working in and visiting the hotel

These goals will be achieved if the E&M department meets its responsibilities in the areas of designing and constructing the building (engineering), maintaining the building (maintenance), and periodically renovating and modernizing it (design and renovation).

Engineering

Many hotel managers use the terms "**engineering**" and "**maintenance**" interchangeably. Thus, you are just as likely to find the department responsible for the care of the hotel called engineering, as you are to find it called maintenance, or some combination of both terms.

HOTEL TERMINOLOGY AT WORK

Engineering: Designing and operating a building to ensure a safe and comfortable atmosphere.

Maintenance: The activities required to keep a building and its contents in good repair.

■

Engineering, as a building specialty, however, is distinct from maintenance. The engineering of a building refers to the application of physics, chemistry, and mathematics to design and operate buildings that provide a comfortable atmosphere for guests and employees. For example, in a lobby area that must be air-conditioned, the building engineer calculates the amount of air-conditioned air required to properly cool the lobby. Factors that must be taken into consideration in such a calculation include the temperature and humidity of the outside air, the desired lobby temperature, the temperature at which air-conditioned air enters the lobby, and the movement of the air once it is inside the lobby. Based on these calculations, the size of the air-conditioning unit required to cool the lobby is determined, as is the optimum number and location of air vents delivering the cold air to the area. The knowledge required to balance each of these features and to make the proper decisions is significant. G.M.s do not usually have the engineering background required to make unassisted decisions about the engineered systems within a hotel and must, therefore, look to the chief engineer for assistance.

Improperly engineered facilities can result in underpowered (or overpowered) equipment, increased building deterioration, excessive energy usage, and higher-than-necessary operating costs. Typically, the chief engineer in an operating hotel will not have actually designed the **HVAC** systems within the building; however, he or she must be knowledgeable about these systems, as well as the engineering of the electrical, water, and waste systems operating within the building. If the chief engineer is not, even routine maintenance will be difficult to perform (or even worse, performed improperly).

HOTEL TERMINOLOGY AT WORK

HVAC: A shorthand term for "heating, ventilating, and air conditioning."

■

THE INTERNET AT WORK

Engineering a building's heating, refrigeration, ventilation, and air conditioning systems is quite complex, and special knowledge is required to manage it. To familiarize yourself with an organization whose members specialize in this field, go to the Web site of the American Society of Heating, Refrigerating, and Air Conditioning Engineers, Inc., at:

www.ashrae.com.

Maintenance

As the term implies, maintenance, refers simply to "maintaining" the hotel's physical property. It has been said that maintenance costs are like taxes; if they are not paid one year, they will be paid in the next year,—and with a penalty!

The maintenance-related costs of a hotel vary with the hotel's age. As a building ages, its maintenance costs generally increase. Even brand-new hotels, however, require **POM**-related expenditures. These costs include staff wages and benefits, replacement parts, contract services, and energy costs that are listed separately on the P&L.

HOTEL TERMINOLOGY AT WORK

POM: Short for "Property Operation and Maintenance." The term is taken from the Uniform System of Accounts for Hotels and refers to the segment of the income statement that details the costs of operating the E&M department.

■

A G.M. should expect that the E&M department maintain the property in the most effective manner possible given the budget assigned to it. To do so, hotel maintenance must be:

- *Planned.* From routinely changing air filters in heating and cooling units to awarding a contract for tree trimming, the E&M department performs too many tasks to leave these activities to chance. An effective chief engineer is a careful administrator who reviews every piece of equipment and required activity in the hotel and then plans what should be done, when it should be done, and who should do it.

- *Implemented.* Some chief engineers know what should be done in their properties and have good intentions of completing all the required tasks, yet do not do so. Shortages of budget or properly trained staff, lack of supervisory skills, insufficient tools, and/or underestimation of the time required to perform a given task can impact the ability of an E&M department to achieve it goals.

   There are many excellent checklists and suggested activities that have been developed for E&M departments. Virtually every franchisor offers such checklists free of charge to its franchisees because it is in the best interest of the franchisor if all hotels in the system represent the brand well.

   Checklists and suggested activities, however, which are not properly implemented, will not result in an acceptable maintenance program. Thus, for a G.M. evaluating the E&M department, the important factor is not whether an acceptable maintenance program has been planned for a hotel, but rather the degree to which the planned programs have been effectively implemented.

- *Recorded.* Record keeping is an immensely important maintenance function. Routine, scheduled maintenance tasks cannot be properly planned unless E&M personnel know when these tasks have last been performed. For example, if the plan is to lubricate hot water pumps every six months, a written record must be kept of the last time the pumps were lubricated. In a similar manner, if a faucet in a guest room is replaced, a record should be kept of when the replacement was made. In doing so, the E&M department will be able to evaluate the quality (life) of faucets used, as well as take advantage of any warranty programs that apply to the replacement parts and to new equipment purchased by the hotel.

   In many cases, such as fire suppression systems and elevators, local ordinances or laws may require that records documenting the performance of system maintenance be kept on file or displayed publicly. Even when it is not mandated by local ordinance, however, excellent record keeping in all areas of the E&M department is a good indicator of overall departmental effectiveness.

Design and Renovation

The cost of maintaining a building is very closely related to its original design and size and the facilities it includes. Those hotels with, for example, food service and banquet facilities, swimming pools, and exercise rooms will experience greater maintenance costs than limited service hotels without these facilities. High-rise facilities will require elevator systems that must be maintained whereas one-story hotels will not. Resort facilities spread over multiple acres will require greater landscape care costs than those located on smaller plots of ground.

In a similar manner, the quality of construction used in building the hotel will affect POM costs. A hotel that has an exterior that must be painted will experience exterior painting costs whereas a hotel made of masonry will not. Energy costs will also be affected by construction. Those hotels built with good insulation and well-made windows will generally experience lower energy costs than those that are not built this way.

The finishes and equipment specified for installation by the hotel's builders have a tremendous impact on the E&M department. Durable finishes and high-quality, long-life equipment may have higher purchase prices, but will generally reduce operating and maintenance costs.

Despite the very best of maintenance programs, however, hotels do wear out with use and must be renovated to compete against newer hotel properties. Hotel buildings have a predictable life span that directly affects their maintenance and renovation needs. Figure 11.1 details the typical life span of a hotel. As can be seen, as a building ages, the challenges of maintaining it increase.

Because renovation and refurbishment will, at some point, be needed, G.M.s must take steps to reserve funds for the time when renovation is undertaken. This is done through the establishment of an **FF&E reserve.**

HOTEL TERMINOLOGY AT WORK

FF&E Reserve: Funds set aside by management today for the future furniture, fixture, and equipment replacement needs of a hotel.

■

FIGURE 11.1   Hotel Life Span

Building Age	Building Characteristics and Requirements
1–3 years	Low maintenance costs incurred
3–6 years	Maintenance costs increase
6–8 years	Refurbishment required; average maintenance costs incurred
8–15 years	Minor renovation and refurbishment required
15–22 years	Major renovation as well as refurbishment required
22+ years	Restoration required; high-maintenance costs incurred

Generally, FF&E reserves should average 2 to 4 percent of a hotel's gross sales revenue. If designated funds are not reserved, the hotel will not be able to carry out needed minor renovation, major renovation, or restoration when needed. Figure 11.2 lists specific items that must be considered when planning a hotel's short- and long-term renovation program.

Refurbishment and minor renovation is actually an ongoing process in most hotels. Major renovation should take place every six to ten years. Costs are high each time a hotel undergoes renovation. Extra cleaning costs are likely to be incurred during construction. It is almost inevitable that guest services will be disrupted, resulting in unhappy guests who must be soothed and in lost revenue from out-of-service areas that normally generate revenue.

Restoration occurs when a hotel undergoes renovation that is so complete that walls are relocated, rooms and public space are totally reconfigured, and mechanical systems are replaced to modernize the hotel.

HOTEL TERMINOLOGY AT WORK

Restoration: Returning a hotel to its original (or better than original) condition.

■

The typical hotel undergoes a restoration every twenty-five to fifty years. When restoration occurs it is a challenging time for management, the E&M department, and guests. If restoration is not undertaken when needed, however, the revenue-producing potential of the hotel will likely decline.

FIGURE 11.2   Selected Hotel Renovation and Replacement Considerations

	Minor Renovation	**Major Renovation**
Guest Rooms	Drapes, bedspreads	Bed frames, mattresses
	Lamps, shades	Wall lights
	Carpets	Wall vinyl
	Upholstered furniture	Case goods
	Faucets	Sinks, countertops
	Mattresses	Televisions
Food and Beverage	Carpets, chairs, reupholster booths	Decorative lighting
	Table top décor	Tables
	Dishes, flatware	Serving equipment
		Wall coverings
Public Space	Table lamps, lobby furniture	Overhead lighting
	Lobby carpet	Corridor carpet
	Lobby wall coverings	Corridor vinyl
	Meeting rooms	Restrooms

MANAGERS AT WORK

"Well Chief," J.D. Ojisima, the hotel G.M., looking up, asked Marion Lott, the hotel's chief engineer, "Where is that noise coming from?"

Marion called down from the space between the hotel's lobby ceiling and the underside of the building's roof, "It's the bearing on the air handler shaft."

J.D., in the course of the normal "walk around" done each morning, had noticed a high-pitched sound coming from above a lobby seating area and had immediately called the chief.

Later, in the G.M.'s office, Marion explained to J.D.: "The bearings on the shaft that turns the fan, that blows chilled air into

the lobby is going bad. That's what's causing the annoying sound you heard," said Marion.

"Unfortunately," continued the chief, "the shaft itself is old, and not in great condition. It may not accept a new bearing for long. We might get a week out of it, or we might get five years. It's hard to say. I could try and replace the bearings only, but the best solution would be to replace the bearings and the shaft. Either way, the lobby will be without air conditioning for two days to tear the air handler apart."

"What is the cost difference between repair and replacement"? asked J.D.

"Well, I'm checking into that now, but I would estimate $22,000 for complete shaft and bearing replacement. If we only replace the bearings, maybe $4,000 time and material."

What would you advise J.D. to do in this case? Assume that total bearing and shaft replacement involved spending from a capital improvement budget, while any repairs to the existing shaft would be expensed on the month's P&L. Would these factors influence your decision? Why? Would it matter if you owned the hotel?

STAFFING THE DEPARTMENT

Perhaps more so than any other department, the talent employed in the maintenance staff crucially affects a hotel's profitable operation. This is true because so much of a guest's impression of the quality of a hotel is dependent on the work of the E&M department. Thus, the quality of the maintenance staff and the quality of their work will, in the guest's eyes, represent the quality of the hotel. When maintenance work is performed poorly or not at all, it shows. The solution to this problem lies in the selection of an excellent E&M department head and appropriate assistants.

Chief Engineer

In the hotel industry, the head of E&M is referred to as the chief engineer or maintenance chief. This person has a significant role to play on the executive committee and as the leader of one of the hotel's most important departments.

In smaller hotels the chief engineer may take a very hands-on role in the maintenance effort. This could involve actually performing maintenance and repair tasks. In larger hotels with larger staffs, the chief engineer serves a more administrative role that consists of planning work, organizing staff, directing employee efforts, and controlling the POM budget. Regardless of a hotel's size, the chief engineer must be well organized, pay great attention to detail, and be a cooperative member of the management team.

Maintenance Assistants

In addition to the chief engineer, the E&M department will employ one or more individuals with varying degrees of skill in the areas of:

- Engineering
- Mechanics
- Plumbing
- Electricity
- Carpentry
- Water treatment (for pools and spas)
- Landscaping
- Grounds maintenance

The needs of a specific hotel will dictate the actual skill, makeup, and number of E&M staff required. It is difficult to find one person skilled in all of the technical E&M areas encountered in a hotel. When the skills or manpower needs of an E&M department exceed the capabilities of the in-house staff, the chief engineer and the G.M. must decide to outsource work. The ability to effectively determine which tasks are best performed by in-house E&M staff versus being contracted to outside help is the real mark of an excellent chief engineer.

MANAGING MAINTENANCE

The maintenance of a building occurs after it has been designed, engineered, and built. Maintenance in a hotel can be examined in a variety of ways, but one helpful way to view its management is to consider maintenance as routine, preventative, or emergency.

Routine Maintenance

When managing a hotel's routine maintenance the chief engineer is simply directing the customary care of the facility. For example, in hotels with lawns and plant beds around entrances or parking areas, it is customary and routine to periodically cut and edge the grass and to maintain the visual integrity of the plant bed by pulling weeds and replacing foliage as needed. If this work is not done, the curb appeal of the hotel suffers. Cleaning interior windows, picking up trash in the parking lot, and shoveling snow in those climates that require it are additional examples of routine maintenance. Often only limited employee training is required to adequately complete routine maintenance tasks.

Generally, the chief engineer, with input from the G.M., decides whether to perform routine maintenance work in-house or to pay an outside vendor to perform it. Regardless of the decision, an effective chief engineer routinely must be concerned with both the exterior and interior of the hotel.

Exterior

On the outside of the hotel, lawn care, landscaping, and leaf and snow removal are important issues. Just as important is the attention to detail required by the actual hotel building. This includes such items as routine roof inspection and repair, window cleaning and window seal inspection, and the care and painting, if required, of the building's exterior finishes. The location of the hotel will dictate, to a large degree, the items that must be considered for routine exterior maintenance. A resort hotel in Florida will have needs different from those of a downtown high-rise hotel in the upper Midwest. Regardless of the setting, however, maintaining the outside of the hotel impacts curb appeal, operational costs, and, ultimately, the building's value. The G.M., working with the chief engineer, must ensure that routine exterior maintenance is being performed well and in a timely manner.

Interior

Inside the hotel, E&M staff also must perform routine maintenance. Some areas include the care of indoor plants, the washing of interior windows (if not assigned to housekeeping), and, in some cases, the care and cleaning of floors and carpets.

One significant task nearly always assigned to the E&M department is the changing of lightbulbs. Lightbulbs, regardless of their type, will burn out and then must be replaced. In some instances, individual lightbulbs are immediately replaced when they burn out. That is, the E&M department implements a **replace as needed** program for bulbs.

HOTEL TERMINOLOGY AT WORK

Replace as Needed: A parts or equipment replacement plan that delays installing a new, substitute part until the original part fails or is in near failure. For example, most chief engineers would use a "replace as needed" plan for the maintenance of refrigeration compressors.

■

The cost to a hotel of replacing a lightbulb consists of two components. These are the price of the bulb itself and the labor dollars required to change the bulb. Therefore, in special cases, such as the lightbulbs in a multistory hotel with high ceilings that require special lifts or ladders for access, the hotel may implement a **total replacement** program that involves changing all bulbs, including those that have not burned out, on a regularly predetermined schedule.

HOTEL TERMINOLOGY AT WORK

Total Replacement: A parts or equipment replacement plan that involves installing new or substitute parts based on a predetermined schedule. For example, most chief engineers would use a "total replacement" approach to the maintenance of lightbulbs in high-rise exterior highway signs.

■

This approach, while it involves the discarding of some bulbs or lamps with life remaining, significantly reduces bulb replacement labor costs and makes the hotel's total bulb replacement costs lower.

Another form of routine maintenance involves guest room and public space–related items that must be attended to on a regular basis when they malfunction, wear out, or break and need fixing or replacement. For example, a room attendant in a guest room may notice that a chair leg is broken, or that the tub drains slowly. A front desk agent may report that a guest has complained about poor television reception or of a toilet that does not flush properly. When events such as these occur, the E&M department is notified via a **work order,** or maintenance request. Figure 11.3 shows a sample work order.

HOTEL TERMINOLOGY AT WORK

Work Order: A form used to initiate and document a request for maintenance. Sometimes referred to as a "maintenance request."

■

In a well-managed hotel, any staff member that sees an area of concern can initiate a work order. Work orders are prenumbered, multicopy forms that, depending on the number of copies preferred by the G.M., are used to notify E&M, the front desk, housekeeping, the G.M., and others who may need to know when a maintenance request is initiated or completed. In some hotels, blank work order forms are actually placed in the guest room for guests to initiate.

Regardless of their original source, the work orders, once received by E&M, are reviewed and prioritized. For example, a work order indicating an inoperable guest room lock would take higher priority than one addressing a crooked picture in another guest room. An E&M employee completes the task(s) called for on the work order, informs the proper areas, and the infor-

FIGURE 11.3 Work Order

Waldo Hotel Work Order

Work Order Number: _____*(Preassigned)*_____   Initiated By: _____

Date: _____   Time: _____   Room or Location: _____

Problem Observed: _____

_____

_____

Received On: _____   Assigned To: _____

Date Corrected: _____   Time Spent: _____

E&M Employee Comments: _____

_____

_____

_____

_____

_____

Chief Engineer Comments: _____

_____

_____

_____

_____

mation related to the work performed is carefully retained. In a well-run department, the chief engineer keeps a room-by-room record of replacements or repairs made. In this manner, decisions that must be made about repairing or replacing in-room items can be more easily made because a history of the room and its contents has been preserved.

Some G.M.s evaluate the effectiveness of their entire E&M department based on the rapidity with which maintenance work orders are completed. While the timely completion of maintenance requests should not be the only criteria for judging the successfulness of a maintenance department, it is indeed a key indicator of effectiveness and efficiency. When work orders are not completed promptly (or at all), the E&M department loses credibility in the eyes of the hotel's staff and with guests. An effective G.M. monitors the speed at which work orders are prioritized and completed and then takes corrective action if needed.

Preventative Maintenance

Even when not performing routine maintenance or responding to a work order, the E&M department has a large number of maintenance-related tasks that must be performed. In fact, in the eyes of most G.M.s, the most important type of maintenance that is performed in a hotel is called **PM,** or a **preventative maintenance program.**

HOTEL TERMINOLOGY AT WORK

PM (Preventative Maintenance) Program: A specific inspection and activities schedule designed to minimize maintenance-related costs and to prolong the life of equipment by preventing small problems before they become larger ones.

■

An effective PM program will save your hotel money in a variety of ways, including reducing:

- Long-term repair costs by the prolonging of equipment life
- Replacement parts costs because purchases of these parts can be planned
- Labor costs by allowing PM to be performed in otherwise slow periods
- The dollar amount of refunds and charge backs due to guest dissatisfaction
- The costs of emergency repairs by minimizing their occurrence

In addition to saving money, a good PM program reduces guest complaints, eases the job of the sales staff, improves the eye appeal and functionality of the hotel, and improves employee morale.

Schedules for PM programs can come from a variety of sources. Equipment suppliers often suggest maintenance activities; franchisors may mandate PM schedules; local ordinances may require specific PM activities; and, most important of all, the skill and experience of the chief engineer, combined with his or her knowledge of the hotel's needs, dictate PM schedules. Most PM activities involve basic inspection, replacement, cleaning, and lubrication. PM is not generally considered to be a repair program nor should it be viewed as one. Repairs must be completed as they are needed, while PM activities should be performed as scheduled.

Some chief engineers design PM programs that are segmented by those activities that must be performed daily, weekly, monthly, semiannually, and annually. Others prefer a system that segments the hotel into major areas, (i.e., food service, laundry, etc.) and then develop area-specific PM schedules. In both cases, the PM program should identify what is to be done, when it is to be done, how it is to be done, and should provide an easy method to document the completion of the activity.

Figure 11.4 is a sample daily, monthly, and annual PM task list for a dryer in the laundry area.

The Chief Engineer should have a written and complete PM program in place. All equipment such as furnaces, air conditioners, water heating equipment, elevators and the like must have individual PM programs. In addition, the E&M department should create a specific PM program for the following areas:

- Public space
- Guest rooms
- Food service
- Laundry
- Other equipment

FIGURE 11.4   Sample PM Task List for Laundry Area Dryer

PM Activity: LAUNDRY AREA DRYER

DAILY

- Clean lint trap
- Wipe down inside chamber with mild detergent
- Clean and wipe dry the outside dryer shell

MONTHLY

- Vacuum the inside of dryer (upper and lower chambers)
- Tighten, if needed, the bolts holding dryer to floor
- Check all electrical connections
- Check fan belt for wear; replace if needed
- Lubricate moving parts

ANNUALLY

- Check pulley alignment
- Adjust rotating basket if needed
- Lubricate motor bearings
- Lubricate drum bearings if needed

Public Space

Public space PM programs are vitally important, but simple to develop. In public spaces such as lobbies, corridors, and meeting areas, PM programs should include items such as windows, HVAC units, furniture, lights, elevators, and carpets. In fact, for an E&M department, carpet care is one of the most challenging PM areas of all. Carpet care duties are often shared between housekeeping and the E&M department, with housekeeping taking responsibility for minor (spot) cleaning issues, and the E&M department responsible for long-term carpet PM.

THE INTERNET AT WORK

Carpet and area rug care can be complex, but a variety of resources are available to help you determine how to best care for these items. To view one such free resource, go to the Web site of the Carpet and Rug Institute at:

www. carpet-rug.com.

Obviously, it is important that public space appearances be well maintained, as they significantly influence guest's opinions about the entire hotel. G.M.s know that a good first impression goes a long way toward ensuring a satisfactory guest stay.

Guest Rooms

Perhaps the most important, and certainly the most extensive, areas for PM are the hotel's guest rooms. Unfortunately, some G.M.s are not fully aware of the quality of the guest room PM program in place at their hotels. This is a huge mistake. The guest room PM program is critical to the sales effort, to the hotel's ability to retain guests, and to the maintenance of the asset's monetary value. In fact, there are few things a G.M. should pay more attention to than the P.M. program used for guest rooms.

An effective P.M. program requires a quarterly, or more frequent, inspection of guest rooms with a careful examination of each item on the guest room **PM Checklist.**

HOTEL TERMINOLOGY AT WORK

PM Checklist: A tool developed to list all of the critical areas that should be inspected during a PM review of a room, area, or piece of equipment.

∎

The checklist for any PM area should be developed to help maintenance staff with their inspections. Figure 11.5 is a sample PM checklist used for guest rooms.

FIGURE 11.5   Guest Room PM Checklist

Hotel Waldo Guestroom PM Checklist

Place an "x" by any item not meeting hotel standards

Year _____   Room Number _____

Area Inspected	Item Inspected	1	2	3	4	Area Inspected	Item Inspected	1	2	3	4
Entrance	Number sign					**Bathroom**	Floor tile/grouting				
Door	Exterior Finish					**continued**	Telephone				
	Interior Finish						Blow Dryer				
	Peep hole						GFI plug operational				
	Door closer					**Drapes**	Drape Hooks				
	Deadbolt						Drape wand				
	Lock/lock plate						Valance				
	Evacuation/fire safety plan						Drape rods and brackets				
	Innkeeper's laws frame					**Bedroom**	Entrance ceiling				
	Hinges						Room ceiling				
Closet	Shelf Stable						Night stand				
	Clothes Hooks						Night stand drawers				
	Clothes Rod						Dresser				
	Carpet/Covebase						Dresser drawers				
	Luggage Rack						Headboard				
	Vinyl/Walls						Desk				
	Closet door finish						Desk chair				
	Closet door operation						Upholstered chairs				
	Closet door mirror						Bed frames				
Fixtures,	Entry light						Mattress (condition)				
lights and	Closet light						Mattress (turned)				
bulbs	Swing lamps						Mirrors				
	Dresser lamps						Art work				
	Desk lamp						Wall vinyl				
	Pole lamp						Electrical switches				
	Bathroom					**HVAC**	Filters changed				
	Smoke Detector						Fan				
	Sprinkler head						Motor				
Bathroom	Door finish						Controls				
	Door lock						Condensate pan				
	Ceiling condition						Wiring				
	Overhead Fan					**TV/Radio**	Picture quality				
	Toilet operation						Swivel				
	Toilet caulking						Lock down				
	Tub driver spout						Volume				
	Tub tile/grouting						Remote control				
	Tub stopper						Cabinet condition				
	Shower head						Connections				
	Curtain rod secure						Video game controls				
	Safety bar secure					**Telephone**	Line 1				
	Nonskid surface						Line 2				
	Sink Faucet						Jacks secure				
	Sink stopper					**Connecting**	Interior Finish				
	Piping					**Door**	Exterior Finish				
	Aerator						Frame				
	Toilet Paper holder						Door stop				
	Towel rack						Lock(s) operation				
	Mirrors						Doorknob				
	Vinyl/Walls						Hinges				
						Other					

Inspector Initials _____

Waldo Hotel, 20XX

Note that the checklist in Figure 11.5 is extensive and must be tailored for each property. Those hotels, for example, that have in-room microwaves and refrigerators must add these items to the guestroom PM checklist. If some guest rooms contain whirlpool-type tubs, these should be included. It is the responsibility of the G.M. and the chief engineer to develop a custom PM checklist and inspection schedule for guest rooms, and then it is the responsibility of the chief engineer to perform the inspections on the agreed-upon schedule. When this is done, guest room quality complaints will be minimized and long-term repair costs will be reduced because small problems will be uncovered and attended to before they become big ones.

Food Service

In the food service area, there are three major PM concerns. The first is back of the house equipment. The ovens, ranges, griddles, fryers, and other production equipment in the kitchen are heavily used and, of course, must be maintained. Specialty equipment such as dishwashers, fryers, and convection ovens may require the PM expertise of specifically trained technicians. If so, these vendors should be selected and their work scheduled by the chief engineer or the F&B director. In all cases, every piece of kitchen as well as mechanical bar equipment should be included in the PM program. The second area of PM concern within the food services area is the dining space used by guests. Included in this program would be tabletops and bases. An especially annoying PM issue for guests involves table leveling; there is simply no excuse for wobbly tables or for foreign objects placed under tables to make them level. In addition, PM must include chairs and booths, self-serve salad or buffet areas, lighting fixtures, and guest check processing equipment.

A third area of PM concern within F&B, and one that is often overlooked, is that required for meeting and conference rooms and equipment. Included in this PM program are light fixtures, tables, chairs, and wall coverings within the hotel's meeting rooms, as well as food service equipment. In addition, the PM program must include transport carts and the audio-visual-related items owned by the hotel. These may include flip chart stands, TVs, overhead projectors, computer projection units, speaker telephones, and the like.

Laundry

In the laundry, the washers, dryers, folding equipment, water supply lines, drains, lighting fixtures, and temperature control units require PM programs. An especially important concern (because of the potential for fire) is the clothes dryer. Dryer drum temperatures can be very high, and the lint buildup that occurs during the natural drying process requires vigilance on the part of the E&M department, as well as housekeeping. Lint traps should be cleaned once per day (or more), and they should be thoroughly inspected monthly.

In many cases, the company supplying laundry chemicals to the hotel maintains the equipment used to dispense chemicals into the washers. This does not mean that the E&M department need not concern itself with this area. In fact, if chemical usage is too high, the chemical supplier may have adjusted equipment to overdispense chemicals in an effort to sell more product. For this reason, as well as the fact that improperly maintained chemical dispensing units may result in substandard laundry quality, the E&M department should make chemical dispenser maintenance an important part of the laundry PM program, even if it is performed in conjunction with the dispensing equipment supplier.

Other Equipment

Additional areas of concern when developing a PM program include those related to pools and spas, front desk equipment, electronic locks (if not included in the guest room maintenance program), exterior door locks, motor vehicles, and in-hotel transportation equipment (i.e., housekeepers carts, luggage carts, etc.), to name but a few. As can be seen, the number of pieces of equipment and the number of areas involved in a quality PM maintenance program are vast. As a G.M., you will count on your chief engineer to develop, maintain, and document an effective and comprehensive PM program that both reduces repair costs and preserves the image of the hotel.

THE INTERNET AT WORK

A comprehensive PM program for hotels is sometimes easier to maintain than to begin because there are so many pieces of equipment that must be included. Today, software exists that can help a chief engineer decide what must be maintained and how frequently to schedule PM. To view one software company's hotel-oriented PM program, go to:

www.attr.com.

Emergency Maintenance

The strongest rationale for implementing well-designed and aggressive routine and preventative maintenance programs is the ability to manage repair costs; however, despite the very best routine and preventative maintenance efforts of the chief engineer and the E&M staff, your hotel will sometimes experience the need for emergency maintenance. Emergency maintenance items are generally defined as those that:

- Are unexpected
- Threaten to negatively impact hotel revenue

- Require immediate attention to minimize damage
- Require labor and parts that may need to be purchased at a premium

For example, assume that, in the middle of the night, a water pipe bursts in one of the hotel's unoccupied guest rooms. A short time later, the guests in the room one floor below the room with the broken pipe call the front desk to complain about water coming into their room from the ceiling. Clearly, this situation requires emergency maintenance. If not attended to immediately, extensive repair work to the pipe as well as the ceilings and walls around the leak may be required.

As a G.M., you certainly want to be notified about any significant emergency maintenance required in the hotel. This is true not only so that you may help plan or evaluate the hotel's response, but also because, generally, emergency maintenance repairs may require the authorization of overtime for E&M staff or outside repair personnel. In addition, needed repair parts that might normally be purchased through customary sources may need to be secured quickly (and often at a premium price) from noncustomary sources.

An effective chief engineer will keep the G.M. informed of significant emergency maintenance items and will seek the G.M.'s advice on the best course of action for responding to these items. In addition, maintaining accurate records about the cost of emergency repairs will help when budgeting for routine and preventative maintenance costs. Generally, the stronger the routine and PM programs, the fewer the dollars spent on emergency repairs.

MANAGERS AT WORK

"The telephone is ringing off the hook!" Dani Pelley, the front office manager, told J.D. Ojisima, the hotel's G.M. "I called maintenance, and they said they were looking into it."

"It" was a complete outage of the satellite system used to deliver television reception to the hotel. The Pay-Per-View features of the hotel (which were VCR based) still worked, but the Free-to-Guests channels were completely down, and guests were calling the front desk to complain or to request a repair on their television sets.

J.D. picked up the telephone, called the chief engineer, and got the bad news. Satellite reception was down. It was not an equipment failure on the hotel's part, but, rather, the satellite service provider was experiencing equipment difficulty. The chief had just gotten off the telephone with them to report the problem, and they estimated a repair time of between two and twenty-four hours. Until the problem was fixed, there would be no Free-to-Guests channels reception. J.D. hung up the telephone and went to talk with Dani Pelley about what to do next.

Given that the televisions may be out for two to twenty-four hours, what steps would you take to inform guests? Employees? Why is it important for all employees to be aware of the repair status of the televisions?

What should the front desk say to a guest who calls requesting a television repair?

What would you do if, the next day, after the televisions were working again, a guest demanded a full refund for their prior night's stay because they had missed their favorite weekly television show? What factors would influence your decision?

MANAGING UTILITIES

Utility management is a tremendously important part of a hotel's overall operation. Utility costs in hotels include expenses for water and sewage bills, gas, electricity, or fossil fuel for heating and cooling the building, fuel for heating water, and, in some cases, the purchase of steam or chilled water.

Energy-related expenses, which had been taken for granted by most hoteliers, became very important and costly during the energy crisis of 1973. Since that time, these costs have moderated somewhat. When the cost of utilities is relatively low, few Americans, including those in the hotel industry, take strong measures to conserve resources and to implement **energy management** programs. Alternatively, when energy costs are high, managers have a heightened sense of awareness about these costs. Good G.M.s require that the E&M department, as well as each member of the hotel's staff, always practice energy effective management.

HOTEL TERMINOLOGY AT WORK

Energy Management: Specific policies and engineering, maintenance, and facility design activities intended to control and reduce energy usage.

■

It is important to remember that, in most cases, the utilities cost involved in lighting, heating, and operating the equipment required to run a hotel will be incurred regardless of occupancy levels. While it is true that higher hotel occupancy will result in some incremental increase in utility costs, as much as 80 percent of total utility costs for a hotel are actually fixed. A hotel's original design and construction and the age of its buildings affect its energy usage. It is most affected, however, by the regular maintenance and calibration of the equipment consuming energy.

Depending on the location of the hotel, energy costs can represent as much as 3 to 10 percent of total operational costs. In addition, energy is a valuable resource, and, as responsible members of the hotel industry, it is important that we do all we can to conserve it. Thus, it is easy to see why an effective E&M department should be very concerned with conserving energy and controlling utility costs.

Electricity

Electricity is the most common and usually the most expensive form of energy used in hotels. To be effective, the hotel's electrical source must be dependable, and the E&M department must maintain the hotel's electrical systems in a safe manner. While some hotels generate their own electricity in an emergency outage situation through the use of a **backup generator**, most hotels will rely on one or more local power providers to deliver electricity to the hotel.

HOTEL TERMINOLOGY AT WORK

Backup Generator: Equipment used to make limited amounts of electricity on-site. Utilized in times of power failure or when the hotel experiences low supply from the usual provider of electricity.

■

In some locations, electric bills account for well over 50 percent (and sometimes as much as 80%) of a hotel's total utility costs. Controlling electrical consumption, then, can really pay off for a G.M. interested in lowering hotel utility bills.

Electricity is used everywhere in a hotel. It powers the hotel's administrative computers, operates fire safety systems, keeps food cold in freezers and refrigerators, and provides power for security systems, to name but a few uses. When considering the total electrical consumption of hotels, however, the two most important uses of electricity and, therefore, those that the chief engineer must manage most carefully are related to lighting and HVAC systems.

Lighting

The lighting in a hotel is tremendously important to curb appeal, guest comfort, worker efficiency, and property security. Lighting is sometimes referred to as illumination, and light levels are measured in **foot-candles.** Generally, the greater the number of foot-candles present, the greater the illumination. Hotels require varying degrees of illumination in different locations, and the type of light fixtures and bulbs used play a large role in producing the most appropriate light for each hotel setting.

HOTEL TERMINOLOGY AT WORK

Foot-candle: A measure of illumination. One foot-candle equals one lumen per square foot. (The European counterpart of the foot-candle is the Lux, a light intensity of one lumen per square meter.)

■

Artificial light is produced to supplement natural (sun) light. Natural light is, of course, very cost-effective and when used properly can have a very positive impact on utility costs by limiting the amount of artificial light that must be produced. When lighting must be supplemented, the hotel can choose from two basic lighting options. The first of these is **incandescent lamps.**

HOTEL TERMINOLOGY AT WORK

Incandescent Lamp: A lamp in which a filament inside the lamp's bulb is heated by electrical current to produce light.

■

Incandescent lights are the type most people think of when they think of the lightbulbs used in their homes. Incandescent bulbs have relatively short life spans (2,000 hours or less) and thus must be frequently changed. They are fairly inefficient since they produce only 15–20 lumens per watt used. For example, a 100-watt bulb produces 1,500–2,000 lumens when it is turned on. Incandescent lights are popular, however, because they are easy to install, easy to move, inexpensive to purchase, and have the characteristic of starting and restarting instantly. Incandescent lamp bulbs can be made in such a way as to concentrate light in one area (these are known as spot or floodlights).

In cases where a conventional incandescent light is not best suited for a specific lighting need, hotels can select an **electric discharge lamp** as a second lighting option.

HOTEL TERMINOLOGY AT WORK

Electric Discharge Lamp: A lamp in which light is generated by passing electrical current through a space filled with a special combination of gases. Examples include fluorescent, mercury vapor, metal halide, and sodium.

■

Electric discharge lamps do not operate directly from electricity. They must be assisted in the process by the use of a **ballast.**

HOTEL TERMINOLOGY AT WORK

Ballast: The device in an electric discharge lamp that starts, stops, and controls the current to the light.

■

Electric discharge lamps are characterized by longer lives (5,000–25,000 hours) and higher efficiency (40–80 lumens per watt). The most common of this lamp type is the fluorescent, and it is frequently used where high light levels and low operating costs are a consideration. If an electric discharge lamp stops working, either the bulb or the ballast may need replacing.

Other types of electric discharge lamps used include those for parking areas or security lighting. In cases such as these, sodium lamps are a good choice as they can generate 200 lumens per watt used and have extremely long lives. Of course, the cost to purchase and install these lights is greater also.

In the late 1980s, compact versions of fluorescent lights became popular in many hotels. These lights were designed to combine the energy efficiency and long life of a traditional fluorescent light with the convenience and ballast-free operation of an incandescent light. For many applications, they provide an excellent blend between operational savings and convenience.

THE INTERNET AT WORK

Compact fluorescent lights are increasingly popular and cost-effective but do have limitations. To read an in-depth discussion of these lights, their uses, and their special disposal requirements, go to:

www.snopud.com/infouse/cfls.htm.

A hotel can select from a wide choice of lights, bulbs, and fixtures. The proper type, color of light, and operational costs must all be taken into consideration when selecting lighting fixtures and lamps. In all cases, lighting maintenance, including lamp repair, bulb changing, and fixture cleaning, must be an integral part of the hotel's PM program.

HVAC

Another significant consumer of electrical power is the hotel's HVAC system. Heating, ventilation, and air conditioning are considered together within the hotel's maintenance program because they all utilize the hotel's air treatment, thermostats, **duct,** and **air handler** systems.

HOTEL TERMINOLOGY AT WORK

Duct: A passageway, usually built of sheet metal, that allows fresh, cold, or warm air to be directed to various parts of a building.

Air Handlers: The fans and mechanical systems required to move air through ducts and to vents.

■

A properly operating HVAC system delivers air to rooms in the hotel at a desired temperature. The efficiency at which a hotel's HVAC system operates, and thus the comfort of the building is affected by a variety of factors, including:

- The original temperature of the room
- The temperature of the air delivered
- The relative humidity of the air delivered

- The air movement in the room
- The temperature-absorbing surfaces in the room

HVAC systems can be fairly straightforward or very complex, but all will consist of components responsible for heating and cooling the hotel.

Heating Components.   While it is possible that all of a hotel's heating components are run by electricity, this is not normally the case. Heating by electricity, especially in cold climates, is not generally cost-effective. Because of this, hotels generally heat at least some parts of their buildings using natural gas, liquefied petroleum gas (LPG), steam, or fuel oil although electricity can be used to heat small areas.

In most hotels, the heating of hot water is second in cost only to the heating of air. A hotel requires an effective furnace (or heat pump system) for heating air and a properly sized boiler for heating water. Regardless of the heat source, electricity is used by fans or pumps to move warm air produced by the furnace, or hot water produced by the hot water heater, to the appropriate parts of the building. The maintenance of these two heating components can be complex, but an effective chief engineer maintains these in a manner that is safe and cost-effective, performing **calibration** and maintenance tasks in accordance with manufacturer's recommendations and local building code requirements.

HOTEL TERMINOLOGY AT WORK

Calibration: The adjustment of equipment to maximize its effectiveness and operational efficiency.

■

Cooling Components.   Just as a hotel must heat air and water, it must frequently cool them also. The major cost of operating air-cooling or conditioning systems is related to electricity usage.

Essentially, in an air-conditioning system, electrically operated equipment extracts heat from either air or water and then utilizes the remaining cooled air or water to absorb and remove more heat from the building. The effectiveness of a cooling system is dependent on several factors, including:

- The original air temperature and humidity of the room to be cooled
- The temperature and humidity of the chilled air entering the room from the HVAC system
- The quantity of chilled air entering the room
- The operational efficiency of the air-conditioning equipment

Some cooling systems are designed to produce small quantities of very cold air that is then pumped or blown into a room to reduce its temperature;

other systems supply larger quantities of air that is not as cold, but because the quantity supplied is greater, has the same room cooling effect.

The ability of a cooling system to deliver cold air or water of a specified temperature and in the quantity required determines the effectiveness of a cooling system. Many times, especially in hot humid weather, the demands placed upon a hotel's cooling system are intense. The ability of the E&M department to maintain cooling equipment in a manner that minimizes guest discomfort (and the resulting complaints) is critical to the success of the hotel. Effective seasonal and PM maintenance on cooling equipment is a crucial part of the chief engineer's job in climates where air conditioning is a frequent need.

Natural Gas

In some geographic areas, natural gas, because it is plentiful and cost-effective, is used by hotels to heat water for guest rooms and to power laundry area clothes dryers. In addition, natural gas is used in many hotel power plants to directly or indirectly provide heat to guest rooms and public spaces. Interestingly, the overwhelming majority of chefs and cooks also prefer natural gas when cooking because of its rapid heat production and the degree of temperature control it allows.

Managed properly, natural gas is an extremely safe source of energy. If a hotel is using natural gas equipment of any type, each gas hot water heater, furnace, or other piece of equipment should have a PM program designed specifically to minimize the operating costs, ensure safety, and maximize the efficiency of the unit. This is especially important because the combustible nature of natural gas requires that gas leaks be avoided at all times. In addition, the calibration of the oxygen and fuel mixture required to maximize the efficiency of the combustion process must be continually and carefully monitored. As a G.M., there are few areas of PM that are more important to evaluate and review regularly than those related to natural gas equipment.

THE INTERNET AT WORK

Gas equipment manufacturers are understandably proud of their products. For more information on gas-operated food service equipment, as well as managerial tips and restaurant operations information, go to:

www.cookingforprofit.com.

Water

Aggressively managing a hotel's water consumption is very cost-effective because it pays three ways. Conserving water:

1. Reduces the number of gallons of water purchased

2. Reduces the amount the hotel will pay for sewage (water disposal)
3. In the case of hot water, reduces water-heating costs because less hot water must be produced

Water costs can be dramatically reduced if the E&M department conscientiously monitors water usage in all areas of the hotel. Figure 11.6 lists, for several areas, just a few of the activities hotel E&M departments can undertake to help reduce water-related costs. Working together, the G.M. and the chief engineer should implement all of those water saving activities that truly impact the hotel's bottom line and do not negatively affect guest satisfaction.

FIGURE 11.6   Sample Water Conservation Techniques

Guest Rooms

- Include inspection of all guest room faucets on the PM checklist
- Inspect toilet flush valves monthly; replace as needed
- Consider installing "water-saver" showerheads
- Investigate "Earth Friendly" procedures designed to enlist the aid of guests in the water conservation process.

Public Space

- Include inspection of all public rest room faucets on the PM checklist
- Install automatic flush valves in men's room urinals
- Where practical, reduce hot water temperatures in public rest rooms
- Check pool and spa fill levels and water pump operation daily

Laundry

- Include, as part of the PM program, the monthly inspection of water fittings on all washers
- Presoak stained terry and linen rather than double washing
- Use the lowest hot water wash setting possible while still ensuring clean terry and linen.

Food Service

- Serve water to diners only on request
- Operate dishwashers only as needed
- Use sprayers, not faucets, to prerinse dishes and flatware intended to be machine washed
- Use chemical sanitizers, rather than excessively hot water to sanitize pots and pans
- Use sprayers, not faucets, to rinse/wash produce prior to cooking or storage

Outdoors

- Inspect sprinkler systems for leaking and misdirected spraying daily
- Utilize the sprinkler system only when critically needed. Do not overwater
- Minimize the use of sprayed water for cleaning (driveway and parking areas for example). Sweep and spot clean these areas instead

Waste

Hotels generate a tremendous amount of solid waste or trash. Sources of waste include packaging materials such as cardboard boxes, crates, and bags that were used in the shipping of hotel supplies, kitchen garbage, guest room trash, and even yard waste generated from the hotel's landscaping efforts. Increasingly, the hotel industry has come to realize that excessive waste and poorly conceived waste disposal methods are detrimental to the environment and represent a poor use of natural resources. In addition, as landfills become scarce, the cost of solid waste disposal has risen. Because of this, hotels have encouraged manufacturers who ship products to them to practice **source reduction** and have aggressively implemented creative programs to reduce the generation of their own solid waste.

HOTEL TERMINOLOGY AT WORK

Source Reduction: The effort by product manufactures to design and ship products so as to minimize waste resulting from the product's shipping and delivery to a hotel.

■

Recycling, minimizing waste generation, and wise purchasing can all go a long way toward reducing waste disposal costs. They should be implemented wherever possible.

THE INTERNET AT WORK

A growing proportion of the population, including many hoteliers, aggressively embraces earth-friendly hotel-operating procedures. The "Green" Hotels Association is one such group. For an overview of the group's philosophy, go to:

http://www.greenhotels.com.

Once there, review the "Meeting Planner's Questionnaire" found at the site to see the types of activities this group encourages hotels to undertake.

In addition to improving conservation efforts and controlling costs, effective waste management means keeping inside and outside trash removal areas clean and, to the greatest degree possible, attractive. This can be achieved by proper sanitation procedures and by enclosing the trash removal areas with fencing or other eye-appealing materials.

Poorly maintained trash removal areas are unsightly and can attract insects, rodents, and other scavenging animals. The chief engineer should regularly inspect these areas for preventative maintenance of fencing or other surrounds and for the quality of sanitation in the trash removal areas.

HOTEL TERMINOLOGY AT WORK GLOSSARY

The following terms were defined within this chapter. If you are not familiar with each of them, please review the segment of the chapter that contains the term.

Engineering	Work order	Electric discharge lamp
Maintenance	PM (preventative mainte-	Ballast
HVAC	nance) program	Duct
POM	PM checklist	Air handler
FF&E reserve	Energy management	Calibration
Restoration	Backup generator	Source reduction
Replace as needed	Foot-candle	
Total replacement	Incandescent lamp	

ISSUES AT WORK

1. For many routine maintenance replacement items, the G.M. has a choice between doing all of the maintenance at once (such as changing air filters in guest rooms quarterly), and doing it as needed (such as replacing hot water heater pumps as they go out). In still other cases, such as parking lot lightbulb replacement or fan belts on motors, the G.M. has a choice between systematic total replacement and a "replace as needed" approach. Assume you were required to make the replacement type decision for exterior parking lot lights in a hotel with parking for 500 cars. What factors would influence your decision? Discuss at least three of these in addition to replacement cost.

2. Lawn care is a good example of the many maintenance items that can be done in-house or contracted to an outside vendor. Assume you operate a 350-room hotel with three acres of total lawn and landscape area. Prepare a list of questions you would ask a potential provider of lawn and landscape services. What factors would most influence your decision to select an outside vendor for your lawn and landscape work?

3. Often repair and maintenance costs are highest when occupancy rates are lowest. This is true because much repair and maintenance work, (damaged ceiling repair for example) can only be done when guest rooms are empty for extended periods. This makes POM costs highest when hotel revenues are lowest. What are some steps management can take to minimize this effect?

4. Many hotels have implemented aggressive recycling programs. Assume an employee group within the hotel approached you about starting a comprehensive recycling program. What factors would influence the time and financial resources you would be willing to commit to such an effort?

5. For major hotel repairs that cannot be done in-house, some chief engineers prefer to establish a relationship with one major contractor in each area, (i.e., plumbing, heating, electrical, etc.), and then employ that contractor for the needed repairs. Other chief engineers prefer to solicit competitive bids for each major project and then select the best bidder. What are the advantages and disadvantages of each approach? Which approach would you suggest to your own chief engineer?

12

Franchise Agreements and Management Contracts

This Chapter at Work

From the perspective of the traveling public, perhaps one of the most misunderstood aspects of hotels is the question of who owns them and who manages them. This is due to the fact that in most cases, hotels are owned by a business entity that elects, for the good of that business, to affiliate with a group of similar hotels and operate under the name of that hotel group. These hotel groups are called brands, flags, or chains. The company administering and directing the brand itself is not, in most cases, an owner of hotels, but rather, as a franchise company, it is responsible for the growth of the brand.

Hotel operations can be further complicated by the fact that the business entity owning the hotel and choosing brand affiliation may also elect to hire a management company that will actually select a G.M. and operate the hotel. Thus, a typical traveler is likely to be staying at a hotel owned by one business entity that has elected to affiliate the hotel with a brand (a second entity) and entrust the management of the hotel to a management company (a third entity), who actually hires the G.M.

Good G.M.s are operational professionals who may, at various times, find themselves working directly for those who own the hotel and, at other times, for a management company selected by the owners to operate the hotel. In most cases, a franchise company will be involved also. Because that is true, it is important for G.M.s to know about both the relationship that exists between a hotel's owners, (the franchisee) and the hotel brand (the franchisor) when both parties sign a franchise agreement and the special relationship that exists between owners and a management company when a management contract is in place.

In this chapter you will learn about major franchise companies and the brands they operate. The owners of hotels often ask experienced G.M.s their opinions about the best brand to be selected for a specific hotel. Therefore, you will also learn how to evaluate alternative brand options with the goal of choosing the best brand for a specific hotel. Managing a franchised hotel presents special challenges to the G.M. This chapter reviews the advantages of brand affiliation from the perspectives of both the owners of a hotel and the franchisor with an emphasis on how the franchise agreement, which is the legal document governing the relationship between the hotel and the managers of the selected brand, affects the work of the G.M.

Just as brand affiliation influences the activities of the G.M., so, too, does the special situation in which the G.M. is employed not directly by the hotel, but rather by the management company selected to operate the hotel. In this chapter you will learn about how some of the major hotel management companies operate. In addition, you will review how the management contract, which is the legal document governing the relationship between the owners of a hotel and the company selected to operate the hotel, affects the day-to-day responsibilities of the G.M.

Chapter 12 Outline

THE HOTEL FRANCHISE RELATIONSHIP

Franchising is a business strategy that allows one business entity to use the logo, trademarks and operating systems of another business entity for the benefit of both. As a result, franchising is a network of interdependent business relationships that allows a number of people to share a brand identification, a successful method of doing business, and, hopefully, a strong marketing and distribution system.

For the franchisee, franchising helps reduce risk. Proven operational methods, developed by the franchisor, are used to manage the business. The franchisee gives up the freedom of being completely independent to become part of a group committed to building a brand and increasing their group's market share. A franchise system can (but may not) also provide group-buying power to reduce the franchisee's operating expenses. The trade-offs for the franchisee are the fees paid to the franchisor for the operating license and the restrictions that are imposed by the franchisor. For the franchisor, franchisees and their financial capital expand the brand faster than it would ever be possible for the franchisor to do so alone.

Hotel Franchising

One of the biggest challenges faced by those who would buy or build a hotel is that of which **flag**, if any, the property should "fly." The question is an important one both to the owners of the property and to the G.M. who operates it.

HOTEL TERMINOLOGY AT WORK

Flag: A term used to refer to the specific brand with which a hotel may affiliate. Examples of currently popular flags include brands such as Comfort Inns, Holiday Inn Express, Ramada Inns, Hampton Inns, Residence Inns, Best Western, and Hawthorn Suites. The hotels affiliated with a specific flag are sometimes referred to as a chain. For example, "Which flags are you considering for your new hotel project?"

■

A hotel **franchise** relationship exists when the owners of a hotel choose a flag and enter into a **franchise agreement** with the managers of that specific brand.

HOTEL TERMINOLOGY AT WORK

Franchise: An arrangement whereby one party (the brand) allows another (the hotel owners) to use its logo, name, systems, and resources in exchange for a fee.

Franchise Agreement: The legal contract between the hotel's owners (the franchisee) and the brand managers (the franchisor), which describes the duties and responsibilities of each in the franchise relationship.

■

It is important to note that, unlike some other franchise industries, the majority of hotel brand managers (franchisors) do not operate hotels. They operate franchise companies. Hotel owners (the franchisees) and their G.M.s are the operating entities in nearly all hotel franchise relationships.

Origin and Structure

Franchising has long been a part of American business. The history of hotel franchising, however, is relatively short. Many in the hotel industry believe that the first significant hotel franchising arrangements began in the 1950s with Kemmons Wilson and his Holiday Inn chain.

In a combination of what may well be part historical fact and part hotel lore, the story is told of how, in 1951, Wilson, a resident of Memphis, Tennessee, loaded his wife and five children into the family car and drove to Washington, D.C., for a vacation. He was quite unhappy with the motel accommodations he found along the way. The rooms he encountered were, he believed, too small, too expensive, and in many cases, not clean. Wilson returned to Tennessee convinced that he could build a chain of hotels across the country that would operate under the same name and provide the traveling public with a lodging experience they could count on to be clean, comfortable, and moderately priced. He hired an architect to draw up the plans for a prototype hotel. The architect, according to legend, was watching an old Bing Crosby movie titled *Holiday Inn* while he was working, and sketched that name on the top of the plans he was drawing. Wilson, upon seeing the plans, liked them and the name at the top as well. As a result, the Holiday Inn was born. The first Holiday Inn opened in Tennessee in 1952 and the 400th Holiday Inn franchise began operation in December 1962. Today, Holiday Inns franchises its name as part of the InterContinental hotel group that consists of over 1,500 properties worldwide, including the brands Inter-Continental Hotels, Holiday Inn, Holiday Inn Select, Holiday Inn Express, Holiday Inn Crown Plaza, and Staybridge Suites.

Today hotel owners increasingly elect to affiliate their hotels with other hotels under a common brand name. In fact, as we saw in chapter 1 (Figure 1.6), the great majority of hotels in the United States currently operate as part of a regional or national brand. Many of these brands are grouped under a common brand management group. For example, Choice Hotels International manages the Clarion, Quality, Comfort Inn, Comfort Suites, Sleep Inn, MainStay Suites, Roadway Inn, and Econolodge brands. Cendant, as of the time of writing this book, manages the Amerihost, Day's Inn, Howard Johnson, Knights Inn, Ramada, Super Eight, Travelodge, and Wingate Inn brands, as well as other franchised names including Avis (car rental) and Century 21 (real estate sales).

While the actual brands managed by any single franchisor change as these brands are bought and sold, the ten largest brands at the time of this writing are included as Figure 12.1.

Each brand will, depending on the parent company's structure, have a brand manager or president responsible for growing the number of hotels in the brand and maintaining the quality standards that have been established for that brand. It is important to understand that in the overwhelming majority of cases franchise companies do not actually own the hotels operating under their brand names. Companies such as these own, instead, the right to sell the brand name and determine the standards that will be followed by those hotel owners who do elect to affiliate with their brands.

With the ownership of a hotel vested in one business entity and the responsibility for brand standards resting with another business entity, it is not surprising that conflict can arise between the hotel's owners and the brand managers. For example, assume the managers of a given brand decide that the logo for their brand, and thus the exterior building signage identifying the brand to the traveling public, has become dated and is in need of modernization. The brand managers may have the authority, because of the

FIGURE 12.1 Ten Largest Brands

Brand	Properties	Rooms
1. Best Western International	4,008	304,664
2. Holiday Inn	1,576	295,252
3. Days Inns Worldwide	1,947	164,023
4. Marriott Hotels, Resorts & Suites	433	160,540
5. Comfort Inns and Comfort Suites	2,065	159,619
6. Sheraton Hotels & Resorts	399	133,200
7. Super 8 Motels	2,092	127,533
8. Ramada Franchise Systems	971	118,114
9. Hampton Inn/ Hampton Inn and Suites	1,175	120,589
10. Holiday Inn Express	1,351	109,186

franchise agreement, to require affiliated hotel owners to update their hotel signage. The owners, however, facing significant purchase and instillation costs for replacing signs that are in perfectly good working order but that have been declared "dated" by the brand managers, may well attempt to resist the purchase of the new signs. In fact, these hotel owners may disagree with the brand managers about numerous operating issues.

As a G.M., it is important for you to understand that if you are operating a branded hotel, you have a responsibility to your employer; however, you also have a responsibility to abide by the franchise agreement signed by your hotel's owners. That agreement will always include a section that requires your best efforts in maintaining the established standards of the brand. Conflicts can and do arise between hotel owners and brand managers. As a G.M., it is your responsibility to balance the legitimate interests of your hotel and the brand in a manner that reflects positively on your own professionalism.

Unlike the history of some other industries, the history of hotel franchising does not include widespread cases of franchisor fraud or deception. Despite that fact, hotel franchise relationships are subject to the same federal and state laws that have been enacted to protect franchisees from unscrupulous franchisors in all industries.

Governmental Regulations Related to Franchises

In the past, some companies offering franchises to individual business owners did so in ways that were unscrupulous and often illegal. In an effort to level the playing field between those who sell and those who would buy franchises, the **Federal Trade Commission (FTC)** in 1979, issued regulations with the full force of federal law. This set of laws are titled "Disclosure Requirements and Prohibitions Concerning Franchising and Business Opportunity Ventures." Commonly referred to as the "Franchise Rule," the

---

HOTEL TERMINOLOGY AT WORK

Federal Trade Commission (FTC): The FTC enforces federal antitrust and consumer protection laws. It also seeks to ensure that the nation's business markets function competitively and are free of undue restrictions caused by acts or practices that are unfair or deceptive.

■

THE INTERNET AT WORK

To read the entire "Franchise Rule" developed by the FTC and to familiarize yourself with the requirements placed upon those who sell franchises, go to:

www.ftc.gov/bcp/franchise/16cfr436.htm.

---

rules spell out the obligations of franchisors when they attempt to sell their franchises to potential franchisees.

Essentially, the Franchise Rule requires that franchisors:

- Supply potential franchisees with a disclosure document at the earlier of the first face-to-face meeting or ten business days before any money is paid by the franchisee to the franchisor
- Provide evidence, in writing, of any earnings claims or profit forecasts made by the franchisor
- Disclose the number and percentage of franchisees achieving the earnings rates advertised in any promotional ads that include earnings claims
- Provide potential franchisees with copies of the basic franchise agreement used by the franchisor
- Refund promptly any deposit monies legally due to potential franchisees that elected not to sign a franchise agreement with the franchisor
- Not make claims orally or in writing that conflict with the written disclosure documents provided to the franchisee

In addition to federal laws and regulations, most states also have franchise investment laws that require franchisors to provide a presale disclosure document known as an **FOC (franchise offering circular)** to potential franchisees.

HOTEL TERMINOLOGY AT WORK

FOC (Franchise Offering Circular): A franchise disclosure document that is prepared by a franchisor and then is registered and filed with the state governmental agency responsible for administering franchise relationships in that state.

■

These states prohibit the sale of a franchise inside their borders until a franchisor's FOC has been filed with the proper state authorities. While these states, like the FTC, impose disclosure requirements on franchisors, neither verifies the accuracy of the information in the disclosure documents. Verification of a franchisor's claims is the responsibility of the buyer (franchisee). For example, a hotel franchise company can make a claim that its 800 number provides the average franchisee with fifty sold guest rooms per night. This claim will *not* be verified as accurate by either the FTC or the state in which the franchisor files an FOC. The potential franchisee should seek verification of any item in the FOC that is questionable prior to signing a franchise agreement.

FOCs are typically designed to comply with both the laws of the state in which they are filed and the FTC's Franchise Rule and will generally include information about:

- The name of the franchisor and the type of franchise it offers for sale
- The business experience of the franchise company's officers
- Fees and royalties that must be paid
- Initial investment requirements
- Rights and obligations of the franchisor and franchisee
- Territorial protection offered by the franchisor
- Required operating policies
- Renewal, transfer, and termination procedures
- Earnings claims
- Current franchisees
- A sample franchise agreement
- Specific information required by each state in which the FOC is to be filed
- The name and address of the legal representative of the franchisor

It is important to remember that hotel franchise FOCs must be prepared to meet the same requirements as those in any other industry. Companies issuing FOCs should be honest, but those who read them should be prepared to verify every important claim made in the document.

THE INTERNET AT WORK

Potential franchisees can learn a great deal about buying and operating a franchise by joining the International Franchise Association (IFA). To review the type of information they provide to their members, go to:

www.franchise.org.

The Franchise Agreement

When a hotel's owners elect to affiliate their hotel with a brand, they will sign a franchise agreement with the franchisor's brand managers. The franchise agreement will spell out, in great detail, the responsibilities of both the brand managers (franchisors) and the hotel owners (franchisee). In the past, many owners within the hotel community felt that brand managers had too much power to control the terms and conditions contained in the franchise agreements. More recently, vocal groups of owners, led chiefly by the **Asian American Hotel Owner's Association (AAHOA),** have proposed, and actively campaigned for, fundamental changes in the basic franchise agreements that have long been in use. These proposed changes seek to give hotel owners more control over the content of franchise agreements and a more equal say in the operation of their hotels.

HOTEL TERMINOLOGY AT WORK

AAHOA (Asian American Hotel Owners Association): An association of hotel owners who, through an exchange of ideas, seek to promote professionalism and excellence in hotel ownership.

■

THE INTERNET AT WORK

The Asian American Hotel Owners Association (AAHOA) has been at the forefront of promoting fairness in hotel franchising. Their associate members interact with many brand management companies. To learn more about AAHOA and to review their 12 Points of Fair Franchising, go to:

www.aahoa.com.

Major Elements

A franchise agreement is simply a written contract between a franchisor (the brand managers) and a franchisee (the hotel owner). While each brand will develop its own franchise agreement, the following information is typically included:

- *Names of the parties signing the agreement.* In this section, the name of the legal entity representing the brand as well as the corporation, partnership, or sole proprietor owning the hotel is listed.

- *Detailed definitions.* In this section, any definitions used in the agreement that could be subject to misinterpretation by the parties to the agreement are defined. For example, many franchisee agreements base the fees to be paid by owners on the gross room revenue achieved by the hotel. In this section of the agreement, the franchisor would detail exactly what gross room revenue means. The following is an example of a definition that describes the term in great detail and is of the type found in this section of the document: *"Gross rooms revenue"* means the revenue from the rental of sleeping rooms and meeting rooms at the hotel. It does not include revenue from Internet access fees, telephone calls, in-room safes or minibars, vending machines, food and beverage sales, or room service.

- *License grant.* Here the franchisor will describe the manner in which the hotel owner is allowed to use the brand's logos, signage, and name in the operation of the hotel.

- *Term (length of agreement).* The beginning and ending date of the agreement will be spelled out in detail. The most common franchise agreements are written for a length of twenty years. Most, however, also contain a **window** at the fifth, tenth, and fifteenth, years. More recently some agreements have been written with **early outs** as franchisors aggressively seek to entice hotel owners to choose their brands.

HOTEL TERMINOLOGY AT WORK

Window: A clause in a franchisee agreement that grants both the franchisor and the franchisee the right, with proper notification, to terminate the agreement.

Early Out: A clause in a franchisee agreement that grants both the franchisor and the franchisee the right, with proper notification, to terminate the agreement after it has been in effect for a relatively short period of time. When this clause exists, a window may be granted after only one, two, or three years.

■

- *Fees.* This section details the fees the franchisee must pay to the franchisor. While each brand is free to set its fees as it wishes, the typical fees in a hotel franchise agreement will include:
  - Affiliation fees. These are flat fees, paid up front (upon signing the agreement), to affiliate with the brand.
  - Royalty fees. These fees are paid based upon an agreed upon formula and are typically tied to the level of revenue generated by the hotel.

- Marketing fees. These fees are also determined by the hotel's revenue levels and are to be used exclusively to advertise the brand name. Such marketing efforts may include ads placed on national or regional radio, magazines, newspapers, or television.
- Reservation fees. These are collected to operate the brand's reservation system (800 number).
- *Reports.* This section lists any monthly or annual reports that must be provided by the hotel owner to the franchisor and when such reports are due. Examples may include reports related to room revenue generated, occupancy levels, and **occupancy taxes** paid and average daily rate (ADR).

HOTEL TERMINOLOGY AT WORK

Occupancy Tax: Money paid by a hotel to a local taxing authority. The room revenue generated by the hotel determines the amount paid. This tax is also known, in some areas, as the "bed" tax. For example, "In our city, the occupancy tax is 4 percent."

■

- *Responsibilities of the franchisor.* This section details the obligations of the franchisor under the agreement and lists what the hotel owner will receive in exchange for paying fees and royalties. It will include items such as inspection schedules, marketing efforts, and brand standards enforcement.
- *Responsibilities of the franchisee.* This section details what the hotel owner will do in exchange for the right to use the name of the franchisor's brand. It will include items such as signage requirements, operational standards that must be implemented, and payment schedules that must be met.
- *Assignment of agreement.* Here the ownership transfer and its affect upon the agreement are detailed. In most cases, the hotel owner must have the approval of the franchisor to transfer (assign) their rights in the agreement to another; however, the franchisors are typically free to assign the agreement to any business entity they choose without the approval of the franchisee.
- *Termination or default.* The events that permit a termination, or define a default, by either party are detailed in this section. In most cases, a default on the part of the franchisee will result in penalties that must be paid by the franchisee to the franchisor.
- *Insurance requirements.* To protect both parties, the hotel owner will be required to provide insurance. In this section the types and amounts of required insurance will be listed. Typical requirements include proof

of general indemnification policies, automobile insurance, and mandatory workers' compensation (injury) insurance.

- *Requirements for alteration.* This section details the rights of the franchisor to change the agreement.
- *Arbitration and legal fees.* In this section, the responsibilities of each party related to legal disputes are detailed. Also included in this section is information about the geographic location of the court where such disputes are to be resolved. In most franchise agreements, disputes are to be resolved in the state in which the franchisor is incorporated.
- *Signature pages.* The authorized representatives of the brand, as well as the owners of the hotel, will sign the franchise agreement.

Advantages to the Franchisee

The primary advantages to a hotel of buying a franchise are that doing so allows the hotel's owners to acquire a brand name with regional or national recognition and to connect the hotel to the Global Distribution System (GDS). As seen earlier, connectivity to the GDS is, in today's hotel market, a necessity. An independent hotel can, in fact, purchase this connectivity; however, it is costly.

Affiliation with a strong brand increases the hotel's sales and thus its profitability. The total fees paid by the hotel owner to the brand managers are related to the strength of the brand name and the revenue that the name will bring to the hotel. While the fees related to a franchise agreement are sometimes negotiable, they will, on average, equal from 3 to 15 percent of a hotel's gross room revenue.

In addition to increased sales levels, affiliation with a brand affects the ability of a hotel's owner to secure financing. When owners seek financing from banks or other lending institutions, they find that these lenders will, almost without exception, require an affiliation with an established brand prior to considering the hotel for a loan.

Additional advantages, depending on the franchisor selected, may include assistance with on-site training, advice on purchasing furnishings and fixtures, reduced operating costs resulting from vendors who give brand operators preferred pricing, and free interior design assistance.

Advantages to the Franchisor

The greatest advantage to a franchisor of entering into a franchise agreement with a hotel owner is the increase in fee payments to the brand that will result from the agreement. Like all businesses, franchise companies desire growth. The greater the number of hotels that operate under a single brand name the greater, in general, the value of the name and thus the fees that can be charged for using that name. In addition, each additional hotel that affiliates with a hotel brand helps to pay for the fixed overhead of operating that brand. Therefore, additional hotel properties operating under the same brand name result in greater profits for the franchise company. As a result, franchisors are aggressive in soliciting agreements with hotel owners even if these owners are affiliated with another brand. As well, franchisors actively pursue those owners developing new hotels who have not yet selected a franchise brand.

Selecting a Franchisor

Perhaps one of the most useful services a hotel G.M. can provide to an owner is that of assistance in the selection of a hotel brand when such assistance is requested. It is simply true that an experienced G.M., more so than an inexperienced owner or the franchisor (who has a vested interest in the sale), is in the best position to provide advice about how well a given brand name will "fit" a specific hotel property. It is also true that many hotel brands go through a life cycle that includes early buildup, in which nearly every property entering the system is newly built. Later in the development of the brand, and in an effort to promote unit growth, brand managers may allow **conversions.**

HOTEL TERMINOLOGY AT WORK

Conversion: As a verb: The process of changing a hotel's flag from one franchisor to another. Also known as "reflagging." For example, "We need a G.M. experienced in managing a hotel conversion."

As a noun: The term used to describe a hotel that has changed its flag from one franchisor to another. For example, "Has this hotel always been a (brand name), or is it a conversion?"
∎

Conversions can be beneficial to a brand because they allow the brand to grow more quickly. They can be a detriment to the brand, however, if the converted properties do not have the features and quality levels of the hotels already in the brand.

For a hotel's owners, purchasing a hotel franchise is actually very much like purchasing the long-term services of other professionals, such as attorneys or accountants, who help the owner maximize the value of their asset. For example, when selecting a franchise, there will be a number of companies (franchisors) offering the service. These service providers offer a variety of experience, skills, and knowledge. In addition, the prices charged for their services will vary. Last, as is true in many relationships, the franchisor is likely to have a unique "style" of doing business that attracts (or detracts!) potential franchisees.

Basic Considerations

As a G.M. advising an owner about franchise selections available, it is important to know as much about a potential franchisor as possible so that your advice will be as accurate as it can be. As we have seen, franchisors are required, by law, to disclose a great deal of information. This information should be reviewed carefully by potential franchisees. Even more information can be obtained through a diligent process of investigation and interview. For the purpose of illustrating the procedure of selecting a franchise brand, assume that you are approached by an investment group that has decided to build a new 150-room limited service hotel. They want to hire you to advise them on selecting the best possible brand for the hotel. While you will have much to investigate, some of the factors that you would certainly want to consider before making a recommendation would be:

- *The quality and experience of the brand managers.* Brand management, like hotel management, is complex. Those brand managers who are experienced in their work will operate the brand better than those who are not. In addition, when brand managers are experienced, it is possible for the hotel's owners to see a track record of success (or failure) on the part of the managers. The relationship between a franchisor and a franchisee is not, despite the claims of the franchisor, a true partnership because, in the case of losses incurred by the hotel, the brand and its managers are not financially responsible. In fact, no brand available today bases the fees it collects on the achieved profits, rather than the achieved revenue, of its branded hotels. As a result, it is the hotel owners, not the brand managers, who bear the financial risk of poor brand management. Because that is true, it is critical that the brand managers be experienced and talented and that they demonstrate great integrity in dealings with their franchisees.

- *Perceived quality/service level of the brand.* Travelers associate some brands with higher quality, service levels, and cost, than other brands. A Holiday Inn Crown Plaza, for example, will likely be perceived by most travelers as having more services (and thus a higher ADR) than a Holiday Inn Express. In most cases, franchisors, in an attempt to offer a franchise product that appeals to hotel owners at a variety of desired investment levels, will offer brands at a range of quality and guest services provided. Those hotel owners who elect to operate the highest quality brand offered by a franchisor will spend, on average, more to build or renovate each of their hotel rooms than if they selected a lower quality level. In addition, total operating costs are likely to be higher with brands that offer guests more services, although ADRs are also likely to be higher in these cases. Of course, a well-managed, lower-cost, limited-service brand can be more profitable for an owner than a poorly managed, limited-service brand property with a higher **systemwide** ADR. Hotel owners that seek to maximize their return on investment must select a brand that is both well managed and that is appropriate (meets quality/service expectations) for the travelers to which the hotel is marketed.

HOTEL TERMINOLOGY AT WORK

System-Wide: The term used to describe all hotels within a given brand. Used for example, in: "Last year, the system-wide ADR for the brand was $115.20, with an occupancy rate of 63.7%."

■

- *The amount of fees paid to the franchisor.* Far too many hotel owners, when evaluating alternative franchisors, focus only on the fees the hotel will pay to the brand. While the fees paid to a franchisor are certainly one factor to be considered, it is not the only factor, nor is it even the most important. Nearly all hotel owners feel the franchise fees they pay are too high; conversely, nearly all franchisors feel that what their franchisees receive in exchange for their fee payments is a great value to the hotel. In fact, the fees paid to a franchisor are a negotiable part of the franchise agreement and should be considered seriously only after the hotel owner has narrowed down the list of potential franchisors to those that meet other criteria the owner has established for selecting the brand.
- *Direction of the brand.* By far the most important factor in the long-term success of the franchisor/franchise relationship is the future direction of the brand. Obviously, it is impossible to predict the future, yet knowing how a brand will be perceived by the public in five, ten, or twenty years is important when signing a franchise agreement for that same number of years. Clues to the future success of the brand can be detected by asking the franchisor about
  - The number of hotels currently operating under the brand name.
  - The percentage of hotels, on an annual basis, that have elected to leave the brand in the past five years.
  - The number of new properties currently being built under the brand's name.
  - The number of existing hotels converting to the brand (if conversions are allowed).
  - The ADR trend for the last five years in comparison to the ADR trend for the industry segment in which the brand competes.
  - The occupancy rate trend for the last five years in comparison to the occupancy rate trend for the industry segment in which the brand competes.

- The percentage of total hotel room revenue contributed by the brand's reservation system and the percentage of hotels within the brand that achieve that average rate of contribution.

The Franchisor Questionnaire

One way for a potential franchisee to begin the process of narrowing down the number of prospective franchisors to be selected is through the use of a structured series of questions to which all franchisors under consideration must respond. Lists of and addresses for hotel franchise companies can be easily obtained on the Internet.

THE INTERNET AT WORK

Lists of hotel franchisors, their mailing addresses, and the individual(s) responsible for each brand they manage can be quickly obtained on the Internet. For one such source of hotel franchisor contact information, go to:

www.franchisehelp.com.

Once a list of potential franchisors has been obtained, it is possible to begin the selection process. Figure 12.2 shows a survey that could be used to search for a franchisor.

HOTEL TERMINOLOGY AT WORK

Area of Protection (AOP): The geographic area, which is designated by a franchisor, and granted to a franchisee, in which no directly competing franchisees will be sold. Used, for example, in, "The AOP the franchisor is proposing consists of a five-mile radius around the hotel and lasts for five years."

■

While the questions that are important to any specific hotel owner will determine the information requested on the franchisor survey, using the results of the information gathered in a survey such as that presented in Figure 12.2, owners of the prospective hotel would contact, and then interview in person, the franchisor finalists.

The Product Improvement Plan (PIP)

While a large number of hotels are built each year, an even larger number of brand conversions are undertaken each year. A brand conversion may occur for a variety of reasons, including a franchisor/franchisee dispute, because the owners of the hotel decide the future prospects for the brand they are cur-

FIGURE 12.2 Franchisor Survey

MEMO

To: POTENTIAL FRANCHISORS
From: J.D. Ojisima
Subject: Attached Franchisor Questionnaire
Date   1/1/20XX

I represent an ownership group that will be building a 150-room, limited-service hotel in our city. The investors have asked me to assist them in evaluating options for flagging the property. In an effort to fairly compare the offerings of alternative potential franchisors, please respond, in writing, to the following questions if your brand has an interest in being considered as a potential franchise partner. Please e-mail your responses to J.D. Ojisima at the following e-mail address: JDOJISIMA@ournewhotel.com.

In addition, our group would like to receive any print materials available regarding your brand. Thank you in advance for your interest in our project.

1. **Application Fees:**
   - What (if any) franchise fees are required as an up-front affiliation (nonoperating revenue) fee to join the brand?
   - Can the above fee be waived or reduced?
   - If so, what is the name and address of the individual in your organization authorized to waive such fees?
   - Who in your organization will determine the exact date that the property may be promoted, signed as, and advertised as your brand?
2. **Area of Protection:**
   - What is the **area of protection (AOP)** proposed by your organization?
   - Does your AOP restrict any other brands you operate (or will operate in the future) from this AOP? If so, name those brands.
   - Does your AOP give our organization the right of first refusal for any brand(s) you currently operate? If so, name those brands.
3. **Reoccurring Fees**
   - Please identify your proposed fee structure for EACH of the first five years of this agreement. Include all fees, that is,
     - Royalty
     - Marketing
     - Reservation
     - All other (including required purchases)
   - Is there flexibility in regard to these fees? If so, who in your organization is authorized to negotiate these fees?
4. **Standards**
   - Please identify the scoring range used in your brand inspection program, as well as the number of times the property will be inspected each year.
   - Please identify the average score (past three years) of all properties in this brand that are within 150 miles of our city.   *(continued)*

FIGURE 12.2 *(Continued)*

- Are inspection scores published? If so where?
- What is the current number of properties operating under this brand? How many of those properties are operating as three diamond (or higher) properties (under AAA inspection standards)?

5. **Mandatory Service Programs**
   - Please describe any mandatory food and beverage programs required by the brand, that is, room service, breakfasts, manager receptions, and so forth.

6. **Operating Performance**
   - Please identify for the previous two years, the brandwide statistics related to
     - ADR
     - Occupancy percent
     - RevPar
     - Reservation system room night contribution
   - Location of all branded (your proposed brand) hotels in our state that are now open or will open next year
   - List of any hotels in our state converting out of your brand last year
   - Address of Web site listing all current properties.

7. **FOC**
   - Please send an up-to-date FOC to our address.

8. **Fair Franchising**
   - Do you subscribe to AAHOA's published 12 Points of Fair Franchising? If not, with which points do you disagree?

9. **Financing Assistance**
   - Please describe the assistance your organization can supply us in the area of securing funding for our hotel project.
   - Please identify the individual within your organization who would supply such assistance.

10. **Termination**
    - What is the length of your proposed agreement?
    - Please describe the penalties incurred and the procedures used should the franchisee elect to take advantage of early termination.

rently affiliated with are not good, or because a new brand appears to offer a better financial return on the owner's investment.

Selecting a new franchisor when converting a hotel from one brand to another is complicated by the fact that the new brand managers are likely to impose renovation, repair, or upgrade conditions on the hotel's owners. For example, a new franchisor may agree to enter into a franchise agreement only if a hotel's owners are willing to replace older carpets and furniture in the hotel's guest rooms with new carpets and furniture. Brand managers want to make sure that each hotel converting into the system will meet the **brand standards** established for the brand they manage.

HOTEL TERMINOLOGY AT WORK

Brand Standard: A hotel service or feature that must be adopted by any property entering a specific hotel brand's system. Used, for example, in, "The franchisor has determined that 'free local telephone calls' will become a new brand standard effective January 1st."

■

In some cases, the renovation and replacement requirements imposed upon a hotel will be quite extensive. Major construction, room additions, and far-reaching facility upgrades may be required. In all cases, installing new outdoor signage and purchasing new and removing old logo items required by the previous franchisor would also need to be done. In general, a conversion will always require some facility modification and, in some cases, these can be quite costly.

Some hotels are reflagged because the hotel's owners have determined that it is not in their best interest to continue to meet the brand standards enforced by the brand managers in charge of their current flag. These owners will take advantage of the windows or early outs available to them to end their relationship with their current franchisor and switch to a new brand. In cases such as these, the owners will often seek a franchise that has lower brand standards. These lowered standards may include everything from a reduced weight of the towels that must be used in the guest bathrooms to the quality of carpet used in corridors. Lower standards generally mean the owners are unlikely to incur large expenses for improving the property prior to joining the new franchise. In fact, reflags such as this can happen in a matter of only several weeks or months because the main changes involve replacement of some interior signage and the logos on guest room items. Even in these cases, however, the hotel's owners will typically be required to complete some physical modifications of the property (e.g., new exterior signage) prior to being accepted into the new franchise system.

Since all conversions will require at least some property change and improvement, owners contemplating a brand conversion will want to know the extent of the changes they must implement prior to being accepted by the new brand. When a potential franchisor inspects a hotel property whose owners are interested in a conversion, a **PIP (product improvement plan)** will be prepared.

HOTEL TERMINOLOGY AT WORK

PIP (Product Improvement Plan): A document detailing the property upgrades and replacements that will be required if a hotel is to be accepted as one of a specific brand's franchised properties. Used, for example, in, "We estimate the PIP on the property to be $4,000,000 if we decide to go with that brand."

■

While hotel franchisors will not, as a rule, estimate the expenses required for implementing the PIPs they prepare, the hotel's owners must do so to obtain a true total cost of the improvements necessary for converting to the new flag. An aggressive PIP can increase an owner's conversion costs by many thousands of dollars, therefore, a thorough review of the required PIP is always crucial prior to beginning the franchise agreement negotiation process.

Negotiating the Franchise Agreement

The franchise agreement is, in the final analysis, simply a contract between the brand's managers and the hotel's owners. As such, it is negotiable. The stronger the position of each side, the more power each will bring to the negotiating process. It is always in the best interest of the hotel's owners, as well as the G.M. advising them, to be represented by an attorney during the franchise agreement finalization period because these agreements are detailed and complex. In the opinion of many in the hotel industry, franchise agreements, which are drafted by the franchisor, tend to be written in the favor of the franchisor. Because this is true, owners should carefully read every line of the franchise agreement to determine exactly what the hotel must do to stay in compliance with the agreement, as well as the penalties that will be incurred if the hotel does not stay in compliance.

Owners should certainly evaluate all components of their proposed franchise agreements; however, one area of special concern, especially to those managing and investing in a hotel, is the relatively new matter of the **impact study**, that is, when these studies should be undertaken, and who should pay for them.

HOTEL TERMINOLOGY AT WORK

Impact Study: An in-depth evaluation of the effect on occupancy percent and ADR that a new hotel in a given market will have on an existing hotel(s) in that same market.

■

To illustrate, assume that, in our example, J.D. Ojisima and the hotel's owners, after a thorough investigation, select the "Sleep Well" brand as the franchise affiliation for their proposed 150-room, limited-service hotel. Assume also that the "Sleep Well" brand is managed by the same corporation (Excalibur Hotels) that manages the "Sleep Better" brand. The "Sleep Better" brand is also a limited-service hotel; however, unlike a "Sleep Well" hotel, franchisees selecting this brand must offer a swimming pool, as well as provide guests a complimentary hot breakfast each morning. Neither of these requirements exists for a "Sleep Well."

If the AOP granted J.D.'s group excludes only the building of additional "Sleep Well" properties within the protected area, it may be the opinion of

Excalibur Hotels, after seeing how well the original hotel performed in the market (recall that franchisors have a right to review the revenue records of their franchisees), that it is in the best interest of Excalibur Hotels to franchise a "Sleep Better" hotel directly across the street from J.D.'s hotel. Of course, a question then arises as to the potential "impact" such a decision will have on the hotel franchised by J.D.'s group. The issue of negative impact has become increasingly important as brand consolidation places more and more hotel brands in the hands of fewer and fewer franchisors. Increasingly, hotel owners have demanded that impact studies, prepared by an independent party, be undertaken and paid for, when appropriate, by the franchisor. This is because impact studies are most likely to be needed when a franchisor that manages two similar hotel brands seeks to grant franchise rights to one brand, within the AOP granted to another brand's franchisee. If the impact study indicates that the granting of a competitive franchise could damage the value of the original franchisee's hotel, compensation for that damage should, in the opinion of many hotel owners, become a negotiable part of the franchise agreement.

Franchise agreements are complex and are increasingly important. They should be entered into only after a great deal of consideration and with expert assistance. The fact, however, is that only a few hotels can survive without a nationally recognized brand name. As a result, G.M.s must become adept at operating hotels in the best interest of their owners, as well as in compliance with their owner's franchise agreement.

MANAGERS AT WORK

"We wanted to get your input, J.D., because you are closest to the operation," said Daniel Flood. Daniel, known to J.D. as "Dan," was the head of the investment group that owned the 350-room full-service hotel at which J.D. was the G.M.

"As you know," continued Dan, "we have a window coming up on our franchise agreement with Premier Hotels. If we are going to switch flags, we need to make a decision within the next sixty days."

J.D. was aware that meetings had been held between the owners of his hotel and an alternative franchise company. In their efforts to secure a franchise agreement with Flood's group, the new franchisor was offering very attractive reductions in royalty and reservation fees for the first three years of the agreement.

"What we need to understand better," said Dan, "is exactly what the impact would be of changing flags. We are especially concerned about conversion costs in their PIP and the new franchise company's short-term ability to drive revenues through their 800 number."

What are some of the factors J.D. should discuss with the hotel's owners? How do you think a name change would affect the hotel's management staff? How would it affect guests? How could it affect the hotel's standing within the community?

THE HOTEL MANAGEMENT COMPANY RELATIONSHIP

If you are a G.M. in the hotel industry for very long, you will likely work, or have the opportunity to work, for a hotel management company. As discussed in chapter 1, a management company is an organization formed for the express purpose of managing one or more hotels. Hotel owners sign **management contracts** that clearly establish the fees, operating responsibilities, and length of time for which the management company will operate their hotel. When a management company secures a contract to operate a hotel, it must provide a G.M. In such a situation, the management company itself, rather than the hotel's owners, employs the G.M. As a result of the popularity of management companies, most G.M.s will spend at least a portion of their careers working, not directly with a hotel's owners but rather directly for a management company.

HOTEL TERMINOLOGY AT WORK

Management Contract: An agreement between a hotel's owners and a hotel management company under which, for a fee, the management company operates the hotel. Also sometimes known as a management agreement.

■

Management Companies

In many cases, those who invest in hotels are not the same individuals as those who want to manage the hotels. These nonoperating hotel owners can either hire individual G.M.s to direct their hotels, or, if they desire, they can hire a management company to do so. In some cases, the owners of a hotel have absolutely no interest in managing or even in the continued ownership of the hotel. For example, assume that a bank has loaned money to a hotel owner to develop a property. The owner opens the hotel, but, over time, fails to make the required loan repayments. As a result, the bank is forced to repossess the hotel. In a case such as this, the bank, which is now the owner, will likely seek a management company that specializes in distressed properties to manage the hotel until it is put up for sale and purchased by a new owner.

The hospitality industry, because it is cyclical, sometimes experiences falling occupancy rates and ADRs. Sometimes these cycles result in properties that fall into receivership and lenders who face the consequence of becoming involuntary owners. In cases such as these, effectively managing a hotel may simply mean optimizing the property's value while offering it for sale. Management companies that specialize in helping lenders maintain repossessed properties until they can be resold will:

- Secure, and if it has closed, reopen the hotel
- Implement sales and marketing plans to maximize the hotel's short- and long-term profitability

- Generate reliable financial statements
- Establish suitable staffing to maximize customer and employee satisfaction
- Show the hotel to prospective buyers
- Report regularly to the owners about the hotel's condition

Clearly, in the situation above, a management company provides a vital service to the bank. While an individual G.M. might be able to provide the same services (and usually at a lower initial cost), many hotel investors and owners prefer to hire management companies.

While the actual number of hotels managed by any single management company varies from year to year, the ten largest management companies based on annual revenue and the number of properties they manage at the time of this writing are included as Figure 12.3.

Origin and Purpose

The financial success of any lodging facility is dependent, in large measure, on the quality and skill of its on-site management. In the time period before the mid-1950s, the owners of a hotel hired the best G.M. they could find to operate the hotel(s) they owned. If they needed a manager with a specific level of skill or experience, they would try to find one. Even talented G.M.s, however, may not have had experience in specific tasks that owners needed to be undertaken. When that was the case, the result was often less than satisfactory for both the owner and the hotel's G.M.

In the 1950s and later, as more hotels became franchised and as hotel owner groups purchased ever larger numbers of hotels, these owner's inabil-

FIGURE 12.3   Ten Largest Management Companies

Company	Properties	Gross Annual Revenues[*]
1. Interstate Hotels and Resorts (with 2002 MeriStar merger)	357	2,800.0
2. Destination Hotels & Resorts	29	545.0
3. Tishman Hotel Corp.	17	521.8
4. Prime Hospitality Corp.	198	485.0
5. Lodgian	106	448.0
6. John Q. Hammonds	56	436.7
7. Kimpton Hotels & Restaurant Group	34	400.0
8. Outrigger Enterprises	39	400.0
9. Ocean Hospitalities	93	339.0
10. Sunstone Hotel Investors	52	293.0

[*] In millions of dollars.

ity to actively recruit, train, and supervise the many G.M.s they required to manage their properties resulted in the growth of companies that were formed simply to manage hotels under ordinary as well as out-of-the ordinary circumstances. Today, with the advent of large (and small) management companies, owners often find that, because a hotel management company employs many managers, one or more of those managers has the exact experience that the owner is looking for. In many cases, owners face special circumstances in the operation of the hotels they own. Some of these special situations include:

- Reflagging a hotel from a lower quality brand to a higher one
- Reflagging a hotel from a higher quality brand to a lower one
- Managing/directing a major (complete) renovation of a hotel
- Operating a hotel in a severely **depressed market**
- Bankruptcy/repossession of the hotel
- Managing a hotel that is slated for permanent closing
- Managing a hotel as a result of the unexpected resignation of the hotel's G.M.
- Managing a hotel for an extended period of time for owners who elect not to become directly involved in the day-to-day operation of the property

HOTEL TERMINOLOGY AT WORK

Depressed Market: The term used to describe a hotel market area where occupancy rates and/or ADRs are far below their historic levels. Used, for example, in, "The permanent closing of the military base in that town resulted in depressed market conditions in the entire county."

■

As a G.M., it is important for you to fully understand the relationship that exists when a hotel owner signs a management contract with a hotel management company. One way to understand the relationship better is to contrast the restaurant business with the hotel business. In the restaurant business, the owner of a restaurant who elects not to operate it, but wishes to continue ownership, will often lease the space to another restaurateur. In that situation, the person(s) owning the new business entity that leases the restaurant pays the restaurant's owner an agreed-upon amount and assumes responsibility for all the expenses associated with operating the business. If the restaurant makes money, the benefit goes to the person(s) who leased the space. If the restaurant loses money, the same person(s) are responsible for the loss.

Unlike the restaurant business, in most cases hotel owners find they cannot lease their properties to management companies. Rather it is the management company that receives a predetermined monthly fee from the hotel's owners in exchange for operating the property, and it is the owners who assume a passive position regarding operating decisions, while at the same time assuming responsibility for all working capital, operating expenses, and debt service. The fees charged by management companies to operate a hotel vary, but commonly range between 1 and 5 percent of the hotel's monthly revenue. Thus, regardless of the hotel's operating performance, the management company is paid the fee for its services and the hotel's owners receive the profits (if any) after all expenses are paid.

In some cases, hotel owners do negotiate contracts that tie, at least to some degree, management company compensation to the hotel's actual operating performance. In some cases, this is acceptable, especially with hotels that are proven profitable. In other cases, however, it can take months or even years to turn an unprofitable hotel into a profitable one. Often, it is the owners of unprofitable or distressed market hotels that seek the assistance of management companies. Understandably, however, few hotel management companies are willing to enter into risky management contracts that may result in them financially subsidizing investors who own a hotel that either has been poorly managed in the past or that is not likely to be a profitable hotel in its current condition.

Hotel Management Company Structures

Hotel management companies can be examined from a variety of different viewpoints. One way to view management companies is to consider whether they are **first tier** or **second tier.** The term "tier" refers simply to whose name is on the hotel the management company is operating. Tiering does not refer to the quality of the management operating, or G.M.s working for, the management company.

HOTEL TERMINOLOGY AT WORK

First Tier: Management companies that operate hotels for owners using the management company's trade name as the hotel brand. Hyatt, Hilton, and Sheraton are examples.

Second Tier: Management companies that operate hotels for owners who have entered into an agreement to use one of a franchisor's flags as the hotel brand. American General Hospitality, Summit Hotel Management, and Winegardner and Hammons, Inc. are examples.

■

Another way to examine management companies is by the number of hotels they operate. Because a hotel management company that operates one resort hotel with 750 rooms is likely to employ more managers and have responsibility for higher revenue than another hotel management company that operates three limited-service hotels, each of which consists of 100 rooms, historically hotel management companies have been ranked (in size) by the number of "rooms" they manage, rather than the number of hotels they manage. The hospitality trade press publishes rankings of the largest hotel management companies periodically.

While the size of a hotel management company may indeed say something about the successfulness of the company, it is often more useful to segment hotel management companies by the manner in which they participate, or do not participate, in the actual risk and ownership of the hotels they manage. As a result, these companies can be examined based upon their participation in one (or more than one) of the following arrangements.

- *The management company is neither a partner in nor an owner of the hotels they manage.* In this situation, the hotel's owners hire the management company. This is common, for example, when lenders involuntarily take possession of a hotel. In other cases, the management company may, for its own philosophical reasons, elect to concentrate only on managing properties and will not participate in hotel investing (ownership).

- *The management company is a partner (with others) in the ownership of the hotels they manage.* A common arrangement within the hotel community is that of a management company, partnering with an investor(s) to jointly own and manage hotels. Frequently, in this situation, the management company either buys or is given a portion of hotel ownership (usually 1%–20%), and then assumes the management of the hotel. Those hotel owners who prefer this arrangement feel that the partial ownership enjoyed by the management company will result in better performance by them. On the other hand, if the hotel experiences losses, the management company may share these losses, and this fact can also help serve as a motivator for the management company!

- *The management company only manages hotels it owns.* Some management companies are formed simply to manage the hotels they themselves own. These companies want to participate in the hotel industry as both investors and managers. Clearly an advantage of this situation is that the management company will benefit from its own success if the hotels it manages are profitable. If the company is not successful, however, it will be responsible for any operating loses incurred by its hotels.

- *The management company owns, by itself, some of the hotels it manages, and owns a part, or none at all, of others it manages.* Some management companies will vary their ownership participation depending on the hotel involved. Thus, a given management company may:

- Own all of a specific hotel as well as manage it
- Manage and be an owning partner in another hotel
- Manage, but not own any part of, yet another hotel property

Each of the above structure types has advantages and disadvantages both to the management company and to those with whom it partners. If a management company employs you as a G.M., it is important for you to know your company's ownership participation level in the specific hotel you are managing so that you can better understand the company's operating philosophy, as well as advise your staff about the ownership of the hotel.

THE INTERNET AT WORK

Management companies concentrate on a variety of specialty areas. Swan Inc. is one of the most technologically advanced. To view its site and services, go to:

www.swanhost.com.

The Management Operating Agreement

There are as many different contracts between those who own hotels and the management companies they employ to manage them, as there are hotels under management contract. Every hotel owner will, depending on the management company selected, have a unique management contract, or operating agreement, for each hotel owned. In some cases, these contracts may include preopening services that are provided even before the hotel is officially open. Preopening activities may include hiring and training staff, purchasing inventories, and other operational activities that must be done before the first guest can be housed. Because you now understand the business relationship that can exist between an owner of a hotel and a management company, it is important that you, as a G.M., know about the basic elements found in a management company's operating agreement.

Major Elements

In his 1980 book, *Administration of Hotel and Restaurant Management Contracts,* James Eyster detailed many of the components typically included in a management agreement. Considered a classic work in the field of hotel management contracts, it is an excellent addition to the serious G.M.'s personal library.

While times have changed, and certainly each specific management contract is different, many of the negotiable issues identified in Eyster's book

THE INTERNET AT WORK

To order a copy of James Eyster's book *Administration of Hotel and Restaurant Management Contracts,* published by Cornell University Press, go to:

www.amazon.com.

In the "Search" field, enter "Books" and then enter the author's name or the book's title.

must still be addressed by owners and prospective management companies when they are discussing a potential management agreement. Today, major elements of management agreements include:

- The length of the agreement
- Procedures for early termination by either party
- Procedures for extending the contract
- Contract terms in the event of the hotel's sale
- Base fees to be charged
- Incentives fees earned or penalties assessed related to operating performance
- Management company investment required or ownership attained
- Exclusivity (Is the management contract company allowed to operate competing hotels?)
- Reporting relationships and requirements (how much detail is required and how frequently will these reports be produced)
- Insurance requirements of the management company (who must carry insurance and how much)
- Status of employees (Are the hotel's employees employed by the hotel owner or the management company?)
- The control, if any, that the owner has in the selection or removal of the G.M. and other managers employed by the management company and working at the owner's hotel

Advantages to the Hotel Owner

A variety of benefits can accrue to hotel owners who select a qualified management company to operate their hotels. Among these are:

- *Improved management quality.* In some cases, a management company is able to offer talented G.M.s a better employment situation than that afforded by an individual hotel owner. A G.M.'s opportunities for advancement, increased training prospects, and employment security are frequently enhanced by working for a management company. As a result, owners benefit from the efforts of G.M.s who are more highly skilled. In addition, a management company may have specialists on staff that can assist the property G.M. in areas such as hospitality law, accounting, and food and beverage management. In many cases, the hotel's owners could not supply these additional resources.

• *Targeted expertise can be obtained.* Some hotels have special needs. Reflagging, renovation, and repositioning skills are not equally possessed by all G.M.s. A management company may well have managers on its staff that are experts in these areas, and this expertise can be used to the hotel owners' advantage.

• *Documented managerial effectiveness is available.* Banks, mortgage companies, and others who are asked supply investment capital to owners want to know that the hotel the owners are purchasing or for which loans are sought will, in fact, be operated with professional hotel managers. The selection of an experienced management company with documented evidence of past success in running hotels similar to the one for which investment is requested adds credibility to loan applications submitted by hotel owners.

• *Payment for services can be tied to performance.* While most management companies charge a revenue-based fee to operate a hotel, owners can negotiate additional payment incentives that help assure the very best management company performance possible. In this way, all of the resources of the company can be utilized in ways that benefit both the company and the hotel. Good management companies welcome such arrangements because they allow for above average fees to be earned in exchange for above average management performance.

• *Partnership opportunities are enhanced.* Many hotel owners are involved in multiple properties. When that is the case, an established management company and an ownership entity can work together in a variety of hotels. The management company will become knowledgeable about the owner(s) and the goals the owner has for its hotels. The owner will become familiar with the abilities as well as the limitations of the management company. A long-term partnership can, in cases such as these, be synergistic.

Disadvantages to the Hotel Owner

Despite many advantages, hotel owners face some disadvantages inherent in the selection of a management company. These include:

• *The owner cannot control selection of the on-site G.M. and other high-level managers.* Throughout this book we have tried to demonstrate the importance of the G.M. to the success of a hotel property. When using a management company, the hotel's owner (who may be allowed some input) will not typically choose the hotel's G.M. As a result, the quality of G.M. employed may be related more to the choice of G.M.s available (currently employed by) the management company than to the quality needed by the hotel. Experienced owners know the importance of quality on-site management and should insist upon the best G.M. (as well as other managers) that the management company can provide.

• *Talented managers leave frequently.* Assume you were the owner of a hotel management company. You have contracts to operate large hotels (that pay you large fees) and smaller hotels (where the fees you earn are less). One of your G.M.s shows considerable talent operating a smaller hotel. The owner of the property is very happy with her. An opening for a G.M. arises at one of your larger hotels. Do you move the G.M.? In many cases, the answer is probably "yes." In those cases, hotel owners may experience frequent turnover of G.M.s, especially if the hotel owned is smaller, is in a less popular geographic location, or for some other reason is not viewed as desirable by G.M.s within the management company that has the contract for operating it.

• *The interests of hotel owners and the management companies they employ sometimes conflict.* On the surface, it would seem that the interests of a hotel owner and the management company selected to operate the hotel would always coincide. Both are interested in operating a profitable hotel. In fact, disputes arise because hotel owners typically seek to minimize the fees they pay to management companies (because reduced fees yield greater profits), while management companies seek to maximize their fees. As a result, hotel owners who hire management companies often have serious disagreements with those companies over whether the hotels are indeed operated in the best interest of the owners. Examples of such disagreements are evident in news reports such as that in Figure 12.4, a story reported on www.Lodgingnews.com, the Web site of the American Hotel and Lodging Association.

• *The costs of management company errors are borne by the owner.* Unlike a lease arrangement, in a management contract it is the owner, not the management company, that is responsible for all costs associated with operating the hotel. As a result, the unnecessary costs incurred as a result of any errors in marketing or operating the hotel are borne not by the management company making the errors, but rather by the hotel's owner.

• *Transfer of ownership may be complicated.* The term (length) of a management contract, especially if the hotel is large, can be several years. As a result, if the owners decide to put the hotel up for sale dur-

FIGURE 12.4   Example of Hotel Owners and Management Company Disagreements

---

April 18, 2002

Marriott Charged

Marriott International is facing a lawsuit from **CTF Hotel Holdings,** a unit of Hong Kong–based **New World Development Co. Ltd.,** over alleged violations of laws dealing with racketeering, commercial bribery, and price fixing, according to reports from Reuters, the *Wall Street Journal,* and *Travel Management Daily.*

Unnamed industry experts told Reuters that the suit, which also names Marriott's **Renaissance Hotel Operating Co.** unit and **Avendra LLC,** a procurement company Marriott cofounded, is typical of the often-fractious relationship between hotel management companies and the property owners who pay them to run their hotels. Neither Marriott nor the plaintiff would comment on the suit, though *TMD* reports that it stems from the manner in which Marriott accounts for spending at hotels it manages on behalf of **CTF,** which owns an unidentified number of hotels in the United States.

"We're reviewing it, and we'll respond as soon as we move through it," says Marriott spokesperson Tom Marder.

Meanwhile, the CTF action mirrors that of a case against **Hilton Hotels Corporation** that is currently in arbitration. According to Bill Brewer, the attorney representing the Hilton Palacio del Rio hotel in San Antonio, Texas, the hotel's owners are seeking $100 million in damages for "overcharging [by Hilton] in virtually all of the services they provide" to the property.

---

ing the life of the contract, those potential buyers who either operate their own hotels, or use a different management company, may not be interested in buying. If the contract is written in such a way as to have a **buyout** of the contract, the cost of the buyout may be so high that the owner can only sell to those potential buyers willing to pay the very highest price for the property, which limits the number of potential buyers.

HOTEL TERMINOLOGY AT WORK

Buyout: An arrangement in which both parties to a contract agree to end the contract early as a result of one party paying the other an agreed-upon financial compensation.
■

Issues Affecting the General Manager

As a professional G.M., you are likely to find yourself, at one time or another during your career, managing a hotel in one of the following situations related to franchisors and management companies:

MANAGERS AT WORK

"I wanted you to know up-front, J.D.," said William Zollars to J.D. Ojisima, the manager of a 350-room full-service hotel.

J.D. was meeting for breakfast at William's request, and the purpose of the meeting had become clear almost immediately.

As the regional vice president for sales, it was William's job to secure new management contracts for Richerland Hospitality, one of the largest management contract companies in the United States.

"Thanks for letting me know Bill," said J.D., "but I had already heard from our hotel owners that you were going to present a proposal." In fact, the owners of the hotel had let J.D. know that Richerland had approached them with the idea of assuming the management of the hotel. Because the hotel J.D. operated had high visibility in the city, and because it was very profitable, it was not unusual that a management company would attempt to secure a management contract for it. It happened almost every year.

"Don't be concerned, J.D.," continued William. "Our proposal will recommend that we keep most of your management team in place, including you . . . of course."

What factors would cause hotel owners to think about selecting a management company to operate their hotel rather than hiring J.D. directly? What types of owners' groups do you believe are best served hiring management companies? Do you believe J.D. should inform the others on his management team that a proposal for a management contract is being submitted to the hotel's ownership? Why or why not?

- The hotel is operating as a franchise.
- The hotel is operating under a management contract.
- The hotel is a franchise operating under a management contract.

When franchise agreements and/or management contracts exist, they will affect your role as a G.M., as well as how you perform your job. In this section we examine how working in a branded property affects the G.M., as well as how working for a management company can impact the G.M.'s daily efforts.

Managing the Franchise Relationship

Most hotels are affiliated with a franchise. This is especially true of hotels with more than seventy-five rooms. As a result, it is likely that you will manage a hotel where the owners and a brand's managers have signed a franchise agreement. As the G.M., this agreement will affect your relationship with:

- *The hotel's owners.* It is a simple fact that hotel owners often find themselves in conflict with, or at the very least in disagreement with, brand managers about how to best operate the brand itself, as well as how to operate the individual hotels making up the brand. Unfortunately, when these disagreements occur, it can put the hotel's G.M. in the middle of the conflict.

Assume, for example, that the brand managers for your hotel have, as a brand standard, established breakfast hours for the hotel's complimentary continental breakfast to be from 6:00 A.M. to 9:00 A.M. The hotel's owners, however, instruct you to begin the breakfast at 7:00 A.M., rather than 6:00 A.M. on the weekends, to reduce labor costs. If you follow the directive of the brand managers, you violate your owner's wishes, however, if you follow the instructions of your hotel's owner, you will be in violation of a brand standard.

When owners instruct G.M.s to violate or ignore brand standards, the resulting influence on the hotel's relationship with the brand can be negative. Alternatively, when brand managers seek the G.M.'s compliance with acts that may be in the best interest of the brand managers, but not the hotel's owners, difficulties may also arise. Issues regarding loyalty to owner/employers and ethical standards for functioning as a professional G.M. are always present, but these take on extra complexity when a hotel is operated as part of a franchised chain.

• *The hotel's franchise service director (FSD).* Each franchise company assigns an individual to monitor the franchisee's compliance with the franchise agreement. The title of the individual who performs this task is the **FSD (franchise service director).**

HOTEL TERMINOLOGY AT WORK

FSD (Franchise Services Director): The representative of a franchise hotel brand who interacts directly with the franchised hotel's G.M.s.

■

While the title of this individual may vary somewhat, the position is always responsible for the day-to-day relationship between the franchisor and the franchisee. In some cases, the FSD may perform the quality assurance inspections required by the franchisor. Other routine tasks include assisting the hotel's sales effort, monitoring and advising about the hotel's use of the franchise-provided reservation system and advising the franchisee on the availability and use of franchisor resources.

Legitimate differences of opinion and conflicts can arise between a hotel G.M. and the franchisor's representative. The personal relationship, however, that ultimately develops between the FSD and the G.M. is an important one. When the relationship is good, the FSD is viewed as a valuable resource. When it is not good, conflicts between the FSD and yourself could escalate to the point that they negatively impact your ability to effectively operate the hotel.

- *The brand.* Even when a hotel's owners do not initiate brand-related conflict with a G.M. and the G.M.'s relationship with the FSD is good, personal conflict may still arise between a G.M. and the brand's managers. Assume, for example, that those brand managers responsible for selling franchises to owners were successful in convincing those who own your hotel to reflag the property to their brand. After one year of operation, the owners complain to the franchise company that the number of reservations received through the franchisor's national reservation center is not consistent with the amounts promised by the sales representatives. In fact, complain the owners, the volume of reservations received is only one-half of that promised. In cases such as these, it is not at all unusual, and in fact is most likely, that the brand managers will claim that it is the G.M., the work of the EOC (Executive Operating Committee), and the operation of the hotel itself that is the cause of the shortfall. Not surprisingly, as the hotel's G.M., you are highly unlikely to agree with this assessment. The potential for resulting conflict is clear.

  While the example above is simply one instance of possible brand conflict, there are certainly many others. The important factor to remember in cases such as these is that the hotel industry is relatively small and G.M.s (as well as brand managers) can quickly develop reputations that will follow them throughout their careers. As a professional G.M., it is always in your best interest to approach any potential conflict situation with brand managers in a way that is credible, principled, and straightforward.

- *Your staff.* Your staff will also be influenced by the requirements of your franchisor. Examples of this are numerous, from standards related to the appearance and content of room attendant's carts, to emergency equipment that should be available in hotel shuttle vans, to the hours room service must be available, brand standards will affect every department in the hotel. In some cases, these standards may conflict with your instructions to your staff. When they do, you must manage that conflict.

  Assume, for example, that a guest checks in to your hotel. The guest is tired and irritable. The hotel is busy because a tour bus, with many check-ins arrived just before this guest and as a result it takes nearly ten minutes to get the guest checked in. The guest complains to the FOM about the time it has taken to get registered. The FOM, realizing that the front desk staff was working at their top speed, apologizes, explains that other guests had arrived first, but takes no other action. When the guest demands that his room be "comped," the FOM declines to do so. The guest, upon arriving in his room, calls the brand's national guest service telephone number, to complain that check-in took nearly "thirty minutes," and demands, according to the brand's "satisfaction guaranteed" program, that his room be "comped." Depending on the brand managers decision about this guest, as a G.M. you may well have to explain to your FOM that his or her decision must be overturned in order to comply with the brand standard of "satisfaction guaranteed."

This example is simply one of many in which the policies used and decisions made by staff may be influenced by the requirements of a brand. As the hotel's G.M., it is part of your job to blend the operating policies that you and the hotel's owner prefer with those dictated by the brand and explain your actions to your staff if conflict between the two approaches should arise.

- *Your guests.* Kemmons Wilson's vision for Holiday Inn was a chain of hotels where arriving guests knew exactly what to expect from their stay. This same vision exists in the minds of most brand managers today. In fact, however, hotels as well as those who operate them can and will vary. As a result, guest experiences can vary also. When the guest's expectations are exceeded, this variation can be good. Unfortunately, that same guest may expect the same experience at the next hotel affiliated with the brand, and they may, in fact, be disappointed.

  For example, assume a hotel brand allows hotel owners to charge guests for local telephone calls (some brands do not allow this). As the G.M. in a competitive market, you determine that many of your guests will expect free local calls because that is what your competitors offer. If you implement the free local call policy, your guests will be pleased, but these same guests may be unhappy if they later stay at one of the other hotels in your chain that does *not* offer complimentary local calls. These guests may, in fact, be disappointed because they believed, and justifiably so, that all hotels affiliated with your brand offered free local calls. As a G.M., when it is your own hotel that falls short of a feature offered by another hotel within your brand, you may be challenged to satisfy a guest whose expectations exceed that which your hotel is able to meet.

Managing for a Management Company

As we have seen, sometimes a management company owns the hotel it operates. When that is the case, the property G.M. is, of course, working directly for the hotel's owners. In many cases, however, the management company does not own the hotel it operates. When that is so, the G.M., because he or she does not work directly for the hotel's owners, may be faced with special challenges. These can include:

- *Career management challenges.* When you work for a management company, advancement in your organization comes through satisfying the desires of the company, not necessarily the owners of the hotel you are managing. An example that involves positive conflict points to one of the challenges you may face in your own career working for a management company. Assume you are a talented G.M. operating a 350-room hotel. Your management company has just gained a ten-year contract to operate a 550-room hotel in your hometown. The hotel will require a G.M., and it is a position you would very much like to assume, yet the owners of your current hotel are adamant that they want you to remain and have even threatened the management company that they will not renew the management contract when it expires if you are allowed to transfer. This problem (and it is a good one!) as well as others like it can occur when long-term career advancement with your management company conflicts with the desires of the hotel owners for whom you are currently managing. In a situation such as this, your company will evaluate your long-term employment worth (just as you also must evaluate it), as well as the course of action that is best for the long-term growth of the management company. Clearly, however, it will not be possible to, at the same time, satisfy your desire for promotion with your hotel owner's desire for G.M. stability.

- *Dual loyalty issues (owners vs. management company).* As the G.M. of a hotel operated by a management company, there may be times that the business interests of the owners of the hotel you are managing conflict with the business interests of your employer. It is important to remember that, in these cases, you will most often be rewarded for loyalty to your management company. For example, assume that the contract for managing the hotel at which you are the G.M. is up for renewal. Most unbiased observers would maintain that it is in the best interest of the hotel's owners to negotiate as short a contract length as possible and one that holds the management company responsible for financial results that fall short of expectations. These same observers would likely state that it is in the best interest of the management company to negotiate as long a contract as possible and one that holds the hotel's owners, not the management company, financially responsible in the event that hotel operating performance does not meet anticipated levels. As a G.M. working for a management company, you may not, at all times, be in a position to advise the hotel owner of their best course of action because, in fact, that course of action works against the best interests of your own company.

- *Strained EOC relationships.* An important part of a G.M.'s job is to assure each member of the EOC that he or she is a valuable partner in the hotel's ultimate success. Certainly this partnership is easier to maintain when the management company is not threatened by the loss of the contract to manage the hotel. When the management company is in danger of loosing the contract, the partnership the G.M. wishes to develop may be strained by the fact that some members of the EOC enjoy greater job security than others.

  Consider, for example, the hotel in which an owner is considering changing a tier-two management company. If the change takes place, it is likely that the G.M., the director of sales and marketing, the controller and, if it is a full-service hotel, the food and beverage director will be replaced. Other department heads, such as the FOM, the executive housekeeper, and the maintenance chief are much less likely to be replaced. This is true because a management company winning a new contract does not, as some believe, replace every employee at the hotel. In fact, to do so would disrupt the hotel tremendously. Thus, depending on the size of hotel and philosophy of the management company assuming the contract, the G.M. (almost always), as well as some number of managers (but generally not all), will be replaced.

  The result is that, despite the fact that the same management company currently operating the hotel employs all EOC members; some may feel more loyalty to the hotel and its owners than to the company. As a G.M., it is not hard to understand these managers' perspective, yet as the leader of the hotel operating team, you must do your best to prevent this dichotomy of interests from influencing the experience that guests in your hotel receive.

- *Affected and concerned employees.* G.M.s working for management companies know to whom they directly report and generally will be familiar with the employment policies and procedure of the management company employing them. Hourly employees may not be as familiar with the management company, and this can be a real concern when an owner chooses to employ a new management company. When, for example, an owner decides to allow one management contract to expire and elects to choose a different management company, the hotel's employees will likely, under the terms of the contract, be terminated by the first management company and "hired" by the new company, even though they may have been at the hotel for many years. A variety of employment-related issues may arise. For example, assume that Maria, a housekeeper, has been at the hotel for fifteen years as an employee of Management Company #1. That company loses its management contract to Company #2. As a result, Maria's employment with the first company is terminated. As a fifteen-year employee of Management Company #1, Maria was entitled to three weeks' paid vacation per year. Management Company #2, however, views Maria as a new employee, and under its policies Maria will qualify for only two weeks' vacation per year. In fact, she must be employed by the new company for a minimum of six months before she is allowed any vacation at all! The impact on Maria is obvious, as are the resulting challenges a G.M. faces when a new management company must implement its benefit, pay, seniority, and related employment policies in place of those of a previous management company.

- ***Conflicts with brand managers.*** Some management companies have excellent relations with the brands they manage for owners but others do not. As a G.M., you may find that some of the wishes or even the directives of the brand managers are in conflict with those of your management company. For example, a franchise company may, in an effort to promote business, send to the hotel large, exterior banners that advertise a special rate or hotel feature. Obviously, the brand would like these signs displayed on the property. The management company's sales philosophy, however, may not include hanging exterior banners because it believes such banners cheapen the image of the hotel. As a result, the banners are not displayed. It is likely that the FSD will complain to the G.M. who was, quite rightly, simply following the directive of the management company to whom he or she reports.

   Conflicts with brand managers can range from the very minor to the very serious. As the owner's representative to the brand, virtually any conflict that could arise between a franchisor and an owner could arise between a franchisor and the owner's management company. As a professional G.M., you must be aware of these potential conflicts and be ready to act in the long-term best interests of your employer.

HOTEL TERMINOLOGY AT WORK GLOSSARY

The following terms were defined within this chapter. If you are not familiar with each of them, please review the segment of the chapter that contains the term.

Flag	AAHOA	Brand standard
Franchise	Window	PIP (product improvement
Franchise agreement	Early out	plan)
Federal Trade Commission (FTC)	Occupancy tax	Impact study
	Conversion	Management contract
FOC (franchise offering circular)	Systemwide	Depressed market
	Area of Protection (AOP)	First tier

Second tier   FSD (franchise services
Buyout   director)

ISSUES AT WORK

1. Some G.M.s believe that they can best further their careers by choosing to manage only hotels affiliated with a specific brand (i.e., Hyatt, Westin, Holiday Inn, etc.). Other G.M.s believe they are most marketable if they have experience managing several different hotel brands. Assume you were a hotel owner. Which type of G.M. do you think would be most valuable to your hotel? Would the brand with which you are affiliated affect your decision? Would your opinion be altered if you were considering changing the flag at your property? Why or why not?

2. Some hotel managers believe that the "brand" name on a hotel is critical to its success whereas others feel profitable hotels can still be operated as independents or that the brand name on the hotel is actually less important than it once was. What do you believe are the major obstacles faced by independent hotels? How can an effective management team overcome these? Do you believe the trend toward an increased number of hotels affiliated with brands will continue? What is the likely impact on independent hotels?

3. Product segmentation in the hotel industry is typically good for franchise companies because it allows them to maximize the number of hotels they have in a given geographic area and thus maximize the fees they receive. Critics contend, however, that excessive product segmentation unfairly pits hotel owners against other owners operating virtually identical hotel products (albeit with different brand names) within the same franchise group and in the same geographic area. As fewer and fewer franchise companies own increasingly larger numbers of brands, this debate will likely intensify. As a G.M. concerned about guest satisfaction, how, if at all, does this issue affect guests? Consider both positive and negative impacts. Do the positives outweigh the negatives? Why or why not?

4. Traditionally, management companies have been paid a monthly fee (usually a percentage of gross rooms revenue) to manage a hotel. More recently, management fees are tied to actual hotel performance as measured by RevPar indexes generated by the STAR Report (see chapter 10). Critics of this newer approach contend that, while the STAR Report measures the sales ability of the management team, it does not measure the team's ability to control costs and maximize profitability. If you formed a management company, would you propose to manage hotels for a percentage of the gross rooms revenue, for a fee determined by your

STAR Report results or for a fee determined by the hotel's profitability? Why? Which do you believe would appeal most to hotel owners? As a professional G.M., under which system would you most like to manage?

5. G.M.s sometimes face difficult decisions when they are employed by a management company and operate a branded hotel. In such a situation, the G.M.'s loyalty can be tested because of the conflicting interests of staff, guests, the brand, the management company, and the hotel's owners. Consider a situation in which the financial interests of two (or more) of these groups directly conflict (e.g., management companies seek to maximize management fees while hotel owners seek to minimize them). What would be in the best interests of each party in your example? To whom do you believe G.M.s owe their greatest loyalty? Why?

13
Purchasing a Hotel

This Chapter at Work

Just as many restaurant managers desire to someday own their own restaurant, many G.M.s aspire to personal hotel ownership. While it is true that large corporations own many hotels (especially very large hotels), it is also true that many hotels are owned and managed by an individual or family. In fact, some G.M.s manage their own hotels so well that they become the owners of multiple properties. This chapter identifies the process of buying and opening a smaller to midsize hotel. The process begins with the decision about whether to buy an existing property or to develop a new one. The second step in the process and one that is very important is that of establishing a purchase price that is reasonable. This chapter identifies several methods that are used to establish a hotel's fair market value.

Very few individuals purchase a hotel without obtaining a mortgage or seeking investors. Securing financing, however, is always a challenge for a hotel project, and the chapter identifies some sources of loans you may investigate as you seek funding for your hotel, as well as the information a lender will require you to provide. Typically, this will involve securing an appraisal on the hotel, preparing a detailed business plan, and projecting (forecasting) sales revenue to demonstrate that the hotel will be able to repay those who invest in it or who lend you the money you will need to buy it.

When a purchase price has been established and financing is secured, the real work of opening the hotel begins. This chapter (as well as this book) concludes with a detailed listing of the many activities G.M.s must undertake prior to opening their own (or any) new hotel. These are presented in time-line fashion, beginning six months prior to opening and concluding with the activities a G.M. must undertake after the hotel's "Grand Opening" has been held.

It is the authors' real hope that this chapter inspires many enterprising, talented hotel G.M.s to "go for it" when considering buying or developing their own hotel property. This is our hope because we believe individuals with a thorough understanding of the hotel business own the best managed hotels, and those who understand hotel management best, we believe, are the owners who have been lucky enough to be G.M.s.

Chapter 13 Outline

SELECTING A PROPERTY

If you are interested in buying a hotel, you can choose between buying an existing hotel and developing a new property. In either case, you are likely to be considering self-ownership for the same reasons any individual **entrepreneur** wants to own a business. These reasons may include financial rewards, a sense of accomplishment, freedom of operation, and long-term investment potential.

HOTEL TERMINOLOGY AT WORK

Entrepreneur: A person who assumes the risk of owning and operating a business in exchange for the financial rewards the business may produce.

■

It is important to understand that, when you own a hotel, you own two distinctly different assets. The first asset is the real estate involved. This includes the land, building(s), furnishings, and fixtures that make up the hotel. The second asset involved in owning a hotel is the operating business itself. For example, in a hotel that is currently operating, the value of the hotel consists of both its real estate value and the profits (if any) that are made by running the hotel. In a hotel that has yet to be built, the value of the real estate may be known and building costs can be estimated, but the value of the operating business must be projected. Because that is true, it is usually easier to establish the worth of a hotel that is operating than the worth of one that has yet to be built.

Buying an Existing Property

Hotels are bought and sold on a regular basis. Buyers and sellers are typically brought together through the use of a hotel **broker.**

Hotels are sold for a variety of reasons, including the retirement of the hotel's owner, the owner's desire for the cash that results from the sale, or to

---

HOTEL TERMINOLOGY AT WORK

Broker: An entity that, for a fee, lists (offers) hotels for sale on behalf of the hotels' owners and solicits buyers for the hotels it lists. Used, for example, in, "I know that hotel is listed with Joe Johnson, a broker with Mid-State Hotel Brokers."

■

THE INTERNET AT WORK

If you are interested in buying a hotel or selling a hotel you own, you are likely to use the services of one or more hotel brokers. These companies list hotels for sale and solicit bids for those hotels from interested buyers. To view the Web site of one such broker, go to:

www.hotel-broker.com.

---

allow the owner to reap the rewards of fully developing a hotel property and selling it for a profit.

An owner of an existing hotel who wishes to sell it typically will contact a hotel broker and enter into a contractual agreement that authorizes the broker to solicit offers to buy the property. As a G.M., you may be contacted by a broker to buy a hotel, or you may contact a broker yourself to determine if a hotel you are interested in purchasing has been listed for sale with the broker. If the hotel you are interested in buying has, in fact, been listed, the broker will send you information on the hotel, including the number of rooms it contains, a summary of its most recent financial performance, current STAR Reports (see chapter 10), the listed (asking) purchase price, and additional information that the broker believes a potential buyer would find useful.

After reviewing the broker-supplied information for an operating hotel and probably visiting the property, you would be in a position to make a most important determination. That determination is whether the hotel is operating at reasonable levels of performance, or if, for some known or unknown reason, it is not operating at a reasonable level of performance.

A hotel that is performing well will most likely have a sales price that reflects that performance. A hotel that is underperforming will generally be sold for less on a per room basis because there is no guarantee that, even with the proper investment and management, it will be able to perform better than it does currently. As a result, there is a significant difference between buying "performance" and buying "potential performance." As a buyer, you must understand this difference very clearly.

Buying Performance

Assume you own a very profitable hotel. Assume also that the hotel outperforms its STAR Report competitive set in both occupancy percentage and ADR and that it is flagged with a very popular and widely known brand. Further, assume that the hotel's location is excellent; its quality assurance scores are among the top 5 percent within its brand; its preventative maintenance program is strong and has been in place for many years; and its measured customer satisfaction levels were also among the highest in its brand. A hotel such as this is performing very well, and its sales price, should you decide to sell it, would likely reflect the excellent performance of the property. A buyer of this hotel would receive not only the real estate involved, but also an exceptionally solid operating business.

As a potential buyer of this hotel, you would likely pay more, per room, for a hotel of this type than for one that was not performing as well. Indeed, it would be worthwhile, in many cases to pay more because, with continued proper management, the hotel is likely to continue to perform at its high level. In addition, those who would lend money to buy such a hotel could be confident that they are assisting in the purchase of a strong business that is most likely able to repay the money loaned to buy the business.

Buying a strong performing hotel is often a safer investment than buying one that is not performing as well. Of course, with that safety comes the probable case that the hotel will be, on a per room basis, a higher priced property to buy than if it were not performing as well.

Buying Potential Performance

When a hotel buyer considers purchasing a hotel that is not operating near its peak potential, that buyer is said to be considering the purchase for it's **upside potential.**

HOTEL TERMINOLOGY AT WORK

Upside Potential: The possibility that, with the proper investment and management, a hotel will yield significant increases in real estate value and/or operational profitability. Used, for example, in, "The broker says the hotel is priced right because, with its location and proper management, it has tremendous upside potential."

■

Nearly all sellers of an underperforming hotel will maintain that their property has strong upside potential. As a potential buyer, however, you must be assured that this is true because, even though an underperforming hotel will sell for less on a per room basis than will one that is performing well, the risk involved in buying an underperforming hotel is, in most cases, greater than the risk of buying an established, more profitable property.

Hotels may be underachieving for a variety of reasons. Assume, for example, that a hotel's RevPar is not comparing favorably with its STAR Report competitive set. The reason may be that the hotel needs a renovation to effectively compete in its market. The hotel's current owners may not, for a variety of reasons, be able to fund the needed renovations. A new owner, with the proper renovation funds in place, may well be able to take advantage of the upside potential in such a property. Alternatively, assume that a hotel is not performing well because it is older, is in a poor location, and the city in which it is located has had many newer and more modern hotels built in recent years. In a situation such as this, it may be much harder for a buyer to develop upside potential. The price, however, of such a hotel will likely be lower to reflect the difficulty inherent in developing this hotel's upside potential.

Many hotel investors look exclusively for underperforming properties with strong upside potential, because if that potential truly exists and the cost of acquiring the hotel is low enough, the likelihood of making significant profits on the future operation or sale of the hotel also exists.

Buying a Property to Be Built

In some cases, the best hotel to purchase may be one that does not yet exist. Assume, for example, that you are a G.M. managing a hotel and that you are looking for an ownership opportunity. You learn that a large shopping complex is to be built on the north side of your city and you believe that the demand for hotel rooms in that area will be significant because no hotels are located nearby. In a case such as this, it may make the most sense for you to pursue the ownership and development of a new hotel constructed in that area.

Building a new property is a complex task and not one to be undertaken without the assistance of hotel professionals, including architects, designers, builders, franchise professionals, and attorneys. Often those who seek to build a hotel will encounter multiple hurdles, including building codes, zoning requirements, restrictions on height or signage allowed, and mandates on the number of parking spaces that must be built to support the hotel. The building process can be challenging. While each element in the process can be very complex, the steps required to build a new hotel are essentially the same for each property. These are:

- *Step 1: Secure the site.* Securing a site involves its purchase or lease, as well as the determination that local building codes will allow the construction of a hotel on the site.
- *Step 2: Select a franchisor.* In nearly every case, a new hotel will be affiliated with a franchise. Because each franchise company has differing requirements for their properties (e.g., number of rooms, room size,

amenities, furnishings, etc.), it makes sense to identify the franchise requirements you must meet prior to beginning construction of the hotel.

- *Step 3: Design the building.* Based upon the site, the requirements of the franchisor, and your own ideas, an architect will be selected to design the hotel building. An experienced G.M. can be of great assistance to an architect in this phase of the project because a properly designed hotel will be easier to manage, and more profitable, than one that is poorly designed.

- *Step 4: Coordinate the building process.* This is done by consistently meeting with the architect, franchise representatives, and builder to ensure that all building, design, and construction plans meet local building code requirements, the requirements of the franchisor, and the desires of the hotel's owner.

- *Step 5: Build the hotel.* Constant monitoring and coordination is required as the actual building process is undertaken.

- *Step 6: Furnish the hotel.* In most cases, the franchisor will dictate the quality and type of furnishings to be installed. In some cases, the franchisor may also suggest vendors who can supply these furnishings, but the hotel's owners will make the final decisions about furnishings suppliers.

- *Step 7: Perform preopening and* **grand opening** *activities.* Before a hotel can actually open, there are many activities that must be undertaken. Many of these are detailed later in this chapter. In all cases, it is important that a hotel, when it opens, is able to immediately provide the excellent service and positive guest experiences that its owners intend to offer.

HOTEL TERMINOLOGY AT WORK

Grand Opening: An event held at a hotel that marks the "official" opening of that hotel. It can be held several days or even weeks after the hotel actually opens and is intended to market the hotel to its client base and the local community.

■

SECURING HOTEL FINANCING

Hotels are expensive. The purchase price of a small (sixty-five-room), limited-service hotel that is newly built will average from a low of $30,000 **per key** to a high of $150,000 or more per key, plus the cost of land. As a result, the purchase of a hotel is generally a multimillion dollar real estate transaction.

—————————————————————— **MANAGERS AT WORK** ——————————————————————

"J.D., you're the only one I'm going to talk to about this project," said Ray Schwan. "I think it's a great opportunity for you . . . and for me."

J.D. listened carefully. Ray Schwan had been a friend since the time, three years ago, when Schwan had stayed for five months in the hotel J.D. managed. As a long-term stay guest, J.D. had many opportunities to see Mr. Schwan around the property, and they had chatted frequently about the hotel business and the new manufacturing plant Mr. Schwan had come to town to develop. Since that time they had seen each other often at Chamber of Commerce events as well as the charity fund-raisers they both fre-quently attended. J.D. considered Schwan a professional colleague and a good friend.

"My business is booming," said Schwan, "and the hotel adjacent to my plant could be a gold mine . . . for both of us! We have to buy it!" continued Mr. Schwan.

J.D. knew about the hotel Schwan was proposing that they buy. It was the Hardley Plaza hotel, located on the city's far west side. It was an older, full-ser-vice property, but one that enjoyed a great location, and it was near Schwan's new manufacturing plant. For the past two hours, Schwan had carefully laid out to J.D. how the property could be purchased and renovated.

"You'll need to pick a fran-chisor for us, J.D.," said Schwan, "and operationally, it's all you. We'll be 50–50 partners. I'll front the down payment for us, you manage the hotel. The way I see it, with good management, in three or four years we stand to make 2 to 3 million dollars by improving the operation then refinancing or selling. Split two ways, that's not too bad! Are you in?"

If you were advising J.D., would you suggest involvement in the proposed venture with Mr. Schwan? What factors would influence your decision? What risks are involved in the new pro-ject? What are the potential bene-fits of J.D.'s involvement?

HOTEL TERMINOLOGY AT WORK

Per Key: A term used to describe the cost of a hotel acquisition based on the number of rooms (keys) purchased. Its value comes in allowing comparison between hotels of unequal size (number of rooms). It is computed as:

Total Hotel Cost / Number of units (rooms) in the hotel = Cost Per Key.

Used, for example, in, "The hotel has 220 rooms, and is selling at a cost of $58,000 per key."

∎

With purchase prices of new and existing properties so high, most hotel transactions involve the use of borrowed money. The purchase of a hotel is complex, and one of the most difficult aspects is that of securing financing. Many lending institutions are wary of making hotel loans because of the complexity of the hotel business. If you are to succeed in obtaining a loan to buy a hotel, you must be prepared to demonstrate the true value of the prop-erty, as well as your ability to service (repay) the debt.

Although each purchase is different, it is important for the individual investor/owner to understand the basics of how a hotel's **market value** is established, the potential sources of funding that may be available, and the supporting documentation these funding sources are likely to require before lending money for a hotel purchase.

HOTEL TERMINOLOGY AT WORK

Market Value: The estimated worth of a hotel. Hotels may, of course, be purchased below, at, or above market value.

■

Establishing Property Market Values

Even for real estate experts, it has always been difficult to determine the true "value" of a hotel. For example, assume a hotel is in a good location and is in good physical condition, but is poorly managed and thus is not profitable. Should the selling price of such a hotel be based on its current profitability or the profitability that it might achieve with better management? If you were the seller of the hotel, you would certainly take the position that the hotel is more valuable than it first appears because, with proper management, its worth would increase. As a buyer, you would seek to purchase the hotel at the lowest possible price and thus would likely take the position that improved management may indeed improve the hotel, but no guarantee exists that it would do so.

Current profitability is often one important factor in establishing the value of a hotel; other factors include annual revenues achieved, physical condition, location, brand, and the quality and experience of the hotel's staff. Additional factors that are often considered in establishing a hotel's value include the hotel's STAR Report results, its competition, the number of new hotels to be built in the area, and the growth (or lack of growth) in the market within which the hotel is located.

Traditionally, hotel values have been established through the use of one or more of the following:

- *Replacement approach.* This approach assumes that a buyer would not be willing to pay more for a hotel than the amount required to build (replace) a similar hotel in a similar location. For example, if a buyer could build an equivalent hotel for $70,000 per key, that buyer would be unlikely to pay the owner of an existing hotel more than that amount. While this approach is useful for many new hotel construction projects, it is less useful, for example, when attempting to estimate the value of a hotel when no replacement hotel has recently been or could be built in the area.

- *Revenue stream approach.* This approach views a hotel primarily as a producer of revenue. Thus, a hotel's value is established as a multiple of its room's revenue. The more revenue that is produced, the more valuable the hotel. Under this system, hotels in good condition will generally sell for between 2 and 4 times their most recent annual room revenue. For example, a hotel with room revenue of $5 million per year might be valued at between $10 million (2 times revenue) and $20 million (4 times revenue), depending on other conditions affecting the hotel. Hotel brokers often use this approach when developing advertisements offering hotels for sale.

- *Sales comparison approach.* This evaluation system assumes that similar type hotels in a given area should sell for similar per key prices. For example, assume that five hotels are located adjacent to a large city's airport. Two of those hotels are of similar age, size, and quality level. If the first of these hotels sold on January 1 of a given year for $100,000 per key, that selling price would be used, during that year, to help establish the value of the second, similar hotel. Using the sale of comparable properties to help establish the value of a property offered for sale is common in the residential real estate market and is also popular in the commercial hotel real estate market. This system is, of course, less reliable to use in a market where no hotels have been recently sold, or where no hotels that are truly comparable to the one being offered for sale have recently been sold.

- *Income capitalization approach.* The income capitalization approach is often used to establish a value for income producing properties such as apartment complexes and hotels. Essentially, this system seeks to develop a mathematical relationship (capitalization rate) between a hotel's projected income, expenses, and its market value. While the computations used are complex and well beyond the scope of this text, the method essentially:
  - Estimates a hotel's potential gross revenue
  - Estimates the hotel's operating expenses
  - Estimates the hotel's net income
  - Performs a value analysis of the hotel based upon the real costs of acquiring the property

  This approach, while the most complex, is also the most widely used.

- *Return on investment approach.* In this approach, a hotel's value is based upon the owner's anticipated return on investment (ROI). For example, assume that a buyer has a choice of two similar hotels. In the case of the first hotel, the purchase would likely yield a ROI of 11 percent. The second hotel has a potential ROI of 15 percent. Using the ROI approach, the value of the second hotel would be higher than the first. In practicality, a potential owner would establish the desired rate of return first, and then use that rate to establish a hotel's market value.

While each of the above approaches to hotel valuation has its advocates and detractors, as a G.M. interested in borrowing money to purchase a hotel, it is most critical that you understand the importance of not paying more for a hotel than it is truly worth.

THE INTERNET AT WORK

Some companies specialize in helping potential sellers and buyers establish the fair market value of hotels. To view the Web site of one of the largest and most well known of these go to:

www.hvsinternational.com.

THE INTERNET AT WORK

Hotel G.M.s and others who are interested in learning more about hotel investment strategies will find solid information on the topic available.

Hotel Investments: Issues and Perspectives, second edition, is published by the Educational Institute of the American Hotel and Lodging Association. It is an excellent addition to the library of the serious potential hotel owner. To purchase the book, go to:

www.ei-ahla.org.

Select: "Products" in the Search bar.

Next, select: "Financial Management."

Finally, select "*Hotel Investments: Issues and Perspectives.*"

Applying for the Loan

In most cases, potential hotel owners will find that it is to their advantage to borrow money to help buy the hotels in which they are interested. While it may be possible for a hotel buyer to pay 100 percent of the purchase price at the time of **closing,** few hotel buyers elect to do so.

Instead, much like the case with personal home ownership, the buyer will elect to put a down payment on the property, and seek a **mortgage** for the balance of the purchase price because the use of borrowed money helps buyers **leverage** their own funds.

HOTEL TERMINOLOGY AT WORK

Closing: The legal process of transferring property ownership from a seller to a buyer. Used, for example, in, "The closing for our new hotel is set for May 22 at the Trans American Title Company offices on Main Street."

■

HOTEL TERMINOLOGY AT WORK

Mortgage: A legal document that specifies an amount of money a lender will lend for the purchase of a real estate asset (hotel), as well as the terms for the loan's repayment.

Leverage: The use of borrowed funds to increase purchasing power.

■

For example, assume you are considering buying two different hotels, each of which makes a 35 percent gross operating profit (GOP). One has a purchase price of $4 million with annual sales of $2 million. The other has a purchase price of $8 million with annual sales of $4 million. Assume also that you have raised and/or saved $4 million of your own funds. While it is possible for you to buy the first hotel and own it "free and clear" (no debt), it may be to your advantage to use your own funds as a down payment on the larger hotel because that hotel may produce, even after debt service, a better ROI for you than the first hotel. Effectively leveraging funds can be a complex process, and the advice of a professional **CPA** experienced in hotel real estate transactions is extremely helpful in determining how much borrowed money it is best to seek for each hotel purchase you are considering.

THE INTERNET AT WORK

To find a CPA in your own area who is experienced in real estate transactions, look for one on the home page of the American Institute of Certified Public Accountants at:

www.aicpa.org.

Of course, seeking a loan is not the same thing as actually getting a loan. Many borrowers seek loans because it is in their own best interests to do so. Those borrowers who actually receive loans get them because the lender feels that the loan is in the best interests of both the entity seeking the loan *and* the institution providing the funds. To demonstrate that your own proposed hotel purchase or project is worthy of a loan, you must be able to show, at the time you apply for the loan, your ability to comply with the loan repayment schedule that will be established by the lender.

Liability for Repayment

When an individual applies for and receives a loan, the lending institution will, of course, hold that same individual responsible for repayment of the loan. When it is a business that receives the loan, the same principle holds true, and the lender will look to the business that borrowed the money to repay the loan. If the loan is not repaid, the lender has **recourse.** Funds are lent to individuals or businesses are classified as either full recourse, limited recourse, or nonrecourse loans and the assets that are used to secure the loan vary for each type.

HOTEL TERMINOLOGY AT WORK

Recourse: The right to demand assets as payment for a loan. Loans can be full recourse, limited recourse, or nonrecourse.

■

A full recourse loan refers to the right of the lender to take any (and all) assets of the borrower if repayment is not made. A limited recourse loan only allows the lender to take assets specifically named in the loan agreement. A nonrecourse loan limits the lender's rights to the specific asset being financed. The nonrecourse loan is common, for example, in most home mortgages, as well as for many hotel loans.

A lender's rational for preferring to make full and limited recourse loans becomes more clear when you realize that lenders typically do not want to own or operate the hotel upon which they have **foreclosed.**

HOTEL TERMINOLOGY AT WORK

Foreclose: The process in which a lender terminates the borrower's interest in a property after a loan is defaulted.

■

In a foreclosure, the lender will typically sell the property in an effort to recover the defaulted loan amount. The process can be long and cumbersome with no guarantee to the lender that all funds loaned will actually be recovered. In addition, operating the hotel until the time of its sale can be difficult because lenders are in the lending business, not the hotel business. As a result, a lender will generally feel more comfortable lending to a hotel borrower if the hotel for which the funds are sought, as well as additional borrower assets, are pledged as security for the loan. Borrowers, understandably seeking to protect their personal and company assets from repossession if the hotel encounters financial difficulty and thus cannot repay funds loaned to it, prefer to seek and secure noncourse funding whenever possible.

Funding Sources

The funds required to purchase a hotel can come from a variety of sources. In most cases a traditional local bank will not be the source of a hotel loan because of the high-risk factor. In nearly all cases, however, if you seek funding to buy or develop a hotel property, you must be willing to face initial rejection of your loan application because all lenders are very cautious about making loans to hotels. To acquire a hotel loan, you must be committed, aggressive, and willing to compromise on key aspects of the loan. Figure 13.1 identifies the type of lender and the range of funding they typically supply for a hotel's purchase or development project.

HOTEL TERMINOLOGY AT WORK

SBA: Short for the United States Small Business Administration. Established in 1953, the SBA provides financial, technical, and management assistance to help Americans start, run, and expand their businesses. The SBA is the nation's largest single financial backer of small businesses.

■

Different lenders have different goals for the loans they make. Some lenders prefer low-risk loans on which they make less money whereas other lenders are willing to assume more risk in exchange for greater profit on the loans they make. Regardless of how conservative or aggressive the lender may

FIGURE 13.1 Funding Sources for Hotels

Hotel Type	Funding Source	Loan Amounts
Luxury Hotels	Life insurance companies Pension funds	$15,000,000 or more
First-Class Hotels	Life insurance companies Credit companies International banks National banks	$3,000,000–$30,000,000
Midmarket Hotels	Credit companies International banks National banks Regional banks Community banks	$1,000,000–$15,000,000
Economy/Budget Hotels	Regional banks Community banks **SBA** loan providers	($5,000,000 or less)

THE INTERNET AT WORK

The SBA is an excellent potential source of funds for those individuals seeking to buy properties with purchase prices in the $1,000,000–$5,000,000 range. To view their Web site and learn about the many services they offer to small business owners, go to:

www.sba.gov.

be, borrowers must be able to demonstrate the following to successfully secure a loan:

- *A strong market.* Lenders prefer to lend money to purchase or develop hotels in markets that are strong and that are likely to stay strong. As a result, hotels in the largest twenty-five to thirty urban markets tend to attract the greatest lender interest. In addition, hotels in smaller cities located close to proven demand generators such as airports, colleges, universities, tourist attractions, and highways also are preferred. Hotels that are located in undeveloped or underdeveloped areas (particularly properties that are yet to be built) are often very difficult to finance because lenders are wary of funding hotels in unproven locations and markets.
- *Appropriate equity.* Lenders will not lend a buyer 100 percent of the money required to buy a hotel. In fact, lenders may require borrowers to have as much as 50 percent **equity** in the property they wish to purchase.

HOTEL TERMINOLOGY AT WORK

Equity: The value of an asset beyond the total amount owed on it for mortgages and other loans.

■

For example, assume you are interested in building a hotel that will cost $10 million. A lender might require that you have 50 percent equity ($5 million) as a down payment to secure the loan. This equity rate can also be expressed as the relationship between a property's value and the amount that a lender will lend on the property. This relationship, known as the loan to value ratio, is computed as:

$$\frac{\text{Amount of loan requested}}{\text{Property value}} = \text{Loan to value ratio}$$

Many lenders require loan to value ratios of up to 50 percent; however, the average for non-SBA loans is generally in the 20 to 60 percent loan to value range. SBA loans can approach 85 percent or more loan to value. The variance in loan to value requirements is typically determined by the size and risk involved in the project under consideration.

- *Strong franchise affiliation.* Few lenders will lend money to a non-branded property. Those potential hotel buyers who seek to save money by not paying franchise-related fees quickly discover that funding for their project is nearly impossible to obtain. The best franchise names, such as, for example, Marriott, Hyatt, Hilton, and Sheraton, yield the greatest lender interest. Lesser-known brands, or those with lower perceived quality, often attract less lender interest. As a result, brand managers who sell lesser known or less desirable franchise names must often identify specific lenders who look favorably upon their brands and who will lend money to develop hotels under these franchises.

- *Proven operational and/or development experience.* Lenders do not want to lend money to hoteliers that learn the hotel business at the lender's expense. As a result, it is always important to clearly demonstrate to a lender that the property for which you are seeking funds will have experienced and talented management on-site. In addition, when a new hotel is proposed, the lender must be confident that those who will develop the hotel have experience in the site selection, construction, and hotel opening skills required for a successful venture.

- *Defensible appraisal, business plan, and revenue forecasts.* As a buyer, it is important that you do not pay more for a hotel than it is worth. Lenders also know that it is important that they not lend more money to a hotel owner than that owner's hotel would be worth if the loan repayments were not made and the lender had to assume possession of the hotel. The best way to establish the true market value of a hotel is to conduct a professional **appraisal.** Nearly all lenders require that an appraisal be done prior to funding a loan for an existing hotel.

HOTEL TERMINOLOGY AT WORK

Appraisal: The establishment of (real estate) value.

■

In addition, to an appraisal, nearly all hotel lenders will require that a **business plan** be submitted as part of any application for a loan.

HOTEL TERMINOLOGY AT WORK

Business Plan: A written document that details an owner/manager's strategy for operating a hotel.

■

The business plan is an important document and is discussed in detail later in this chapter. A critical part of the business plan and one that all lenders will require is a realistic forecast (prediction) of the hotel's future revenue and expense.

The Hotel Appraisal.   Before lenders will lend money for the purchase of an existing hotel, they will want to review the appraisal for the property. When a hotel does not exist, a lender will likely request that a **feasibility study** be substituted for the appraisal and submitted in support of the loan request.

HOTEL TERMINOLOGY AT WORK

Feasibility Study: A determination that a proposed (hotel) development will (or will not) meet the expectations of its investors. The study should include the estimated market demand for the property, as well as its economic viability.

■

For example, assume you want to build a new hotel on the beach in a popular area of Florida. The value of that hotel cannot be established by an appraisal because it does not yet exist. In such a case, the feasibility study would serve as a substitute for the appraisal.

The hotel appraisal that is submitted in support of a loan request is much more than an estimate of a hotel's market value. As we saw earlier in this chapter, there are a variety of methods that can be used to establish a hotel's estimated market value. When a funding source requests that an appraisal be supplied in support of a loan application, the potential lender wants to know:

- The legal description of the property and the land upon which it is located
- The physical condition of the property
- An assessment of market conditions affecting the geographic area in which the hotel is located
- An assessment of market conditions affecting the hotel
- Current valuation of property for tax purposes
- The valuation method(s) used to estimate the property's market value
- The qualifications/certifications of the individual or company conducting the appraisal
- Assumptions used in developing the appraisal
- The date the appraisal was conducted
- The estimated market value of the property

It is important to realize that an appraisal is performed to benefit both the individual seeking to purchase a hotel and the lender who is asked to help fund the purchase. A hotel purchase (or new construction) consists of three essential components. These are the land, the building, and the furnishings. It is imperative that these components be in balance if the hotel is to be financially successful.

For example, it is not surprising that new budget or economy hotels are rarely built on New York's Manhattan Island, or in the most densely populated areas of Paris or Tokyo. The land costs in these areas are so high that an economy hotel is generally not economically feasible. For a full-service hotel, land costs should generally comprise between 10 to 20 percent of the total project's cost. In a limited service hotel, land costs may rise as high as 25 percent of the total project cost. Land costs above these levels could seriously jeopardize a hotel's economic viability.

Similarly, a hotel buyer/developer who buys or leases land at a good price, but who then builds too expensive a building, or furnishes the hotel with excessively expensive artwork, furniture, and fixtures, will also find it difficult to be financially successful.

True market value is an elusive concept. In a free market society, the value of an item is, ultimately, a reflection of what a willing buyer will pay. Sometimes, however, hotel buyers are willing to pay too much to acquire a property. This is especially true with inexperienced buyers or those who ignore professional appraisals. Lenders generally will not ignore a professional appraiser's estimate of market value. That is the reason an appraisal is a required part of the loan application process.

The Hotel Business Plan.   Once the market value for a hotel has been established by a professional appraiser, a lender will want to know your specific plans for making the hotel you want to buy a successful one. If the hotel is to be newly built, the lender will want to know when the building project will be completed, how operating losses that will be incurred in the initial opening months will be funded, and how long it is likely to be before the hotel will show profits.

If the hotel is an older property that is to be renovated, the lender will want to know when the renovations will begin, how much they will cost, and the likely impact of the renovations on future sales. If the property is an existing one that does not require extensive renovation, the lender will still want to know your plans for improving (or maintaining) sales and for operating the hotel. Additional information the lender will require may also be included in the business plan.

A business plan should always begin with a cover letter that explains why the plan has been sent to the reader. Traditionally, the business plan begins with a title page, followed by a table of contents. The plan's actual content should start with an overview statement summarizing the plan's content. It should also include a specific request for the amount of money you wish to borrow as well as a brief description of your plan for paying the money back.

While the order of information may vary, the business plan should always address:

- A physical description of the hotel
- The plan to marketing the hotel
- The hotel's financial management plan
- The hotel's operating (management) plan.

In addition, the business plan should include, as addendums or appendices, any data required to support the assumptions or statements made in it. The specific contents of a business plan may be somewhat different based upon lender requirements; however, Figure 13.2 is an example of a business plan outline that would meet the general information requirements of most lenders.

A well-written business plan can play an important part in securing financing for a hotel. For those potential hotel buyers who need help in preparing a business plan, there are many hospitality consultants and specialized companies offering this specific assistance. It is important to remember, however, that the best business plans secure funding because they demonstrate to the lender that the hotel project being proposed is sound, the risk to the lender is reduced to the greatest degree possible and the individuals involved in the project have both experience and integrity.

THE INTERNET AT WORK

Regardless of the type of business, a well-developed business plan is essential for anyone seeking to borrow money to start or buy a business. Some software companies have developed programs to assist in developing professionally written business plans. To view the site of one of the most popular of these companies, go to:

http://www.bplans.com.

The Hotel Revenue Forecast.   Regardless of whether the hotel for which you seek a loan is an existing property or requires new construction, your lender will want to know the sales revenue that you expect the hotel to produce. The lender may want to see your revenue forecast for one-**quarter**, one year, five years, or even longer.

HOTEL TERMINOLOGY AT WORK

Quarter: A three-month period. Often used to summarize accounting data. Used, for example in "What is our sales forecast for the first quarter of next year?"

∎

It is important that this sales forecast be as accurate as possible. If your forecast is too conservative, you may not show enough revenue to convince

FIGURE 13.2 Sample Business Plan Outline

1. Cover letter to lender
2. Table of contents page
3. Plan summary/overview
4. Description of hotel
   a. Location description
      i. Property size, features, and physical condition
      ii. Construction/renovation plan (if applicable)
      iii. Appraisal summary
5. Marketing plan
   a. Description of hotel's primary market
      i. Competition
      ii. Current marketing efforts and results
      iii. Proposed marketing efforts
      iv. Anticipated future results
6. Financial plan
   a. Statement of equity available/funding requested
      i. Revenue Forecast
      ii. Forecasted revenue and expense
      iii. Forecast assumptions
      iv. Hotel breakeven analysis
      v. Balance sheet of individual/business seeking funds
7. Management plan
   a. Description of current management team
      i. Description of proposed management team
      ii. Operational philosophy/strategy
      iii. Resumes of proposed owners and managers
8. Supporting documentation
   a. Appraisal
   b. Copy of proposed purchase agreement (price)
   c. Franchise agreement (if a franchised property)
   d. Management contract (if a management company is involved)
   e. Other supporting documentation

the lender that you can make the required loan repayments. If, however, your forecast is unrealistically high, knowledgeable lenders may deny the loan because they lack confidence in your forecast ability and business plan. Also, if the forecast is unrealistically high, you may be successful in securing the loan; however, because you will not likely achieve your forecasted revenue amounts, you may lack the ability to repay the loan as promised.

The best sales forecasts include estimates of hotel revenue and expenses. An accurate revenue and expense forecast can be developed if you use realistic assumptions regarding:

- The hotel's opening date
- Achievable occupancy rates
- Achievable ADR
- Required operating expenses

In an existing hotel, these assumptions may be easy to make because you know the hotel's current revenue and expense levels. In a hotel that will be built or that requires extensive renovation, the income and expense levels may be harder to predict. Franchisors can be helpful in providing information about average operating costs, as can a number of industry sources that publish such data on an annual basis. Additional sources of information regarding probable revenues may be obtained through the local Visitor's and Convention Bureau or your state's Hotel and Lodging Association. There are also hospitality industry consultants that can be employed to help you develop a revenue and expense forecast that is realistic and that will help maximize your chances of securing a loan.

Figure 13.3 is an example of a revenue and expense forecast that might be required by a lending institution. Note that it projects:

- Revenues (sales) for a four-year period
- Expenses for the same period
- An increasing occupancy percentage
- An increasing ADR

It is highly likely that a lender will ask for backup information about how these assumptions were made, and perhaps, independent verification that they are realistic.

HOTEL START-UP

When you have selected a hotel to buy, secured financing, and arranged to build (or take possession) of your hotel, the real work has just begun. There are essentially three scenarios involved in starting up a new hotel. These are:

- A new hotel is built
- An existing hotel is purchased and operated under the same flag
- An existing hotel is purchased and **reflagged**

HOTEL TERMINOLOGY AT WORK

Reflag: To change a hotel from one franchise brand to another (see Conversion). Used, for example, in, "We can buy the property, reflag it and reposition it in the upper-scale transient market."

■

FIGURE 13.3 Example of Revenue and Expense Forecast

New Hotel Forecast For Fiscal Years One thru Four
Financial Summary Detail

Description	Year 1	Pct	Year 2	Pct	Year 3	Pct	Year 4	Pct
Revenue (Sales)								
Rooms	4,835,520	67.44%	5,555,186	69.18%	6,317,078	70.96%	6,944,695	71.27%
Food	1,750,000	24.41%	1,850,000	23.04%	1,925,000	21.62%	2,100,000	21.55%
Beverage	350,000	4.88%	385,000	4.79%	410,000	4.61%	450,000	4.62%
Telephone	135,000	1.88%	130,000	1.62%	125,000	1.40%	120,000	1.23%
Other Income	100,000	1.39%	110,000	1.37%	125,000	1.40%	130,000	1.33%
Total of Departmental Sales	7,170,520	100.00%	8,030,186	100.00%	8,902,078	100.00%	9,744,695	100.00%
Direct Operating Expenses								
Rooms	1,250,000	17.43%	1,350,000	16.81%	1,425,000	16.01%	1,450,000	14.88%
Food	1,575,000	21.96%	1,665,000	20.73%	1,732,500	19.46%	1,890,000	19.40%
Beverage	175,000	2.44%	192,500	2.40%	205,000	2.30%	225,000	2.31%
Telephone	150,000	2.09%	175,000	2.18%	195,000	2.19%	225,000	2.31%
Other Expenses	100,000	1.39%	110,000	1.37%	120,000	1.35%	130,000	1.33%
Total of Direct Operating Expenses	3,250,000	45.32%	3,492,500	43.49%	3,677,500	41.31%	3,920,000	40.23%
Gross Operating Income	3,920,520	54.68%	4,537,686	56.51%	5,224,578	58.69%	5,824,695	59.77%
Undistributed Expenses								
Admin & Gen.	650,000	9.06%	675,000	8.41%	690,000	7.75%	700,000	7.18%
Sales & Marketing	450,000	6.28%	475,000	5.92%	500,000	5.62%	525,000	5.39%
Franchise Fees (5% room rev.)	241,776	3.37%	277,759	3.46%	315,854	3.55%	347,235	3.56%
Utility Costs	300,000	4.18%	325,000	4.05%	350,000	3.93%	375,000	3.85%
Property Operations and Maintenance	375,000	5.23%	400,000	4.98%	425,000	4.77%	450,000	4.62%
Total of Undistributed Expenses	2,016,776	28.13%	2,152,759	26.81%	2,280,854	25.62%	2,397,235	24.60%
Gross Operating Profit	1,903,744	26.55%	2,384,927	29.70%	2,943,724	33.07%	3,427,461	35.17%
Fixed Charges								
Management Fees (3%)	215,116	3.00%	240,906	3.00%	267,062	3.00%	292,341	3.00%
Taxes	225,000	3.14%	250,000	3.11%	250,000	2.81%	275,000	2.82%
Insurance	45,000	0.63%	50,000	0.62%	55,000	0.62%	60,000	0.62%
Depreciation	450,000	6.28%	450,000	5.60%	450,000	5.05%	450,000	4.62%
Mortgage Loan Payment	1,200,000	16.74%	1,200,000	14.94%	1,200,000	13.48%	1,200,000	12.31%
FF&E Reserve (3%)	215,116	3.00%	240,906	3.00%	267,062	3.00%	292,341	3.00%
Total of Fixed Charges	2,350,231	32.78%	2,431,811	30.28%	2,489,125	27.96%	2,569,682	26.37%
Net Profit or (Loss)	−446,487	−6.23%	−46,885	−0.58%	454,599	5.11%	857,779	8.80%
Hotel Room Count	250		250		250		250	
Annual Rooms Sold	46,720		51,556		57,168		61,594	
Annual Rooms Available (250 × 365)	91250		91250		91250		91250	
Occupancy %	51.20%		56.50%		62.65%		67.50%	
ADR	$103.50		$107.75		$110.50		$112.75	
RevPar	$52.99		$60.88		$69.23		$76.11	

Regardless of the scenario you have undertaken, as the new owner/G.M. there are a variety of tasks for which you will be responsible. Most of these should be accomplished before the hotel officially opens, but some, as you will see, require ongoing attention. While it is not possible to detail every required management task to be accomplished before and after a hotel is opened, the following pre- and postopening responsibilities suggest some of the many activities you will undertake or supervise.

Selected Preopening Responsibilities of the G.M./Owner

Opening a new hotel is a daunting task. In fact, some management companies have developed special opening teams specifically trained to accomplish the preopening, opening day, and postopening tasks required. In other cases, the opening "team" may consist only of the G.M./owner. Regardless of the size of the opening team, however, there are many tasks to be completed. The following list, though not exhaustive, provides a sense of the scope and variety of preopening responsibilities for which you, as the G.M./owner, will be responsible. In keeping with the majority of hotel development projects today, the activities list assumes the hotel will be operated as a franchise. In addition, some of these tasks are unique to a hotel reflag (conversion) project, and these are italicized.

Six Months Prior to Opening

- G.M. arrives on-site (the office is in an on-site trailer when the project involves new construction)
- Office supplies, business cards, stationary, and envelopes ordered
- Office telephone, answering machine, and fax lines installed
- Begin search for EOC members (especially DOSM and chief engineer)
- Secure all required franchisor operating manuals
- Order hotel telephone system and in-room telephones, and determine information to be listed on the telephone faceplates
- Install "Coming Soon" sign with hotel name on the site
- Join local Chamber of Commerce; subscribe to local and state business magazines
- *Inform GDS contact(s) of new property affiliation and projected opening date*
- Establish hotel depository account(s) with local bank
- Establish petty cash account
- Order hotel courtesy van (if one is to be used)
- Order property walkie-talkies or wireless communication system
- *Coordinate, with telephone vendor, all PMS requirements and cabling needs*

- Assure interface capability of PMS and all required interfaces
- Enter contract with landscaper
- Order all needed exterior signs
- *Order all necessary interior signs*
- Plan direct mail campaign and begin implementation of sales plan
- Order needed laundry and maintenance equipment
- Setup accounts payable system
- Open needed vendor accounts, including:
  - FedEx
  - Office supply store
  - Florist
  - Printer
  - Trash removal
  - Hardware store
  - Building supply store
  - Gas station
- File for all necessary licenses (liquor) and operating permits
- Order vending machines
- Place Yellow Pages ad
- Create area information guide with location of restaurants and attractions
- Obtain federal tax I.D. number
- Prepare job descriptions
- Order cable channels/movie services

Three Months Prior to Opening

- DOSM selected and begins work
- Chief engineer selected and begins work
- *Order business cards for known EOC members*
- Food and beverage suppliers selected
- Undertake wage survey in area to determine prevailing local wages
- Contact newspaper to begin employee solicitation/advertising process
- Begin FOM and executive housekeeper search
- Determine policies necessary for processing reservations, including:
  - Pets
  - Check-in, check-out times
  - Cancellations
  - Credit card requirements
- *Order customized folio paper, keycard holders, and assorted front office forms*
- Purchase exterior trash receptacles

- Confirm orders for:
  - Fitness equipment
  - Kitchen supplies
  - Housekeeping supplies (terry, linen, etc.)
  - In-room directories
  - Guest in-room amenities
- Executive housekeeper arrives on property
- FOM arrives on property
- Secure credit card accounts and assure that authorization system is in place
- Select pest control vendor
- Order employee time clock
- Place order for Bibles with Gideons
- Order phone books
- Order audiovisual equipment/meeting room furniture
- *Select local laundry dry cleaner; order laundry tags from printer*
- Order insurance liability cards for guest room doors
- Order roll-away beds, cribs, and high chairs
- Order ADA compliance items
- Secure/install emergency master key box for fire department
- Conclude supervisory hiring
- Plan grand opening party

One Month Prior to Opening

- Review all insurance policies/coverage with insurance carrier
- Install guest safety deposit boxes
- Install decals (logos) on courtesy van
- Select fire extinguisher service company
- Begin hiring hourly employees
- Establish partnerships with local restaurants to encourage referrals
- Mail grand opening invitations
- Order employee uniforms
- *Order franchise directories*
- Designate smoking/nonsmoking rooms, install signage
- Contact health department for F&B facility inspections
- Purchase first aid and biohazard kits
- Install cellular telephone/CB in van
- Begin training of hourly employees

- Purchase laundry chemicals and dispensing equipment
- Prepare MSDS binders for affected areas
- Test fire alarm system
- *Inform vendors of name change*
- *Inform current direct bill guests of name change*
- *Do mass FAX to travel agents announcing change of hotel name*
- Secure all remaining in-room amenities and supplies
- Plan rooms preventative maintenance program
- Purchase tools, jumper cables, and other maintenance supplies

One Week Prior to Opening
- Test all systems
  - Electronic locks
  - Credit card processing
  - Safety systems
  - Televisions/remotes
  - Water
  - HVAC
  - Cable/in-room movies
  - Room telephones/voice mail
- Send grand opening party press release to local news media
- Conduct practice meals in the room service, breakfast, lunch, and dinner areas
- Host grand opening party
- "Keep smiling"

Selected Postopening Responsibilities of the G.M./Owner

After the grand opening party has been held, the real work of operating the hotel continues. As a G.M., you will find that there are many postopening tasks that must be completed, and although you or the G.M. is not responsible for each of these, you are responsible for ensuring that they are undertaken and completed.

Postgrand Opening Activities
- Mail thank-you cards to grand opening attendees
- Follow-up on all leads made during the grand opening party
- Thank the media for attending
- Thank all hotel employees for their assistance during the opening

Ongoing Activities

- Train staff, train staff, train staff!
- Improve constantly through continued study of the hospitality field
- Spend time daily with:
  - Each department head
  - Your hourly staff
  - Your guests
  - Your family
- Assist the hotel sales effort whenever possible (because by doing so you will continue to better understand your client's wishes and needs)
- Manage your hotel (because only you know how to do it best).

Serving as G.M. of a hotel is, without a doubt, one of the best, most rewarding jobs in the world. Owning the hotel you manage is even better. While it is not at all the authors' belief that everything you must know about operating a hotel is contained in this book, it *is* our firm belief that, by carefully studying it, you can begin your journey into the fascinating world of hotel management and, perhaps, ownership. We wish you the best of luck in your hotel career!

MANAGERS AT WORK

"Well, Leroy, October seems strong, but what is the forecast for room sales in November and December?" asked J.D. Ojisima, the hotel's new owner, at one of the first weekly EOC meetings since J.D. assumed ownership of the property. It was late August and final planning was well underway for the year's fourth quarter.

"November starts well, then softens in the last week, because business travelers stay home for Thanksgiving. Then we get a bump up in occupancy in the first two weeks of December, but then nothing much until January. Nobody wants to travel for business around the holidays," replied Leroy Gates, the DOSM.

The controller spoke up, "The way I see it, if we don't cut expenses, and I mean significantly cut expenses, we could actually show a loss in the fourth quarter. As a property that targets business travelers, I know this hotel has traditionally been slow in the fourth quarter and does great in the second and third quarters, but I think we need to plan our fourth quarter budget cuts now."

"But my housekeepers are always the first to be cut," protested Maggie Pennycuff, "and the holidays are a poor time to ask them to reduce their hours and their take-home pay. J.D., I hope we can avoid that this year!"

Assume that you are J.D. and that you have forecasted a decline in occupancy percentage of 10–15 points for a given quarter of the year. What specific steps could you take to increase sales and/or reduce expenses in that quarter? What are additional steps that could be taken through the year to prepare for such a quarter? Given the choice, do you think a hotel should reduce room rates, cut expenses, or increase spending on sales efforts in anticipation of a down period? Who should make such decisions? Do you believe J.D.'s experience as a G.M. will help in this decision making? Why or why not?

HOTEL TERMINOLOGY AT WORK GLOSSARY

The following terms were defined within this chapter. If you are not familiar with each of them, please review the segment of the chapter that contains the term.

Entrepreneur	Closing	Equity
Broker	Mortgage	Appraisal
Upside potential	Leverage	Business plan
Grand opening	Recourse	Feasibility study
Per key	Foreclose	Quarter
Market value	SBA	Reflag

ISSUES AT WORK

1. With some notable exceptions, the concept of the owner/on-site manager is not as common in the hotel business as it is in the restaurant business. Why do you think that has been the case? List five factors that would lead you to want to own your own hotel(s). Are there factors that would make you seek an alternative investment for your time and money? What are they?

2. Some hotel buyers are interested only in properties with strong upside potential (a distressed property), while others prefer to purchase hotels with known levels of profitability. If you were buying a hotel, which would you choose? Why? How do you think your ability to secure investor support would be influenced by your decision?

3. One of the most difficult (but also most important aspects involved in buying a hotel) is the determination of the appropriate price to pay. This chapter presented several approaches to establishing a hotel's market value. Some valuation systems place great emphasis on the hotel's real estate value, while others place a greater emphasis on the hotel's ability to generate operating profits. Which do you think is more important? List three factors that support your point of view.

4. Financing sources usually feel most comfortable lending funds to experienced hotel operators. If you were a bank loan officer who was evaluated, in part, by the quality of loans you approved, how many years experience would you want a G.M. to possess before approaching your lending institution for funding to buy a hotel? What type(s) of experience would you want that G.M. to have? How would you determine the quality of the G.M.?

5. The time (number of hours worked per week) involved in the preopening of a hotel is extensive. What are some specific nonwork activities you

could do to keep balance in your life while managing the preopening of your own hotel? What could you suggest for your top management staff to keep the same balance in their lives? Do you think most G.M.s buy their own hotel for its financial rewards or for the freedom of managing their own hotel? Which would appeal most to you?

Glossary

AAHOA (Asian American Hotel Owners Association)   An association of hotel owners who, through an exchange of ideas, seek to promote professionalism and excellence in hotel ownership.

Accountability   An obligation created when a person is delegated duties/responsibilities from higher levels of management.

Accounts Payable   The sum total of all invoices owed by the hotel to its vendors for credit purchases made by the hotel. Also called A.P.

Accounts Receivable   Money owed to the hotel because of sales made on credit. Sometimes referred to as "AR" for short.

Accounts Receivable Aging   A process by which the average length of time money owed to the hotel because of sales made on credit is determined.

ADR   Short for "average daily rate," the average selling price of all guest rooms for a given time period. The formula for ADR is Total Room Revenue/Total Number of Rooms Sold = ADR.

Agitation   Movement of the washing machine resulting in friction as fabrics rub against each other.

Air Handler   The fans and mechanical systems required to move air through ducts and to vents.

Allowances and Adjustments   Reductions in sales revenue credited to guests because of errors in properly recording sales or to appease a guest for property shortcomings.

Amenities   Hotel products and services designed to attract guests.

Appraisal   The establishment of (real estate) value.

Area of Protection (AOP)   The geographic area, which is designated by a franchisor, and granted to a franchisee, in which no directly competing franchisees will be sold.

Attrition   The difference between the original request and the actual purchases of a group. For example, a group might reserve one hundred rooms, but actually use only fifty. The hotel's standard group contract may, in such a case, stipulate that the group pay a penalty for "overreserving."

At-Will Employment   The employment relationship that exists when employers can hire any employee as they choose and dismiss that employee with or without cause at any time. The employee can also elect to work for the employer or terminate the work relationship anytime he or she chooses.

Audiovisual (AV) equipment   Those items including DVD players, laptops, LCD projectors, microphones, sound systems, flip charts, overhead projectors, slide projectors, TVs, and VCRs that are used to communicate information to meeting attendees during their meetings.

Audit   An independent verification of financial records.

Auditor   The individual(s) who conducts an independent verification of financial records.

Authority   The power to tell others to do or not to do something in efforts to attain the hotel's objectives.

Authorize   To validate.

Back Office System   The accounting system used by the controller to prepare the hotel's financial documents such as the balance sheet, income statement, and so on.

Backup Generator   Equipment used to make limited amounts of electricity on-site. Utilized in times of power failure or when the hotel experiences low supply from the usual provider of electricity.

Backup Systems   Redundant hardware and/or software operated in parallel to the system it serves. Used in times of failure or power outages, these are often operated by battery systems. For example, a backup system to the hotel's telephones would enable outside calling even if the main digital telephone system were to shut down.

Ballast   The device in an electric discharge lamp that starts, stops, and controls the current to the light.

Banquet   A food and/or beverage event held in a function room.

Banquet Event Order (BEO)   A form used by the sales, catering, and food production areas to detail all requirements for a banquet. Information provided by the banquet client is summarized on the form, and it becomes the basis for the formal contract between the client and the hotel.

Bell Staff   Those uniformed attendants responsible for guest services, including luggage handling, valet parking, airport transportation, and related guest services. The title originally arose because, in earlier years, the staff would come to the "front" (desk) to assist a guest when a bell was rung as a summons to them.

Benefits   Indirect financial compensation consisting of employer-provided rewards and services other than wages or salaries.

Bid   An offer by the hotel to supply sleeping rooms, meeting space, food and beverages, or other services to a potential client at a stated price. If the bid is accepted, the hotel will issue the client a contract detailing the agreement made between the hotel and the client.

Biohazard Waste Bag   A specially marked plastic bag used in hotels. Laundry items that are blood or bodily fluid stained and thus need special handling in the OPL are placed into these bags for transporting to the OPL.

Blackout Dates   Specific days in which the hotel is "sold-out" and/or is not accepting normal reservations.

Block   Rooms reserved exclusively for members of a specific group. As in, "We need to create a block of fifty rooms for May 10 and 11 for the Society of Antique Furniture Appraisers."

Blood-Borne Pathogen   Any microorganism or virus, carried by blood, that can cause a disease.

Bond(ing)   Purchasing an insurance policy against the possibility that an employee will steal.

Bonified Occupational Qualifications (BOQs)   Qualifications to perform a job that are judged reasonably necessary to safely or adequately perform all tasks within the job.

Booking   Hotel jargon for making a confirmed sale. As in, "What is the current booking volume for the month in the Food and Beverage department?" or "How many out-of-state tour buses were booked into the hotel last month?"

Brand   The name of a hotel chain. Sometimes referred to as a "flag."

Brand Standard   A hotel service or feature that must be adopted by any property entering a specific hotel brand's system. Used, for example, in, "The franchisor has determined that 'free local telephone calls' will become a new brand standard effective January 1st."

Broker   An entity that, for a fee, lists (offers) hotels for sale on behalf of the hotels' owners and solicits buyers for the hotels it lists. Used, for example, in, "I know that hotel is listed with Joe Johnson, a broker with Mid-State Hotel Brokers."

Bucket Check   A procedure used to verify, for each guest, the accuracy of that guest's registration information.

Business Plan   A written document that details an owner/manager's strategy for operating a hotel.

Buyout   An arrangement in which both parties to a contract agree to end the contract early as a result of one party paying the other an agreed-upon financial compensation.

C.P.A.   Certified Public Accountant. An individual designated by the American Institute of Certified Public Accountants as competent in the field of accounting.

Calibration   The adjustment of equipment to maximize its effectiveness and operational efficiency.

Call Accounting   The system within the hotel used to document and charge guests for their use of the telephone.

Call Brand Beverages   High-priced and higher-quality alcoholic beverages that are sold by name (such as Johnny Walker Red Scotch or Bombay Gin) rather than sold by type of liquor (scotch or gin) only.

Cancellation Number   A series of numbers and/or letters that serve to identify the cancellation of a specific hotel reservation.

Capital Expenditure   The purchase of equipment, land, buildings, or other fixed assets necessary for the operation of the hotel.

Career Ladder   A plan that projects successively more responsible professional positions within an organization/industry. Career ladders also allow one to plan/schedule developmental activities judged necessary to assume more responsible positions.

Cash Bars   A beverage service alternative where guests desiring beverages during a banquet function pay for them personally.

Catering   The process of selling and carrying out the details of a banquet event.

Centralized Accounting   A financial management system that collects accounting data from an individual hotel(s), then combines and analyzes the data at a different (central) site.

Certified Public Accountant (C.P.A.)   An individual designated by the American Institute of Certified Public Accountants as competent in the field of accounting.

Chamber of Commerce   An organization whose goal is the advancement of business interests within a community or larger business region.

Closed-Circuit Television (CCTV)   A camera and monitor system that displays, in real time, the activity within the camera's field of vision. A CCTV consisting of several cameras and screens showing the camera's fields of vision may be monitored in a single hotel location.

Closing   The legal process of transferring property ownership from a seller to a buyer. Used, for example, in, "The closing for our new hotel is set for May 22 at the Trans American Title Company offices on Main Street."

Coaching   A process whose goal is helping staff members, and the hotel team, reach their highest possible levels of performance.

Coding   The process of assigning incurred costs to predetermined cost centers or categories.

Cold Calling   Making a sales visit/presentation to a potential client without having previously set an appointment to do so.

Collusion   Secret cooperation between two or more hotel employees for the purpose of committing fraud.

Commercial Food Service Operation   Food Services offered in hotels and restaurants and other organizations whose primary purpose for existence involves generation of profits from the sale of food and beverage products.

Comp (Complimentary)   Short for "complimentary" or "no-charge" for products or services.

Compensation   All financial and nonfinancial rewards given to management and nonmanagement employees in return for the work they do for the hotel.

Compensatory Damages   Also known as actual damages, this monetary amount is intended to compensate injured parties for actual losses or damage they have incurred. This typically includes items such as medical bills and lost wages.

Competitive Set   The group of competing hotels to which an individual hotel's operating performance is compared.

Concierge   The individual(s) within a full-service hotel responsible for providing guests with detailed information regarding local dining and attractions, as well as assisting with related guest needs.

Confirmation Number   A series of numbers and/or letters that serve to identify a specific hotel reservation.

Consortia   Groups of hotel service buyers organized for the purpose of reducing their client's travel-related costs. A single such group is a consortium.

Contact Alarms   A warning system that notifies (contacts) an external entity such as the fire or police department if the alarm is activated.

Continuous Quality Improvement (CQI)   Ongoing efforts within the hotel to better meet (or exceed) guest expectations and define ways to perform work with better, less costly, and faster methods.

Contribution Margin   The amount that remains after the product (food) cost of a menu item is subtracted from its selling price.

Controller   The individual responsible for recording, classifying, and summarizing the hotel's business transactions. In some hotels, this position is referred to as the comptroller.

Convention and Visitors Bureau (CVB)   An organization, generally funded by taxes levied on overnight hotel guests, that seeks to increase the number of visitors to the area it represents. Also called the "CVB" for short.

Conversion   The process of changing a hotel's flag from one franchisor to another. Also known as "reflagging." For example, "We need a G.M. experienced in managing a hotel conversion." As a noun: The term used to describe a hotel that has changed its flag from one franchisor to another. For example, "Has this hotel always been a (brand name), or is it a conversion?"

Corkage Fee   A charge levied by a hotel when a guest brings a bottle (e.g., of a special wine) to the hotel for consumption at a banquet function or in the hotel's dining room.

Cost Center   A hotel department that incurs costs in support of a revenue center. Two examples are the housekeeping and maintenance departments.

Cost per Occupied Room   Total costs incurred for an item or area, divided by the number of rooms occupied in the hotel for the time period examined.

Cross-Selling   Messages designed to advertise the availability of other hotel services.

CTA   "Closed to Arrival." In this situation, the hotel declines reservations for guests attempting to arrive on this specific date.

Curb Appeal   The term used to indicate the initial visual impression the hotel's parking areas, grounds, and external building aesthetics create for an arriving guest.

Damages   The actual amount of losses or costs incurred due to the wrongful act of a liable party.

Data Mining   Using technology to analyze guest (and other) related data to make better marketing decisions.

Decentralized Accounting   A financial management system that collects accounting data from an individual hotel site and combines and analyzes that data at the same site.

Deep Cleaning   The intensive cleaning of a guestroom, typically including the thorough cleaning of items such as drapes, lamp shades, carpets, furniture, walls, and the like.

Delegation   The process of assigning authority (power) to others to enable subordinates to do work that a manager at a higher organizational level would otherwise do.

Demand Generator   An organization, entity, or location that creates a significant need for hotel services. Examples in a community include large businesses, tourist sites, sports teams, educational facilities, and manufacturing plants.

Depreciation   The part of a fixed asset's cost that is recognized as an expense in each accounting period because it is assumed to have been "used up" during that period.

Depressed Market   The term used to describe a hotel market area where occupancy rates and/or ADRs are far below their historic levels. Used, for example, in, "The permanent closing of the military base in that town resulted in depressed market conditions in the entire county."

Direct Bill   An arrangement whereby a guest is allowed to purchase hotel services and products on credit terms.

Discipline   Activities designed to reinforce desired performance (positive discipline) or to correct undesired performance (negative discipline).

Discrepancy Report   A daily comparison between the status of rooms as listed by the PMS at the front office, and the status of rooms as listed by the housekeeping department.

Distribution Channel   A distinct and definable source of hotel rooms or services sales. For example, the Internet is one distribution channel, and meeting planners are another.

DOSM   Short for "Director of Sales and Marketing." Variations include DOS (Director of Sales) and DOM (Director of Marketing).

Downsizing   Reducing the number of employees and/or labor hours for cost-containment purposes.

Drop In   A potential buyer (guest) who arrives at the hotel without an appointment.

Duct   A passageway, usually built of sheet metal, that allows fresh, cold, or warm air to be directed to various parts of a building.

Early Out   A clause in a franchisee agreement that grants both the franchisor and the franchisee the right, with proper notification, to terminate the agreement after it has been in effect for a relatively short period of time. When this clause exists, a window may be granted after only one, two, or three years.

E.I. (Educational Institute of the AH&LA)   The shortened version of the name given to the Educational Institute of the American Hotel and Lodging Association (AH&LA). Located in Orlando, Florida, and Lansing, Michigan, E.I. is the professional development and certification subsidiary of the AH&LA.

Electric Discharge Lamp   A lamp in which light is generated by passing electrical current through a space filled with a special combination of gases. Examples include fluorescent, mercury vapor, metal halide, and sodium.

Embezzlement   The theft of a company's financial assets by an employee.

Emergency Plan   A document describing a hotel's pre-determined, intended response to a safety/security threat encountered by the hotel.

Employee Handbook   Written policies and procedures related to employment at a hotel. Also sometimes called an employee "manual."

Employment Agreement   A document specifying the terms of the work relationship between the employer and employee that indicates the rights and obligations of both parties.

Empowerment   The act of granting authority to employees to make key decisions within the employees' areas of responsibility.

Energy Management   Specific policies and engineering, maintenance, and facility design activities intended to control and reduce energy usage.

Engineering   Designing and operating a building to ensure a safe and comfortable atmosphere.

Entrepreneur   A person who assumes the risk of owning and operating a business in exchange for the financial rewards the business may produce.

Executive Operating Committee (EOC)   Those members of the hotel's management team (generally department heads) responsible for departmental leadership and overall property administration.

Equity   The value of an asset beyond the total amount owed on it for mortgages and other loans.

Ethics   Standards used to judge the "right" and "wrong" (or fairness) of one's actions when dealing with others.

Executive Housekeeper   The individual responsible for the management and operation of the housekeeping department.

Expenses   The amount of money spent to generate revenues.

External Audit   An independent verification of financial records performed by accountants who are not employed by the organization operating the hotel.

External Recruiting   Tactics designed to attract persons who are not current hotel employees for vacant positions.

F&B   Shortened term for "food and beverage." Used, for example as in the following: "Please let the F&B Director know about the changes the guest has requested."

Feasibility Study   A determination that a proposed (hotel) development will (or will not) meet the expectations of its investors. The study should include the estimated market demand for the property, as well as its economic viability.

Federal Trade Commission (FTC)   The FTC enforces federal antitrust and consumer protection laws. It also seeks to ensure that the nation's business markets function competitively and are free of undue restrictions caused by acts or practices that are unfair or deceptive.

FF&E (furniture, fixtures, and equipment)   The term used to refer to the furniture, fixtures, and equipment used by a hotel to service its guests.

FF&E Reserve   Funds set aside by management today for the future furniture, fixture, and equipment replacement needs of a hotel.

First Tier   Management companies that operate hotels for owners using the management company's trade name as the hotel brand. Hyatt, Hilton, and Sheraton are examples.

Fixed Charges   Those expenses incurred in the purchase and occupation of the hotel itself. These include rent, property taxes, insurance, interest, and depreciation and amortization.

Fixed Labor Costs   The minimum number of labor hours and associated labor costs that are required to operate the food service operation whenever it is open regardless of the number, if any, of guests that are served.

Flag   A term used to refer to the specific brand with which a hotel may affiliate. Examples of currently popular flags include brands such as Comfort Inns, Holiday Inn Express, Ramada Inns, Hampton Inns, Residence Inns, Best Western, and Hawthorn Suites. The hotels affiliated with a specific flag are sometimes referred to as a chain.

FOC (Franchise Offering Circular)   A franchise disclosure document that is prepared by a franchisor and then is registered and filed with the state governmental agency responsible for administering franchise relationships in that date.

Folio   The detailed list of a hotel guest's room charges, as well as other charges authorized by the guest or legally imposed by the hotel.

FOM   Short for front office manager.

Food and Beverage Director   The individual responsible for the operation of a hotel's F&B program(s).

Foot-candle   A measure of illumination. One foot-candle equals one lumen per square foot. (The European counterpart of the foot-candle is the Lux, a light intensity of one lumen per square meter.)

Foreclose   The process in which a lender terminates the borrower's interest in a property after a loan is defaulted.

Franchise   An arrangement whereby one party (the brand) allows another (the hotel owners) to use its logo, name, systems, and resources in exchange for a fee.

Franchise Agreement   The legal contract between the hotel's owners (the franchisee) and the brand managers (the franchisor), which describes the duties and responsibilities of each in the franchise relationship.

Franchisee   Those who own the hotel and buy the right to use the brand name for a fixed period of time and at an agreed-upon price.

Franchisor   Those who manage the brand and sell the right to use the brand name.

Free-to-Guests   A service provided at no additional charge (beyond normal room rental charges) to the hotel guest. Examples could include making local telephone calls, access to premium cable television channels such as HBO or Showtime, and use of the hotel's pool or workout facilities. (Ultimately, the hotel must absorb the cost(s) of providing these services to guests, but guests are not charged on a per usage basis. Therefore, the term does not mean that the services that are provided are free to the hotel.)

Front Desk   The area within the hotel used for guest registration and payment.

Front Office   The department within the hotel responsible for guest reservations, registration, service, and payment.

FSD (Franchise Services Director)   The representative of a franchise hotel brand who interacts directly with the franchised hotel's G.M.s.

Full-Service Hotel   A hotel is considered "full-service" when it provides guests with extensive food and beverage products and services.

Function Room   Public space such as meeting rooms, conference areas, and ballrooms (which can frequently be subdivided into smaller spaces) that are available in the hotel for banquet, meeting, or other group rental purposes.

General Manager (G.M.)   The traditional title used to identify the individual at a hotel property who is responsible for final decision making regarding property-specific operating policies and procedures. Also the leader of the hotel's management team.

Global Distribution System (GDS)   Referred to as the GDS for short, this system connects those travel professionals worldwide who reserve rooms with hotels offering rooms for sale.

Globalization   The condition in which countries and communities within them throughout the world are becoming increasingly interrelated.

GOP   Short for gross operating profit. This popular term is taken from a pre-1990 version of the Uniform System of Accounts for Hotels (USAH) published by the New York Hotel Association. It refers to hotel revenue less those expenses typically controlled at the property level. It is generally expressed on the income statement and in the industry as both a dollar figure and percent of total revenue.

Grand Opening   An event held at a hotel that marks the "official" opening of that hotel. It can be held several days or even weeks after the hotel actually opens and is intended to market the hotel to its client base and the local community.

Group Contract   A legal document used to summarize the agreement between a hotel and its group client.

Group Sale   A large sale (in number of rooms or dollar volume) of the hotel's rooms or services. The sales and marketing department, not the front desk, book sales of this type.

Group Sales   Rooms and services sold primarily through the efforts of the hotel's sales and marketing department, and given to the front office for recording and servicing.

Guarantee   A contractual agreement about the number of meals to be provided at a banquet event. Typically, a guarantee must be made several days in advance of the event. At that time, the entity contracting with the hotel for the event agrees to pay for the larger of the actual number of guests served or the number of guests guaranteed.

Guest   A hotel visitor. Most guests rent rooms and/or purchase food or beverages in a hotel outlet or a banquet function.

Guest Check Average   The average amount spent by a guest in a room service or dining room order. The guest check average typically includes the food and alcoholic beverage sales. Guest check average = total revenue ÷ total number of guests served.

Guest Service Agent   An employee working in the front desk area of the hotel. Also referred to by some in the industry as a "desk clerk."

H.R.   Short for human resources.

Head Table   Special seating at a banquet reserved for guests of honor.

Headquarter Hotel   The hotel that hosts the main group of attendees during an event in which there are multiple host hotels.

Horizontal Communication   Communication between individuals at the same organizational level.

Hospitality Suites   A guest room rented by a supplier/vendor usually during conventions/conferences to provide complimentary food and/or beverages to invited guests.

Hosted Bars   A beverage service alternative in which the host of a function pays for beverages during all or part of the banquet event; also called an "open" bar.

Hosted Events   Functions served by a hotel, which are complimentary to invited guests because costs are borne by the event's sponsor.

Hotel Chain   A group of hotels with the same brand name.

Hoteliers   Those who work in the hotel business.

House Brand Beverages   Alcoholic beverages that are sold by type (scotch, gin, etc.) rather than by brand name and that are served when a call brand beverage is not requested. Sometimes referred to as "Well" brands.

House Count   An estimate of the number of guests staying in a hotel on a given day.

House Person   The individual responsible for the cleaning of public spaces (the house). Also sometimes referred to as a PA (public area cleaner) or porter.

House Phone   A publicly located telephone within the hotel used to call the front desk, or in some cases, the front desk and guest rooms.

Human Relations   Skills needed to understand and effectively interact with other people.

HVAC   A shorthand term for "heating, ventilating, and air conditioning."

Impact Study   An in-depth evaluation of the effect on occupancy percent and ADR that a new hotel in a given market will have on an existing hotel(s) in that same market.

Incandescent Lamp   A lamp in which a filament inside the lamp's bulb is heated by electrical current to produce light.

Incident Report   A document prepared to record the details of an accident, injury, or disturbance, and the hotel's response to it.

Inclusive   A single price that includes all charges.

Inspector (Inspectress)   The individual(s) responsible for physically checking the room status of guest rooms, as well as other tasks as assigned by the executive housekeeper.

Institutional (Noncommercial) Food Service Operation   Those food services provided by health care, educational, military, religious, and numerous other organizations whose primary reason for existence is not to generate a profit from the sale of food/beverage products but rather is to support another organizational purpose.

Interfaced   The term used to describe the process in which one data generating system shares its data electronically with another system.

Internal Alarms   A warning system that notifies an area within the hotel if the alarm is activated.

Internal Audit   An independent verification of financial records performed by members of the organization operating the hotel.

Internal Recruiting   Tactics to identify and attract currently employed staff members for job vacancies that represent promotions or lateral transfers to similar positions.

Interstate Commerce   The commercial trading or transportation of people or property that occurs between and/or among states.

Job Description   A list of tasks that an employee working in a specific position must be able to effectively perform.

Job Specification   A list of the personal qualities judged necessary for successful performance of the tasks required by the job description.

Keycards   The electromagnetic card used in a recodable locking system.

Laundry Par Levels   The amount of laundry in use, in process, and in storage.

Lead   Information about a prospect who is likely to buy from the hotel.

Leverage   The use of borrowed funds to increase purchasing power.

Liable   Legally bound to compensate for loss or injury.

Limited-Service Hotel   A lodging property that offers no or very limited food services; sometimes a complimentary breakfast is served, but there is no table service restaurant.

Line Departments   Hotel divisions that are in the "chain of command" and are directly responsible for revenues (such as front office and food/beverage) or for property operations (such as housekeeping and maintenance and engineering).

Line-Level   Those employees whose jobs are considered entry level or nonsupervisory. These are typically positions where the employee is paid an hourly (rather than salary) compensation. Examples include positions such as guest service agents, room attendants, and food and beverage servers.

Linen   A generic term for the guest room sheets and pillowcases and tablecloths and napkins washed and dried in the laundry area.

Link   A relationship between two Web sites. When Web site users select a link at one site, they are taken to another Web site address. An external link leads to a Web page other than the current one; an internal link leads elsewhere on the current page.

Maintenance   The activities required to keep a building and its contents in good repair.

Management   The process of planning, organizing, staffing, directing, controlling, and evaluating human, financial, and physical resources for the purpose of achieving organizational goals.

Management Company   An organization that operates a hotel(s) for a fee. Also sometimes called a "Contract Company."

Management Contract   An agreement between a hotel's owners and a hotel management company under which, for a fee, the management company operates the hotel. Also sometimes known as a management agreement.

Marketing Plan   A calendar of specific activities designed to meet the hotel's sales goals.

Market Segmentation   Efforts to focus on a highly defined (smaller) group of travelers.

Market Share   The percentage of the total market (typically in dollars spent) captured by a property.

Market Value   The estimated worth of a hotel. Hotels may, of course, be purchased below, at, or above market value.

Material Safety Data Sheet (MSDS)   A written statement describing the potential hazards of, and best ways to handle, a chemical or toxic substance. An MSDS is provided by the manufacturer of the chemical or toxic substance to the buyer of the product and must be posted and made available in a place where it is easily accessible to those who will actually use the product.

Mentor   A senior employee of a hotel who provides advice and counsel to less experienced staff members about matters relating to the job, organization, and profession.

Minibars   Small, in-room refrigerated or unrefrigerated cabinets used to store beverages, snacks, and other items the hotel wishes to offer for sale to guests.

Minimum Wage   The lowest amount of compensation that an employer may pay to an employee covered by the FLSA or applicable state law. Minimum wage provisions cover most hotel employees; however, exceptions can include youthful employees being paid a training wage for the first ninety days of employment and some tipped employees.

Minutes per Room   The average number of minutes required to clean a guest room. Determined by the following computation: total number of minutes worked by room attendants/total number of guest rooms cleaned = minutes per room.

MLOS   "Minimum Length of Stay." In this situation, the hotel declines reservations for guests seeking to stay for fewer days than the minimum established by the hotel.

MOD   Manager on Duty. The individual on the hotel property responsible for making any management decisions required during the period he or she is MOD.

Moments of Truth   Any (and every) time that a guest has an opportunity to form an impression about the hotel. Moments of truth can be positive or negative.

Mortgage   A legal document that specifies an amount of money a lender will lend for the purchase of a real estate asset (hotel), as well as the terms for the loan's repayment.

Motivation   An inner drive that a person has to attain a goal.

Negotiated Rate   A special room rate, offered for a fixed period of time, to a specific client of the hotel. As in "What is the negotiated rate we should offer the Travelsavers consortium next year?"

Networking   The development of personal relationships for a business-related purpose. For example, a Chamber of Commerce–sponsored breakfast open to all community business leaders interested in improving local traffic conditions would be an excellent example of a networking opportunity for a member of a hotel's sales team.

Night Audit   The process of reviewing for accuracy and completeness the accounting transactions from one day to conclude or "close" that day's sales information in preparation for posting the transactions of the next day.

Night Auditor   The individual who performs the daily review of guest transactions recorded by the front office.

Nonprogrammed Decisions   Decisions that occur infrequently and require creative and unique decision-making abilities.

No-show   A guest who makes a confirmed room reservation but fails to cancel the reservation or arrive at the hotel on the date of the confirmed reservation.

Occupancy Rate   The ratio of guest rooms sold (including comps) to guest rooms available for sale in a given time period. Always expressed as a percentage, the formula for occupancy rate is Total Rooms Sold/Total Rooms Available = Occupancy Percent (%).

Occupancy Tax   Money paid by a hotel to a local taxing authority. The room revenue generated by the hotel determines the amount paid. This tax is also known, in some areas, as the "bed" tax. For example, "In our city, the occupancy tax is 2 percent."

On-the-Job Training (OJT)   Learning activities designed to enhance the skills of current employees. OJT programs are typically offered by management with the intent of improving guest service and employee performance at the hotel. There is generally no charge to the employee for the training.

OPL   Short for "On Premise Laundry."

Orientation   The process of providing basic information about the hotel which must be known by all of its employees.

OSHA   The Occupational Safety and Health Administration. A federal agency established in 1970 that is responsible for developing and enforcing regulations related to assuring safe and healthful working conditions.

Other Revenue   Revenue derived from the sale of hotel products and services that are not classified as rooms, food, or beverages.

Over   A situation in which cashiers have more money in their cash drawer than the official sales records indicate. Thus, a cashier with $10 more in the cash drawer than the sales record indicates is said to be $10 "over."

Overbooking   A situation in which the hotel has more guest reservations for rooms than it has rooms available to lodge those guests. Sometimes referred to as "oversold."

Overbuilt   The condition that exists when there are too many hotel guest rooms available for the number of travelers wanting to rent them.

Overtime   The number of hours of work after which an employee must receive a premium pay rate. This premium rate is generally one and one-half times the basic hourly rate.

Pace Report   A document summarizing confirmed (group) sales made by the sales and marketing department.

P&L   Short for the profit and loss statement, also a synonym for the income and expense statement. The P&L records total hotel revenues and expenses for a specific time period.

Package   A group of hospitality services (such as hotel rooms, meals and airfare) sold for one price. For example, a Valentine's Day getaway package to Las Vegas offered by a T.A. might include airfare, lodging, meals, and show tickets for two people at one inclusive price.

PBX   The system within the hotel used to process incoming, internal, and outgoing telephone calls.

Per Key   A term used to describe the cost of a hotel acquisition based on the number of rooms (keys) purchased. Its value comes in allowing comparison between hotels of unequal size (number of rooms). It is computed as:

Pickup   The actual number of rooms used by a client in a defined time period. As in "What was Travelsavers' pickup last year?"

PIP (Product Improvement Plan)   A document detailing the property upgrades and replacements that will be required if a hotel is to be accepted as one of a specific brand's franchised properties. Used, for example, in, "We estimate the PIP on the property to be $4,000,000 if we decide to go with that brand."

PM (Preventative Maintenance) Program   A specific inspection and activities schedule designed to minimize maintenance-related costs and to prolong the life of equipment by preventing small problems before they become larger ones.

PM Checklist   A tool developed to list all of the critical areas that should be inspected during a PM review of a room, area, or piece of equipment.

PMS   Short for "property management system." This term refers to the computerized system used by the hotel to manage its rooms revenue, room rates, room assignments, and reservations, as well as other selected guest service functions.

Point of Sale (POS) Terminal   A computer system that contains its own input and output components and, perhaps, some memory capacity but without a central processing unit.

POM   Short for "Property Operation and Maintenance." The term is taken from the Uniform System of Accounts for Hotels and refers to the segment of the income statement that details the costs of operating the E&M department.

Post   To enter a guest's charges into the PMS, thus creating a permanent record of the sale, as in "Please post this meeting room charge to Mr. Walker's folio."

Premium Brand Beverages   The highest-priced and highest-quality beverages generally available. Examples include Johnny Walker Black Scotch and Bombay Sapphire Gin; these brands are sometimes referred to as "Super Call" brands.

Prepaid Expenses   Expenditures made for items prior to the accounting period in which the item's actual expense is incurred.

Product Usage Report   A report detailing the amount of an inventoried item used by a hotel in a specified time period (i.e., week, month, quarter, year).

Profitability   Revenue − Expenses = Profit. The G.M.'s assignment of specific revenues and expenses to a given department will, in great measure, dictate profit levels in that department.

Programmed Decisions   Routine or repetitive decisions that can be made after considering policies, procedures, or rules.

Progressive Discipline   A process of negative discipline in which repeated infractions result in an increasingly severe penalty.

Prospect   An individual or group who, while not currently using the hotel, are considered potential clients with a good likelihood of using the hotel in the future.

Public Space   Those areas within the hotel that can be freely accessed by guests and visitors. Examples include lobby areas, public rest rooms, corridors, and stairwells.

Punitive Damages   This monetary amount is assessed to punish liable parties and to serve as an example to the liable party as well as others not to commit the wrongful act in the future.

Quality Inspection Scores   Sometimes called quality assurance (QA) scores, these scores are the result of annual (or more frequent) inspections conducted by a franchise company to ensure that franchisor-mandated standards are being met by the franchisee. In some cases, management companies or the property itself may establish internal inspection systems as well. In general, however, it is the franchise company's quality inspection score that is used as a measure of the effectiveness of the G.M., the hotel's management team, and the owner's financial commitment to the property.

Quarter   A three-month period. Often used to summarize accounting data. Used, for example, in, "What is our sales forecast for the first quarter of next year?"

Rack Rate   The price at which a hotel sells its rooms when no discounts of any kind are offered to the guest. Often shortened to "rack."

Reasonable Care   A legal concept identifying the amount of care a reasonably prudent person would exercise in a specific situation.

Recodable Locking System   A hotel guest room locking system designed such that when a guest inserts their "key" (typically an electromagnetic card) into the guest room lock for the first time, the lock is immediately recoded, canceling entry authorization for the previous guest's key and thus enhancing guest safety.

Recourse   The right to demand assets as payment for a loan. Loans can be full recourse, limited recourse, or nonrecourse.

Reengineering   Reorganizing hotel departments or work sections within departments.

Reflag   To change a hotel from one franchise brand to another (see Conversion). Used, for example, in, "We can buy the property, reflag it, and reposition it in the upper-scale transient market."

Registration (reg) Card   A document that provides details such as guest's name, arrival date, rate to be paid, departure date, and other information related to the guest's stay.

Remote Printer   A unit in the kitchen preparation area that receives and prints orders entered through a point-of-sale terminal located in the dining room, room service order taker's workstation, or other area.

Repeat Business   Revenues generated from guests returning to a commercial operation such as a hotel as a result of positive experiences on previous visits.

Replace as Needed   A parts or equipment replacement plan that delays installing a new, substitute part until the original part fails or is in near failure. For example, most chief engineers would use a "replace as needed" plan for the maintenance of refrigeration compressors.

Resources   Something of value to the organization. Typical resources include money, labor, time, equipment, food/beverage products, supplies, and energy.

Restoration   Returning a hotel to its original (or better than original) condition.

Revenue   Money the hotel collects from guests for the use of rooms or from the purchase of hotel goods and services.

Revenue Center   A hotel department that generates revenue. Two examples are the front office and food and beverage departments.

RevPar   Short for "revenue per available room," the average sales revenue generated by each guest room during a given time period. The formula for RevPar is Occupancy % ($\times$) ADR = RevPar.

RFP   Short for "Request for Proposal." An RFP is a request from a potential client for the hotel to submit its pricing offer (proposal) to the client in writing. An RFP may include questions about the hotel's features and services in addition to the prices it is offering.

ROI   Short for "return on investment." The percentage rate of return achieved on the money invested in a hotel property.

Role-play   A training activity that allows trainees to practice a skill by interacting with each other in simulated roles (such as pretending that one trainee is a guest and the other is an employee interacting with the guest).

Room Attendant Cart   A wheeled cart that contains all of the items needed to properly and safely clean and restock a guest room.

Room Attendants   The individual(s) responsible for cleaning guest rooms. Sometimes referred to as "housekeepers."

Room Mix   The ratio of room types contained in a hotel. For example, the number of double-bedded rooms compared with king-bedded rooms, the number of smoking permitted rooms to no smoking permitted rooms, and the number of suites compared with standard rooms.

Room Service   Food and beverage services delivered to a guest's room.

Room Status   The up-to-date (actual) condition (occupied, vacant, dirty, etc.) of the hotel's individual guest rooms.

Room Type   The term used to designate specific configurations of guest rooms. For example, smoking versus nonsmoking, king bed versus double beds, or suite versus regular sleeping room. Commonly abbreviated (i.e., K for King, NS for Nonsmoking, etc.), the hotel's holding of the proper room type is often as important to guests as whether the hotel, in fact, has a room for them.

Rooms Division Manager   An individual in a hotel responsible for the management of both the front office and the housekeeping departments. (This position does not exist in every hotel.)

Safety   Protection of an individual's physical well-being and health.

Safety and Security Committee   An interdepartmental task force consisting of hotel managers, supervisors and hourly employees charged with the responsibility of monitoring and refining a hotel's safety and security efforts.

Salary   Pay calculated at a weekly, monthly, or annual rate rather than at an hourly rate.

Sales and Marketing Committee   The group of individuals responsible for coordinating the hotel's sales and marketing effort.

Sales Call   A meeting arranged for the purpose of selling the hotel's products and services.

SBA   Short for the United States Small Business Administration. Established in 1953, the SBA provides financial, technical and management assistance to help Americans start, run, and expand their businesses. The SBA is the nation's largest single financial backer of small businesses.

Seasonal Hotel   A hotel whose revenue and expenditures vary greatly depending on the time (season) of the year the hotel is operating. Examples include hotels near ski resorts, beaches, theme parks, some tourist areas, sporting venues, and the like.

Second Tier   Management companies that operate hotels for owners who have entered into an agreement to use one of a franchisor's flags as the hotel brand. American General Hospitality, Summit Hotel Management, and Winegardner and Hammons, Inc. are examples.

Security   Protection of an individual or business's property or assets.

Selection   The process of evaluating job applicants to determine those more qualified (or potentially qualified) for vacant positions.

Sell-out   (1) A situation in which all rooms are sold or oversold. A hotel, area, or entire city may, if demand is strong enough, sell-out. (2) A period of time in which management attempts to maximize ADR.

Service   The process of moving food and beverage products from service staff to the guests.

Service Charges   A mandatory amount added to a guest's bill for services performed by a hotel staff member(s).

Serving   The process of moving food and beverage products from production personnel (cooks and bartenders) to food and beverage servers who will serve them to guests.

Short   A situation in which cashiers have less money in their cash drawer than the official sales records indicate. Thus, a cashier with $10 less in the cash drawer than the sales record indicates is said to be $10 "short."

Sign-In/Sign-Out Program   An arrangement in which individuals taking responsibility for hotel assets (such as hand tools, power equipment, or keys to secured areas) must document their responsibility by placing their signature as well as the date and time on a form developed to identify who last had possession of, and thus responsibility for, the asset.

Site Tour   A physical trip (tour) around the hotel, usually hosted by a sales and marketing staff member, for the purpose of introducing potential clients and other interested parties to the hotel's features.

SMERF   Short for social, military, educational, religious, or fraternal organizations as in, "We should assign Vernon to work the SMERF market next year because he has extensive contacts with these groups."

Solvency   The ability of a hotel to pay its debts as they come due.

Source Reduction   The effort by product manufactures to design and ship products so as to minimize waste resulting from the product's shipping and delivery to a hotel.

Span of Control   The number of people one supervisor can effectively manage.

Staff Departments   Hotel divisions that provide technical, supportive assistance to line departments.

STAR Report   Short for the Smith Travel Accommodations Report. Produced by Smith Travel Research, this report is used to compare a hotel's sales results to those of its selected competitors.

Stay-over   A guest that is not scheduled to check out of the hotel on the day his or her room status is assessed. That is, the guest will be staying at least one more day.

Strategy A method or a plan developed to achieve a long-range goal.

Suite While there is no universally agreed-upon definition, in most cases this term refers to a guest room consisting of at least two physically separated rooms or, at the very least, a hotel room that is extra large when compared with the hotel's standard guest room.

Systemwide The term used to describe all hotels within a given brand. Used for example, in: "Last year, the systemwide ADR for the brand was $115.20, with an occupancy rate of 63.7%."

Tactic An action or method used to attain a short-term objective.

Team A group of individuals who place the goals of the group above their own.

Terry A generic term for the bath towels, hand towels, and washcloths washed and dried in the laundry area.

Test Calls Calls made to a toll-free number or other reservation system to verify the accuracy of information about a specific hotel and/or about the quality of selling done by the reservation center's staff.

Third-Party Liability A legal concept that holds the second party (the hotel serving alcohol) responsible for acts caused by the first party (the drinker), if the drinker subsequently causes harm to a third party (the victim of an accident).

Total Replacement A parts or equipment replacement plan that involves installing new or substitute parts based on a predetermined schedule. For example, most chief engineers would use a "total replacement" approach to the maintenance of lightbulbs in high-rise exterior highway signs.

Tourism Industry All businesses that cater to the needs of the traveling public.

Turnover Rate A measure of the proportion of a workforce that is replaced during a designated time period (i.e., month, quarter, year). Number of employees separated/Number of employees in the workforce = Employee turnover rate.

Trace System A methodical process used to record what has been done in the past and what must be done in the future to maximize sales effectiveness. An effective trace system includes a "contact management" component that allows records to be kept for each individual client (contact).

Transient Guests that are neither part of a group booking or tour group. Transient guests can be further subdivided by traveler demographic to gain more detailed information about the type of guest staying in the property.

Transient Sales Rooms and services sold primarily through the efforts of the front office and its staff.

Travel Agent A hospitality professional that assists clients in planning travel. Also known as T.A.

Tricolumned Statement An income statement that lists (1) actual hotel operating results from a specific time period, as well as (2) budgeted operating estimates for the same time period, and, finally (3) the actual operating results from the prior year's same time period.

Unemployment Claim A claim made by an unemployed worker to the appropriate state agency asserting that the worker is eligible for unemployment benefits.

Unemployment Insurance Funds provided by employers to make available temporary financial benefits to employees who have lost their jobs.

Unemployment Rate The number, usually expressed as a percentage, of employable persons who are out of work and looking for jobs.

Unity of Command Each employee should report to/be accountable to only one boss for a specific activity.

Upselling Tactics used to increase the hotel's average daily rate (ADR) by encouraging guests to rent higher-priced rooms with better or more amenities (view, complimentary breakfast and newspaper, increased square footage, etc.) than those provided with lower-priced rooms.

Upside Potential The possibility that, with the proper investment and management, a hotel will yield significant increases in real estate value and/or operational profitability.

Valet   Originally a term used to identify an individual who cared for the clothes of wealthy travelers; its most common usage now is in reference to those individuals responsible for parking guest vehicles.

Vertical Communication   Communication between individuals that flows up and down throughout the organization.

Wage   Pay calculated on an hourly basis.

Walked   A situation in which a guest with a reservation is relocated from the reserved hotel to another hotel because no room was available at the reserved hotel.

Walk-In   A guest seeking a room who arrives at the hotel without an advance reservation.

Window   A clause in a franchisee agreement that grants both the franchisor and the franchisee the right, with proper notification, to terminate the agreement.

Word-of-Mouth Advertising   Informal conversations between persons as they "discuss" their positive or negative experiences at a hotel.

Work Order   A form used to initiate and document a request for maintenance.

Yield Management   Demand forecasting systems designed to maximize revenue by holding rates high during times of high guest room demand and by decreasing room rates during times of lower guest room demand.

YTD   Short for "year to date." Used when comparing performance from the beginning of the year up through, and including, the present period.

Zero Tolerance   The total absence of behavior that is objectionable from the perspectives of discrimination or harassment. This is done through the issuing of appropriate policies, the conduct of applicable workshops, the development of procedures for employees alleging discrimination or harassment to obtain relief and written protocols for reporting, investigating and resolving incidences and grievances.

Photo Credits

Index